P9-CME-711

BLACK
BRITISH
CULTURAL
STUDIES

Black Literature and Culture
A Series Edited by Houston A. Baker, Jr.

BLACK BRITISH CULTURAL STUDIES

A Reader

Edited by
Houston A. Baker, Jr.
Manthia Diawara
and
Ruth H. Lindeborg

The University of Chicago Press
Chicago & London

Houston A. Baker, Jr., is professor of English and the Albert M. Greenfield professor of Human Relations at the University of Pennsylvania, where he also directs the Center for the Study of Black Literature and Culture. **Manthia Diawara** is professor of comparative literature and director of the Program in Africana Studies at New York University. **Ruth H. Lindeborg** is assistant professor of English at Ohio State University.

The University of Chicago Press, Chicago 60637
The University of Chicago Press, Ltd., London

© 1996 by The University of Chicago
All rights reserved. Published 1996
Printed in the United States of America

05 04 03 02 01 00 99 98 97 96   5 4 3 2 1

ISBN (cloth): 0-226-14480-1
ISBN (paper): 0-226-14482-8

Chapter 12, "British Cultural Studies and the Pitfalls of Identity," is copyright © 1996 by Paul Gilroy

Library of Congress Cataloging-in-Publication Data

Black British cultural studies : a reader / edited by Houston A.
  Baker, Jr., Manthia Diawara, and Ruth H. Lindeborg.
      p.   cm. — (Black literature and culture)
    Includes index.
    ISBN 0-226-14480-1. — ISBN 0-226-14482-8 (pbk.)
    1. Blacks—Great Britain—Civilization.   2. National
characteristics, British.   3. Great Britain—Race relations.
4. Arts, Black—Great Britain.   I. Baker, Houston A.   II. Diawara,
Manthia, 1953–   .   III. Lindeborg, Ruth H.   IV. Series.
DA125.A1B56   1996
941'.00496—dc20   95-42672
                                                              CIP

⊗ The paper used in this publication meets the minimum requirements of the American National Standard for Information Sciences—Permanence of Paper for Printed Library Materials, ANSI Z39.48-1984.

Contents

Acknowledgments

The editors thank the following individuals and organizations for their permission to reprint the following essays:

Stuart Hall, "Race, Articulation and Societies Structured in Dominance." In *Sociological Theories: Race and Colonialism*. Paris: Unesco Publishing, 1980.

Hazel Carby, "White Woman Listen." In *The Empire Strikes Back: Race and Racism in Seventies Britian*, 212–35. Centre for Contemporary Cultural Studies, University of Birmingham. London: Hutchinson, 1982.

Homi Bhabha. "The Other Question." In *Literature, Politics and Theory: Papers from the Essex Conference, 1976–1984*, ed. Francis Barker et al. London: Methuen, 1986.

Robert Crusz, "Black Cinemas, Film Theory and Dependent Knowledge," introduction to *Screen* (London) 26 (1985). Reprinted courtesy of Sankofa, copyright © Sankofa Film and Video, 1985.

Stuart Hall, "Minimal Selves." In *Identity*, ed. Lisa Appignanesi. London: Institute for Contemporary Arts (Document 6), 1987.

Dick Hebdige, "Digging for Britain: an Excavation in Seven Parts." 1987. Rev. and rpt. in *Come on Down: Popular Media Culture in Postwar Britain*, ed. Dominic Strinatti and Stephen Wagg. London: Routledge, 1992.

Stuart Hall, "New Ethnicities," 1987. Rpt. in *Race, Culture and Difference*, ed. J. Donald and A. Rattansi. London: Sage Publications Ltd., 1992.

Judith Williamson, "Two Kinds of Otherness; Black Film and the Avant-Garde." 1987. Rev. and rpt. in *Deadline at Dawn: Film Criticism 1980–1990*. London, Marion Boyars, 1993.

Jim Pines, "The Cultural Context of Black British Cinema." In *Blackframes: Critical Perspectives on Black Independent Cinema,* ed. Mbye Cham and Claire Andrade-Watkins. Cambridge: MIT Press, 1988. Copyright © 1988 MIT.

Isaac Julien and Kobena Mercer. "De Margin and De Centre," *Screen* 29, no. 4 (1988), *The Last "Special Issue" on Race?,* pp. 2–11.

Stuart Hall, "Cultural Identity and Cinematic Representation." 1989. Rev. and rpt. as "Cultural Identity and Diaspora." In *Identity,* ed. Jonathan Rutherford. London: Lawrence and Wishart, 1990.

Gilane Tawadros, "Beyond the Boundary: The Work of Three Black Women Artists in Britain." *Third Text* (London) 8/9 (1989): 121–50.

Kobena Mercer, "Just Looking for Trouble: Robert Mapplethorpe and Fantasies." In *Sex Exposed: Sexuality and the Pornography Debate,* eds. Lynne Segal and Mary McIntosh. London: Virago, 1992.

Chapter 15, "Black British Cinema: Spectatorship and Identity Formation in *Territories,*" originally appeared in *Public Culture* 3, no. 1 (1990), © 1990 by the Center for Transnational Cultural Studies. Rights reserved.

Sonia Boyce. "The Art of Identity," *Transition* 55 (1992). Reprinted by permission of Oxford University Press.

. . .

We are also indebted to Rasheed Araeen, Sutapa Biswas, Sonia Boyce, and especially to Lubaina Himid for permission to reproduce their work. We also thank the Arts Council Collection of the South Bank Centre, London for permission to reproduce Ms. Boyce's *Lay Back, Keep quiet and think what Made Britain so Great.*

The editors gratefully acknowledge the support of the University of Pennsylvania and Ohio State University in making this volume possible.

Representing Blackness/ Representing Britain: Cultural Studies and the Politics of Knowledge

Houston A. Baker, Jr.

Stephen Best

and Ruth H. Lindeborg

We would argue . . . that critical theories are just beginning to recognize and reckon with the kinds of complexity inherent in the culturally constructed nature of ethnic identities, and the implications this has for the analysis of representational practices.

Isaac Julien and Kobena Mercer

There have been black men willing even to die, and not for an abstract freedom they teach you in grammar school which be-longs largely to dead patriots masquerading as Indians, but for the simple need to say exactly what they think, and explain exactly what they think America is. But any black American who ever tried to say something factual about the black man's life in America, even in the uncomplicated circumstance of slavery, was either killed or, as the slave ship grew more sophisticated and gave a few Negroes radios or air conditioning in the hold, driven crazy or driven away for daring to protest.

LeRoi Jones

This collection of essays offers a sampling of black British cultural studies as it has unfolded over the past decade and a half. The collection is not intended to define cultural studies as a whole. It does not attempt to challenge any one camp's reigning notions of how cultural studies has developed or should develop in the United Kingdom or anywhere else. Nor does the collection pose as the announcement of a new intellectual paradigm. Black British cultural studies is an established and productive field of work. It has existed as a serious intellectual field for almost two decades. Key documents of the project, such as Stuart Hall's essay "New Ethnicities" (see this volume, chap. 7), are quoted often enough to be considered classics. However, until now, there has existed no single volume bringing together the type of representative culling offered by the following pages.

Writers like Hall, Paul Gilroy, Kobena Mercer, and others who make their home in Britain have exerted such a strong influence on the United States academy in recent years that it seems a useful act to bring them together in a single volume. The risk of such an act is that readers will expect a

1

full theorization of black British cultural studies as part of the apparatus—and such an account is impossible. It is impossible because a full account would involve tracing in detail the entire cultural studies story in Britain, a task far too heroic for an anthology. A full account is also impossible because black British cultural studies is still evolving. It continues to assume strategic and ever-changing roles in various scholarly inquiries such as cinema studies and postcolonial critique.

Nevertheless, the present volume would be remiss if it did not give some account of its own principles of selection and offer an explanation of its own interests in, and interpretations of, the black British cultural studies project. The essays that are included in the following pages were chosen because they have exerted significant influences or played defining roles in both practical and academic discussions of race and representation, colonial and postcolonial discourse, and black expressive cultural theory during the past two decades. They were chosen as well because they are motivated by and themselves form parts of an identifiable field of intellectual alliances. These alliances appear both as a set of seemingly immutable links between black British cultural studies' chief practitioners themselves and as a more flexible set of affiliations among practitioners and workers in other fields, such as critical social theory, psychoanalysis, sociology, feminism, and African-American literary theory. In fact, the flow between black British cultural studies and these other discursive fields is so generous that it is difficult at times to say precisely what *is* and what *is not* black British cultural studies. Black British cultural studies has as many intellectual currents and eddies as it has practitioners, and sometimes the project seems to be as much "history" as it is "autobiography." Yet a narrativization is possible by threading together a persistent, if somewhat chimerical, array of questions.

A newcomer to black British cultural studies might feel reassured that key words, questions, and assumptions continually reappear and bind together what can at times seem a radically heterogeneous and mercurial field. This newcomer might also be reassured by the fact that such key terms and assumptions all bear some relationship to the relatively more settled body of knowledge known as British cultural studies, especially as that body of knowledge has made two discrete scholarly appearances in the academy.

The first appearance is suggested by the cultural materialist traditions of what has come in the academy to be called the "culture and society" school—a school that counts among its distinguished scholars Richard Hoggarth, E. P. Thompson, Raymond Williams, and of course, the more conservative elder statesman F. R. Leavis. The second scholarly appearance of this general British cultural studies tradition is a Marxist line that traces its influences to Antonio Gramsci and members of the Frankfurt school.

From the Leavisites, British cultural studies drew an admittedly broad description of "culture" as "those patterns of organization, those characteristic forms of human energy which can be discovered as revealing themselves . . . within or underlying all social practices." In this intellectual tradition, culture is not, as it is sometimes believed to be, an "ideal" state of human perfection, or a signifier of a "universal human condition." Furthermore, in this tradition culture is not held to be a documentary and fixed body of intellectual and imaginative work, "the best that has been thought and said in the world." Rather, according to the British cultural materialists, culture is a synthesis of the ideal and the documentary into a social and sensuous human praxis. Culture thus manifests itself in the systematic patterns of human activity and energy constituted by distinctive and heterogeneous human practices—that is to say, the *forms* of culture. The analysis of culture—"cultural studies" for the British materialists—therefore involves the apprehension of "how the interactions among these [human] practices and patterns are lived and experienced as a whole . . . 'structure of feeling' " (Hall 1980).

To the seemingly ambitious set of scholarly objectives of the materialists, British cultural studies subsequently appended—in a second appearance, as it were—a critical interrogation of Marxist critical practice itself. As cultural studies burrowed farther and farther into the interior of Marxism's base and superstructure model, it discovered a repressed consciousness as well as the source of profound silences surrounding questions of ideology, language, and the symbolic. The second wave of British cultural studies realized clearly that such silences and their subjects were decisively questions of culture.

And to the extent that Marxism's Achilles heel was, in fact, to be found in such silences, cultural studies was able—through the work of the Frankfurt school and the structuralist interventions of Claude Lévi-Strauss, Louis Althusser, and Ferdinand de Saussure—to learn more about the nature of culture. Cultural studies was able to demand of culture what its synchronicities were with notions such as "class," "the state," and "false consciousness." Cultural studies could research the causes of culture's profound inertia within the base and superstructure model. And such new demands upon culture opened the way for black scholars in the social sciences and the humanities to begin to interrogate how "culture," "class," "false consciousness," and "the state" were implicated with notions of "nation," "imperialism," "racism," and most explicitly, "ethnicity."

The initiation of black interrogation can perhaps be seen as the founding of the tradition we now call black British cultural studies. In the interest of its own self-clarification, black British cultural studies had to reflect on its relationship to British cultural studies as a whole. And this meant, among other things, exploring black British cultural studies' relationship to Marxism. Black cultural workers in Britain had to ask: How does ethnicity's equivalence with nationalism, imperialism, racism, and the state produce the specific ethnicities of "Britishness," and more abstractly, "Englishness" (this volume, chap. 7)? How have the metaphors of Britishness (e.g., "the British nation," "this Island Race," "the Bulldog Breed") served to coalesce white English class differences into "nation," a *United* Kingdom, in fact, that stands almost always united against blacks and metaphors of blackness (Gilroy 1982, 276–314)?

These and other questions formed the original acts of correspondence and dissimilarity, identification and distancing, between British cultural studies, Marxist critical theory, and a distinctively black line of inquiry. The first and most celebrated casualty of the black British cultural studies enterprise was the thoroughly naturalized link between "race" and "ethnicity." Under black British cultural studies' scrutiny, this link appeared to be anything but natural; it emerged, instead, as a specific manifestation of post–World War II racism. It also manifested itself—in its seeming naturalness—as a crippling silence in the intellectual traditions of British Marxism, as well as in the work of the "culture and society" school.

Black British cultural studies began to accept, as one of its founding premises, that the specifically British conflation and naturalization of race and ethnicity was a function of a constructed field of "belongingness" and "homogeneity." Black British cultural studies thus discovered that the supposed fixity of "race" had generally been articulated in Britain through images of ethnic inclusion and exclusion—"Britons" and "aliens." A convergence of race and ethnicity had produced what seemed to be clear national boundaries. Enoch Powell, paterfamilias to modern British racism, had after all confidently and provocatively proclaimed: "It is . . . truly when he looks into the eyes of Asia that the Englishman comes face to face with those who would dispute with him the *possession* of his native land."[1] The border wars and a moral panic about "rivers of blood" were thus deconstructed by black British cultural studies as a political end product of that naturalization of race, ethnicity, and nation. The moral panic itself was a conservative reaction to the rapid increase in African, Asian, and West Indian immigration that marked Britain in the late 1960s. Its fervor was equivalent to the sound and fury surrounding California's Proposition 187 in the 1990s.

Moreover, the race-and-ethnicity nexus, as black British cultural studies was quick to disclose, was not confined to the rabid rhetoric of right-wing politicians. Surprisingly, it could also be discovered in the work of Raymond Williams, a much honored and radical member of the culture and society school's pioneering assault on conservative hegemony in England. It was Williams, after all, who observed in *Toward 2000,* which he calls a contribution to a "new and substantial kind of

1. Emphasis added. Powell quoted in Gilroy 1991, 45.

socialism," that "an English working man (English in the terms of sustained modern integration) protests at the arrival or presence of 'foreigners' or 'aliens' and now goes on to specify them as 'black.' "[2] Now although this phrasing may seem innocently descriptive, Paul Gilroy argues that it is in fact expressive of a complicity between Williams's scholarship and a postindustrial English conservative racism and nationalism.

In Gilroy's view, Williams shares an ideological posture with Powell, at least insofar as Williams claims (or seems to claim) that Britain's race problems began with immigration. The ethnic identity of "Englishness" is, in both Powell's and Williams's readings, seen as a product of "long experience" or "rooted settlement." The manner in which the racial signifier "black" creeps into Williams's analysis suggests that it lies somehow outside the discursive fields of both "rooted" and "settlement." For Williams, "black" in effect domesticates a heterogeneous field of transient others (Pakistanis, Jamaicans, Guyanese, etc.). They come together under a single sign of alterity—black—irrespective of the time of their own particular "rooted settlements" in the United Kingdom itself. (The silent complicity of Williams's use of "black" signals repression rather than flagrant offense. Such use seems almost inescapable, as we shall see later, for it is precisely the employment of "black" to corral a heterogeneous field that constitutes a fundamental strategy of black British cultural studies.) "Black" thus makes ethnicity a temporal configuration, one that is made to appear always in tension with a fixed "Englishness." Phrased otherwise, "Englishness" as "ethnicity" is the forever receding vanishing point of "blackness" as "race." And as the Powell and Williams examples suggest, insofar as race can be articulated as ethnicity, both can be conflated as a national Englishness, which brings us directly to another of black British cultural studies' principal interrogations.

In Britain, the more intensely "social identity" wound itself around structures of race and ethnicity, the greater became the proliferation of metaphors of war, invasion, and infection (border wars of their own symbolic kinds, of course). Hence, both race and ethnicity were deliberately unwound, so to speak, as a kind of ideological razor wire to be strung along the "English" nation's imagined borders. Nationalism in Britain goes to work with racism, in other words, to translate and transform the "impassable symbolic [and constructed] boundaries" (Hall, this volume, chap. 7) of race into fixed and naturalized differences between national, patriotic, "English" belongingness, on one hand, and villainous, traitorous, criminal alienage, on the other.

"The politics of 'race' in [Britain] is fired," according to Gilroy, "by conceptions of national belonging and homogeneity which not only blur the distinction between

2. Williams quoted in Gilroy 1991, 50.

'race' and nation, but rely on that very ambiguity for their effect" (1991, 45). The black British cultural studies posture on racism and nationalism therefore stands in sharp contrast to the position staked out by, for example, Benedict Anderson in his influential study of nationalism, *Imagined Communities*. Anderson contends that "nationalism thinks in terms of historical destinies, while racism dreams of eternal contaminations transmitted from the origins of time through an endless sequence of loathsome copulations" (1983, 136). Such "loathsome copulations" are precisely the nightmare emerging from the dark side of Britain's conservative "English" national unconscious. Of course, the "dirtiness" of these bad English dreams is but the detritus of Britain's own imperial adventurousness across the non-European globe. Race, then, indexes today in Britain both the cartography of past imperial splendor and the whirlwind's inevitable return as a black diasporic assault. Race, or specifically, blackness, is the "return of the [imperial] repressed" seen by conservatives as a continuing immigrant "invasion." And as Gilroy concludes on these matters, "What must be sacrificed is the language of British nationalism . . . stained with the memory of imperial greatness. What must be challenged is the way that these apparently unique customs and practices are understood as expressions of a pure and homogeneous nationality" (1991, 69).

Gilroy's clear statement of a challenge to be met surrounding race, nation, and ethnicity is only one of the strategic interventions of the project called black British cultural studies. It correlates in intriguing ways with that same project's energetic attempts to open up the general narrative of "nation" by re-siting and re-presenting Britain itself as postcolonial territory. Gilroy's attention to imperial nostalgia and desire points to the existence of an alternative history of Britain, a counternarrative, as it were, that would dismantle fantasies of imperial benevolence and triumph.

Analysis as counternarrative describes the most crucial way in which black British cultural studies has engaged with, and contributed to, the work of postcolonial studies in recent years. Postcolonial studies itself and black British critique are, perhaps, most strongly allied in their mutual emphasis on counterhistories of modernity. Such counterhistories demand accompanying critical accounts of the roles of knowledge and representation in the development of European imperial power. They involve, that is, what might decisively be called a "politics of knowledge." Edward Said has written that the key task of postcolonial intellectuals is, in fact, the production of "potentially revised visions of the past tending towards a future" (1985, 55). For black British cultural studies this task of revised historiography takes three broad forms.

First, black re-vision produces narratives that retell the histories of blackness and Britishness from new vantage points. This includes the narration of stories previously excluded from the national public sphere. Black Audio Film Collective's

Handsworth Songs (1986) offers an example of such a retelling. The film is an alternative documentary that traces the "ghosts of old [colonial] stories of slavery, racism, oppression, and capitalist exploitation" in a brilliant analysis of contemporary race riots in Birmingham.

Second, black British cultural studies' new historiography has manifested a deep engagement with Africa's diasporic roots, especially the hybrid pasts and possibilities of black subjectivity that provide spaces of resistance to homogenizing narratives of Englishness. As a politics of knowledge production, black British cultural studies also explores the transformative potential of presenting new stories in new ways. For example, it takes seriously such processes as "sampling," "remixing," and "constant repetition" (versioning) in black music of the diaspora. In Gilroy's estimate, such processes can produce "an alternative sense of time and the historical process" (1991, 209).

An engagement with the politics of knowledge points to postcolonial and black British cultural studies' investment and interest in the political power of representation itself. Both critiques sample the power of new forms of knowledge to unseat dominance by unseating dominant representations of race and cultural values. Both look toward a more democratic social narrative to be derived from alternative styles of representation.

Looking back over the 1980s, Stuart Hall suggests that such concerns with representation are marked by two phases. Hall describes the first phase as a reversal of the binary logic of black and white. This he sees as largely a period of protest that contests racist, stereotypical imagery in political and cultural media, demanding black rights of access to representation. The second phase, according to Hall, confronts the notion of identity as a complex problem for black cultural politics. The problem is rendered enormously difficult both by the tenacity of racist representation and by the challenge of portraying blackness following what Hall calls "the end of the innocent notion of the essential black subject" (this volume, chap. 7). (We shall have more to say later about Hall's general account of black "protest" politics—their origins, audience, and effects.)

Hall's identification of the difficulties facing a black cultural politics of representation points to a dilemma that very recently has assumed increasing importance for black British and postcolonial studies. Identities—even "black" and "postcolonial" themselves—begin to fail under the pressures of both antiessentialist critiques and more finely nuanced social analyses of race, class, and ethnicity. Identity becomes a site of problematic conjuncture rather than an embodied political venue, which creates nearly insurmountable pressures of articulation, even (or perhaps inevitably) for any type of radical praxis.

In an influential discussion of power, representation, and postcolonial critical intervention, Gayatri Spivak points out that representation always involves negotiation between portraying (*Darstellung*) and speaking for (*Vertretung*). Looking at the attempts of Third World intellectuals to narrate subaltern histories, Spivak suggests that postcolonial cultural politics reaches its limits when it is engaged to speak for subjects and experiences that cannot be spoken in or to dominant discourses.[3] Spivak's words illuminate in uncanny ways the crisis that did, in fact, transform black British and postcolonial cultural studies in the late 1980s. That crisis was occasioned by publication of Salman Rushdie's novel *The Satanic Verses.*

In Britain, Muslim-led protests against Rushdie's work shattered the analytically useful but ultimately untenable coherence of British "blackness." The heterogeneity of nonwhite experiences and values in Britain—and worldwide—was made blazingly clear. From the vantage point of Spivak, such protests as those in Britain can be understood in part as the refusal of an elite representation of nonwhite subalternity and, at the same time, as a radical (fundamentalist) refusal of tactical misrepresentations of Rushdie himself as an "other" avant-garde intellectual.

To engage the *Satanic Verses* controversy in this fashion is to highlight major shifts in the politics of race and nation in Britain. It is to highlight a crisis in the agendas of both black British and postcolonial cultural studies. For in Britain, the dominant discourse of race and nation had begun to shift even before the publication of Rushdie's novel so outraged Islamic fundamentalism. A renewed melting of ethnicity into nationality had begun politically and academically to construct principles of inclusion and exclusion according to "Englishness"—both its "rooted" civilities and its capitalist productivity.[4]

In many ways a logical outcome of Thatcherism, this revised definition of Englishness drew its borders not simply along racial lines per se, but also along the fissures between dangerous aliens on one hand and profitable and productive ones on the other. Certainly the Rushdie controversy—complete with its avant-garde other as British novelist—supplies a plenitude of images and arguments that appear to affirm the validity of such a sociopolitical divide. On one side, "English" commentators see book-burning Muslims who appear to threaten British codes of conduct; on the other, an emerging, and apparently quietist, "brown" middle class moving into civility and across the Atlantic to profitable American academic posts.[5]

Following the tension and ideological turmoil of the Rushdie controversy, the analyses of both black British and postcolonial studies have in some respects collapsed. They have been replaced, in some instances, by new approaches to transna-

3. Spivak makes this complex argument in "Can the Subaltern Speak?" (1988, 271–313).
4. It is important to note that many protests were led by other elites, especially religious figures.
5. See, for example, "Britain's Browns," *Economist,* 28 October 1989, 21–24.

tional cultural studies that are deeply attentive to what Arjun Appadurai describes as the contemporary disjunctures and differences of a global cultural economy.[6] Black British cultural studies, let it be added, is thriving today—but in altered form. No longer making nation and nationalism the crucial reference points of their politics, its theorists and practitioners seem to be moving in at least two opposing directions. Either they are engaged with the global diasporic experience of "blackness" or they are defining themselves locally in terms of the British politics of town councils and national parliament: global generalizations of blackness on one hand; local politics on the other.

It would be irresponsible to address only the present state of black British cultural studies as an endpoint of this introduction, however, without engaging a strategic conjuncture that has indisputably led to much of the popularity and influence of black British cultural studies in the United States. In one sense its felt presence is simply representative of what we have identified as Appadurai's notion of information flows of a global "public sphere." The Internet and the ease and speed of travel have produced an interplay of knowledge and ideas that is unprecedented. Discussions of blackness and its multiple significations can no longer be conducted in a single "national" context. Yet to the extent that the British project has recently seemed to attract a unique intellectual currency for "blackness" in the American academy, it is mandatory to explore in some detail the connection between black British cultural studies and black studies in the United States. First, then, the difference.

Perhaps the most striking difference between theorists and practitioners of black cultural production in Britain and black American cultural workers of, say, the black arts and black power movements, is their assumed sites of enunciation. In the United States, the black arts and black studies movements of the 1960s and 1970s were direct outgrowths of civil rights and black power politics. These politics—whether southern nonviolent direct action or northern urban rebellions—were always mass oriented. They were bound by and operated within the everyday life of most black Americans. Thus, when these politics gave birth to black studies and the black arts, it was inevitable that such projects orchestrated their missions and goals to accord with the vernacular resonances of the majority of the black United States.

The aim of black studies and the black arts in the United States was to employ the rhythms, tone, kinesthetics, cultural memory, and common sense of the black masses to create new spaces of inquiry within the academy and new grounds for creativity within the arts. The work was unabashedly referential (a far better description we think than "essential"), positing always a mass black constituency as its

---

6. Appadurai maps this alternative basis for transnational cultural study in "Disjuncture and Difference in Global Cultural Economy" (1993, 269–95).

source of cultural influence and as its ideal audience. Its determinative question was captured by the title of a Sonia Sanchez drama, *Uh Huh, but How Do It Free Us?*

"Blackness" was the idea that bridged the distance between the black masses and black cultural workers who occupied black studies seats in universities and leadership roles in the arts. Blackness was defined in myriad ways. But it seems generally to have signified in the United States a congeries of historical, cultural, sociopolitical, and genetic properties and experiences shared by United States citizens of African descent. It was blackness that allowed disparate subject positions to converge under the sign of a politically engaged "we."

To reclaim the word "black" in the name of a valued group history was considered in itself a revolutionary act. No term in the Western lexicon, with the possible exception of "Satan," has been more imbued with negative connotations. To endorse "black" in an energetically nationalistic negation of negation was for United States blacks of the 1960s and 1970s to establish a project with extraordinary global possibilities. Just as the black American masses in their civil rights and black power politics had mounted a globally recognized challenge to the structures and promises of capitalism and democracy, so too black studies and the black arts brought international attention to bear on existing Western regimes of intellectual knowledge and aesthetic power. If exclusions, mistakes, and pseudointellectual arrogance sometimes marked sites where blackness was reborn in the United States, nevertheless the overall effect of black studies and the black arts was an irreversible shift of a Western politics of knowledge and structures of cultural and aesthetic feeling.

Africa, the Caribbean, and Europe all responded to the polemics, poetry, music, drama, rhetoric, and rhythms of a newly emergent United States blackness with varying degrees of affirmation and identification. Malcolm X, LeRoi Jones, June Jordan, Stokeley Carmichael, and many other black spokespersons became models for cultural nationalist struggles in the arts and politics of emergent African universities and Caribbean popular arts movements alike. Europe's endorsement of United States black nationalist scholarship and art was akin to its legendary adoption of black American music. Black American literature and literary study of the 1960s and early 1970s, for example, gained far more currency and support from certain French, English, and German scholars than from the United States academy as a whole. At points during the late 1960s and early 1970s, it seemed as if black studies and the black arts offered an international precedent for radically challenging white Western hegemony.

Entering the stage of history and speaking in a vernacular voice, the black studies politics of knowledge and art in the United States offered a unique blend of rough-and-tumble theorizing, robust critical polemic, and striking artistic prodigality. This much is certain: no combination of circumstances and participants has produced a nexus of black mass energy in combination with black artistic, intellectual, and po-litical production like that represented by the workings of blackness in the United States of the 1960s and 1970s. One has only to experience again the fierce originality of an anthology like LeRoi Jones and Larry Neal's *Black Fire,* or to reread the stir-ring rhetoric of the Yale conference proceedings titled *Black Studies in the Univer-sity,* to realize what a dramatic rupture was effected in traditional discourses by the desire and language of United States black studies and black arts.

To turn from *Black Fire* or *Black Studies in the University* to recent writings of theorists and practitioners of black cultural work in Britain is to experience, as our foregoing discussions of the analytical nuances of black British cultural studies surely anticipate, a dizzying shift. In the work of British theorists, the site of enuncia-tion of the signifier "black" alters in quite remarkable ways. And the signifier's U.S. history—through a curiously forceful amnesia that always marks the romantic drive for originality—seems scarcely remembered.

Stuart Hall, who is arguably the most popular scholar in the field of black British cultural studies, and to whose analysis we promised to return, writes:

> [There was a] moment when the term "black" was coined as a way of refer-encing the common experience of racism and marginalization in Britain and came to provide the organizing category of a new politics of resistance, among groups and communities with, in fact, very different histories, tradi-tions, and ethnic identities. In this moment, politically speaking, "The Black Experience," as a singular and unifying framework based on the building up of identity across ethnic and cultural difference between the different com-munities, became "hegemonic" over other ethnic/racial identities—though the latter did not, of course, disappear. Culturally, this analysis formulated itself in terms of a critique of the way blacks were positioned as the unspoken and invisible "other" of predominantly white aesthetic and cultural dis-courses. (This volume, chap. 7)

Hall describes the return of the repressed: "black" employed as a homogenizing sign for a heterogeneous field. For Hall, however, the strategy was significant for its cri-tique of the "representational and discursive spaces of English society." The critique, as we have earlier suggested, was seen by Hall as twofold:

> First, the question of *access* to the rights to representation by black artists and black cultural workers themselves. Second, the *contestation* of the mar-ginality, the stereotypical quality, and the fetishized nature of images of blacks by the counterposition of a "positive" black imagery. These strategies were principally addressed to changing what I would call the "relations of representation."

This formation of a new politics of ethnicity occurs in the late 1970s and early 1980s, born in part out of resistance to the dramatic increase of racist violence in the late 1970s (e.g., Paki-bashing, intensified policing) and out of popular uprisings against institutionalized racism. But from the foregoing, one would hardly deduce that concerted efforts at decidedly "ethnic" coalition building occurred in the United States a good deal earlier than the time frame of Hall's descriptions. And one certainly would not surmise that black cultural workers like LeRoi Jones and others were integrally involved during the 1960s and 1970s in moments like the Newark, New Jersey, mayoral campaign in which the sign "black" served as a marker for a successful coalition politics.

Hall speaks of "black" being "coined" in Britain. What is most striking about his notion of a black British creation de novo is not so much the absence of a traditional historical line acknowledging the existence and agency of the past, but the easy elision of an on-the-ground practical coalition politics—a politics of black liberation, if you will—and an exclusively "cultural politics" based solely on discourse. That is to say, what is both striking and at the same time unsettling is the way in which "black"'s site of enunciation is dramatically shifted away from vernacular politics and rearticulated in the theoretical space of representation.

Rather than the outgrowth of an acknowledged and interested set of black majority political efforts, both cultural politics and the politics of knowledge seem, at least in this late 1980s account, to constitute the only possible politics of blackness. Questions of blackness and representation, that is to say, seem to be naturalized as the only envisionable route to a politics of inquiry, creativity, and "cultural" intervention. However—and here is the great virtue of the black British cultural studies project—even at this already abstracted level of generalization, Hall suggests that it is insufficient for scholars merely to concentrate on relations of representation. To be effective they must engage the "*politics* of representation" (emphasis added). Hall writes:

> My own view is that events, relations, structures do have conditions of existence and real effects *outside* the sphere of the discursive; but only within the discursive, and subject to its specific conditions, limits, and modalities, do they have or can they be constructed within meaning. . . . how things are represented and the "machineries" and regimes of representation in a culture do play a *constitutive,* and not merely a reflexive, after-the-event, role. (First emphasis added)

Black British cultural studies set to work amid the articulations of poststructuralism, deconstruction, new critiques of Marxism, postcolonial inquiries, and Euro-American philosophies and critiques of representation. Announcing, as previously stated, the "end of the essential black subject" as even a "necessary fiction," Hall endorsed post-Althusserian Marxism and the insights of deconstruction for black

British cultural work. His goal was to wrest the concept of "ethnicity" away from its negative associations and to reformulate it to serve as an inclusive category for "new identities." The doors of British identity are thus thrown discursively open by black British cultural studies to all who are willing to doff a naive essentialism.

Earlier it was suggested that black cultural workers in the United States confidently said "we" and assumed the pronoun's reference in mass gatherings of people of color engaged in oppositional politics. It is not nearly as easy, however, to infer who precisely black British cultural workers intend when they say "we." This, of course, returns us to the ever-shifting evolutions and alliances of the project itself—the at times seemingly impossible task of wrestling the project into easy or stable revelations.

Do the boundaries of new "ethnicity" extend so widely that they make "black" into merely an immigrants' omnibus for easy transatlantic excursions? Can poststructuralism's skeptical politics of representation be championed without deep reservations as the sole resource for black people seeking political liberation? Do erudite complexities of postcolonial critique—particularly its psychoanalytic writings—necessitate an intellectual vanguard as a precondition for liberation?

Such thorny questions notwithstanding, Hall and his British colleagues were prescient in their suggestion that the end of a simplistic politics in which a "good" black subject displaces a "bad old essentialist white subject" would be heralded with "extraordinary relief." Indeed, the ascendancy of black British cultural studies did bring relief and a positive sense of new openings on the part of scholars, artists, and critics in both Britain and the United States.

The tentative steps toward theory among black U.S. scholars of the 1970s aroused startling (and sometimes a positively silly) ire and controversy among a black "mass" constituency that remained fundamentally committed into the early 1980s to a black majoritarian and referential politics. In the United States, therefore, black theory was enormously energized by the persuasive and brilliant analyses of black British cultural studies. Nevertheless, even black scholars who had been most influenced by poststructuralism and other new semiotic modes of investigation viewed such modes merely as resources or complements to a black vernacular theory in formation. The theoretical goal of such scholars was not to abandon a black "mass" concern, but rather to combine, in a collage of vernacular and poststructural usefulness, the very terms, history, energy, and interests of that constituency.

As that black majority was assaulted on every front and veritably silenced by the politics of the Reagan-Bush era, however, "blackness" could no longer serve in America as a bridge across the expanding chasm between upper-middle-class academic interests and lower-middle- and working-class interests. Reagan-Bush ideology paralleled Enoch Powell's white nationalism and a triumphal Thatcherism in Britain. It was suddenly baldly naive for any serious cultural worker to champion merely an on-the-ground oppositional politics of black/white reversal, a politics that assumed, for example, that there would continue to be an ever-increasing pool of capital (economic or cultural) for black studies anywhere in the world. A new historical conjuncture was in effect.

Conditions were—and continue to be—defined by conservatism. During the eighties, this produced dramatic intellectual retreats from any form of radical politics and a rash of academic careerist fears. Furthermore, this conservatism proved itself unequivocally more tolerant of the strategies of black British cultural studies than of the roughhewn and oppositional rhetoric of black "mass" vernacularism in the United States. With the growing academic interest in all modes of black cultural production and theory in the United States, a politics that offered both status and "transnational" work for people of diverse "ethnicities" was far more appealing than an academic project such as U.S. black studies, which seemed to require an ideological melanin test for admission. Scholars who were identified neither as "black" nor as in any way intellectually compatible with the "roots" essentialism of the referential liberation politics of black power could, in effect, still come to "blackness" via a politics of representation.

This politics of representation was thoroughly grounded in a new, and potentially redemptive, notion of "ethnicity." The work of this politics, like Lévi-Strauss's revisionist anthropology, could be textually accomplished in the privacy of one's own study, or amid the approbation of quite civil academic conferences and classrooms for "theory."

The shift in sites of enunciation for blackness in recent years has, of course, been enormously productive, as we hope this introduction makes abundantly clear. The move to a cultural politics of representation has given impetus not only to black theory in the United States, but also to works of art and scholarship that have beneficially refigured all terms in black studies in general. To the extent that a specifically *black* British cultural studies has elided with recent analyses of postcolonial discourse and with paradigm-shifting critiques of Marxism and psychoanalysis, a new black politics of knowledge has emerged. It currently offers a means of rewriting the terms of all traditional white Western nationalisms and answering the silences of their epistemological and ideological frameworks.

The scholars represented in the pages that follow employ an impressive theoretical repertoire to counter Western hegemonic definitions of art, creativity, knowledge, and of course, blackness. Music, film, the visual arts, cinema criticism are all reconceptualized in ways that reflect the importance of "diaspora" as a theoretical construct. Traditional disciplinary protocols of Marxist economics and Weberian sociology are subjected to insightful scrutiny. New theoretical working space for black identity formation is offered by Homi Bhabha as he displays the multiple lines and fissures of postcolonial discourse. It is, in fact, Bhabha who sagely alerts us to the ambivalence of the colonial stereotype and the effects of colonialism's irresistible fetishizations. Meanwhile, Manthia Diawara, keenly aware of Bhabha's insights, provides an engaged reading of black oppositional cinema practices.

The general feeling that emerges from this anthology is best suggested by the title of Dick Hebdige's essay. There is a feeling of having arrived at a site of intellectual excavation. Working from within this site called Britain, the scholars represented in the following pages convert the very sign "Britain" into a metonym for international theoretical territories of debate concerning such matters as hegemony and subjectivity, essentialism and representation, diaspora and home. Perhaps what is clearest about this collection is that the master's tools can indisputably be used both to deconstruct the house and to complicate the master's own sense of precisely whose house it is anyway.

Works Cited

Anderson, B. 1983. *Imagined Communities: Reflections on the Origin and Spread of Nationalism.* London: Verso. Rev. ed., London: Verso, 1991.

Appadurai, A. 1993. "Disjuncture and Difference in Global Cultural Economy." In *The Phantom Public Sphere,* ed. Bruce Robbins, 269–95. Minneapolis: University of Minnesota Press.

Gilroy, P. 1982. "Steppin' Out of Babylon: Race, Class, and Autonomy." In *The Empire Strikes Back: Race and Racism in Seventies Britain.* London: Hutchinson.

———. 1991. *There Ain't No Black in the Union Jack.* London: Hutchinson, 1987. Reprint, Chicago: University of Chicago Press.

Hall, S. 1980. "Cultural Studies: Two Paradigms." *Media, Culture, and Society,* no. 2, 57–72.

Said, E. 1985. "Intellectuals in the Postcolonial World." *Salmagundi* 63.

Spivak, G. 1988. "Can the Subaltern Speak?" In *Marxism and the Interpretation of Culture,* ed. C. Nelson and L. Grossberg. Urbana: University of Illinois Press.

One

Race, Articulation, and Societies Structured in Dominance

Stuart Hall

The aim of this paper is to mark out a set of emergent questions and problems in the study of racially structured social formations, and to indicate where some new and important initiatives are developing. In order to do this, it is necessary to situate the breaks which these studies represent from the established field of study; this, in turn, requires a crude characterization of the field. I begin with such a crude sketch, at a very general level of abstraction— offering only passing apologies for the necessary simplification involved. The attempts to deal with the question of "race" directly or to analyze those social formations where race is a salient feature constitute, by now, a formidable, immense, and varied literature, which is impossible to summarize at all adequately. No justice can be done to this complexity and achievement here.

Something important about this field of inquiry can nevertheless be grasped by dividing many of the varied tendencies represented within it into two broad dominant tendencies. Each has generated a great variety of different studies and approaches. But the selection of these two tendencies is not wholly arbitrary. In many

ways, they have come to be understood as opposed to one another. As is often the
case with such theoretical oppositions, they can also be understood, in many respects, as inverted mirror images of one another. Each tries to supplement the weakness of the opposing paradigm by stressing the so-called neglected element. In
doing so, each points to real weaknesses of conceptualization and indicates, symptomatically, important points of departure for more adequate theorizations. Each,
however, I suggest, is inadequate within the operative terms of its present theorization. The break thus constitutes a theoretical rupture, in part or in whole, with each
of these dominant tendencies, and a possible restructuring of the theoretical field
such as might enable important work of a new kind to begin.

For simplification's sake, the two tendencies may be called the "economic" and
the "sociological." Let us begin with the first—the economic. A great range and
variety of studies must, for convenience, be bundled together under this crude head-
ing. These include both differences of emphasis and differences of conceptualization. Thus, some studies within this tendency concentrate on internal economic
structures, within specific social formations (analyses of the economic and racial
structures of South Africa would be a good example). Others are more concerned
with relations between internal and external economic features, however these are
characterized (developed/underdeveloped; imperialist/colonized; metropolitan/
satellite, etc.). Or very different ways of conceptualizing the "economic" are involved, based on radically different economic premises or frameworks. For the purposes of this paper, I shall group together within this tendency—the pertinent
differences will be dealt with later—those which are framed by neoclassical "development" economics (e.g., a dual sector analysis: capitalist and subsistence sectors);
those which adopt a modernization or industrialization model (e.g., based on
something like Rostow's theory of "stages of growth"); those, like the "dependency" theorists of the ECLA school, utilizing a radical theory of the economics of
world underdevelopment; or those like Baran or Gunder Frank, who have employed
a Marxist orientation (how classical it remains, as shall be seen, is a matter of continuing controversy). What allows a characterization of these very different approaches
as belonging to a single tendency is simply this: they take economic relations and
structures to have an overwhelmingly determining effect on the social structures of
such formations. Specifically, those social divisions which assume a distinctively racial or ethnic character can be attributed to or explained principally with reference to
economic structures and processes.

The second approach I have called sociological. Here again—rather tenden-
tiously—a great variety of approaches are placed under a single rubric. Some concentrate on social relations between different racial or ethnic strata. Some deal more
exclusively with cultural differences (ethnicity), of which race is only one, extreme

case. Some pursue a more rigorously plural theory, derived from Furnivall and M. G. Smith and others of that school. Some are exclusively concerned with forms of political domination or disadvantage, based on the exploitation of racial distinctions. In the vast majority of these studies, race is treated as a social category. Biological conceptions of race have greatly receded in importance, though they have by no means wholly disappeared (for example, the revival of biosociology, and the reintroduction of biologically based theories, through the genetic principle, in the recent work of Jensen and Eysenck). The principal stress in this second tendency is on race or ethnicity as specifically social or cultural features of the social formations under discussion.

Again, what distinguishes the contributors to this school as belonging—for the purposes here alone—to a single tendency, is this: however they differ internally, the contributors to the sociological tendency agree on the autonomy, the nonreductiveness, of race and ethnicity as social features. These exhibit, they argue, their own forms of structuration, have their own specific effects, which cannot be explained away as mere surface forms of appearance of economic relations, or adequately theorized by reducing them to the economic level of determination.

Here it can be seen how the two paradigms have been counterposed to one another, each correcting the weakness of its opposite. The first tendency, whether Marxist or not, gives an overall determinacy to the economic level. This, it is said, imparts a hard center—a materialist basis—to the otherwise soft-centeredness or culturalism of ethnic studies. The stress on the sociological aspects, in the second tendency, is then a sort of direct reply to this first emphasis. It aims to introduce a necessary complexity into the simplifying schemas of an economic explanation, and to correct against the tendency of the first toward economic reductionism. Social formations, the second tendency argues, are complex ensembles, composed of several different structures, none of which is reducible to the other. Thus, whereas the former tends to be monocausal in form, the latter tends to be pluralist in emphasis, even if it is not explicitly plural in the theoretical sense.

It will be seen that this debate reproduces, in micro, the larger, strategic debates which have marked out the field of social science in general in recent years. Consequently, developments in the latter, larger, field—whether they take racially structured social formations as their specific objects of inquiry or not—are bound to have theoretical effects for that region of study. Hence, the consequences of such breaks in the paradigms for the "sociological theories of race." The debate is not, however, exclusively a theoretical one. Differences of theoretical analysis and approach have real effects for the strategies of political transformation in such societies. If the first tendency is broadly correct, then what are often experienced and analyzed as ethnic or racial conflicts are really manifestations of deeper, economic contradictions. It is, therefore, to the latter that the politics of transformations must essentially be addressed. The second tendency draws attention to the actual forms and dynamic of political conflict and social tension in such societies—which frequently assume a racial or ethnic character. It points to the empirical difficulty of subsuming these directly into more classical economic conflicts. But if ethnic relations are not reducible to economic relations, then the former will not necessarily change if and when the latter do. Hence, in a political struggle, the former must be given their due specificity and weight as autonomous factors. Theory here, as always, has direct or indirect practical consequences.

Political circumstances—while not sufficient to account for the scientific value of these theories—also provide one of the conditions of existence for theory and have effects for its implementation and appropriation. This has clearly been the case, even if restricted (as is done for a good section of this paper) primarily to Latin America and the Caribbean. The dual sector model—based on an export-led, import-substitution, foreign investment supported type of economic development—sponsored a long and disastrous period of national economic development, which further undermined the economic position of one country after another in the region. The theory of modernization was for long the economic cutting-edge of alliance-for-progress strategies in the continent. Versions of the "dependency" school have been harnessed, under different conditions, to the promotion of anti-imperialist, national-capitalist development of a radical type. The metropolitan/satellite theories of Gunder Frank and others were specifically developed in the context of the Cuban revolution and the strategies of Latin American revolution elaborated by the Organization of Latin American States—represented, for example, in the resolutions to the 1962 Second Declaration of Havana. The whole field, indeed, provides an excellent case study of the necessary interconnections between theory, politics, and ideology in social science.

Each tendency exhibits something of its own rational core. Thus, it may not be possible to explain away race by reference to the economic relations exclusively. But the first tendency is surely correct when it insists that racial structures cannot be understood adequately outside the framework of quite specific sets of economic relations. Unless one attributes to race a single, unitary, transhistorical character—such that wherever and whenever it appears it always assumes the same autonomous features, which can be theoretically explained, perhaps, by some general theory of prejudice in human nature (an essentialist argument of a classic type)—then one must deal with the historical specificity of race in the modern world. Here one is then obliged to agree that race relations are directly linked with economic processes: historically, with the epochs of conquest, colonization, and mercantilist domination, and currently, with the "unequal exchanges" which characterize the economic relations between developed metropolitical and "underdeveloped" satellite economic regions of the world economy. The problem here is not whether economic structures are relevant to racial divisions but how the two are theoretically connected. Can the economic level provide an adequate and sufficient level of explanation of the racial features of these social formations? Here, the second tendency enters its caveat. Similarly, the second tendency is surely correct to draw attention to the specificity of those social formations which exhibit distinctive racial or ethnic characteristics. The critique of economic reductionism is also certainly to the point. The problem here is to account for the appearance of this "something else"—these extraeconomic factors and their place in the dynamic reproduction of such social formations. But these "real problems" also help us to identify what weaknesses are obscured by the inversions which each paradigm practices on the other. If the dominant tendency of the first paradigm is to attempt to command all differences and specificities within the framework of a simplifying economic logic, then that of the second is to stop short with a set of plural explanations which lack an adequate theorization, and which in the end are descriptive rather than analytic. This, of course, is to state the differences in their sharpest and most oversimplified form. It is worthwhile, now, exploring some of the complex terrain and arguments which are contained by this simple binarism.

The first aspect can be pinpointed by looking at some features of the recent controversies which have arisen in the analysis of the South African social formation. South Africa is clearly a "limit case" in the theoretical sense, as well as a "test case" in the political sense. It is perhaps *the* social formation in which the salience of racial features cannot for a moment be denied. Clearly, also, the racial structures of South African society cannot be attributed to cultural or ethnic differences alone: they are deeply implicated with the forms of political and economic domination which structure the whole social formation. Moreover, there can be little argument that this is a social formation in which the capitalist mode of production is the dominant economic mode. Indeed, South Africa is the "exceptional" case of an industrial capitalist social formation, where race is an articulating principle of the social, political, and ideological structures, and where the capitalist mode is sustained by drawing, simultaneously, on what have been defined as both "free" and "forced" labor.

Now substantial parts of the literature on the South African social formation deal with the racial aspects of the society as accounted for, essentially, by the governing economic relations. These relations are characterized as, for all practical purposes, class relations in the classical sense. The structuring of the South African labor force into black and white strata is therefore analyzed as similar to the "fracturing" of the working class, which one finds in all capitalist social formations—with the single exception that, here, race is the mechanism by which this stratification of the class is accomplished. As Wolpe has observed, these analyses assume that white and black working classes stand in essentially the same relation to capital. Hence, the dynamic of social relations will fall within the basic logic of class struggle which capitalist relations or production classically assume. The racial divisions amount to "nothing more than the specific form which the fractionalization of the working class, common to all capitalist modes of production, has taken in the South African social formations" (Wolpe 1976). Such analyses—Wolpe refers to several sources—thus tend to fall into what we have defined as our "first" paradigm: the subsumption of racial structures under the "logic" of capitalist economic relations. This approach can then be easily matched by its immediate, and inverted, opposite. These alternative analyses treat economic class formations as largely irrelevant to the analysis of the social and political structures, where race, rather than class, is treated as the pertinent factor, through which the society is socially structured and around which social conflicts are generated. Such a "sociological" approach can be found in, for example, Kuper 1974 and Van den Berghe 1965.

Much more important—and more difficult to slot easily into either of the two approaches—is the work of John Rex, himself a South African and a distinguished sociologist. Rex has not worked extensively on South African materials. But his writing, though often necessarily programmatic, represents the "sociological" approach at one of its richest and most complex points. Rex's first essay on the subject, "South African Society in Comparative Perspective" (1973), opens with a critique of the failure of both structural-functionalist and Marxist perspectives to deal effectively with race and ethnicity in South African society. He is equally critical of, though he gives more attention to, the "plural" theory of Furnivall and Smith. Smith argued that the different ethnic segments of Caribbean society were "plurally" distinct, held together only through the monopoly, by one of the segments, of political power: "the monopoly of power by one cultural section is the essential precondition for the maintenance of the total society in its current form." Against this, Rex correctly argues that "the dynamics of the society turn upon the involvement of men of differing ethnic backgrounds in the same social institutions, viz., the slave plantation" (1973, 261). The same could be said of the attempts to extend the "plural society" paradigm, with its primacy of attention to cultural segmentation, and its ascription of the factor of cohesion to the instance of political monopoly, to South Africa. However, he is equally critical of any attempt to explain the racial forms in which social conflict appears in such societies as a species of "false consciousness."

Rex bases his own approach on a significant historical fact of *difference*. Whereas "classically" capitalism has been installed through the expansion of market relations, production for which is based on "free labor," capitalism in South Africa arose on the basis of conquest (of the Bantu peoples) and their incorporation into the economic relations on the basis of "unfree labor," "as part of an efficient capitalist system of production." This inaugurates the capitalist mode on very different historic "presuppositions" from those derived from the general account said to be offered by Marx—presuppositions, however, more typical of "colonial" formations, where conquest and colonization have been central features, and thus pertinent to the appearance, in such societies, of "not simply the class struggle engendered by capitalist development, but the 'race war' engendered by colonial conquest" (262). Rex makes a great deal of these differentiating features: the "capacity of the employers to command the use of coercive violence during and after colonial conquest," and the fact that the "central labour institution" is not classical free labor but "migrant labour in its unfree form."

Taking as the central feature of his analysis this quite atypical "central labour institution," Rex is able to delineate more precisely the specific economic mechanisms which have served to "incorporate" the African working class into the capitalist system in ways which *preserve* rather than liquidate its segmentary racial character. The racial structure of the South African social formation is thereby given concrete economic conditions of existence—the link being traceable, precisely, through its "peculiarity," its deviation from the "classical" capitalist path. Rex traces historically the various economic forms of this "unfreedom": the rural reserves, the labor compound, the emergence of the third element of the migrant labor system, the "urban native location." "Nearly all African labour partakes in some measure of the characteristics of the compound worker and the domestic worker's status. All are liable to masters and servants legislation, and none are completely free, even though the development of secondary manufacturing industry may lead to greater flexibility of wages, greater permanence of the labour force and hence greater recognition of the needs of the worker for kinship and community" (278). These "differences," both in the mode of entry and in the status of African labor, are seen by Rex as operating principally through the means by which African labor supply is recruited to capitalist industry. The economic relations are thus the necessary, but not the sufficient, condition of the racial structure of the South African social formation. For this is also preserved by a "non-normative" element—for example, political and legal factors—which stems from the political domination of the state by the white settler capitalist class, and the "workable compromise" between this class and the white working class, which leads both to reap the advantages of confining native labor to its subordinate status in the labor market. In the context of the "classical" line of capitalist development, a capitalism which preserves rather than abolishes such "irrational" features must be, to say the least, a "deviant" case.

There is certainly no simple counterposing of "social" as against "economic" factors here. Rex cannot be accused of neglecting the level of economic relations, as many "culturalists" can. Indeed, it is his concern with the specificity of the *forms* of economic relations peculiar to the South African case which enables him to grasp some of the fundamental features of a social formation which is both identifiably "capitalist" and yet different in structure from "the capitalist type" of social development—as the latter has been derived from one reading of the Marxist literature. The attention to the "central labour institutions" of this formation enables him to bring forward what Marx in another context called the "differentia specifica"—the basis, as he put it, of an adequate historically specific abstraction: "just those things which determine their development, i.e., the elements which are not general and common, must be separated out . . . so that in their unity . . . their essential difference is not forgotten" (Marx 1973, 85).

Nor is there a neglect of class relations and the class struggle. The segmentary approach of "pluralism" is specifically refused. "If there is division, the divisions can be seen as functionally integrated within an over-all pattern of political conflict generated by the capitalist development of the country since the mineral discoveries of 1867 and 1886." The "revision" involved is rather the refusal of any attempt to subsume these into a universal and univocal form—"capitalist class relations" in general. "Clearly what we have here is not something which can be adequately interpreted in terms of some universal Marxist law of class struggle but a specific kind of class struggle there undoubtedly is, namely one in which the classes are groups of varying rights and degrees of rightlessness, according to the kind of conquest or unfreedom which was imposed on them in an earlier period. The history, the structure and the forms of social differentiation which South Africa presents (i.e. its 'racial' aspect) are, as in the case of any former colonial society, the product of such conquest and unfreedom." These two criteria—conquest and "unfree" labor—are the critical conceptual mechanisms through which Rex's analysis is organized. The "origin" of the capitalist mode in conditions of conquest, coupled with the "peculiar institutions" of unfree labor, thus preserve, at the economic level, and secure its continuing racially ascriptive features. This is a capitalism of a very specific and distinctive kind: "there are a number of different relationships to the means of production more subtle than can be comprehended in terms of distinction between owners and non-owners," each of which "gives rise to specific class situations . . . a whole range of class situations." The analysis therefore begins with the economic level but differentiates it from the classical type.

In addition, however, there are other relations which are not ascribable within the "social relations of production." These include distinctions at the level of culture and values—maintained, for example, by such institutional structures as the system of Bantu education and forms of political power—established through the separation of political and economic power, such as the control of political power by the whites. These generate conflicts between groups distinct from "control of the means of production." Here the analysis encompasses the position of social groups—the African "middle class," the Cape Coloureds, the Indian traders—which cannot be easily assimilated to the earlier analysis of economic relations. From them many ascriptive features of South Africa's "closed" structure of social relations also arise.

This analysis, while predicated on the "peculiarity" of the South African system, is not limited to it. Rex has recently proposed a similar sketch as the basis for analyzing ethnic relations in Latin America and the Caribbean. Here, too, the analysis begins with delineating "the basic forms of economic exploitation which can arise in colonial conditions," including "other possible types of capitalist and non-capitalist exploitation and accumulation." In this instance, the range includes forms of "unfree" or "partly free" labor—the *encomie* slavery and the plantation system, the formation of a "dependent peasant." It includes a similar range of social strata—the "settlers," pariah trader groups, middlemen, the caciques, missionaries, administrators. The general form of the argument is very similar to that employed in the South African case. "Some of these groups are opposed to one another as classes in a Marxian sense. All of them, however, form relatively close groups with their own distinctive cultural traits and social organization. The over-all effect is of too much overlap and inter-penetration to justify us in calling it a caste system, but too much closure of avenues of mobility for us to call it a system of social stratification. It is much too complex, involving overlapping modes of production, for it to be described as a situation of class struggle in the Marxian sense. All of these aspects need to be kept in mind when we speak of a colonial system of social stratification" (Rex 1977, 30).

On the broad theoretical plane, we must see this as a model founded on a very specific theoretical revision. Without undue simplification, it combines elements of a Marxist and a Weberian approach. The synthesis is, however, secured on essentially Weberian terrain. I say this, not because Rex constantly counterposes his own approach to what he sees as an inadequate and simplifying application of the "Marxist law of class struggle"—though he does. Rather, this characterization refers to the conceptual structure of Rex's revisions. The synthesis is accomplished, theoretically, in two different, complementary ways. The first is the distancing of the analysis from what is conceptualized as a "classical" Marxist approach. Much depends on how this definition is established. "Classical" Marxism is characterized as a mode of explanation which assumes that all the various instances of conflict are subsumable within and dominated by the class struggle. Classes are defined by economic position—loosely, in terms of the distinction between "owners and nonowners" of the means of production. They are economic groups "in themselves" which can be organized, through the pursuit of their distinct class interests in competing market situations, by means of the class struggle, to become "classes-for-themselves." The

Marxist approach is also identified, here, with a set of propositions as to the form, the path, and the logic of capitalist development. The classical form is that in which free labor confronts the capitalist in the labor market. (Capitalism "can spring to life only when the owner of the means of production and subsistence meets in the market with the free labourer selling his labour power. And this one historical condition comprises a world's history" [Marx 1961, 170].) The classical path is that which makes this struggle between owners and nonowners the typical, dominant, and determining set of relations in all social formations in which the capitalist mode is dominant. The classical logic is that the "economic rationality" of capitalist market relations sooner or later prevails over and transforms those relations stemming from previous, now displaced, modes of production, so that capitalist relations "net" the latter within their sway. Rex distances himself from this "classical" account, in terms of the pertinent differences between it and the actual social formations it is required to explain. True, he concedes that where there is capitalism, there will be economic struggles of a capitalist type—class struggles. However, social formations of a colonial type exhibit different forms which take a different path and obey a different logic. In addition, there are in such social formations other structural relations which are not attributable to class relations of a classical capitalist type.

The second feature is a recuperation of these problems within the framework of a "classical" Weberianism. By this we mean that, contrary to those who have adopted Weber against Marx, as a way of moving decisively from economic-structural to more "superstructural" features, Rex always works from that often-forgotten side of Weber's work which treats extensively of economic relations, including, of course, economic class conflict of a capitalist type as one among a range of possible types of such relations. This is a distinctive stress, which allows Rex to encompass Marxian analysis of class relations as one, limited case within a more inclusive range of economic relations, defined as a set of "ideal-types." This "one among a range" approach thus also permits the elaboration of other economic relations to explain peculiar features of social formations which do not exhibit Marx's hypostasized classical capitalist structure. For Weber, economic class conflicts were conceptualized as one among a range of possible market situations, in relation to which groups, differently composed, struggled in competition. For Weber, these different market relations do not overlap into anything which can be called the general form of the class struggle. Groups competing in the struggle over prestige or status may not be the same as groups competing over the power over scarce resources. Thus, in his work on immigration and housing, Rex distinguishes between and within economic groups in terms of the stratification of the housing market—in relation to which he identifies a set of distinct "housing classes." It follows that the groups dominant in each market situation do not cohere into anything so singular as a single ruling class in the Marxian sense. Instead, one must generate, according to each empirical case, a range of ideal-typical market situations, the sum of these plural structures constituting the social formation. This does not mean that the analysis excludes questions of exploitation. This is not, however, a general feature but one which remains to be specified in each individual case. It is, thus, Weber in this "harder" form—Weber, so to speak, "corrected for" by Marx—which is the theoretical basis of the synthesis Rex proposes. The solution to a limited, one-sided form of Marxian explanation is the adoption of a powerful and distinctive "left Weberianism." It should be pointed out here that this "solution" is not restricted exclusively to those who are opposed to the "totalism" of Marxian forms of explanation. It has been noted (cf. McLennan 1976 and Schwarz 1978) that some Marxist theorists, when required to integrate political and ideological structures into an economic analysis of a Marxist kind, sometimes also attempt to deal with these levels by a somewhat untheorized appropriation of Weberianism. (This, it has been suggested, is sometimes the case with the work of so distinguished a Marxist economic historian as Maurice Dobb.) So what has been pinpointed here is something like a "theoretical convergence," operated at one time or another from arguments which begin from either the Marxist or the Weberian pole of the debate.

Significantly, there is one point where Rex challenges both Marx and Weber—a point where, incidentally, they both appear to agree. This is the contention that "free labour was the only form of labour compatible in the long run with the logic of rational capitalism" (Rex 1973, 273). This argument—founded, in Weber, by his particular ideal-type definition of "capitalist rationality," and in Marx, by his historical analysis of the "typical" path of capitalist development, based on the English case— is contested by Rex on both fronts. Instead, Rex argues that historical deviations from this "modal" type can often be found in social formations of a "specifically colonial type." Here, in contrast, conquest and a variety of forms of "unfree labour" (based on apparently irrational forms of ascriptive relations, such as those founded on racial differences) can be possible conditions of existence for the emergence and development of an "effective" capitalist mode of production. Lying behind this analytic distinction is, undoubtedly, a theoretical-political point: namely, a refusal of the "Euro-centeredness" of Marxism, based as it is on extrapolating to other social formations forms of development, paths, and logics peculiar to, and illegitimately generalized from, European cases (especially, of course, the English case, which forms the basis for the analysis in Marx's *Capital*).

With this important qualification, we can now identify the dominant tendency of this synthesis (the following passage may stand for many other instances in Rex's work): "Of course, one problem in adopting terms like 'caste' and 'estate' . . . is that all of them seem to omit what is essential to the Marxist definition of class, i.e. relationships to the means of production. What we wish to suggest here, however, departs from simple Marxism in a twofold sense. First it recognizes that at the level of relationships to the means of production there are more possible positions and potentialities for class formation than simple European Marxism seems to allow; and second, that over and above the actual means of production, there are a number of social functions and positions and that these functions are appropriated by closed groups which, thereafter, have their own interests and their own power position vis-à-vis society as a whole." When this "Marx plus Weber" theoretical position is then translated to the domain of politics, it yields a "Marx plus Fanon" sort of argument (Rex 1977, 23–24, 45).

The position, the synthesis of which has been outlined here, has of course been criticized in the context of its application to South Africa. For example, Wolpe (1976) points out that the distinction between "free" and "forced" labor is not an adequate way of conceptualizing the relations of production of a capitalist social formation, since, for Marx, even in its classical form, free labor is "free" only in a very specific and formal sense: it is, after all, subject to economic compulsions to sell its labor power as a commodity. Thus, in the South African case, the free/unfree couple, while effective in distinguishing the different constraints which structure the availability of black and white labor in the market, is not theoretically powerful enough to establish, for black labor, a relation to capitalist production of a conceptually distinct kind: "all labour-power is in some way and in some degree unfree, the type, gradation or continuum of degrees of unfreedom 'merely' affect the intensity of exploitation but not its mode" (Wolpe 1975, 203). Second, this distinction does not encompass what for Marx was central to "relations of production"; namely, the mode of appropriation of surplus labor. Third, such an approach abstracts the labor market and its constraints from the system of production relations proper, which are in fact the central preoccupation of a Marxian analysis. Fourth, the absence of an adequate theorization at the mode of production level leaves us with a political and ideological definition of "classes" which are then too easily homogenized with the main racial groupings. However, a detailed analysis of the position of the black and white working class in South Africa, in terms both of their complex relations to capitalist production and their internal stratifications, does not allow us to "treat racial groups" as "homogeneous in their class composition." Wolpe, indeed, uses Carchedi's recent work on the identification of social classes to say that the "functions" of even the white working class with respect to capital are not homogeneous. Fifth, Wolpe argues that political and ideological positions cannot be ascribed as a bloc to classes defined at the economic level: "A social class, or fraction or stratum of a class, may take up a class position that does not correspond to its interests, which are defined by the class determination that fixes the horizon of the class struggle" (Carchedi

1977). The example taken is that of the "labour aristocracy." This leads on to a more general argument, that the analysis of classes and class struggle must begin from the level of the relations of production, rather than from political and ideological criteria; but that the latter have their specific forms of "relative autonomy" which cannot be ascribed to the place of a class or class fraction in the relations of production.

I am not concerned to assess in detail the merits of these arguments as they relate to the South African case. Instead, I want to use the example of this exchange to establish the basis of a more general argument. Rex's arguments may not be entirely satisfactory in themselves, but undoubtedly they win effective ground from what he calls "simple Marxism"—as Wolpe is obliged to concede. These represent real theoretical gains, against some of the weaknesses and lacunae in what has become the dominant form in which the classical Marxist paradigm has been applied. These gains are not wholly offset by pointing, correctly, to the ways in which Rex sometimes misrepresents Marx and distorts Marx's real theoretical effectivity. Second, Wolpe's response shows that these weaknesses can only be "corrected for," while retaining the broad outline of a Marxist approach, by significantly modifying the dominant form in which the Marxist paradigm has been applied: by means of a more scrupulous or rigorous application of Marx's protocols (which have often, over time, been subject to severe theoretical simplification and impoverishment) and/or by bringing to the fore aspects and arguments which, though they can be shown not to contradict Marx, have not tended to play a very significant part when applied to the peculiar features of postconquest or postcolonial social formations. This paper's interest in certain new approaches to these problems, from within a substantially new application of Marxist protocols of analysis, arises precisely from a concern to indicate where and how these new emphases are beginning to develop.

Wolpe himself concedes some of the points, at least. He acknowledges that Rex "was right to insist upon the need for a more comprehensive and more refined conceptualization of class than was encompassed by the bare reference to property relations." This, however, he suggests, means moving away from the attention which Rex gives to market relations and constraints on the labor supply, into a fuller analysis of the relations of production and "modes of production" analysis. He acknowledges that Rex was correct to draw attention to pertinent differences in the conditions affecting the entry into the labor market of "black" and "white" labor: though he would add that the distinction between free/unfree labor is then too sharply and simply applied. Wolpe also recognizes that Rex brings forward a point of great theoretical interest by his reference to the form of the "political compromise" between the white capitalist and the white working classes, and the consequent "supervising and policing" functions which white labor exerts over black. It follows from this that some of the more simplistic political recipes based on the call for "black" and "white" labor to sink their differences in a common and general class struggle against capital—the famous call to "unite and fight"—are abstract political demands, based on theoretically unsound foundations, since they do not adequately grasp the structurally different relations in which "white" and "black" labor stand in relation to capital.

Indeed, on this point, Wolpe may not have gone far enough. For a larger argument is involved here, even if only implicitly. Rex is arguing that the South African social system shows no strong or "inevitable" tendencies to be gradually assimilated to the more "rational" forms of "free" labor, which Marx suggested was a necessary precondition for the establishment and reproduction of the capitalist mode of production. Hence, he would argue, the racial fractioning of the South African working classes has a real and substantial basis, with pertinent effects at the economic, as well as at the political and ideological, level. Rex thus points to the need for a definition of "the capitalist mode" which is able to deal with "other types of capitalist and noncapitalist exploitation and accumulation"—that is, to a "capitalist" system founded quite securely on forms of labor other than traditionally free and mobile labor. This formulation may be criticized as being, finally, too plurally descriptive. It avoids the necessity to specify the articulating mechanisms, and the modes of dominance, between these different "types." But Rex has clearly succeeded, once again, in putting into question an analysis predicated unquestioningly on a general and necessary classical path of capitalist development, with a classical and irreversible sequence of evolutionary stages. To put this more broadly: he opens up the crucial theoretical question of the teleological and evolutionary form in which Marx's work on the necessary preconditions and optimal line of development of the capitalist mode has been interpreted—from the famous assertion, in *The Communist Manifesto*, that "the bourgeoisie . . . compels all nations on pain of extinction, to adopt the bourgeois mode of production . . . it creates a world after its own image," through to the legendary discussion on the "sequence of stages" which is often derived from the section on "precapitalist forms"—the so-called *Formen*—in the *Grundrisse* (Marx 1965). Against this teleological extrapolation, it must be said that the fact of conquest, and thus the very different conditions in which preconquest social strata have been inserted into the capitalist mode, have not, on the whole, played a central role in the versions of Marxist theory usually applied to such postconquest societies. (The difficulty of deciding precisely what was the nature of the American slave systems—clearly inaugurated within yet separate from the expanding mercantile capitalist phase—is an aspect of the same theoretical problem [Genovese 1965; Hindess and Hirst 1975].)

These, then, represent some of the gains which Rex's critique makes against a too-simple Marxism. What I am concerned to show, now, is how current Marxist theorizings on these questions have begun, through their own internal critique of what earlier passed as "classical" or orthodox Marxism, to rectify some of the weaknesses correctly pinpointed by the critics of reductionism. These departures are, at once, rich and complex, often only at a rudimentary stage of formulation, and—as is often the case at a critical moment of paradigm-shift—locked in an intricate internal debate. Only certain indications of some of the main directions in this work can be provided in this review.

We might begin, here, by looking at one, very distinctive formulation with respect to the development of the social formations of Latin America, which not only defines itself within "classical" Marxism, but which develops, in what is held to be a Marxist direction, one of the lines of argument which the critique by Rex and others has put in question: namely, the work of Gunder Frank, and critiques of Frank's work from within a transformed Marxist perspective.

One distinctive but seminal application of what is taken to be the Marxist paradigm is to be found in the work of A. Gunder Frank. Frank's work was itself counterposed to the dominant and formative school of "dependency" theorists, grouped around the United Nations Economic Commission for Latin America (ECLA), which was established in 1948. This school adopted a more rigorously structural analysis to explain the "underdevelopment" of the underdeveloped countries of the region. As against earlier developmentalist models, the ECLA "school" insisted that development and underdevelopment had to be treated within the single framework of a world economic system. The "underdeveloped" countries were the dependent sectors of such a world economy: as Furtado (1971) put it, "the theory of underdevelopment turns out to be essentially a theory of dependence." This starting point within a global economic framework had much in common, in a "broadly" Marxist way, with those writers who had attempted to deal with modern aspects of capitalist development on a world scale in terms of a "theory of imperialism" (e.g., Lenin, Luxemburg, Hilferding, and Bukharin). The ECLA theorists accepted some such general framework of imperialism, giving of course greater attention than the classical theorists did to the effects of this world system at its peripheries. They were not necessarily Marxist in any other sense. These general relations of dependency, they argued, had created internal structures promoting a form of what they called "dependent capitalist development" in those sectors, and among those classes, closely linked with the imperialist chain, while marginalizing other sectors, including the great mass of the population, especially the peasantry. "The differences between the internationalized sector and the non-industrialized or marginal sector are the direct result of capitalist expansion, and become a form of structural dualism" (O'Brien 1975). However, the "school" promulgated a variety of different strategies for overcoming this externally induced sectoral imbalance—often of a technical-economic rather than of a political kind.

Frank certainly shares with the dependency theorists the necessity to begin from a world capitalist system in which development and underdevelopment were structurally related. However, he explicitly argued against the possibility of a genuine, indigenous program of economic development, of, say, a national-bourgeois type, as a possible path for Latin America out of its phase of dependent development. And this argument was supported by a startling thesis, which takes us back to the problems posed earlier. Frank argued that Latin America had been thoroughly incorporated into capitalist world relations since the period of the conquest by the European powers in the sixteenth century. Its underdevelopment stemmed from this dependent nature of its early insertion into the world capitalist market. Implicit in this thesis was the view that no structural differences remained between the more- and the less-developed sectors of these dependent social formations. "Dependency," he argued, was no recent phenomenon in the region. It was only the latest form of the long-standing "satellitization" of the Latin American economies within the framework of imperialist economic relations. The "expansion of the capitalist system over the past centuries effectively and entirely penetrated even the most isolated sectors of the underdeveloped world." The fundamental term for understanding this penetration and subversion by capitalist relations which had brought about the structural coupling of development and underdevelopment was that of a single continuum—the "metropolis-satellite polarization[,] . . . "one and the same historical process of the expansion and development of capitalism" which continues to generate "both economic development and structural underdevelopment." This was the imperialist chain, which "extends the capitalist link between the capitalist world and the national metropolises to the regional centres . . . and from these local centres and so on to the large landowners or merchants who expropriate surplus from small peasants or tenants, and sometimes even from these latter to the landless labourers exploited by them in turn" (Frank 1969).

The most telling critique of Frank's work is offered in Ernesto Laclau's review essay, "Feudalism and Capitalism in Latin America" (republished in Laclau 1977). Laclau's specific criticisms are easily resumed. The object of his critique is Frank's assertion that Latin America has "been capitalist from the beginning"—a single process, which must, for Frank, be "identical in all its aspects from the sixteenth to the twentieth century." Laclau, first, criticizes Frank's conception of "capitalism." Frank defines this as a system of production for the market, of which profit forms the driving motive. This, Laclau argues, differs fundamentally from Marx's conception of mode of production insofar as it dispenses with Marx's principal criteria for defining a "mode"—the relations of production. This "error" leads Frank to assume that, wherever there is capital accumulation, then Marx's "law"—the rapid and inevitable transformation of the social formation by capitalist relations—must follow.

However, as Laclau shows, for Marx, the accumulation of commercial capital is perfectly compatible with the most varied modes of production and does not by any means presuppose the existence of a capitalist mode of production: e.g., "However, not commerce alone, but also merchant's capital is older than the capitalist mode of production, is in fact historically the oldest free state of existence of capital" (Marx 1974, 319–21). This leads Laclau to mount a further critique of Frank's lack of historical specificity—exploitative situations as different as the Chilean *inquilinos,* the Ecuadorian *huasipungeros,* West Indian plantation slaves, and Manchester textile workers being, for all practical purposes, subsumed into a single relation, declared "capitalist." The same can be said in more detail of the troublesome case of plantation slavery in the New World. This is, of course, the site of a protracted, and still unresolved debate. Ulrich B. Phillips—who, despite his offensive antislave viewpoint, Genovese correctly praises for a seminal analysis of the political economy of slavery—argued, long ago, that plantation slavery was a form of capitalism. That was, indeed, the basis of his objection to it (cf. Genovese 1971). Genovese himself argues (1977) that slavery had a distinct set of exploitative relations—a "seigneurial society [which] created a unique society, neither feudal . . . nor capitalist." Hindess and Hirst constitute plantation slavery as its own distinctive "mode," using primarily formal criteria. Williams, early on, subsequently Genovese, and Banaji, among others, have concentrated on the relationship between plantation slavery—whatever its characteristic "mode"—and the global capitalist economy. Fogel and Engerman have described slavery as a profitable form of "capitalist agriculture" (Hindess and Hirst 1977; Williams 1966; Genovese 1971; Banaji 1977; Fogel and Engerman 1974).

Frank quotes Marx's observation in the *History of Economic Doctrines*—which describes the plantations as "commercial speculations, centres of production for the world market"—as proof that Marx regarded them, too, as "capitalist." Laclau reminds us that Marx, pertinently, added, "if only in a formal way." Actually, Marx seemed to be arguing the opposite to Frank; for he insists that plantation slavery could only be "formally capitalist," "since slavery among the Negroes excludes free-wage labour, which is the base on which capital production rests. However, those who deal in slave-trading are capitalists." As Beechey (1978) has recently argued, slavery certainly presupposed private property, a class of owners, and a propertyless class. However, whereas under capitalism the worker owns his own labor power which he sells as a commodity to the capitalist, slaveholders owned both the labor power and the slave. "The slaveholder considers a Negro, whom he has purchased, as his property, not because the institution of slavery as such entitles him to that Negro, but because he has acquired him like any other commodity through sale and purchase" (Marx 1974, 776). However, both the slave trade itself, and the extraction of the commodities so produced, were funded by mercantile capital and circulated within the global circuits of capital. As Beechey (1978) puts it, with great clarity: "Slaveholders were both merchants, dealing with the purchase and sale of commodities on the world market, and slaveholders exploiting their slaves within the plantation system, which emerged as a specialized agricultural region, a kind of internal colony within the expanded world market."

What Marx was describing, then, was something radically different from Frank's interpretation: namely, an articulation between two modes of production, the one "capitalist" in the true sense, the other only "formally" so: the two combined through an articulating principle, mechanism, or set of relations, because, as Marx observed, "its beneficiaries participate in a world market in which the dominant productive sectors are already capitalist." That is, the object of inquiry must be treated as a complex articulated structure which is, itself, "structured in dominance." Slave plantation owners thus participated in a general movement of the world capitalist system: but on the basis of an internal mode of production—slavery in its modern, plantation form—not itself "capitalist" in character. This is a revolutionary proposition in the theoretical sense, since it departs from that very teleological reading of Marx which produced, in Frank, the indefensible thesis that Latin America has been "capitalist" since the conquest. What we have now, in opposition to the thesis of "inevitable transformation" of precapitalist modes and their dissolution by capitalist relations, is the emergent theoretical problem of an articulation between different modes of production, structured in some relation of dominance. This leads on to the definition of a social formation which, at its economic level, may be composed of several modes of production "structured in dominance" (cf. Althusser and Balibar 1970; Hindess and Hirst 1975, 1977; Poulantzas 1973). This has provided the basis for an immense amount of formative work, especially on "precapitalist modes of production," offering a more rigorous approach to that reading of Marx, rightly criticized—on this very point—by Rex, while retaining the systematic terms of a Marxist analysis. This work is, of course, pitched principally at the level of economic relations. Though it has clear consequences for other levels of the structure of social formations (class formations, alliances, political and ideological structures, etc.), these have not been spelled out (for example, in Laclau's essay quoted here: though for related developments pertaining to these levels, see Laclau, and others referred to more extensively below). It has, for example, quite pertinent effects for any analysis of the way this articulated combination of modes inserts economic agents drawn from different ethnic groups into sets of economic relations which, while articulated into a complex unity, need not be conceptualized as either necessarily the same or inevitably destined to become so.

This emergent problematic constitutes perhaps the most generative new theoretical development in the field, affecting the analysis of racially structured social formations. The emergent theoretical position is grounded by its proponents in a certain "rereading" of the classical Marxist literature. It is part of that immense theoretical revolution constituted by the sophisticated return to the "reading" of Marx's *Capital* which has had such a formative intellectual impact over the past decade. It is also currently being developed in a range of different theoretical fields. Laclau puts the essential argument in a strong form: "the precapitalist character of the dominant relations of production in Latin America was not only not incompatible with production for the world market, but was actually intensified by the expansion of the latter." Marx, in a passage less well known than the *Communist Manifesto* "scenario" quoted earlier, spoke of the fact that "the circuit of industrial capital . . . crosses the commodity circulation of the most diverse modes of social production. . . . No matter whether commodities are the output of production based on slavery, of peasants . . . of State enterprise . . . or of half-savage hunting tribes . . . they come face to face with the monies and commodities in which industrial capital presents itself. . . . The character of the process of production from which they originate is immaterial. . . . They must be reproduced and to this extent the capitalist mode of production is conditional on modes of production lying outside of its own stage of development" (Marx 1956, 109). Bettelheim, who may appear to take a more "classical" view, argues that the *dominant* tendency is toward the dissolution of other modes by the capitalist one. But this is often combined with a secondary tendency—that of "conservation-dissolution": where noncapitalist modes, "before they disappear are 'restructured' (partly dissolved) and thus subordinated to the predominant capitalist relations (and so conserved)" (Bettelheim 1972).

Using this schema, Wolpe shows that certain problems of the South African social formation, referred to earlier, which could not be satisfactorily explained within the older reading, and which Rex among others correctly criticized, begin to be resolvable through the use of these new theoretical instruments and in a manner which throws significant light on the racial fracturing of class relations in South Africa. While the detailed outlines of this attempted "solution" cannot be entered into here (Wolpe 1975), its broader consequences are worth quoting. Wolpe (1972) suggests, for example, that the reliance of the capitalist sector in South Africa on the noncapitalist sectors in the African areas for both cheap labor supply and subsistence reproduction enables capital to pay for labor-power below the cost of its reproduction, while having always available a plentiful labor supply whose costs of subsistence it does not fully bear. He employs both the "articulation" and the "dissolution-conservation" variants of the thesis. In South Africa, the tendency of capital accumulation to dissolve other modes is cross-cut and blocked by the counteracting tendencies to conserve the noncapitalist economies—on the basis that the latter are articulated in a subordinate position to the former. Where capitalism develops by means, in part, of its articulation with noncapitalist modes, "the mode of political domination and the content of legitimating ideologies assume racial, ethnic and cultural forms and for the same reasons as in the case of imperialism . . . political domination takes on a colonial form" (Wolpe 1975). He adds: "The conservation of noncapitalist modes of production necessarily requires the development of ideologies and political policies which revolve around the segregation and preservation and control of African 'tribal' societies"—that is, the relation assumes the forms of ideologies constructed around ethnic, racial, national, and cultural ideological elements.

In short, the emergent theory of the "articulation of different modes of production" begins to deliver certain pertinent theoretical effects for an analysis of racism at the social, political, and ideological levels. It begins to deliver such effects—and this is the crucial point—not by deserting the level of analysis of economic relations (i.e., mode of production) but by posing it in its correct, necessarily complex, form. Of course, this may be a necessary but not a sufficient starting point. In this respect, Wolpe's term "requires" may go too far, suggesting a necessary correspondence, of a too-functionalist kind, between the structure of modes of production and the specific forms of political domination and ideological legitimation. The level of economic analysis, so redefined, may not supply sufficient conditions in itself for an explanation of the emergence and operation of racism. But, at least, it provides a better, sounder point of departure than those approaches which are obliged to desert the economic level, in order to produce "additional factors" which explain the origin and appearance of racial structuring at other levels of the social formation. In this respect, at least, the theoretical advances briefly outlined here have the merit of respecting what we would call two cardinal premises of Marx's "method": the materialist premise—that the analysis of political and ideological structures must be grounded in their material conditions of existence; and the historical premise—that the specific forms of these relations cannot be deduced, a priori, from this level but must be made historically specific "by supplying those further delineations which explain their *differentiae specificae.*" Both premises are well expressed in one of the most justly famous passages from *Capital:* "The specific economic form, in which unpaid labour-surplus is pumped out of direct producers, determines the relationship of rulers and ruled, as it grows directly out of production itself and, in turn, reacts upon it as a determining element. Upon this, however, is founded the entire formation of the economic community which grows up out of the production relations themselves, thereby simultaneously its specific political form" (the materialist premise). But "this does not prevent the same economic basis—the same from the standpoint of its main conditions—due to innumerable different empirical circumstances, natural environments, racial relations, external historical influences, etc., from showing infinite variations and gradations in appearance, which can be ascertained only by analysis of the empirically given circumstances" (the historical premise) (Marx 1974, 791–92). Both premises are indeed required, if the conditions of theoretical adequacy are to be met: each, on its own, is not sufficient. The first, without the second, may lead us straight back into the impasse of economic reductionism; the second, without the first, snares us in the toils of historical relativism. Marx's method, properly understood and applied, provides us with the conditions—though not, of course, the guarantee—of a theoretical adequacy which avoids both. (For a further elaboration of the "basic premises" of Marx's method, see Johnson et al. 1978a,b; for a condensed version of the argument outlined by Wolpe, as applied to Latin American and Caribbean social formations, see Hall 1977b.)

The application of the "articulation" thesis, briefly outlined here, has had revolutionary theoretical consequences in other fields of inquiry, which can only be shortly noted here since they fall outside of our principal concern. They can be found, in the English context, in the work on "precapitalist modes" and social formations by Hindess and Hirst (1975, 1977); in Banaji (1977); in work on "colonial modes of production" (e.g., Alavi 1975); in the *Review of African Political Economy, Critique of Anthropology,* and *Economy and Society;* also, in a related form, in the renewed debate about "transition," sparked off by the reissue of the formative set of essays on *The Transition from Feudalism to Capitalism* (Hilton 1976); and in the work on Jamaica by Post (1978). In France, it is most noteworthy in the context of the revived interest in the new "economic anthropology" to which such writers as Godelier, Meillassoux, Terray, Rey, and Dupré have made outstanding contributions (cf. the selection by Seddon 1978). (For interpretive overviews and critiques in English, see, inter alia, Clammer 1975; Bradby 1975; Foster-Carter 1978; Seddon 1978; Wolpe 1980.) Meillassoux principally deals with "self-sustaining" agricultural social formations, and their dissolution-transformation, when they have grafted on to them production for external "capitalist" markets. This has certain theoretical consequences for those articulated social formations where the noncapitalist sector is "able to fulfil functions that capitalism prefers not to assume in the under-developed countries" (cf. Wolpe's development of this argument, above)— and thus for such societies as the South African one, where (as Clammer extrapolates) "people who are obliged to become wage-labourers in a neo- and quasi-colonial situation are forced back on the 'traditional' sector to obtain precisely those services which the capitalist does not provide." Clammer correctly points out that this revives the "dual sector" analysis—though in a radically new form; since (Meillassoux argues) it is precisely the ideological function of "dual sector" theories to "conceal the exploitation of the rural community, integrated as an organic component of capitalist production" (Meillassoux 1972, 1974; for a more extended critique, see Clammer 1975).

Rey's work deals principally with "lineage" societies and, like Meillassoux's, derives from African fieldwork: but wider extrapolations of a theoretical nature have been made from this terrain (Rey 1971, 1973, 1975; Rey and Dupré 1973). It differs from other work in the French "economic anthropology" tradition by being concerned, in part, with problems of extending the "articulation" argument—as the title of his second book indicates—to the question of class alliances, and thus to the political level. Rey also departs somewhat from the problematic of "articulation." He is concerned with the "homoficence" of capitalism—what Foster-Carter calls the problem of the "parallelism of action" of capitalism (cf. Foster-Carter 1978; also for a more substantive review/critique both of Rey and of the "articulation" literature). A major distinction in Rey's work is, however, the attempt to periodize this " parallelism of action" as a process, into three principal stages, marked by the character of the articulation in each. These are (i) the period of the slave trade, where the European market acquires supplies, through relations of exchange, "essentially by playing on the internal contradictions of the lineage social formations"; (ii) a transitional phase—colonialism in the full sense—where capitalism takes root, grounding itself in the precapitalist mode and gradually subordinating it; (iii) a new type of social formation, with the capitalist mode of production internally dominant; frequently, then, dependent on a metropolitan capitalism (neocolonialism). To each phase a different set of class alliances corresponds. Rey is also much concerned with the way the lineage societies are interrupted and disarticulated by the exterior force of capital—often through violence and what Marx called the "fact of conquest" (Foster-Carter 1978). Rey sees the "rooting" of capitalism in these precapitalist modes as possible only with the implantation of "transitional modes"—precisely the function of the colonial period. While giving to this phase a seminal role not normally accorded to it, or even distinctly remarked, Rey's approach leaves the history of capital and the mechanism of transition as one largely "written outside such social formations," and he tends to treat the relations of exchange as the central articulating feature (for a wider critique, see Clammer 1975; Foster-Carter 1978; Terray 1972; Bradby 1975).

The term "articulation" is a complex one, variously employed and defined in the literature here referred to. No clear consensus of conceptual definition can be said to have emerged so far. Yet it remains the site of a significant theoretical rupture (*coupure*) and intervention. This is the intervention principally associated with the work of Althusser and the "school" of structuralist Marxism. The term is widely employed, in a range of contexts, especially in the *For Marx* essays (1965), and the succeeding volume, with Balibar, *Reading Capital* (1970). At least two different applications are particularly relevant to our concerns here (though, interestingly, the term is not defined in the "Glossary," prepared by Ben Brewster and sanctioned by Althusser himself, which appeared in the English editions of both books). Aside from these particular usages, the term has a wider reference of both a theoretical and a methodological nature.

Foster-Carter correctly suggests that "articulation" is a metaphor used "to indi-cate relations of linkage and effectivity between different levels of all sorts of things"—though he might have added that these things require to be linked because, though connected, they are not the same. The unity which they form is thus not that of an identity, where one structure perfectly recapitulates or reproduces or even "ex-presses" another; or where each is reducible to the other; or where each is defined by the same determinations or has exactly the same conditions of existence; or where each develops according to the effectivity of the same conditions of existence; or even where each develops according to the effectivity of the same contradiction (e.g., the "principal contradiction" so beloved, as the warrant and guarantee of all argu-ments, by so-called orthodox Marxists). The unity formed by this combination or articulation is always, necessarily, a "complex structure," a structure in which things are related, as much through their differences as through their similarities. This requires that the mechanisms which connect dissimilar features must be shown—since no "necessary correspondence" or expressive homology can be as-sumed as given. It also means—since the combination is a structure (an articulated combination) and not a random association—that there will be structured relations between its parts, i.e., relations of dominance and subordination. Hence, in Althusser's cryptic phrase, a "complex unity, structured in dominance."

Many of the classic themes of the Althusserian intervention are resumed in and through his various uses of this term: for example, his argument that Marx's "unity" is not the essentialist "expressive unity" to be found in Hegel, and that, therefore, Marx's dialectic is not merely an inversion, but a theoretical advance over Hegel. This is the critique against conceiving Marx's "totality" as an "expressive totality," which grounds Althusser's early critique of the attempts to rescue Marx's work from "vulgar materialism" by way of a detour through Hegelianism (see Althusser's *For Marx,* especially the chapter "On the Marxian Dialectic"). It also founds Althusser's critique of the attempt to read Marx as if he meant that all the structures of a social formation could be reduced to an "expression" of the economic base; or as if all the instances of any historical conjuncture moved in a relation of direct correspondence with the terms of the "principal contradiction" (that of the "base," between forces and relations of production)—this is Althusser's critique (the opposite of that against Hegelian idealism) against "economic reductionism." Marx's "complex unity," Althusser argues, is neither that in which everything perfectly expresses or corresponds to everything else; nor that in which everything is reducible to an expression of "the Economic." It operates, instead, on the terrain of articulation. What we find, in any particular historical conjuncture (his example, in "Contradiction and Overdetermination" in *For Marx*, is Russia, 1917) is not the unrolling of the "principal contradiction," evenly, throughout all the other levels of the social formation, but, in Lenin's terms, the "merger," "rupture," condensation of contradictions, each with its own specificity and periodization—"absolutely dissimilar currents, absolutely heterogeneous class interests, absolutely contrary political and social strivings"—which have "merged . . . in a strikingly 'harmonious' manner" (Lenin, *Letters from Afar*, no. 1). Such conjunctures are not so much "determined" as overdetermined, i.e., they are the product of an articulation of contradictions, not directly reduced to one another.

Althusser and Balibar, then, employ this general theoretical concept in a variety of different contexts. They conceive of a social formation as composed of a number of instances—each with a degree of "relative autonomy" from one another—articulated into a (contradictory) unity. The economic instance or level, itself, is the result of such a "combination": the articulation between forces and relations of production. In particular social formations, especially in periods of "transition," social formations themselves may be an "articulated combination" of different modes with specified, shifting terms of hierarchical ordering between them. The term also figures in the Althusserian epistemology, which insists that knowledge and the production of knowledge are not directly produced, as an empiricist reflection of the real "in thought," but have a specificity and autonomy of their own—thought, "established on and articulated to the real world of a given historical society" (Althusser and Balibar 1970, 42). The scientific analysis of any specific social formation depends on the correct grasping of its principle of articulation: the "fits" between different instances, different periods and epochs, indeed different periodicities, e.g., times, histories. The same principle is applied, not only synchronically, between instances and periodizations within any "moment" of a structure, but also, diachronically, between different "moments." This connects with Althusser's objections to the notion of a given and necessary sequence of stages, with a necessary progression built into them. He insists on the nonteleological reading of Marx, on the notion of "a discontinuous succession of modes of production" (204), whose combined succession—i.e., articulation through time—requires to be demonstrated. Indeed, "scientificity" itself is associated with "the problem of the forms of variation of the articulation" of the instances in every social structure (207). The same is said of the relations between the economic and the political and ideological forms of their appearance. This, too, is thought on the analogy of an articulation between structures which do not directly express or mirror each other. Hence, the classical problem for Marxism—the problem of determinancy of the structure, the "determination in the last instance by the economic" (which distinguishes Marxism from other types of social scientific explanation)—is itself redefined as a problem of "articulation." What is "determined" is not the inner form and appearance of each level, but the mode of combination and the placing of each instance in an articulated relation to the other elements. It is this "articulation of the structure" as the global effect of the structure itself—or what has been called, by Balibar, "the matrix role of the mode of production"—which defines the Althusserian concept of determination: as a structural causality (220). It is this conception, on the other hand, which has provided the basis for the critique by Hindess and Hirst (1975) of Althusser's "determinacy of articulation by the structure" as itself an "expressive totality"—a Spinozian eternity. Dealing with the example of the relation between feudal ground rent and the feudal relation of lordship and servitude, Balibar treats it as a reduced instance of the articulation of *two* different instances, an "economic" instance and a "political" instance. Likewise, Balibar defines the concept of mode of production as itself the result of a variant combination of elements (object of labor, means of labor, labor power). What changes, in each epoch, is not the elements, which are invariant (in the definitional sense), but the way they are combined: their articulation. While it is not possible to "tell" the whole of the Althusserian intervention through the terms of a single concept, like articulation, it must be by now apparent that the concept has a wide and extensive reference in the works of the structuralist Marxists.

Though we cannot go into the theoretical and methodological background to the emergence of the concept, we can at least note in passing two pertinent provenances. The first is that of structuralist linguistics, which provided the master-model of a substantial part of the whole "structuralist" venture. Saussure, the "founder" of this school, who argued that language is not a reflection of the world but produces meaning through the articulation of linguistic systems upon real relations, insists that meaning is no mere "correlation between signifier and signified, but perhaps more essentially an act of simultaneously cutting out two amorphous masses, two 'floating kingdoms' . . . language is the domain of *articulations*" (Barthes 1967). More pertinent, perhaps, is the warrant which Althusser and others have found in Marx's most extensive "methodological" text—the 1857 *Introduction to "The Grundrisse"*—for a theory of the social formation as what Marx himself calls an "articulated hierarchy" (*Gliederung*)—or, as Althusser translates him, "an organic hierarchized whole." "In all forms of society," Marx wrote, "it is a determinate production and its relations which assign every other production and its relations their rank and influence" (1973). If this represents a slender warrant for the construction of the whole structuralist edifice, it is certainly clear that, in that text, Marx was decisively opposing himself to any notion of a simple identity between the different relations of capital (production, circulation, exchange, consumption). He spoke, at length, of the complexity of determinations between these relations, the sum of whose articulations, nevertheless, provided him (in this text) with the object of his inquiry (adequately constructed in a theoretical sense); and, in *Capital,* with the key to the unraveling of the necessarily complex nature of the relations between the different circuits operating within the capitalist mode (cf. Hall 1973). This is the real burden of Marx's extensive criticisms in the 1857 *Introduction* against treating the different relations which compose the capitalist mode as a "regular syllogism"—an "immediate identity." "To regard society as one single subject is . . . to look at it wrongly; speculatively." "The conclusion we reach is not that production, distribution, exchange and consumption are identical, but that they all form the members of a totality of distinctions within a unity" (Marx 1973). In the same way, there seems to be a clear warning issued against any simple notion of an evolutionary sequence or succession of stages in that development: " Their sequence is determined, rather, by their relation to one another in modern bourgeois society, which is precisely the opposite of that which seems to be their natural order or which corresponds to historical development. The point is not the historic position of the economic relations in the succession of different forms of society." This last point indicates what we would want to call (in addition to those already signaled) the third premise of Marx's method: the structural premise. It is, above all, the employment of the structural premise in the later, mature work of Marx, and the manner in which this has been appropriated and developed by Althusser and the structuralists, which produces, as one of its theoretical results, the extensive-intensive concept of articulation.

The term itself is by no means unproblematic, indicating here a certain approach, rather than providing in itself a theoretical resolution to the problems it indexes. It has been subjected to a searching critique. In itself, the term has an ambiguous meaning, for, in English, it can mean both "joining up" (as in the limbs of the body, or an anatomical structure) and "giving expression to" (cf. Foster-Carter 1978). In Althusserian usage, it is primarily the first sense which is intended. There are, in any case, theoretical objections to the notion that one structure "gives expression to" another: since this would be tantamount to seeing the second structure as an epiphenomenon of the first (i.e., a reductionist conception), and would involve treating a social formation as an "expressive totality"—precisely the object of Althusser's initial critique of Hegelianism. Some notion of an "expressive" link—say, between the economic and political structures of a society remains, even in Althusserian usage, but this is elaborated by other terms which break up or break into any residual sense of a perfect and necessary "correspondence." Thus, in addition to insisting on the specificity, the nonreductiveness, the "relative autonomy," of each level of the society, Althusser always uses such terms as "displacement," "dislocation," "condensation," in order to demonstrate that the "unity" which these different relations form are not univocal, but mislead through "overdetermination." Another criticism, then, is that the concept of "articulation" may simply leave two dissimilar things yoked together by a mere external or arbitrary connection: what Marx once called "independent, autonomous neighbours . . . not grasped in their unity" (1973, 90). Althusser attempts to overcome this "mere juxtaposition" by using the concept of "overdetermination," and by always speaking of "articulation" as involving hierarchical as well as lateral relations, i.e., relations of dominance and subordination (cf. Marx's discussion of money in different historical epochs, which does not "wade its way through all economic relations" but is defined by where it plays a "dominant" or a "subordinate" role). This, however, leads on to other criticisms. The schema constructed around articulation has, often with justice, been described as too "formalist." Thus, in the full-blown "structural causality" of Althusser and Balibar's *Reading Capital,* the "economic" determines "in the last instance" not substantively but principally by "giving the index of effectivity" in the structure to one or another level: i.e., in a *formal* way. (But Althusser [1976] retreats from some of these more formalist excesses.) While the whole attempt to develop such an analysis is predicated on the need for an approach which is not reductive, it has been criticized as giving rise to a conception of "structure" which—since it contains within itself all the conditions of its own functioning—is itself that "expressive totality" which Althusser seeks to avoid (cf. Hindess and Hirst 1975; Hirst 1976). The framework is also open to the criticism that it leaves the internal elements of any "structural combination" unchanged, with change or transition being limited to the variations (different articulations) through which the "invariant elements" are combined. This weakens the historicity of the approach—contravening what we have called the historical premise of Marx's work (but again see Althusser 1976). This notion of the variation between invariant elements has resulted in a very formalist way of defining a "mode of production" (following, especially, Balibar): so that some of the real advances made in attempting to ground analysis in a more developed and sophisticated understanding of modes of production and their combination can easily be vitiated by a sort of formalist hunt for one, separate "mode of production" after another. Nevertheless, we would continue to insist on the potentially generative value of the term and its cognate concepts, which give us a start in thinking about the complex unity and *differentiae specificae* of social formations, without falling back on a naive or "vulgar materialist" reductionism, on the one hand, or a form of sociological pluralism, on the other.

So far, I have been speaking, exclusively, of the application of the term "articulation" to the economic structure of complex social formations. But I have also said that the social formation itself can be analyzed as an "articulated hierarchy." At the economic level, this may involve the articulation of a social formation around more than one mode of production. Some of the political and ideological features of such societies can then be explained with reference to this particular combination. But it is also possible to conceptualize the different levels of a social formation as an articulated hierarchy. Since we must assume no "necessary correspondence"—no perfect replication, homology of structures, expressive connection—between these different levels, but are nevertheless required to "think" the relations between them as an "ensemble of relations" (marked by what Marx in his 1857 *Introduction,* when dealing with these issues, defined as the "law of uneven development")—then it is, once more, to the nature of the articulations between them to which we must turn. The attention—of a more detailed and analytic kind—to the nature of modes of production helps to ground these other aspects of the social formation more adequately at the level of the economic structures (the materialist premise). However, we cannot thereby deduce a priori the relations and mechanisms of the political and ideological structures (where such features as racism make a decisive reappearance) exclusively from the level of the economic. The economic level is the necessary but not sufficient condition for explaining the operations at other levels of the society (the premise of nonreductionism). We cannot assume an express relation of "necessary correspondence" between them (the premise of historical specificity). These are, as Marx put it, "a product of historical relations and possess their full validity only for and within these relations." This is an important, indeed a critical, qualification. It requires us to demonstrate—rather than to assume, a priori—what the nature and degree of "correspondence" is, in any specific historical case. Thus, through this opening, some of the criticisms which, as was noted earlier, are made from the perspective of "sociological" explanations—for example, the requirement to be historically specific—begin to be met, within the framework of this seminal revision.

Here, however, different positions within the general problematic of "articulation" can be identified. Some theorists argue that all we can do is to deal with each level, in terms of its own specificity, and the "conditions of existence" which must be fulfilled for it to function (e.g., the economic relations of the capitalist mode require, as a condition of existence, some extraeconomic, juridical framework, which secures the "contract" between buyer and seller of labor power). But, it is argued, the internal forms and specificities of the extraeconomic levels can neither be prescribed or identified from the economic level which "requires it," as a formal necessity of its functioning. This is tantamount to a theory of the "autonomy" (not "relative autonomy") of the different levels (Hirst 1976; Cutler et al. 1977). This, however, fails to deal with social formations as a "complex unity" (Marx's "unity of many determinations").

Other approaches recognize that there may well be "tendential combinations":

combinations which, while not prescribed in the fully determinist sense, are the "preferred" combinations, sedimented and solidified by real historical development over time. Thus, as is clear from, say, the Latin American case, there is no "necessary correspondence" between the development of a form of capitalism and the political forms of parliamentary democracy. Capitalism can arise on very different political foundations. Engels, himself, showed how capitalism can also harness and adapt very different legal systems to its functions. This does not prevent us from arguing that the advent of capitalism has frequently (tendentially) been accompanied by the formation of bourgeois parliamentary democratic regimes: or even from accepting Lenin's percipient observation that parliamentary democracy provides "the 'best possible' political shell for capitalism." We must, however, see these "combinations" as historically specific, rather than specified a priori: as "laws of tendency"— which can be countermanded by "counteracting tendencies." To take a pertinent example: in Europe, the rise of capitalism is consequent upon the destruction of feudal ties and the formation of "free labor"—of "labor power" as a commodity. It is hard to think of a capitalist formation in which there would be no form of labor power available to capital in its "free" form. This, in turn, means that, whatever the specific legal form with which capitalist development "corresponds," it must be one in which the concept of the juridical "contract" between "free persons" appears, which can legally regulate the forms of contract which "free labor" requires. This "requirement" is something more than a mere, empty, or formal "condition of existence." However, this does not mean that the tendency to combine capitalism with "free labor" cannot, under specific historical conditions, be cross-cut or countermanded by a counteracting tendency: namely, the possibility of certain of the conditions of existence of capitalism being effectively secured by combining "free labor" with certain forms of "unfree" or "forced" labor. Once we move away from European to postconquest or postcolonial societies, this combination—free and "unfree" labor, on the basis of a combination of different modes of production— becomes more and more the paradigm case. This leaves almost everything of importance, still, to be done in developing a better understanding of the "laws of motion" of capitalist formations which are structured in this alternative manner. Naturally, it has consequences, then, for political and legal structures. In such "deviant" social formations (deviant only in the sense of departing from the European paradigm-case), there will be political structures which combine (or may combine) forms of parliamentary democracy with other forms of political representation—or legal structures which elaborate more than one form of citizen status. The "articulation" of "free" and "forced" labor, the combination of "equal" and "restricted" franchises, the position of the chiefs and the Bantustan "internal colonies," and the different legal statuses of "white" and "black" citizens, in the South African social formation, perfectly represent the elements of such a "variant" case—one which is in no sense "noncapitalist"; provided, that is, we read Marx's "laws of development and motion" as laws of tendency (and countertendency) rather than as a priori laws of necessity.

Where, then, the relations between the different levels of a social formation are concerned, one needs additional concepts, i.e., to supply further determinations, to those which have been mobilized for the analysis of the economic "mode of production" levels. And one needs to acknowledge that the economic level, alone, cannot prescribe what those levels will be like and how they will operate—even if their mechanisms are not fully specifiable without attending to the level of the economic. Here, the work of Althusser, and of the "Althusserians"—for example, Poulantzas's work on "the state"—requires to be supplemented by the work of another Marxist theorist whose elaboration, at this level, constitutes a contribution to the development of a rigorously nonreductionist Marxism of the very first importance. This is the work of Gramsci. Gramsci's work is more fragmentary (much of it written in prison, under the eyes of the censor, in one of Mussolini's jails), far less "theorized" than that of Althusser. Gramsci has been formative for the development of Althusser's problematic: though, since in certain respects Gramsci remained a "historicist," the relationship between Althusser and Gramsci is a complex one. In a review of this relationship, we have expressed it in terms of Gramsci providing the "limit case" of historicity for Marxist structuralism (Hall, Lumley, and McLennan 1977).

We cannot elaborate in any depth, here, on Gramsci's concepts (for a review, see Hall, Lumley, and McLennan 1977; Anderson 1977; Mouffe 1979). The central concept in his work is that of hegemony. Hegemony is that state of "total social authority" which, at certain specific conjunctures, a specific class alliance wins, by a combination of "coercion" and "consent," over the whole social formation, and its dominated classes: not only at the economic level, but also at the level of political and ideological leadership, in civil, intellectual, and moral life as well as at the material level, and over the terrain of civil society as well as in and through the condensed relations of the state. This "authority and leadership" is, for Gramsci, not a given a priori but a specific historical "moment"—one of unusual social authority. It represents the product of a certain mastery of the class struggle, certainly, but it is still subject to the class struggle and the "relations of social forces" in society, of which its "unstable equilibrium" is only one, provisional, outcome or result. Hegemony is a state of play in the class struggle which has, therefore, to be continually worked on and reconstructed in order to be maintained, and which remains a contradictory conjuncture. The important point, for Gramsci, is that, under hegemonic conditions, the organization of consent (by the dominated classes to the "leadership" of the dominant class alliance) takes precedence (though it does not obliterate) the exercise of domination through coercion. In such conditions, the class struggle tends to assume the form, not of a "frontal assault" on the bastions of the state ("war of maneuver") but of a more protracted, strategic, and tactical struggle, exploiting and working on a number of different contradictions (Gramsci's "war of position"). A state of hegemony enables the ruling class alliance to undertake the enormous task of modifying, harnessing, securing, and elaborating the "superstructure" of society in line with the long-term requirements of the development of the mode of production—e.g., capital accumulation on an expanded scale. It enables such a class alliance to undertake the educative and formative tasks of raising the whole social formation to what he calls a "new level of civilization," favoring the expanded regime of capital. This is no immediate and direct imposition of the narrow, short-term, "corporate" class interests of a single class on society. It forges that unity between economic, political, and ideological objectives such that it can place "all the questions around which the struggle rages on a 'universal' not a corporative level, thereby creating a hegemony of a fundamental social group over a series of subordinate groups." This is what Gramsci calls the "educative and formative role of the State. . . . Its aim is always that of creating new and higher types of civilization; of adapting the 'civilization' and the morality of the broadest popular masses to the necessities of the continuous development of the economic apparatus of production"—the formation of a "national-popular will," based on a particular relationship between the dominant and dominated classes. This, then, depends, not on a presumed, necessary, or a priori correspondence between (economic) structure and (political and ideological) superstructures but precisely on those historically specific mechanisms—and the concrete analysis of those historical "moments"—through which such a formative relationship *between* structure and superstructures comes to be forged. For Gramsci, the object of analysis is always the specificity of this "structure-superstructure" complex—though as a historically concrete articulation. "It is the problem of the relations between structure and superstructure which must be accurately posed and resolved if the forces which are active in history . . . are to be correctly analysed." This is a rigorously nonreductionist conception: "How then could the whole system of superstructures be understood as distinctions within politics, and the introduction of the concept of distinction into a philosophy of praxis hence be justified? But can one really speak of a dialectic of distincts, and how is the concept of a circle joining the levels of the superstructure to be understood? Concept of 'historical bloc', i.e. . . . unity of opposites and distincts. Can one introduce the criterion of distinction into the structure too?" Gramsci, clearly, answers these questions in the affirmative. He is especially sharp against any form of vulgar economism: "It is therefore necessary to combat economism not only in the theory of historiography, but also and especially in the theory and practice of politics. In this field, the struggle can and must be carried on by developing the concept of hegemony." (All the quotes are from two essays in Gramsci 1971.)

Gramsci's theoretical contribution has only begun, recently, to be recognized—though his role as an outstanding militant in Italian politics in the 1920s and 1930s has long been acknowledged. His analysis bears, in a specially rich and productive way, on the analysis of the great bourgeois social formations of a developed capitalist type in Europe—Western Europe, where a reductionist economistic analysis, clearly, will not suffice to account for the depth of the transformations involved. Perhaps for this very reason, he has been thought of as, par excellence, the Marxist theorist of "Western capitalism." His work has, therefore, hardly been applied or employed in the analysis of non-European formations. There are, however, very strong grounds for thinking that it may have particular relevance for non-European social formations—for three, separate reasons. First, Gramsci may help to counteract the overwhelming weight of economism (Marxist and non-Marxist) which has characterized the analysis of postconquest and "colonial" societies. Perhaps because the weight of imperialist economic relations has been so powerfully visible, these formations have virtually been held to be explainable by an application of "imperialism" as essentially a purely "economic" process. Second, these societies present problems as to the relation in the "structure-superstructure complex" equal in complexity to those about which Gramsci wrote. Naturally, no simple transfer of concepts would be advisable here: Gramsci would be the first to insist on historical specificity, on difference. Third, Gramsci viewed the problem of "hegemony" from within the specific history of the Italian social formation. This gave him a particular, and highly relevant, perspective on the problem. For long periods Italy was marked precisely by the absence of "hegemony": by an alliance of ruling classes governing through domination rather than through hegemonic class leadership (direction). So his work is equally relevant for societies in which, according to the rhythm and punctuation of the class struggle, there have been significant movements into and out of a phase of "hegemonic direction." Moreover, Italy was/is a society brutally marked by the law of uneven development: with massive industrial capitalist development to the north, massive underdevelopment to the south. This raises the question of how the contradictions of the Italian social formation are articulated through different modes of production (capitalist and feudal), and through class alliances which combine elements from different social orders. The problem of the state, and the question of strategic alliances between the industrial proletariat and the peasantry, the "play" of traditional and advanced ideologies, and the difficulties these provide in the formation of a "national-popular will" all make his analysis of Italy specially relevant to colonial societies.

Gramsci's work has recently been taken up and developed in a structuralist manner—especially in Althusser's essay "Ideological State Apparatuses" (1971). This seminal essay differs from Gramsci's work, specifically, in posing the problem in terms of "reproduction." But the concerns which underlie this approach are not all that distant from those of Gramsci. The economic relations of production must themselves be "reproduced." This reproduction is not simply economic, but social, technical, and above all, ideological. This is another way of putting Gramsci's observation that, to achieve its full development, capitalist social relations require to be coupled with an elaborate development and elaboration at the "noneconomic" levels of politics, civil society, and culture, through moral, intellectual, and ideological leadership. Althusser then shares with Gramsci a classical concern for the manner in which the "hegemony" of a ruling class alliance is secured, at these other levels, through a formative and educative class leadership or authority over the social formation as a whole. Both of them argue that this enlarged or expanded hegemony is specific to the institutions, apparatuses, and relations of the so-called superstructures of the state and civil society. Both Althusser and Gramsci, then, insist that ideology, while itself a contradictory site and stake in the class struggle, has a specific function in securing the conditions for the expanded reproduction of capital. It is, therefore, a pertinent and distinctive level of struggle, where leadership is secured and contested: with mechanisms and sites of struggle "relatively autonomous." Both also maintain that "ideology" is not a simple form of false consciousness, to be explained as a set of myths or simple false constructions in the head. All societies require specific ideologies, which provide those systems of meaning, concepts, categories, and representations which make sense of the world, and through which men come to "live" (albeit unconsciously, and through a series of "misrecognitions"), in an imaginary way, their relation to the real, material conditions of their existence (which are only representable to them, as modes of consciousness, in and through ideology). Althusser sometimes tends to represent ideology as rather too functionally secured to the rule of the dominant classes: as if all ideology is, by definition, operative within the horizon of the "dominance ideas" of the ruling class. For Gramsci, ideologies are thought of in a more contradictory way—really, as sites and stakes in the class struggle. What interests Gramsci is how the existing ideologies— the "common sense" of the fundamental classes—which are themselves the complex result of previous moments and resolutions in the ideological class struggle, can be so actively *worked upon* so as to transform them into the basis of a more conscious struggle, and form of intervention in the historical process. Both insist, however, that ideologies are not simply "in the head," but are material relations—what Lenin called "ideological social relations"—which shape social actions, function through concrete institutions and apparatuses, and are materialized through practices.

Gramsci insists on the process which transforms these great "practical ideologies" of fundamental social classes. Althusser, for his part, adds that ideologies operate by constituting concrete individuals as the "social subjects" of ideological discourses—the process of what, following Laclau, he calls "interpellating subjects."

These propositions have been taken forward in a seminal intervention by Laclau (1977). In the essays "Populism" and "Fascism," Laclau argues that the individual elements of these ideologies (e.g., nationalism, militarism, racism, "the people," etc.) have, in themselves, no necessary class-belonging, "no necessary class connotation." We cannot assume a priori that these elements necessarily "belong" to any specific class, or indeed that a class, as a single homogeneous entity, has a single unitary and uncontradictory "world view" which, as Poulantzas (1973) says, it carries around with it, through history, "like a number plate on its back." Ideologies, as concrete discursive formations do exhibit a peculiar "unity" of their own. This unity arises, first, through what Laclau calls "condensation": where each element "fulfils a role of condensation with respect to others. When a familial interpellation, for example, evokes a political interpellation, or an aesthetic interpellation, and when each of these isolated interpellations operates as a symbol of the others, we have a relatively unified ideological discourse." (This has been defined as "ideological unity" through a process of connotative condensation—cf. O'Shea 1978.) Second, unity is secured through "the specific interpellation which forms the axis and organizing principle of all ideology. In trying to analyse the ideological level of a determinate social formation, our first task must be to reconstruct the interpellative structures which constitute it." If separate ideological elements have no necessary class-belonging, and classes do not have paradigmatic ideologies assigned or ascribed to them, what then is the relationship between classes and ideologies? As might be assumed, this relation is understood in terms of the way the class struggle articulates the various ideological discourses. "Articulation requires . . . the existence of non-class contents—interpellations and contradictions—which constitute the raw materials on which class ideological practices operate. The ideology of the dominant class, precisely because it is dominant, interpellates not only the members of that class but also members of the dominated class." It succeeds to the extent that it articulates "different ideologies to its hegemonic project by an elimination of their antagonistic character." Ideologies are therefore transformed "through the class struggle, which is carried out through the production of subjects and the articulation/disarticulation of discourses." This follows Gramsci's general line, which argued that ideologies cannot be reduced to the transparent, coherent "class interests" of their class-subjects, and that ideologies are transformed, not by one class imposing a unitary "world vision" upon all other classes, but by "a process of distinction and of change in the relative weight possessed by the elements of the old ideology . . . what was secondary or subordinate or even incidental becomes of primary importance, it becomes the nucleus of a new doctrinal and ideological ensemble" (Mouffe 1979; see also Mouffe for a seminal elaboration of this argument in relation to Gramsci).

There are problems with Laclau's tentative formulations: for example, what are "class practices" which can operate to transform ideologies but which are, themselves, presumably, without any specific ideological elements which "belong" to them? Despite these difficulties, these theorists begin to give us the tentative elements by means of which we can attempt to construct a nonreductionist theory of the superstructural or extraeconomic aspects of social formulations—once again, powered through the use of the concept of articulation.

What I have tried to do in this paper is to document the emergence of a new theoretical paradigm, which takes its fundamental orientation from the problematic of Marx's, but which seeks, by various theoretical means, to overcome certain of the limitations—economism, reductionism, "apriorism," a lack of historical specificity—which have beset certain traditional appropriations of Marxism, which still disfigure the contributions to this field by otherwise distinguished writers, and which have left Marxism vulnerable and exposed to effective criticism by many different variants of economistic monism and sociological pluralism. This is a survey of an emergent field, not a comprehensive critical account. It must in no sense be assumed that the solutions attempted have been fully demonstrated, or that they are as yet adequately developed or without serious weaknesses and lacunae. With respect to those racially structured social formations, which form the principal objects of inquiry in this collection, the problematic has hardly begun to be applied. Thus all that I have been able to do is to indicate certain strategic points of departure in such a potential field of application, certain protocols of theoretical procedure. Specifically, there is as yet no adequate theory of racism which is capable of dealing with both the economic and the superstructural features of such societies, while at the same time giving a historically concrete and sociologically specific account of distinctive racial aspects. Such an account, sufficient to substitute those inadequate versions which continue to dominate the field, remains to be provided. Nevertheless, in the hope of sponsoring and promoting such a development, it might be useful to conclude with a brief outline of some of the theoretical protocols which—in my view, of necessity—must govern any such proposed investigation.

This would have to begin from a rigorous application of what I have called the premise of historical specificity. Racism is not dealt with as a general feature of human societies, but with historically specific racisms, beginning with an assumption of difference, of specificity rather than of a unitary, transhistorical, or universal "structure." This is not to deny that there might well be discovered to be certain common features to all those social systems to which one would wish to attribute the designation "racially structured." But—as Marx remarked about the "chaotic" nature of all abstractions which proceed at the level of the "in-general" exclusively—such a general theory of racism is not the most favorable source for theoretical development and investigation: "even though the most developed languages have laws and characteristics in common with the least developed, nevertheless, just those things which determine their development, i.e. the elements which are *not* general and common, must be separated out . . . so that in their unity . . . their essential difference is not forgotten" (Marx 1973). Racism in general is a "rational abstraction" insofar as "it really brings out and fixes the common element and saves us repetition." Thus it may help to distinguish those social features which fix the different positions of social groups and classes on the basis of racial ascription (biologically or socially defined) from other systems which have a similar social function. However, "some determinations belong to all epochs, others only to a few. Some will be shared by the most modern epoch and the most ancient." This is a warning against extrapolating a common and universal structure to racism, which remains essentially the same, outside of its specific historical location. It is only as the different racisms are historically specified—in their difference—that they can be properly understood as "a product of historical relations and possess . . . full validity only for and within those relations." It follows that there might be more to be learned from distinguishing what, in common sense, appear to be variants of the same thing: for example, the racism of the slave South from the racism of the insertion of blacks into the "free forms" of industrial-capitalist development in the postbellum North; or the racism of Caribbean slave societies from that of the metropolitan societies like Britain, which have had to absorb black workers into industrial production in the twentieth century.

In part, this must be because one cannot explain racism in abstraction from other social relations—even if, alternatively, one cannot explain it by reducing it to those relations. It has been said that there are flourishing racisms in precapitalist social formations. This only means that, when dealing with more recent social formations, one is required to show how thoroughly racism is reorganized and rearticulated with the relations of new modes of production. Racism within plantation slave societies in the mercantilist phase of world capitalist development has a place and function, means and mechanisms of its specific effectivity, which are only superficially explained by translating it out from these specific historical contexts into totally different ones. Finley (1969), Davis (1969, 1970), and others have argued that, though slavery in the ancient world was articulated through derogatory classifications which distinguished between the enslaved and enslaving peoples, it did not necessarily entail the use of specifically racial categories, while plantation slavery almost everywhere did. Thus, there can be no assumed, necessary coincidence between racism and slavery as such. Precisely the differences in the roles which slavery played in these very different epochs and social formations may point us to the necessary ground for specifying what this specific coincidence between slavery and racism might secure. Where this coincidence does in fact appear, the mechanisms and effectivity of its functioning—including its articulation with other relations—need to be demonstrated, not assumed.

Again, the common assumption that it was attitudes of racial superiority which precipitated the introduction of plantation slavery needs to be challenged. It might be better to start from the opposite end—by seeing how slavery (the product of specific problems of labor shortage and the organization of plantation agriculture—supplied, in the first instance, by nonblack, indigenous labor, and then by white indentured labor) produced those forms of juridical racism which distinguish the epoch of plantation slavery. The elaboration of the juridical and property forms of slavery, as a set of enclaves within societies predicated on other legal and property forms, required specific and elaborate ideological work—as the history of slavery, and of its abolition, eloquently testifies. The same point may be made, in extenso, for all those explanations which ascribe racism-in-general to some universal functioning of individual psychology—the "racial itch," the "race instinct"—or explain its appearance in terms of a general psychology of prejudice. The question is not whether men-in-general make perceptual distinctions between groups with different racial or ethnic characteristics, but rather, what are the specific conditions which make this form of distinction socially pertinent, historically active. What gives this abstract human potentiality its effectivity, as a concrete material force? It could be said, for example, that Britain's long imperial hegemony, and the intimacy of the relationship between capitalist development at home and colonial conquest overseas, laid the trace of an active racism in British popular consciousness. Nevertheless, this alone cannot explain either the form and function which racism assumed, in the period of "popular imperialism" at the height of the imperialist rivalry toward the end of the nineteenth century, or the very different forms of indigenous racism, penetrating deep into the working class itself, which has been an emergent feature of the contact between black and white workers in the conditions of postwar migration. The histories of these different racisms cannot be written as a "general history" (Hall 1977b; Hall et al. 1978). Appeals to "human nature" are not explanations; they are an alibi.

One must start, then, from the concrete historical "work" which racism accomplishes under specific historical conditions—as a set of economic, political, and ideological practices, of a distinctive kind, concretely articulated with other practices in a social formation. These practices ascribe the positioning of different social groups in relation to one another with respect to the elementary structures of society; they fix and ascribe those positionings in ongoing social practices; they legitimate the posi-

tions so ascribed. In short, they are practices which secure the hegemony of a dominant group over a series of subordinate ones, in such a way as to dominate the whole
social formation in a form favorable to the long-term development of the economic
productive base. Though the economic aspects are critical, as a way of beginning,
this form of hegemony cannot be understood as operating purely through economic
coercion. Racism, so active at the level—"the economic nucleus"—where Gramsci
insists hegemony must first be secured, will have or contract elaborate relations at
other instances, in the political, cultural, and ideological levels. Yet, put in this (obviously correct) way, the assertion is still too a priori. How specifically do these mechanisms operate? What further determinations need to be supplied? Racism is not
present, in the same form or degree, in all capitalist formations: it is not necessary to
the concrete functioning of all capitalisms. It needs to be shown how and why racism
has been specifically overdetermined by and articulated with certain capitalisms at
different stages of their development. Nor can it be assumed that this must take one,
single form or follow one necessary path or logic, through a series of necessary
stages.

This requires us, in turn, to show its articulation with the different structures of
the social formation. For example, the position of the slave in pre-emancipation
plantation society was not secured exclusively through race. It was predominantly
secured by the quite specific and distinctive productive relations of slave-based agriculture, and through the distinctive property status of the slave (as a commodity) and
of slave labor power (as united with its exerciser, who was not however its
"owner"), coupled with legal, political, and ideological systems which anchored this
relation by racial ascription. This coupling may have provided the ready-made rationale and framework for those structures of "informal racism" which became operative when "freed" black labor migrated northward in the United States or into the
"free village" system in the post-emancipation Caribbean. Yet the "coupling" operated in new ways, and required its own ideological work—as in the "Jim Crow"
legislation of the 1880s and 1890s (Van Woodward 1957). The reproduction of the
low and ascribed status of black labor, as a specific fraction of the "free laboring"
classes of industrial capitalism, was secured—with the assistance of a transformed
racism, to be sure, but also through other mechanisms, which accomplished their
structured positioning with respect to new forms of capital in new ways. In the latter
case, pertinent struggles have developed which exploited the gaps, or worked directly on the contradictions between racial ascription and the official ideologies of
"equal opportunity" which were simply not available to black slaves under a plantation system (Myrdal 1962). We treat these differences as "essentially the same" at
our peril. On the other hand, it does not follow that because developed capitalism
here functions predominantly on the basis of "free labor" that the racial aspects of

social relations can be assimilated, for all practical purposes, to its typical class relations (as does Cox 1970, despite many pertinent observations). Race continues to differentiate between the different fractions of the working classes with respect to capital, creating specific forms of fracturing and fractioning which are as important for the ways in which they intersect class relations (and divide the class struggle, internally) as they are mere "expressions" of some general form of the class struggle. Politically and culturally, these combined and uneven relations between class and race are historically more pertinent than their simple correspondence.

At the economic level, it is clear that race must be given its distinctive and "relatively autonomous" effectivity, as a distinctive feature. This does not mean that the economic is sufficient to found an explanation of how these relations concretely function. One needs to know how different racial and ethnic groups were inserted historically, and the relations which have tended to erode and transform, or to preserve these distinctions through time—not simply as residues and traces of previous modes, but as active structuring principles of the present organization of society. Racial categories alone will not provide or explain these. What are the different forms and relations in which these racial fractions were combined under capital? Do they stand in significantly different relations to capital? Do they stand within an articulation of different modes of production? What are the relations of dissolution/conservation between them? How has race functioned to preserve and develop these articulations? What are the functions which the dominated modes of production perform in the reproduction of the dominant mode? Are these linked to it through the domestic reproduction of labor power "below its value," the supply of cheap labor, the regulation of the "reserve army of labor," the supply of raw materials, of subsistence agriculture, the hidden costs of social reproduction? The indigenous "natural economies" of Latin America and the forms of semidomestic production characteristic of the Caribbean societies differ significantly, among and between them, in this respect. The same is true even where different ethnic fractions stand in the same sets of relations to capital. For example, the position of black labor in the industrial North of the United States and of black migration to postwar Britain show highly distinctive patternings along racial lines: yet these situations are not explicable without the concept of the "reserve army of labor." Yet it is clear that blacks are not the only division within the "reserve army": hence race is not the only mechanism through which its size and composition is regulated. In the United States, both white immigrants (e.g., European and Mexican) and women, and in Britain both women and the Irish, have provided a significant alternative element (see Braverman 1975; Castles and Kosak 1973).

The either/or alternatives, surveyed in the opening parts of this paper, are therefore seriously disabling, at a theoretical level, whether it is "metropolitan" or "satellite" formations which are under discussion, and whether it is historical or contemporary forms which are under scrutiny. As I have argued (Hall et al. 1978), the structures through which black labor is reproduced—structures which may be general to capital at a certain stage of development, whatever the racial composition of labor—are not simply "colored" by race: they work through race. The relations of capitalism can be thought of as articulating classes in distinct ways at each of the levels or instances of the social formation—economic, political, ideological. These levels are the "effects" of the structures of modern capitalist production, with the necessary displacement of relative autonomy operating between them. Each level of the social formation requires its own independent "means of representation"—the means by which the class-structured mode of production appears, and acquires effectivity at the level of the economic, the political, the ideological class struggle. Race is intrinsic to the manner in which the black laboring classes are complexly constituted at each of these levels. It enters into the way black labor, male and female, is distributed as economic agents at the level of economic practices, and the class struggles which result from it; and into the way the fractions of the black laboring classes are reconstituted, through the means of political representation (parties, organizations, community action centers, publications, and campaigns), as political forces in the "theater of politics"—and the political struggles which result; and the manner in which the class is articulated as the collective and individual "subjects" of emergent ideologies—and the struggles over ideology, culture, and consciousness which result. This gives the matter or dimension of race, and racism, a practical as well as theoretical centrality to all the relations which affect black labor. The constitution of this fraction as a class, and the class relations which ascribe it, function as race relations. Race is thus, also, the modality in which class is "lived," the medium through which class relations are experienced, the form in which it is appropriated and "fought through." This has consequences for the whole class, not specifically for its "racially defined" segment. It has consequences in terms of the internal fractioning and division within the working class which, among other ways, are articulated in part through race. This is no mere racist conspiracy from above. For racism is also one of the dominant means of ideological representation through which the white fractions of the class come to "live" their relations to other fractions, and through them to capital itself. Those who seek, with effect, to disarticulate some of the existing syntaxes of class struggle (albeit of a corporatist or social-reformist kind) and to rearticulate class experience through the condensed interpellations of a racist ideological syntax are, of course, key agents in this work of ideological transformation—this is the ideological class struggle, pursued, precisely, through harnessing the dominated classes to capital by means of the articulation of the internal contradictions of class experience with racism. In Britain, this process has recently attained a rare and general pitch. But they succeed to the measure that they do because they are practicing on real contradictions within and inside the class, working on real effects of the structure (however these may be "misrecognized" through racism)—not because they are clever at conjuring demons, or because they brandish swastikas and read *Mein Kampf.*

Racism is, thus, not only a problem for blacks who are obliged to suffer it. Nor is it a problem only for those sections of the white working class and those organizations infected by its stain. Nor can it be overcome, as a general virus in the social body, by a heavy dose of liberal innoculation. Capital reproduces the class, including its internal contradictions, as a whole—structured by race. It dominates the divided class, in part, through those internal divisions which have racism as one of its effects. It contains and disables representative class institutions, by neutralizing them—confining them to strategies and struggles which are race-specific, which do not surmount its limits, its barrier. Through racism, it is able to defeat the attempts to construct alternative means of representation which could more adequately represent the class as a whole, or which are capable of effecting the unity of the class as a result: that is, those alternatives which would adequately represent the class as a whole—against capitalism, against racism. The sectional struggles, articulated through race, instead, continue to appear as the necessary defensive strategies of a class divided against itself, face-to-face with capital. They are, therefore, also the site of capital's continuing hegemony over it. This is certainly not to treat racism as, in any simple sense, the product of an ideological trick.

Nevertheless, such an analysis would need to be complemented by an analysis of the specific forms which racism assumes in its ideological functioning. Here, we would have to begin by investigating the different ways in which racist ideologies have been constructed and made operative under different historical conditions: the racisms of mercantilist theory and of chattel slavery; of conquest and colonialism; of trade and "high imperialism"; of "popular imperialism" and of so-called postimperialism. In each case, in specific social formations, racism as an ideological configuration has been reconstituted by the dominant class relations, and thoroughly reworked. If it has performed the function of that cementing ideology which secures a whole social formation under a dominant class, its pertinent differences from other such hegemonic ideologies require to be registered in detail. Here, racism is particularly powerful and its imprint on popular consciousness especially deep, because in such racial characteristics as color, ethnic origin, geographical position, etc., racism discovers what other ideologies have to construct: an apparently "natural" and universal basis in nature itself. Yet, despite this apparent grounding in biological givens, outside history, racism, when it appears, has an effect on other ideological formations within the same society, and its development promotes a transformation of the whole ideological field in which it becomes operative. It can in this way harness other ideological discourses to itself—for example, it articulates securely with the us/them structure of corporate class consciousness—through the mechanism previously discussed of connotative condensation. Its effects are similar to other ideologies from which, on other grounds, it must be distinguished: racisms also dehistoricize— translating historically specific structures into the timeless language of nature; decomposing classes into individuals and recomposing those disaggregated individuals into the reconstructed unities, the great coherences, of new ideological "subjects." It translates "classes" into "blacks" and "whites," economic groups into "peoples," solid forces into "races." This is the process of constituting new "historical subjects" for ideological discourses—the mechanism we encountered earlier, of forming new interpellative structures. It produces, as the natural and given "authors" of a spontaneous form of racial perception, the naturalized "racist subject." This is not an external function, operative only against those whom it disposes or disarticulates (renders silent). It is also pertinent for the dominated subjects—those subordinated ethnic groups or "races" which live their relation to their real conditions of existence, and to the domination of the dominant classes, in and through the imaginary representations of a racist interpellation, and who come to experience themselves as "the inferiors," *les autres.* And yet these processes are themselves never exempted from the ideological class struggle. The racist interpellations can become themselves the sites and stake in the ideological struggle, occupied and redefined to become the elementary forms of an oppositional formation—as where "white racism" is vigorously contested through the symbolic inversions of "black power." The ideologies of racism remain contradictory structures, which can function both as the vehicles for the imposition of dominant ideologies, and as the elementary forms for the cultures of resistance. Any attempt to delineate the politics and ideologies of racism which omits these continuing features of struggle and contradiction wins an apparent adequacy of explanation only by operating a disabling reductionism.

In this field of inquiry, "sociological theory" has still to find its way, by a difficult effort of theoretical clarification, through the Scylla of a reductionism which must deny almost everything in order to explain something, and the Charybdis of a pluralism which is so mesmerized by "everything" that it cannot explain anything. To those willing to labor on, the vocation remains an open one.

Works Cited

Alavi, H. 1975. "India and the Colonial Mode of Production." *Socialist Register* (London).

Althusser, L. 1965. *For Marx.* London: Allan Lane.

———. 1971. *"Lenin and Philosophy" and Other Essays.* London: New Left Books.

———. 1976. *Essays in Self-Criticism.* London: New Left Books.

Althusser, L., and E. Balibar. 1970. *Reading Capital.* London: New Left Books.

Anderson, P. 1977. "The Antinomies of Antonio Gramsci." *New Left Review* (London), no. 100.

Banaji, J. 1977. "Modes of Production in a Materialist Conception of History." *Capital and Class* (London), no. 3.

Barthes, R. 1967. *Elements of Semiology*. London: Jonathan Cape.

Beechey, V. 1978. "The Ideology of Racism." Ph.D. thesis, Oxford University.

Bettelheim, C. 1972. "Theoretical Comments." In *Unequal Exchange,* ed. A. Emmanuel. London: New Left Books.

Bradby, B. 1975. "Capitalist/Precapitalist Articulation." *Economy and Society* (London) 4, no. 2.

Braverman, H. 1975. *Labour and Monopoly Capital*. New York: Monthly Review Press.

Carchedi, G. 1977. *On the Economic Identification of Social Classes*. London: Routledge and Kegan Paul.

Castles, C., and G. Kosak. 1973. *Immigrant Workers and Class Structure in Western Europe*. London: Oxford University Press.

Clammer, J. 1975. "Economic Anthropology and the Sociology of Development." In *Beyond the Sociology of Development,* ed. I. Oxall, T. Barnett, and D. Booth. London: Routledge and Kegan Paul.

Cox, O. 1970. *Caste, Class, and Race*. New York: Monthly Review Press.

Cutler, A., et al. 1977. *Marx's Capital and Capitalism Today*. London: Routledge and Kegan Paul.

Davis, D. B. 1969. "Comparative Approach to American History: Slavery." In *Slavery in the New World,* ed. E. Genovese and L. Foner. Englewood Cliffs, N.J.: Prentice-Hall.

———. 1970. *The Problem of Slavery in Western Culture*. Ithaca: Cornell University Press.

Finley, M. 1969. "The Idea of Slavery." In *Slavery in the New World,* ed. E. Genovese and L. Foner. Englewood Cliffs, N.J.: Prentice-Hall.

Fogel, R., and S. Engerman. 1974. *Time on the Cross*. Boston: Little, Brown and Co.

Foster-Carter, A. 1978. "The Modes of Production Debate." *New Left Review* (London), no. 104.

Frank, A. G. 1969. *Capitalism and Underdevelopment in Latin America*. New York: Monthly Review Press.

Furtado, C. 1971. "Dependencia externa y teoria economica." *El Trimestre Economico,* April–June. Translated by P. O'Brien, in *Beyond the Sociology of Development,* ed. I. Oxall, T. Barnett, and D. Booth. London: Routledge and Kegan Paul, 1975.

Genovese, E. 1965. *The Political Economy of Slavery*. New York: Vintage Books.

———. 1970. *The World the Slaveholders Made*. New York: Vintage Books.

———. 1971. *In Red and Black*. New York: Vintage Books.

———. 1977. "Reply to Criticism." *Medical History Review* (New York), winter.

Gramsci, A. 1971. *Selections from the Prison Notebooks*. London: Lawrence and Wishart.

Hall, S. 1973. "Marx's Notes on Method: A Reading of 'The 1857 Introduction.'" *Working Papers in Cultural Studies* (Birmingham) 6.

———. 1977a. "Continuing the Discussion." In *Race and Class in Post-Colonial Society*. Paris: UNESCO.

———. 1977b. "Pluralism, Race, and Class in Caribbean Society." In *Race and Class in Post-Colonial Society*. Paris: UNESCO.

Hall, S., B. Lumley, and G. McLennan. 1977. "Politics and Ideology in A. Gramsci." *Working Papers in Cultural Studies* (Birmingham) 10.

Hall, S., et al. 1978, *Policing the Crisis.* London: Macmillan.

Hilton, R., ed. 1976. *The Transition from Feudalism to Capitalism.* London: New Left Books.

Hindess, B., and P. Hirst. 1975. *Pre-Capitalist Modes of Production.* London: Routledge and Kegan Paul.

———. 1977. *Modes of Production and Social Formation.* London: Routledge and Kegan Paul.

Hirst, P. 1976. "Althusser's Theory of Ideology." *Economy and Society* (London) 5, no. 4.

Johnson, R., et al. 1978a. "The Problem of 'A-priorism.' " Birmingham: Centre for Cultural Studies. Mimeograph.

———. 1978b. " 'The Histories' in Marx." Birmingham: Centre for Cultural Studies. Mimeograph.

Kuper, L. 1974. *Race, Class, and Power.* London: Duckworth.

Laclau, E. 1977. *Politics and Ideology in Marxist Theory.* London: New Left Books.

Marx, K. 1956. *Capital.* Vol. 2. London: Lawrence and Wishart.

———. 1961. *Capital.* Vol. 1. Moscow: Foreign Languages Publishing House.

———. 1965. *Precapitalist Economic Formations.* Ed. E. Hobsbawm. New York: International Publishers.

———. 1973. *Introduction to "The Grundrisse."* London: Penguin.

———. 1974. *Capital.* Vol. 3. London: Lawrence and Wishart.

McLennan, G. 1976. "Some Problems in British Marxist Historiography." Birmingham: Centre for Cultural Studies. Mimeograph.

Meillassoux, C. 1960. "Essai d'interprétation de phénomène économique dans les sociétiés traditionelles d'auto-subsistence." *Cahiers d'Études Africaines* (The Hague), vol. 4.

———. 1972. "From Production to Reproduction." *Economy and Society* (London) 1, no. 1.

———. 1974. "Imperialism as a Mode of Reproduction of Labour Power." Mimeograph.

Mouffe, C. 1979. Introduction to *Gramsci and Marxist Theory,* ed. C. Mouffe. London: Routledge.

Myrdal, G. 1962. *An American Dilemma: The Negro Problem and Modern Democracy.* New York: Harper and Row.

O'Brien, P. 1975. "A Critique of Latin-American Dependency Theories." In *Beyond the Sociology of Development,* ed. I. Oxall, T. Barnett, and D. Booth. London: Routledge and Kegan Paul.

O'Shea, A. 1978. "A Critique of Laclau's Theory of Interpellation." Birmingham: Centre for Cultural Studies. Mimeograph.

Oxall, I., T. Barnett, and D. Booth, eds. 1975. *Beyond the Sociology of Development.* London: Routledge and Kegan Paul.

Post, K. 1978. *Arise, Ye Starvelings: The Jamaican Labour Rebellion of 1938 and Its Aftermath.* The Hague: Nijoff.

Poulantzas, N. 1973. *Political Power and Social Classes.* London: New Left Books.

Rex, J. 1970. *Race Relations in Sociological Theory.* London: Weidenfeld and Nicholson.

————. 1973. *Race, Colonialism, and the City.* London: Routledge and Kegan Paul.

————. 1977. "New Nations and Ethnic Minorities." In *Race and Class in Post-colonial Society.* Paris: UNESCO.

Rey, P.-P. 1971. *Colonialisme, neo-colonialisme, et transition au capitalisme.* Paris: Maspéro.

————. 1973. *Les alliances de classes.* Paris: Maspéro.

————. 1975. "Reflections on the Lineage Mode of Production." *Critique of Anthropology* (London), no. 3.

Rey, P.-P., and G. Dupré. 1973. "Reflections on the Pertinence of a Theory of Exchange." *Economy and Society* (London) 2, no. 2.

Rose, S., J. Hambley, and J. Haywood. 1973. "Science, Racism, and Ideology." *Socialist Register* (London).

Schwarz, B. 1978. "On Maurice Dobb." In *Economy, History, Concept,* ed. R. Johnson, G. McLennan, and B. Schwarz. Birmingham: Centre for Cultural Studies.

Seddon, D., ed. 1978. Introduction to *Relations of Production.* London: Cass.

Smith, M. G. 1965. *The Plural Society in the British West Indies.* Berkeley: University of California Press.

Terray, E. 1972. *Marxism and "Primitive Societies."* New York: Monthly Review Press.

Van den Berghe, P. 1965. *South Africa: A Study in Conflict.* Middletown, Conn.: Wesleyan University Press.

Vann Woodward, C. 1957. *The Strange Career of Jim Crow.* London: Oxford University Press.

Williams, E. 1966. *Capitalism and Slavery.* Chapel Hill: Russell.

Wolpe, H. 1972. "Capitalism and Cheap Labour in South Africa." *Economy and Society* (London) 1, no. 4.

————. 1975. "The Theory of Internal Colonialism." In *Beyond the Sociology of Development,* ed. I. Oxall, T. Barnett, and D. Booth. London: Routledge and Kegan Paul.

————. 1976. "The White Working Class in South Africa." *Economy and Society* (London) 5, no. 2.

————. 1980. Introduction to *The Articulation of Modes of Production,* ed. H. Wolpe. London: Routledge.

Two

White Woman Listen! Black Feminism and the Boundaries of Sisterhood

Hazel V. Carby

I'm leaving evidence. And you got to leave evidence too. And your children got to leave evidence. . . . They burned all the documents. . . . We got to burn out what they put in our minds, like you burn out a wound. Except we got to keep what we need to bear witness. That scar that's left to bear witness. We got to keep it as visible as our blood.

Gayle Jones, *Corregidora*

The black women's critique of *his*tory has not only involved us in coming to terms with "absences"; we have also been outraged by the ways in which it has made us visible, when it has chosen to see us. *His*tory has constructed our sexuality and our femininity as deviating from those qualities with which white women, as the prize objects of the Western world, have been endowed. We have also been defined in less than human terms (Jordan 1969, 238, 495, 500). Our continuing struggle with *his*tory began with its "discovery" of us. However, this chapter will be concerned with *her*story rather than *his*tory. We wish to address questions to the feminist theories which have been developed during the last decade; a decade in which black women have been fighting, in the streets, in the schools, through the courts, inside and outside the wage relation. The significance of these struggles ought to inform the writing of the herstory of women in Britain. It is fundamental to the development of a feminist theory and practice that is meaningful for black women. We cannot hope to reconstitute ourselves in all our absences, or to rectify the ill-conceived presences that invade herstory from *his*tory,

61

but we do wish to bear witness to our own herstories. The connections between these and the herstories of white women will be made and remade in struggle. Black women have come from Africa, Asia, and the Caribbean and we cannot do justice to all their herstories in a single chapter. Neither can we represent the voices of all black women in Britain; our herstories are too numerous and too varied. What we will do is offer ways in which the "triple" oppressions of gender, race, and class can be understood, in their specificity, and also as they determine the lives of black women.

Much contemporary debate has posed the question of the relation between race and gender, in terms which attempt to parallel race and gender divisions. It can be argued that as processes, racism and sexism are similar. Ideologically, for example, they both construct common sense through reference to "natural" and "biological" differences. It has also been argued that the categories of race and gender are both socially constructed and that, therefore, they have little internal coherence as concepts. Furthermore, it is possible to parallel racialized and gendered divisions in the sense that the possibilities of amelioration through legislation appear to be equally ineffectual in both cases. Michèle Barrett, however, has pointed out that it is not possible to argue for parallels because as soon as historical analysis is made, it becomes obvious that the institutions which have to be analyzed are different, as are the forms of analysis needed.[1] We would agree that the construction of such parallels is fruitless and often proves to be little more than a mere academic exercise; but there are other reasons for our dismissal of these kinds of debate. The experience of black women does not enter the parameters of parallelism. The fact that black women are subject to the *simultaneous* oppression of patriarchy, class, and "race" is the prime reason for not employing parallels that render their position and experience not only marginal but also invisible.

In arguing that most contemporary feminist theory does not begin to adequately account for the experience of black women we also have to acknowledge that it is not a simple question of their absence; consequently, the task is not one of rendering their visibility. On the contrary we will have to argue that the process of accounting for their historical and contemporary position does, in itself, challenge the use of some of the central categories and assumptions of recent mainstream feminist thought. We can point to no single source for our oppression. When white feminists emphasize patriarchy alone, we want to redefine the term and make it a more complex concept. Racism ensures that black men do not have the same relations to patriarchal/capitalist hierarchies as white men. In the words of the Combahee River Collective:

1. My thanks to Michèle Barrett, who, in a talk given at the Social Science Research Council's Unit on Ethnic Relations, helped to clarify many of these attempted parallels.

We believe that sexual politics under patriarchy is as pervasive in Black women's lives as are the politics of class and race. We also often find it difficult to separate race from class from sex oppression because in our lives they are most often experienced simultaneously. We know that there is such a thing as racial-sexual oppression which is neither solely racial nor solely sexual e.g. the history of rape of Black women by white men as a weapon of political repression.

Although we are feminists and lesbians, we feel solidarity with progressive Black men and do not advocate the fractionalisation that white women who are separatists demand. Our situation as Black people necessitates that we have solidarity around the fact of race, which white women of course do not need to have with white men, unless it is their negative solidarity as racial oppressors. We struggle together with Black men against racism, while we also struggle with Black men about sexism. (In Moraga and Anzaldua 1981, 213)

It is only in the writings by black feminists that we can find attempts to theorize the interconnection of class, gender, and race as it occurs in our lives and it has only been in the autonomous organizations of black women that we have been able to express and act upon the experiences consequent upon these determinants. Many black women had been alienated by the nonrecognition of their lives, experiences, and herstories in the women's liberation movement. Black feminists have been, and are still, demanding that the existence of racism must be acknowledged as a structuring feature of our relationships with white women. Both white feminist theory and practice have to recognize that white women stand in a power relation as oppressors of black women. This compromises any feminist theory and practice founded on the notion of simple equality.

Three concepts which are central to feminist theory become problematic in their application to black women's lives: "the family," "patriarchy," and "reproduction." When used they are placed in a context of the herstory of white (frequently middle-class) women and become contradictory when applied to the lives and experiences of black women. In a comprehensive survey of contemporary feminist theory, *Women's Oppression Today,* Michèle Barrett sees the contemporary family (effectively the family under capitalism) as the source of oppression of women:

It is difficult to argue that the present structure of the family-household is anything other than oppressive for women. Feminists have consistently, and rightly, seen the family as a central site of women's oppression in contemporary society. The reasons for this lie both in the material structure of the household, by which women are by and large financially dependent on men, and in the ideology of the family, through which women are confined to a primary concern with domesticity and motherhood. This situation underwrites the disadvantages women experience at work, and lies at the root of the exploitation of female sexuality endemic in our society. The concept of "dependence" is perhaps, the link between the material organisation of the household, and the ideology of femininity: an assumption of women's dependence on men structures both of these areas. (1980, 214)

The immediate problem for black feminists is whether this framework can be applied at all to analyze our herstory of oppression and struggle. We would not wish to deny that the family can be a source of oppression for us but we also wish to examine how the black family has functioned as a prime source of resistance to oppression. We need to recognize that during slavery, periods of colonialism, and under the present authoritarian state, the black family has been a site of political and cultural resistance to racism. Furthermore, we cannot easily separate the two forms of oppression because racist theory and practice are frequently gender-specific. Ideologies of black female sexuality do not stem primarily from the black family. The way the gender of black women is constructed differs from constructions of white femininity because it is also subject to racism. Black feminists have been explaining this since the last century, when Sojourner Truth pointed to the ways in which "womanhood" was denied the black woman.

> That man over there says women need to be helped into carriages, and lifted over ditches, and to have the best place everywhere. Nobody ever helps me into carriages, and lifted over ditches, or over mud-puddles, or gives me any best place! And aint I a woman? Look at me! Look at my arm! I have ploughed, and planted, and gathered into barns, and no man could head me! And aint I a woman? I could work as much and eat as much as a man—when I could get it—and bear the lash as well! And aint I a woman? I have borne thirteen children, and seen most all sold off to slavery, and when I cried with my mother's grief, none but Jesus heard me! And aint I a woman? (Loewenberg and Bogin 1978, 235)

Black women are constantly challenging racist ideologies of black female sexuality in their day-to-day struggles. Asian girls in schools, for example, are fighting back to destroy the racist mythology of their femininity. As Pratibha Parmar has pointed out, careers officers do not offer them the same interviews and job opportunities as white girls. This is because they believe that Asian girls will be forced into marriage immediately after leaving school. The commonsense logic of this racism dictates that a career for Asian girls is thought to be a waste of time. But the struggle in schools is not just against the racism of the careers service:

> "Yes, and then there are some racist students who are always picking on us.

Recently, we had a fight in our school between us and some white girls. We really showed them we were not going to stand for their rubbish. "

Sangeeta and Wahida's statements reflect a growing confidence and awareness amongst young Asian girls about themselves and their situations in a climate of increased racist attacks on black people generally.

Many Asian girls strongly resent being stereotyped as weak, passive, quiet girls, who would not dare lift a finger in their own defence. They want to challenge the idea people have of them as girls "who do not want to stand out or cause trouble but to tip-toe about hoping nobody will notice them." (Parmar and Mirza 1981)

The use of the concept of "dependency" is also a problem for black feminists. It has been argued that this concept provides the link between the "material organisation of the household, and the ideology of femininity." How then can we account for situations in which black women may be heads of households, or where, because of an economic system which structures high black male unemployment, they are not financially dependent upon a black man? This condition exists in both colonial and metropolitan situations. Ideologies of black female domesticity and motherhood have been constructed, through their employment (or chattel position) as domestics and surrogate mothers to white families rather than in relation to their own families. West Indian women still migrate to the United States and Canada as domestics and in Britain are seen to be suitable as office cleaners, National Health Service domestics, etc. In colonial situations Asian women have frequently been forced into prostitution to sexually service the white male invaders, whether in the form of armies of occupation or employees and guests of multinational corporations. How then, in view of all this, can it be argued that black male dominance exists in the same forms as white male dominance? Systems of slavery, colonialism, imperialism have systematically denied positions in the white male hierarchy to black men and have used specific forms of terror to oppress them.

Black family structures have been seen as pathological by the state and are in the process of being constructed as pathological within white feminist theory. Here, ironically, Western nuclear family structure and related ideologies of "romantic love" formed under capitalism are seen as more "progressive" than black family structures. An unquestioned commonsense racism constructs Asian girls and women as having absolutely no freedom, whereas English girls are thought to be in a more "liberated" society and culture. However, one Asian schoolgirl points out:

Where is the freedom in going to a disco, frightened in case no boy fancies you, or no one asks you to dance, or your friends are walked home with boys and you have to walk home in the dark alone? (Parmar and Mirza 1981)

The media's "horror stories" about Asian girls and arranged marriages bear very little relation to their experience. The "feminist" version of this ideology presents Asian women as being in need of liberation, not in terms of their own herstory and needs, but *into* the "progressive" social mores and customs of the metropolitan West. The actual struggles that Asian women are involved in are ignored in favor of applying theories from the point of view of a more "advanced," more "progressive" outside observer. In fact, it is very easy for this ideology to be taken up and used by the state in furtherance of racist and sexist practices. The way in which the issue of arranged marriages has been used by the government to legitimate increased restrictions on immigration from the subcontinent is one example of this process.

Too often concepts of historical progress are invoked by the left and feminists alike, to create a sliding scale of "civilized liberties." When barbarous sexual practices are to be described, the "Third World" is placed on display and compared to the "First World," which is seen as more "enlightened" or "progressive." The metropolitan centers of the West define the questions to be asked of other social systems and, at the same time, provide the measure against which all "foreign" practices are gauged. In a peculiar combination of Marxism and feminism, capitalism becomes the vehicle for reforms, which allow for progress toward the emancipation of women. The "Third World," on the other hand, is viewed as retaining precapitalist forms expressed at the cultural level by traditions which are more oppressive to women. For example, in an article comparing socialist societies, Maxine Molyneux falls straight into this trap of "Third Worldism" as "backwardness."

> A second major problem facing Third World post-revolutionary states is the weight of conservative ideologies and practices; this is often subsumed in official literature under the categories of "traditionalism" or "feudal residues." The impact and nature of "traditionalism" is subject to considerable variation between countries but where it retains any force it may constitute an obstacle to economic and social development which has to be overcome in the formation of a new society. In some societies customary practices tend to bear especially heavily on women. Institutions such as polygyny, the brideprice, child marriages, seclusion, and forms of mutilation such as footbinding or female "circumcision" are woven into the very fabric of pre-capitalist societies. They often survive in Third World countries long after they have been made illegal and despite the overall changes that have occurred. (1981, 3)

Molyneux sees "systems of inheritance and arranged marriages" as being one of the central ways "by which forms of pre-capitalist property and social relations are maintained."

One immediate problem with this approach is that it is extraordinarily general. The level of generality applied to the "Third World" would be dismissed as too vague to be informative if applied to Western industrialized nations. However, Molyneux implies that since "Third World" women are outside of capitalist relations of production, entering capitalist relations is, necessarily, an emancipating move.

> There can be little doubt that on balance the position of women within imperialist, i.e. advanced capitalist societies is, for all its limitations, more advanced than in the less developed capitalist and non-capitalist societies. In this sense the changes brought by imperialism to Third World societies may, in some circumstances, have been historically progressive. (4)

This view of imperialism will be addressed in more detail later in the chapter. At this point we wish to indicate that the use of such theories reinforces the view that when black women enter Britain they are moving into a more liberated or enlightened or emancipated society than the one from which they have come. Nancy Foner saw the embodiment of West Indian women's increased freedom and liberation in Britain in the fact that they learned to drive cars![2] Different herstories, different struggles of black women against systems that oppress them, are buried beneath Eurocentric conceptions of their position. Black family structures are seen as being produced by less advanced economic systems and their extended kinship networks are assumed to be more oppressive to women. The model of the white nuclear family, which rarely applies to black women's situation, is the measure by which they are pathologized and stands as a more progressive structure to the one in which they live.

It can be seen from this brief discussion of the use of the concept "the family" that the terms "patriarchy" and "reproduction" also become more complex in their application. It bears repetition that black men have not held the same patriarchal positions of power that the white males have established. Michèle Barrett argues that the term "patriarchy" has lost all analytic or explanatory power and has been reduced to a synonym for male dominance. She tries therefore to limit its use to a specific type of male dominance that could be located historically.

> I would not . . . want to argue that the concept of patriarchy should be jettisoned. I would favour retaining it for use in contexts where male domination is expressed through the power of the father over women and over younger men. . . . Hence I would argue for a more precise and specific use of the concept of patriarchy, rather than one which expands it to cover all expressions of male domination and thereby attempts to construe a descriptive term as a systematic explanatory theory. (Barrett 1980)

2. Foner also argues that "In rural Jamaica, most women do not smoke cigarettes; in London, many of the women I interviewed smoked, and when I commented on this they noted that such behaviour would not have been approved in Jamaica. Thus in England there is an enlargement of the women's world" (1979, 69–70).

Barrett is not thinking of capitalist social organization. But if we try to apply this more "classic" and limited definition of patriarchy to the slave systems of the Americas and the Caribbean, we find that even this refined use of the concept cannot adequately account for the fact that both slaves and manumitted males did not have this type of patriarchal power. Alternatively, if we take patriarchy and apply it to various colonial situations it is equally unsatisfactory because it is unable to explain why black males have not enjoyed the benefits of white patriarchy. There are very obvious power structures in both colonial and slave social formations and they are predominantly patriarchal. However, the historically specific forms of racism force us to modify or alter the application of the term "patriarchy" to black men. Black women have been dominated "patriarchally" in different ways by men of different "colors."

In questioning the application of the concepts of "the family" and "patriarchy" we also need to problematize the use of the concept of "reproduction." In using this concept in relation to the domestic labor of black women we find that in spite of its apparent simplicity it must be dismantled. What does the concept of reproduction mean in a situation where black women have done domestic labor outside of their own homes in the servicing of white families? In this example they lie outside of the industrial wage relation but in a situation where they are providing for the reproduction of black labor in their own domestic sphere, simultaneously ensuring the reproduction of white labor power in the "white" household. The concept, in fact, is unable to explain exactly what the relations are that need to be revealed. What needs to be understood is, first, precisely *how* the black woman's role in a rural, industrial, or domestic labor force affects the construction of ideologies of black female sexuality which are different from, and often constructed in opposition to, white female sexuality; and second, how this role relates to the black woman's struggle for control over her own sexuality.[3]

If we examine the recent herstory of women in postwar Britain we can see the ways in which the inclusion of black women creates problems for hasty generalization. In pointing to the contradiction between "homemaking as a career" and the campaign to recruit women into the labor force during postwar reconstruction, Elizabeth Wilson (1980, 43–44) fails to perceive migration of black women to Britain as the solution to these contradictory needs. The Economic Survey for 1947 is cited as an example of the ways in which women were seen to form "the only large reserve of labour left," yet, as we know, there was a rather large pool of labor in the colonies that had been mobilized previously to fight in World War II. The industries that the survey listed as in dire need of labor included those that were filled by both male and female black workers, though Elizabeth Wilson does not differentiate them.

3. See Parmar 1982 for an elaboration of this point.

The survey gave a list of the industries and services where labour was most urgently required. The boot and shoe industry, clothing, textiles, iron and steel, all required female workers, as did hospitals, domestic service, transport, and the women's land army. There was also a shortage of shorthand typists, and a dire shortage of nurses and midwives.

This tells us nothing about why black women were recruited more heavily into some of these areas than others; perhaps we are given a clue when the author goes on to point out that women were welcomed into the labor force in a "circumscribed way,"

> as temporary workers at a period of crisis, as part-time workers, and as not disturbing the traditional division of labour in industry along sex lines—the Survey reflected the view which was still dominant, that married women would not naturally wish to work.

Not all black women were subject to this process: Afro-Caribbean women, for example, were encouraged and chose to come to Britain precisely to work. Ideologically they were seen as "naturally" suitable for the lowest paid, most menial jobs. Elizabeth Wilson goes on to explain that "work and marriage were still understood as alternatives . . . two kinds of women . . . a wife and a mother or a single career woman." Yet black women bridged this division. They were viewed simultaneously as workers and as wives and mothers. Elizabeth Wilson stresses that the postwar debate over the entry of women into the labor force occurred within the parameters of the question of possible effects on family life. She argues that "wives and mothers were granted entry into paid work only so long as this did not harm the family." Yet women from Britain's reserve army of labor in the colonies were recruited into the labor force far beyond any such considerations. Rather than a concern to protect or preserve the black family in Britain, the state reproduced commonsense notions of its inherent pathology: black women were seen to fail as mothers precisely because of their position as workers.

One important struggle, rooted in these different ideological mechanisms, which determine racially differentiated representations of gender, has been the black woman's battle to gain control over her own sexuality in the face of racist experimentation with the contraceptive Depo-Provera and enforced sterilizations (OWAAD 1979).

It is not just our herstory before we came to Britain that has been ignored by white feminists; our experiences and struggles here have also been ignored. These struggles and experiences, because they have been structured by racism, have been different to those of white women. Black feminists decry the nonrecognition of the specificities of black women's sexuality and femininity, both in the ways these are constructed and also as they are addressed through practices which oppress black women in a gender-specific but nonetheless racist way.

This nonrecognition is typified by a very interesting article on women in Third World manufacturing by Diane Elson and Ruth Pearson (1981, 95). In analyzing the employment of Third World women in world market factories they quote from an investment brochure designed to attract foreign firms:

> The manual dexterity of the oriental female is famous the world over. Her hands are small and she works fast with extreme care. Who, therefore, could be better qualified by *nature and inheritance* to contribute to the efficiency of a bench-assembly production line than the oriental girl? (Original emphasis)

The authors, however, analyze only the naturalization of gender and ignore the specificity signaled by the inclusion of the adjective "oriental," as if it didn't matter. The fact that the sexuality of the "oriental" woman is being differentiated is not commented upon and remains implicit rather than explicit as in the following remarks:

> It is in the context of the subordination of women as a gender that we must analyse the supposed docility, subservience and consequent suitability for tedious, monotonous work of young women in the Third World.

In concentrating an analysis upon gender only, Elson and Pearson do not see the relation between the situation they are examining in the periphery and the women who have migrated to the metropole. This last description is part of the common-sense racism that we have described as being applied to Asian women in Britain to channel them into "tedious, monotonous work." Elson and Pearson discuss this ascription of docility and passivity and compare it to Frantz Fanon's analysis of colonized people, without putting together the ways in which the women who are their objects of study have been oppressed not by gender subordination alone but also by colonization. The "oriental" sexuality referred to in the advertising brochure is one of many constructions of exotic sexual dexterity promised to Western male tourists to Southeast Asia. This ideology of "Eastern promise" links the material practice of the move from the bench—making microchips—to the bed, in which multinational corporate executives are serviced by prostitutes. This transition is described by Elson and Pearson but not understood as a process which illustrates an example of racially demarcated patriarchal power.

> If a woman loses her job in a world market factory after she has re-shaped her life on the basis of a wage income, the only way she may have of surviving is by selling her body. There are reports from South Korea, for instance, that many former electronics workers have no alternative but to become pros-

titutes. . . . A growing market for such services is provided by the way in which the tourist industry has developed, especially in South East Asia.

The photographs accompanying the article are of anonymous black women. This anonymity and the tendency to generalize into meaninglessness the oppression of an amorphous category called "Third World women" are symptomatic of the ways in which the specificity of our experiences and oppression are subsumed under inapplicable concepts and theories. Black feminists in the U.S. have complained of the ignorance, in the white women's movement, of black women's lives.

> The force that allows white feminist authors to make no reference to racial identity in their books about "women" that are in actuality about white women is the same one that would compel any author writing exclusively on black women to refer explicitly to their racial identity. That force is racism. . . . It is the dominant race that can make it seem that their experience is representative. (hooks 1981, 138)

In Britain too it is as if we don't exist.

There is a growing body of black feminist criticism of white feminist theory and practice, for their incipient racism and lack of relevance to black women's lives.[4] The dialogues that have been attempted have concentrated more upon visible, empirical differences that affect black and white women's lives than upon developing a feminist theoretical approach that would enable a feminist understanding of the basis of these differences.[5] The accusation that racism in the women's movement acted so as to exclude the participation of black women has led to an explosion of debate in the U.S.A.

> from a black female perspective, if white women are denying the existence of black women, writing "feminist" scholarship as if black women are not a part of the collective group American women, or discriminating against black women, then it matters less that North America was colonized by white patriarchal *men* who institutionalized a racially imperialist social or-

4. Much of this critical work has been written in America but is applicable to the women's liberation movement in Britain. Apart from the books cited in this chapter, interested readers should look out for essays and articles by Gloria Joseph, Audre Lourde, Barbara Smith, and Gloria Watkins that represent a range of black feminist thought. In Britain, the very existence of the feminist Organisation of Women of Asian and African descent (OWAAD) is a concrete expression of black feminists' critical distance from "white" feminism. See also Amos and Parmar (1982), who criticize the women's liberation movement for its irrelevance to the lives of black girls in Britain.

5. See Joseph and Lewis 1981 for an attempt at a dialogue that shows just how difficult it is to maintain.

der, than that white women who purport to be feminists support and actively perpetuate anti-black racism. (hooks 1981, 123–24)

What little reaction there has been in Britain has been more akin to lighting a damp squib than an explosion. U.S. black feminist criticism has no more been listened to than indigenous black feminist criticism. Yet, bell hooks's powerful critique has considerable relevance to British feminists. White women in the British women's liberation movement are extraordinarily reluctant to see themselves in the situations of being oppressors, as they feel that this will be at the expense of concentrating upon being oppressed. Consequently the involvement of British women in imperialism and colonialism is repressed and the benefits that they—as whites—gained from the oppression of black people ignored. Forms of imperialism are simply identified as aspects of an all-embracing patriarchy rather than as sets of social relations in which white women hold positions of power by virtue of their "race."

> Had feminists chosen to make explicit comparisons between . . . the status of black women and white women, it would have been more than obvious that the two groups do not share an identical oppression. It would have been obvious that similarities between the status of women under patriarchy and that of any slave or colonized person do not necessarily exist in a society that is both racially and sexually imperialistic. In such a society, the woman who is seen as inferior because of her sex can also be seen as superior because of her race, even in relationship to men of another race. (141)

The benefits of a white skin did not just apply to a handful of cotton, tea, or sugar plantation mistresses; all women in Britain benefited—in varying degrees—from the economic exploitation of the colonies. The pro-imperialist attitudes of many nineteenth- and early-twentieth-century feminists and suffragists have yet to be acknowledged for their racist implications. However, apart from this herstorical work, the exploration of contemporary racism within the white feminist movement in Britain has yet to begin.

Feminist theory in Britain is almost wholly Eurocentric and, when it is not ignoring the experience of black women "at home," it is trundling "Third World women" onto the stage only to perform as victims of "barbarous," "primitive" practices in "barbarous," "primitive" societies.

It should be noted that much feminist work suffers from the assumption that it is only through the development of a Western-style industrial capitalism and the resultant entry of women into waged labor that the potential for the liberation of women can increase. For example, foot-binding, clitoridectomy, female "circumcision," and other forms of mutilation of the female body have been described as "feudal residues," existing in economically "backward" or "underdeveloped" nations (i.e., not the industrialized West). Arranged marriages, polygamy, and these forms of mutilation are linked in reductionist ways to a lack of technological development.

However, theories of "feudal residues" or of "traditionalism" cannot explain the appearance of female "circumcision" and clitoridectomy in the United States at the same moment as the growth and expansion of industrial capital. Between the establishment of industrial capitalism and the transformation to monopoly capitalism, the United States, under the influence of English biological science, saw the control of medical practice shift from the hands of women into the hands of men. This is normally regarded as a "progressive" technological advance, though this newly established medical science was founded on the control and manipulation of the female body. This was the period in which links were formed between hysteria and hysterectomy in the rationalization of the "psychology of the ovary."

> In the second half of the [nineteenth] century . . . fumbling experiments with the female interior gave way to the more decisive technique of surgery—aimed increasingly at the control of female personality disorders. . . . The last clitoridectomy we know of in the United States was performed in 1948 on a child of five, as a cure for masturbation.
>
> The most common form of surgical intervention in the female personality was ovariotomy, removal of the ovaries—or "female castration." In 1906 a leading gynecological surgeon estimated that there were 150,000 women in the United States who had lost their ovaries under the knife. Some doctors boasted that they had removed from fifteen hundred to two thousand ovaries apiece. . . . it should not be imagined that poor women were spared the gynecologist's exotic catalog of tortures simply because they couldn't pay. The pioneering work in gynecological surgery had been performed by Marion Sims on black female slaves he kept for the sole purpose of surgical experimentation. He operated on one of them thirty times in four years. (Ehrenreich and English 1979)

These operations are hardly rituals left over from a precapitalist mode of production. On the contrary, they have to be seen as part of the "technological" advance in what is now commonly regarded as the most "advanced" capitalist economy in the world. Both in the U.S.A. and in Britain, black women still have a "role"—as in the use of Depo-Provera on them—in medical experimentation. Outside of the metropoles, black women are at the mercy of the multinational drug companies, whose quest for profit is second only to the cause of "advancing" Western science and medical knowledge.

The herstory of black women is interwoven with that of white women but this does not mean that they are the same story. Nor do we need white feminists to write our herstory for us: we can and are doing that for ourselves. However, when they write their herstory and call it the story of women but ignore our lives and deny their relation to us, that is the moment in which they are acting within the relations of racism and writing *his*tory.

Constructing Alternatives

It should be an imperative for feminist herstory and theory to avoid reproducing the structural inequalities that exist between the "metropoles" and the "peripheries," and within the "metropoles" between black and white women, in the form of inappropriate polarizations between the "First" and "Third World," developed/underdeveloped or advanced/backward. We have already argued that the generalizations made about women's lives across societies in the African and Asian continents would be thought intolerable if applied to the lives of white women in Europe or North America. These are some of the reasons why concepts which allow for specificity, while at the same time providing cross-cultural reference points—not based in assumptions of inferiority—are urgently needed in feminist work. The work of Gayle Rubin and her use of discrete "sex/gender systems" appears to provide such a potential, particularly in the possibility of applying the concept within as well as between societies. With regard to the problems with the concept of patriarchy discussed above, she has made the following assessment:

> The term "patriarchy" was introduced to distinguish the forces maintaining sexism from other social forces, such as capitalism. But the use of "patriarchy" obscures other distinctions. (Rubin 1975, 167)

In arguing for an alternative formulation Rubin stresses the importance of maintaining

> a distinction between the human capacity and necessity to create a sexual world, and the empirically oppressive ways in which sexual worlds have been organized. Patriarchy subsumes both meanings into the same term. Sex/gender system, on the other hand, is a neutral term which refers to the domain and indicates that oppression is not inevitable in that domain, but is the product of the specific social relations which organize it. (168)

This concept of sex/gender systems offers the opportunity to be historically and culturally specific but also points to the position of relative autonomy of the sexual realm. It enables the subordination of women to be seen as a "product of the relationships by which sex and gender are organized and produced" (177). Thus, in order to account for the development of specific forms of sex/gender systems, reference must be made not only to the mode of production but also to the complex totality of specific social formations within which each system develops. Gayle Rubin argues that kinship relations are visible, empirical forms of sex/gender systems. Kinship here is not limited to biological relatives but is rather a "system of categories and statuses which often contradict actual genetic relationships."

What are commonly referred to as "arranged marriages" can, then, be viewed as the way in which a particular sex/gender system organizes the "exchange of women." Similarly, transformations of sex/gender systems brought about by colonial oppression, and the changes in kinship patterns which result from migration, must be assessed on their own terms, not just in comparative relation to other sex/gender systems. In this way patterns of subordination of women can be understood historically, rather than being dismissed as the inevitable product of pathological family structures.

At this point we can begin to make concrete the black feminist plea to white feminists to begin with our different herstories. Contact with white societies has not generally led to a more "progressive" change in African and Asian sex/gender systems. Colonialism attempted to destroy kinship patterns that were not modeled on nuclear family structures, disrupting, in the process, female organizations that were based upon kinship systems which allowed more power and autonomy to women than those of the colonizing nation. Events that occurred in the Calabar and Owerri provinces of southern Nigeria in the winter months of 1929 bear witness to this disruption and to the consequent weakening of women's position. As Judith Van Allen points out, these events are known in Western social science literature as the "Aba Riots," a term which not only marginalizes the struggles themselves but which makes invisible the involvement of Igbo women. "Riots" implies unsystematic and mindless violence and is a perfect example of the constructions of *his*tory. The Igbo people on the other hand remember this conflict as Ogu Umuniwanyi, the "Women's War."

> In November of 1929, thousands of Igbo women . . . converged on the Native Administration centers. . . . The women chanted, danced, sang songs of ridicule, and demanded the caps of office (the official insignia) of the Warrant Chiefs, the Igbo chosen from each village by the British to sit as members of the Native Court. At a few locations the women broke into prisons and released prisoners. Sixteen Native Courts were attacked, and most of these were broken up or burned. The "disturbed area" covered about 6000 square miles and contained about two million people. It is not known how many women were involved, but the figure was in tens of thousands. On two occasions, British District Officers called in police and troops, who fired on the women and left a total of more than 50 dead and 50 wounded. No one on the other side was seriously injured. (Van Allen 1976, 60)

Judith Van Allen examines in detail the women's organizations that ensured and regulated women's political, economic, and religious role in traditional Igbo society.

Although their role was not equal to that of men they did have "a series of roles—despite the patrilineal organization of Igbo society" (62). Two of the associations that Judith Van Allen finds relevant were the *inyemedi*, or wives of a lineage, and the *umuada*, daughters of a lineage. Meetings of the *umuada* would "settle intralineage disputes among their 'brothers' as well as disputes between their natal and marital lineages." Since these gatherings were held in rotation among the villages into which members had married, "they formed an important part of the communication network of Igbo women." *Inyemedi*, on the other hand, came together in villagewide gatherings called *mikri*, gatherings of women who were in common residence rather than from a common place of birth (*ogbo*).

> The *mikri* appears to have performed the major role in the daily self-rule among women and to have articulated women's interests as opposed to those of men. *Mikri* provided women with a forum in which to develop their political talents and with a means for protecting their interests as traders, farmers, wives and mothers. (69)

Men recognized the legitimacy of the decisions and rules of the *mikri*, which not only settled disputes among women but also imposed rules and sanctions which directly affected men's behavior. The *mikri* could impose fines for violations of their decisions, and if these were ignored, women would "sit on" an offender or go on strike.

> To "sit on" or "make war on" a man involved gathering at his compound at a previously agreed upon time, dancing, singing scurrilous songs detailing the women's grievances against him (and often insulting him along the way by calling his manhood into question), banging on his hut with pestles for pounding yams, and in extreme cases, tearing up his hut (which usually meant pulling the roof off). (61)

A strike, on the other hand, "might involve refusing to cook, to take care of small children or to have sexual relations with their husbands" (61).

British colonizers in Nigeria dismissed all traditional forms of social organization that they found as "organized anarchy," and promptly imposed a system of administration that ignored female political structures and denied Igbo women any means of representation, leave alone any decision-making or rule-instituting power. Coming from sex/gender systems of Britain in the 1920s these colonial males could not conceive of the type of autonomy that Igbo women claimed. When the women demanded that they should serve on the Native Courts, be appointed to positions as District Officers, and further that "all white men should go to their own country," they were scoffed at by the British, who thought they acted under the influence of "savage passions." Their demands were viewed as totally irrational. The war waged by Igbo women against the British was a concerted organized mobilization of their political traditions. The fruits of colonialism were the imposition of class and gender relations which resulted in the concentration of national, economic, and political power in the hands of a small, wealthy elite. We have quoted at length this example from the herstory of Igbo women, in order to illustrate the ways in which an unquestioning application of liberal doses of Eurocentricity can completely distort and transform herstory into *his*tory. Colonialism was not limited to the imposition of economic, political, and religious systems. More subtly, though just as effectively, it sedimented racist and sexist norms into traditional sex/gender systems. Far from introducing more "progressive" or liberating sex/gender social relations, the colonizing powers as

> class societies tend to socialize the work of men and domesticate that of women. This creates the material and organizational foundations for denying that women are adults and allows the ruling classes to define them as wards of men. (Sacks 1975)

Karen Sacks, in her essay "Engels Revisited," examines the ways in which these class societies have domesticated the field of activity for women to the extent that "through their labor men are social adults; women are domestic wards" (1975, 231). Although this work agrees with much white feminist theory, which has focused on the isolation of women within the nuclear family as a prime source of oppression in Western sex/gender systems, it does not necessarily follow that women living in kinship relations organized in different sex/gender systems are not oppressed. What it does mean is that analysis has to be specific and is not to be deduced from European systems. She goes on to explain that in India,

> in Untouchable tenant-farming and village-service castes or classes, where women work today for village communities . . . they "have greater sexual freedom, power of divorce, authority to speak and witness in caste assemblies, authority over children, ability to dispose of their own belongings, rights to indemnity for wrongs done to them, rights to have disputes settled outside the domestic sphere, and representation in public rituals." In short, women who perform social labor have a higher status *vis-à-vis* men of their own class than do women who labor only in the domestic sphere or do no labor. (233)

Unfortunately feminist research has neglected to examine the basis of its Eurocentric (and often racist) framework. In the words of Achola O. Pala:

> Like the educational systems inherited from the colonial days, the research industry has continued to use the African environment as a testing ground

for ideas and hypotheses the locus of which is to be found in Paris, London, New York or Amsterdam. (Pala 1977)

Throughout much of this work, what is thought to be important is decided on the basis of what happens to be politically significant in the metropoles, not on what is important to the women who are under observation. Thus, from her own experience, Achola Pala relates how the major concerns of women are totally neglected by the researcher.

> I have visited villages where, at a time when the village women are asking for better health facilities and lower infant mortality rates, they are presented with questionnaires on family planning. In some instances, when the women would like to have piped water in the village, they may be at the same time faced with a researcher interested in investigating power and powerlessness in the household. In yet another situation, when women are asking for access to agricultural credit, a researcher on the scene may be conducting a study on female circumcision. (10)

The noncomprehension of the struggles and concerns of the African women, which Pala talks about, is indicative of the ways in which much Euro-American feminism has approached the lives of black women. It has attempted to force them into patterns which do not apply and in the process has labeled many of them deviant.

Another problem emerges from the frequently unqualified use of terms such as "precapitalist" and "feudal" to denote differences between the point of view of the researcher and her object of study. What is being indicated are differences in the modes of production. This distinction is subsequently used to explain observable differences in the position of women. However, the deployment of the concept sex/gender system interrupts this "logical progression" and reveals that the articulation of relations of production to sex/gender systems is much more complex. "Precapitalist" and "feudal" are often redundant and nonexplanatory categories which rest on underestimations of the scope and power of capitalist economic systems. Immanuel Wallerstein, for example, has argued that the sixteenth century saw the creation of

> a world-embracing commerce and a world-embracing market . . . the emergence of capitalism as the dominant mode of social organisation of the economy . . . the only mode in the sense that, once established, other "modes of production" survived in function of how they fitted into a politico-socio framework deriving from capitalism. (1974, 77)

Wallerstein continues to dismiss the idea that feudal and capitalist forms of social organization could coexist by stressing that

The world-economy has one form or another. Once it is capitalist, relationships that bear certain formal relationships to feudal relationships are necessarily redefined in terms of the governing principles of a capitalist system. (92)

There are ways in which this economic penetration has transformed social organization to the detriment of women in particular. Work on sexual economics by Lisa Leghorn and Katherine Parker demonstrates that the monetary system and heavy taxation that European nations imposed on their colonies directly eroded the status of women:

> In many nations the impact of the sudden need for cash was more devastating than the steep taxes themselves. Only two mechanisms for acquiring cash existed—producing the new export crops and working for wages—both of which were made available only to men. Men were forced to leave their villages and farms to work in mines, plantations or factories, at extremely low wages. Women were often left doing their own as well as the men's work, while most of the men's wages went to taxes and to support themselves at the higher standard of living in urban areas. As men who remained on the farms were taught how to cash crop, most technological aid and education went only to them, and women were left maintaining the subsistence agricultural economy that sustained themselves and their children. In Africa women still do 70% of the agricultural work while almost all the agricultural aid has gone to men. (1981, 44)

We need to counteract the tendency to reduce sex oppression to a mere "reflex of economic forces" while at the same time recognizing that

> sexual systems cannot, in the final analysis, be understood in complete isolation. A full-bodied analysis of women in a single society, or through out history, must take everything into account: the evolution of commodity forms in women, systems of land tenure, political arrangements, subsistence technology, etc. (Rubin 1975, 203, 209)

We can begin to see how these elements come together to affect the lives of black women under colonial oppression in ways that transform the sex/gender systems in which they live but that are also shaped by the sex/gender system of the colonizers. If we examine changes in land distribution we can see how capitalist notions of the private ownership of land (a primarily economic division) and ideas of male dominance (from the sex/gender system) work together against the colonized.

> Another problem affecting women's agricultural work is that as land ownership shifts from the collective "land-use rights" of traditional village life, in which women shared in the distribution of land, to the European concept of

private ownership, it is usually only the men who have the necessary cash to pay for it (by virtue of their cash-cropping income). In addition, some men traditionally "owned" the land, while women "owned" the crops as in the Cameroons in West Africa. As land becomes increasingly scarce, men begin to rent and sell "their" land, leaving women with no recourse but to pay for land or stop their agricultural work. (Leghorn and Parker 1981, 45)

It is impossible to argue that colonialism left precapitalist or feudal forms of organization untouched. If we look at the West Indies we can see that patterns of migration, for both men and women, have followed the dictates of capital.

When men migrated from the islands for work in plantations or building the Panama Canal, women migrated from rural to urban areas. Both have migrated to labor in the "core" capitalist nations. Domestic, marginal, or temporary service work has sometimes been viewed as a great "opportunity" for West Indian women to transform their lives. But as Shirley-Ann Hussen has shown,

> Take the case of the domestic workers. A development institution should be involved in more than placing these women in domestic jobs as this makes no dent in the society. It merely rearranges the same order. Domestic labour will have to be done away with in any serious attempt at social and economic reorganisation.[6]

If, however, imperialism and colonialism have ensured the existence of a world market, it still remains necessary to explain how it is in the interests of capitalism to maintain social relations of production that are noncapitalist—that is, forms that could not be described as feudal because that means precapitalist, but which are also not organized around the wage relation. If we return to the example of changes in ownership of land and in agricultural production, outlined above, it can be argued that

> the agricultural division of labor in the periphery—with male semi-proletarians and female agriculturalists—contributes to the maintenance of a low value of labor power for peripheral capital accumulation through the production of subsistence foodstuffs by the noncapitalist mode of production for the reproduction and maintenance of the labor force. (Deere 1979, 143)

In other words the work that the women do is a force which helps to keep wages low. To relegate "women of color" in the periphery to the position of being the victims of feudal relations is to aid in the masking of colonial relations of oppression. These relations of imperialism should not be denied. Truly feminist herstory should be able to acknowledge that

6. S.-A. Hussen 1975, 29; quoted in Leghorn and Parker 1981, 52.

> Women's economic participation in the periphery of the world capitalist sys-
> tem, just as within center economies, has been conditioned by the require-
> ments of capital accumulation . . . [but] the economic participation of
> women in the Third World differs significantly from women's economic par-
> ticipation within the center of the world capitalist system. (133)

Black women have been at the forefront of rebellions against land seizures and
struggle over the rights of access to land in Africa, Latin America, and the Caribbean. Adequate herstories of their roles in many of these uprisings remain to be
written. The role of West Indian women in the rebellions preceding and during the
disturbances in Jamaica in 1938, for example, though known to be significant has
still not been thoroughly described. White feminist herstorians are therefore mistaken when they portray black women as passive recipients of colonial oppression.
As Gail Omvedt has shown in her book *We Will Smash This Prison* (1980), women
in India have a long and complex herstory of fighting oppression both in and out of
the wage relation. It is clear that many women coming from India to Britain have a
shared herstory of struggle, whether in rural areas as agricultural laborers or in urban districts as municipal employees. The organized struggles of Asian women in
Britain need to be viewed in the light of this herstory. Their industrial battles, and
struggles against immigration policy and practice, articulate the triple oppression of
race, gender, and class that have been present since the dawn of imperialist domination.

In concentrating solely upon the isolated position of white women in the Western nuclear family structure, feminist theory has necessarily neglected the very
strong female support networks that exist in many black sex/gender systems. These
have often been transformed by the march of technological "progress" intended to
relieve black women from aspects of their labor.

> Throughout Africa, the digging of village wells has saved women enormous
> amounts of time which they formerly spent trekking long distances to obtain
> water. But it has often simultaneously destroyed their only chance to get to-
> gether and share information and experiences. Technological advances such
> as household appliances do not free women from domestic drudgery in any
> society. (Leghorn and Parker 1981, 55)

Leghorn and Parker, in *Women's Worth,* attempt to create new categories to describe, in general terms, the diversity of male power across societies. While they warn
against the rigid application of these categories—few countries fit exactly the category applied to them—the work does represent an attempt to move away from
Euro-American racist assumptions of superiority, whether political, cultural, or economic. The three classifications that they introduce are "minimal," "token," and

"negotiating power" societies. Interestingly, from the black women's point of view, the most salient factor in the categorization of a country has

> usually been that of women's networks, because it is the existence, building or dissolution of these networks that determines women's status and potential for change in all areas of their lives. (60)

These categories cut through the usual divisions of First/Third World, advanced/dependent, industrial/nonindustrial in an attempt to find a mechanism that would "free" thinking from these definitions. Space will not allow for a critical assessment of all three categories but it can be said that their application of "negotiating power" does recognize as important the "traditional" women's organizations to be found in West Africa, and described above in relation to the Igbo. Leghorn and Parker are careful to stress that "negotiating power" is limited to the possibilities of negotiating; it is not an absolute category of power that is held *over* men by women. The two examples of societies given in their book where women hold this negotiating position are the Ewe, in West Africa, and the Iroquois. Both of course are also examples where contact with the whites has been for the worse. Many of the Ewe female institutions disintegrated under colonialism, while the institutions that afforded Iroquois women power were destroyed by European intrusion. In contrast to feminist work that focuses upon the lack of technology and household mechanical aids in the lives of these women, Leghorn and Parker concentrate upon the aspects of labor that bring women together. Of the Ewe they note:

> Women often work together in their own fields, or as family members preparing meals together, village women meeting at the stream to do the wash, or family, friends and neighbours, walking five to fifteen miles a day to market together, sitting near each other in the market, and setting the day's prices together. They share childcare, news, and looking after each other's market stalls. In addition to making the time more pleasant, this shared work enables women to share information and in fact serves as an integral and vital part of the village communications system. Consequently, they have a tremendous sense of solidarity when it comes to working in their collective interest. (88)

It is important not to romanticize the existence of such female support networks, but they do provide a startling contrast to the isolated position of women in the Euro-American nuclear family structure.

In Britain, strong female support networks continue in both West Indian and Asian sex/gender systems, though these are ignored by sociological studies of migrant black women. This is not to say that these systems remain unchanged with migration. New circumstances require adaptation and new survival strategies have to be found.

> Even childcare in a metropolitan area is a big problem. If you live in a village in an extended family, you know that if your child's outside somewhere, someone will be looking out for her. If your child is out on the street and your neighbour down the road sees your child in some mess, that woman is going to take responsibility of dealing with that child. But in Brooklyn or in London, you're stuck in that apartment. You're there with that kid, you can't expect that child to be out on the street and be taken care of. You know the day care situation is lousy, you're not in that extended family, so you have a big problem on your hands. So when they talk about the reduction of housework, we know by now that that's a lie. (Prescod-Roberts and Steele 1980, 28)

However, the transformations that occur are not merely adaptive; neither is the black family destroyed in the process of change. Female networks mean that black women are key figures in the development of survival strategies, both in the past, through periods of slavery and colonialism, and now, facing a racist and authoritarian state.

> There is considerable evidence that women—and families—do not . . . simply accept the isolation, loss of status, and cultural devaluation involved in the migration. Networks are re-formed, if need be with non-kin or on the basis of an extended definition of kinship, by strong, active, and resourceful women. . . . Cultures of resistance are not simple adaptive mechanisms; they embody important alternative ways of organizing production and reproduction and value systems critical of the oppressor. Recognition of the special position of families in these cultures and social structures can lead to new forms of struggle, new goals. (Caufield 1974, 81, 84)

In arguing that feminism must take account of the lives, herstories, and experiences of black women we are not advocating that teams of white feminists should descend upon Brixton, Southall, Bristol, or Liverpool to take black women as objects of study in modes of resistance. We don't need that kind of intrusion on top of all the other information-gathering forces that the state has mobilized in the interest of "race relations." White women have been used against black women in this way before and feminists must learn from history. After the Igbo riots described above, two women anthropologists were sent by the British to "study the causes of the riot and to uncover the organisational base that permitted such spontaneity and solidarity among the women" (in Caufield 1974). The women's liberation movement, however, does need to listen to the work of black feminists and to take account of autonomous organizations like OWAAD (Organisation of Women of Asian and African Descent) who are helping to articulate the ways in which we are oppressed as black women.

In addition to this it is very important that white women in the women's movement examine the ways in which racism excludes many black women and prevents them from unconditionally aligning themselves with white women. Instead of taking black women as the objects of their research, white feminist researchers should try to uncover the gender-specific mechanisms of racism among white women. This more than any other factor disrupts the recognition of common interests of sisterhood.

In *Finding a Voice,* by Amrit Wilson, Asian women describe many instances of racial oppression at work from white women. Asian women

> are paid low salaries and everything is worse for them, they have to face the insults of supervisors. These supervisors are all English women. The trouble is that in Britain our women are expected to behave like servants and we are not used to behaving like servants and we can't. But if we behave normally . . . the supervisors start shouting and harassing us. . . . They complain about us Indians to the manager. (Wilson 1978, 122)

Black women do not want to be grafted onto "feminism" in a tokenistic manner as colorful diversions to "real" problems. Feminism has to be transformed if it is to address us. Neither do we wish our words to be misused in generalities as if what each one of us utters represents the total experience of all black women. Audre Lourde's address to Mary Daly is perhaps the best conclusion.

> I ask that you be aware of how this serves the destructive forces of racism and separation between women—the assumption that the herstory and myth of white women is the legitimate and sole herstory and myth of all women to call for power and background, and that non-white women and our herstories are note-worthy only as decorations, or examples of female victimization. I ask that you be aware of the effect that this dismissal has upon the community of black women, and how it devalues your own words. . . . When patriarchy dismisses us, it encourages our murders. When radical lesbian feminist theory dismisses us, it encourages its own demise. This dismissal stands as a real block to communication between us. This block makes it far easier to turn away from you completely than attempt to understand the thinking behind your choices. Should the next step be war between us, or separation? Assimilation within a sole Western-European herstory is not acceptable. (In Moraga and Anzaldua 1981, 96)

In other words, of white feminists we must ask, what exactly do you mean when you say "WE"??

Acknowledgments

The debt I owe to my sisters, Valerie Amos and Pratihba Parmar, is enormous for the many hours we have spent discussing our experiences as black women and as feminists. Both contributed to the ideas in this chapter but any criticisms for inadequacies should be directed at me. To Paul, John, and Errol, thank you for those transatlantic telephone calls—support and brotherly affection were regularly transmitted. To Susan Willis, I owe especial thanks for her support and friendship in a new job and a new country. To faculty, staff, and students at the Afro-American Studies Program at Yale and the Birmingham Centre for Contemporary Cultural Studies, thank you for your encouragement and enthusiasm for my work.

Works Cited

Amos, V., and P. Parmar. 1982. "Resistances and Responses: Black Girls in Britain." In *Feminism for Girls: An Adventure Story,* ed. A. McRobbie and T. McCage. London: Routledge and Kegan Paul.

Barrett, M. 1980. *Women's Oppression Today.* London: Verso.

Caufield, M. D. 1974. "Cultures of Resistance." *Socialist Revolution* (San Francisco) 4, no. 2 (October).

Deere, C. D. 1979. "Rural Women's Subsistence Production." In *Peasants and Proletarians: The Struggles of Third World Women Workers,* ed. R. Cohen et al. London: Hutchinson.

Ehrenreich, B., and D. English. 1979. *For Her Own Good.* New York: Doubleday Anchor.

Elson, D., and R. Pearson. 1981. "Nimble Fingers Make Cheap Workers: An Analysis of Women's Employment in Third World Export Manufacturing." *Feminist Review* (London), no. 7 (spring).

Foner, N. 1979. *Jamaica Farewell.* London: Routledge and Kegan Paul.

hooks, b. 1981. *Ain't I a Woman.* Boston: South End Press.

Hussen, S.-A. 1975. "Four Views on Women in the Struggle." In *Caribbean Women in the Struggle.* N.p.: Caribbean Church Women of the Caribbean Conference of Churches.

Jones, G. 1975. *Corregidora.* New York: Random House.

Jordan, W. 1969. *White over Black.* Harmondsworth: Penguin.

Joseph, G., and J. Lewis. 1981. *Common Differences: Conflicts in Black and White Feminist Perspectives.* New York: Anchor Doubleday.

Leghorn, L., and K. Parker. 1981. *Women's Worth: Sexual Economics and the World of Women.* London: Routledge and Kegan Paul.

Leis, N. 1974. "Women in Groups: Ijaw Women's Associations." In *Woman, Culture, and Society,* ed. M. Rosaldo and L. Lamphere. Stanford: Stanford University Press.

Loewenberg, J., and R. Bogin, eds. 1978. *Black Women in Nineteenth-Century American Life.* University Park: Pennsylvania State University Press.

Molyneux, M. 1981. "Socialist Societies Old and New: Progress towards Women's Emancipation?" *Feminist Review* (London), no. 8 (summer).

Moraga, C., and J. Anzaldua, eds. 1981. *This Bridge Called My Back: Writings by Radical Women of Color*. Watertown, Mass.: Persephone Press.

Omvedt, G. 1980. *We Will Smash This Prison*. London: Zed Press.

OWAAD (Organisation of Women of Asian and African Descent). 1979. *Fowaad*, no. 2.

Pala, A. O. 1977. "Definitions of Women and Development: An African Perspective." *Signs* (Chicago) 3, no. 1.

Parmar, P. 1982. "Gender, Race, and Class: Asian Women in Resistance." In *The Empire Strikes Back: Race and Racism in Seventies Britain*, ed. Centre for Contemporary Cultural Studies. London: Hutchinson.

Parmar, P., and N. Mirza. 1981. "Growing Angry, Growing Strong." *Spare Rib* (London), no. 111 (October).

Prescod-Roberts, M., and N. Steele. 1980. *Black Women: Bringing It All Back Home*. Bristol (U.K.): Falling Wall Press.

Rubin, G. 1975. "The Traffic in Women: Notes on the Political Economy of Sex." In *Toward an Anthropology of Women*, ed. R. R. Reiter. New York: Monthly Review Press.

Sacks, K. 1975. "Engels Revisited: Women, the Organization of Production, and Private Property." In *Toward an Anthropology of Women*, ed. R. R. Reiter. New York: Monthly Review Press.

Van Allen, J. 1976. "'Aba Riots' or Igbo 'Women's War'? Ideology, Stratification, and the Invisibility of Women." In *Women in Africa Studies in Social and Economic Change*, ed. N. Hafkin and E. Bay. Stanford: Stanford University Press.

Wallerstein, I. 1974. *The Modern World System*. Vol. 1. New York: Academic Press.

Wilson, A. 1978. *Finding a Voice: Asian Women in Britain*. London: Virago.

Wilson, E. 1980. *Only Halfway to Paradise: Women in Postwar Britain, 1945–1968*. New York: Tavistock Publications.

Three

The Other Question:
Difference,
Discrimination, and the
Discourse of Colonialism

Homi K. Bhabha

The genesis of this essay is diverse and discontinuous; its long march of critical contestation tracks my attempts to clear a space for the "other" question. To pose the colonial question is to realize that the problematic representation of cultural and racial difference cannot simply be read off from the signs and designs of social authority that are produced in the analyses of class and gender differentiation. As I was writing in 1982, the conceptual boundaries of the West were being busily reinscribed in a clamor of countertexts—transgressive, semiotic, semanalytic, deconstructionist—none of which pushed those boundaries to their colonial periphery, to that limit where the West must face a peculiarly displaced and decentered image of itself "in double duty bound," at once a civilizing mission and a violent subjugating force. It is there, in the colonial margin, that the culture of the West reveals its *différance*, its limit-text, as its practice of authority displays an ambivalence that is one of the most significant discursive and psychical strategies of discriminatory power—whether racist or sexist, peripheral or metropolitan.

It is the force of ambivalence that gives

the colonial stereotype its currency: ensures its repeatability in changing historical
and discursive conjunctures; informs its strategies of individuation and marginalization; produces that effect of probabilistic truth and predictability which, for the stereotype, must always be in *excess* of what can be empirically proved or logically
construed. The absence of such a perspective has its own history of political expe-
diency. To recognize the stereotype as an ambivalent mode of knowledge and power
demands a theoretical and political response that challenges deterministic or func-
tionalist modes of conceiving of the relationship between discourse and politics, and
questions dogmatic and moralistic positions on the meaning of oppression and discrimination. My reading of colonial discourse suggests that the point of intervention
should shift from the *identification* of images as positive or negative, to an understanding of the *processes of subjectification* made possible (and plausible) through
stereotypical discourse.

My essay is indebted to traditions of poststructuralist and psychoanalytic theory,
especially in their feminist formulation. Equally important is its theoretical reorientation, effected through my reading of the work of Frantz Fanon and Edward
Said. Fanon's insights into the language of the unconscious, as it emerges in the grotesque psychodrama of everyday life in colonial societies, demands a rethinking of
the forms and forces of "identification" as they operate at the edge of cultural authority. Said's work—especially *Orientalism* (1978) and *The Question of Palestine*
(1979)—dramatically shifts the locus of contemporary theory from the Left Bank to
the West Bank and beyond, through a profound meditation on the myths of Western
power and knowledge which confine the colonized and dispossessed to a half-life of
misrepresentation and migration. For me, Said's work focused the need to quicken
the half-light of Western history with the disturbing memory of its colonial texts that
bear witness to the trauma that accompanies the triumphal art of Empire.

Edward Said concludes his essay in *Literature, Politics, and Theory* (Barker et al.
1986) with a perspective on the state of the art, which is both informative and interdisciplinary. Three publications which are representative of developments in the
analysis of "otherness" are *Europe and Its Others* (Barker et al. 1985); " 'Race,'
Writing, and Difference" (1985); and *Black Literature and Literary Theory* (Gates
1984).

. . .

To describe the racist discourse of colonial power as constructed around a
"boundary dispute" is not merely to pun the political with the psychoanalytic. It is
my object to suggest that the construction of the colonial subject in discourse, and
the exercise of colonial power through discourse, demands an articulation of forms
of difference—racial and sexual. Such an articulation becomes crucial if it is held

that the body is always simultaneously inscribed in both the economy of pleasure and desire and the economy of discourse, domination, and power. I do not wish to conflate, unproblematically, two forms of the marking—and splitting—of the subject or to globalize two forms of representation. I want to suggest, however, that there is a theoretical space and a political space for such an articulation—in the sense in which that word itself denies an "original" identity or a "singularity" to objects of difference, sexual or racial. If such a view is taken, as Feuchtwang argues in a different context (1980, 41), it follows that the epithets racial or sexual come to be seen as modes of differentiation, realized as multiple, cross-cutting determinations, polymorphous and perverse, always demanding a specific and strategic calculation of their effects. Such is, I believe, the moment of colonial discourse. It is the most theoretically underdeveloped form of discourse, but crucial to the binding of a range of differences and discriminations that inform the discursive and political practices of racial and cultural hierarchization.

Before turning to the construction of colonial discourse, I want briefly to discuss the process by which forms of racial/cultural/historical otherness have been marginalized in theoretical texts committed to the articulation of *différance, signifiance,* in order, it is claimed, to reveal the limits of Western metaphysical discourse. Despite the differences (and disputes) between grammatology and semiology, both practices share an anti-epistemological position that impressively contests Western modes of representation predicated on an episteme of presence and identity. In facilitating the passage "from work to text" and stressing the arbitrary, differential, and systemic construction of social and cultural signs, these critical strategies unsettle the idealist quest for meanings that are, most often, intentionalist and nationalist. So much is not in question. What does need to be questioned, however, is the *mode of representation of otherness*, which depends crucially on how the "West" is deployed within these discourses.

The anti-ethnocentric stance is a strategy which, in recognizing the spectacle of otherness, conceals a paradox central to these anti-epistemological theories. For the critique of Western idealism or logocentrism requires that there is a constitutive discourse of lack imbricated in a philosophy of presence, which makes the differential or deconstructionist reading possible, "between the lines." As Mark Cousins says, the *desire* for presence which characterizes the Western episteme and its regimes of representation, "carries with it as the condition of its movement and of the regulation of its economy, a destiny of nonsatisfaction" (1978, 76). This could lead, as he goes on to say, "to an endless series of playful deconstructions which manifest a certain sameness in the name of difference." If such repetitiousness is to be avoided, then the strategic failure of logocentrism would have to be given a displacing and subversive role. This requires that the "nonsatisfaction" should be specified *pos-*

itively, which is done by identifying an anti-West. Paradoxically, then, cultural otherness functions as the moment of *presence* in a theory of *différance.* The "destiny of nonsatisfaction" is fulfilled in the recognition of otherness as a *symbol* (not sign) of the presence of *signifiance* or *différance*: otherness is the point of equivalence or identity in a circle in which what needs to be proved (the limits of logocentricity) is assumed (as a destiny or economy of lack/desire). What is denied is any knowledge of cultural otherness as a differential *sign,* implicated in specific historical and discursive conditions, requiring construction in different practices or reading. The place of otherness is fixed in the West as a subversion of Western metaphysics and is finally appropriated by the West as its limit-text, anti-West.

Derrida, for example, in the course of his *Positions* interview (1981), tends to fix the problem of ethnocentricity repeatedly at the limits of logocentricity, the unknown territory mapped neatly onto the familiar, as presuppositions inseparable from metaphysics, merely another limitation of metaphysics. Such a position cannot lead to the construction or exploration of other discursive sites from which to investigate the differential materiality and history of colonial culture. The interiority and immediacy of voice as "consciousness itself," central to logocentric discourse, is disturbed and dispersed by the imposition of a foreign tongue which differentiates the gentleman from the native, culture from civilization. The colonial discourse is always at least twice-inscribed, and it is in that process of *différance* that denies "originality" that the problem of the colonial subject must be thought.

To address the question of ethnocentricity in Derrida's terms, one could explore the exercise of colonial power in relation to the violent hierarchy between written and aural cultures. One might examine, in the context of a colonial society, those strategies of normalization that play on the difference between an "official" normative language of colonial administration and instruction and an unmarked, marginalized form—pidgin, creole, vernacular—which becomes the site of the native subject's cultural dependence and resistance, and as such a sign of surveillance and control.

Finally, where better to raise the question of the subject of racial and cultural difference than in Stephen Heath's masterly analysis of the chiaroscuro world of Welles's classic *A Touch of Evil.* I refer to an area of its analysis which has generated the least comment, that is, Heath's attention to the structuration of the border Mexico/U.S.A. that circulates through the text affirming and exchanging some notion of "limited being." Heath's work departs from the traditional analysis of racial and cultural differences, which identifies stereotype and image, and elaborates them in a moralistic or nationalistic discourse that affirms the *origin* and *unity* of national identity. Heath's attentiveness to the contradictory and diverse sites within the textual system which *construct* national/cultural differences in their deployment of the semes of "foreignness," "mixedness," "impurity," as transgressive and corrupting, is extremely relevant. His attention to the turnings of this much neglected subject, as sign (not symbol or stereotype) disseminated in the codes (as "partition," "exchange," "naming," "character," etc.), gives us a welcome sense of the circulation and proliferation of racial and cultural otherness. Despite the awareness of the multiple or cross-cutting determinations in the construction of modes of sexual and racial differentiation, there is a sense in which Heath's analysis marginalizes otherness. Although I shall argue that the problem of the border Mexico/U.S.A. is read too singularly, too exclusively under the sign of sexuality, it is not that I am unaware of the many proper and relevant reasons for that "feminist" focus. The "entertainment" operated by the realist Hollywood film of the 1950s was always also a containment of the subject in a narrative economy of voyeurism and fetishism. Moreover, the displacement that organizes any textual system, within which the display of difference circulates, demands that the play of "nationalities" should participate in the sexual positioning, troubling the law and desire. There is, nevertheless, a singularity and reductiveness in concluding that:

> Vargas is the position of desire, its admission and its prohibition. Not surprisingly he has two names: the name of desire is Mexican, Miguel . . . that of the Law American, Mike. . . . The film uses the border, the play between American and Mexican . . . at the same time it seeks to hold that play finally in the opposition of purity and mixture which in turn is a version of Law and desire. (Heath 1975, 93)

However liberatory it is from one position to see the logic of the text traced ceaselessly between the Ideal Father and the Phallic Mother, in another sense, in seeing only one possible articulation of the differential complex "race-sex" it half colludes with the proffered images of marginality. For if the naming of Vargas is crucially mixed and split in the economy of desire, then there are other mixed economies which make naming and positioning equally problematic "across the border." For to identify the "play" on the border as purity and mixture and to see it as an allegory of law and desire reduces the articulation of racial and sexual difference to what is dangerously close to becoming a circle rather than a spiral of *différance*. On that basis, it is not possible to construct the polymorphous and perverse collusion between racism and sexism as a *mixed economy*—for instance, the discourses of American cultural colonialism and Mexican dependency, the fear/desire of miscegenation, the American border as cultural signifier of a pioneering, male "American" spirit always under threat from races and cultures beyond the border. If the death of the Father is the interruption on which the narrative is initiated, it is through that death that miscegenation is both possible and deferred; if, again, it is the purpose of the narrative to restore Susan as "good object," it also becomes its project to deliver Vargas from his racial "mixedness." It is all there in Heath's splendid scrutiny of the text, revealed as he brushes against its grain. What is missing is the taking up of these positions as also the *object(ives)* of his analysis.

The difference of other cultures is other than the excess of signification, the *différance* of the trace or trajectory of desire. These are theoretical strategies that may be necessary to combat "ethnocentricism" but they cannot, of themselves, unreconstructed, represent that otherness. There can be no inevitable sliding from the semiotic or deconstructionist activity to the unproblematic reading of other cultural and discursive systems. There is in such readings a will to power and knowledge that, in failing to specify the limits of their own field of enunciation and effectivity, proceed to individualize otherness as the discovery of their own assumptions.

What is meant by colonial discourse as an apparatus of power will emerge more fully as a critique of specific, historical texts. At this stage, however, I shall provide what I take to be the minimum conditions and specifications of such a discourse. It is an apparatus that turns on the recognition and disavowal of racial/cultural/historical differences. Its predominant strategic function is the creation of a space for a "subject peoples" through the production of knowledges in terms of which surveillance is exercised and a complex form of pleasure/unpleasure is incited. It seeks authorization for its strategies by the production of knowledges of colonizer and colonized which are stereotypical but antithetically evaluated. The objective of colonial discourse is to construe the colonized as a population of degenerate types on the basis of racial origin, in order to justify conquest and to establish systems of administration and instruction. Despite the play of power within colonial discourse and the shifting positionalities of its subjects (e.g., effects of class, gender, ideology, different social formations, varied systems of colonization, etc.), I am referring to a form of governmentality that in marking out a "subject nation," appropriates, directs, and dominates its various spheres of activity. Therefore, despite the play in the colonial system which is crucial to its exercise of power, I do not consider the practices and discourses of revolutionary struggle as the under/other side of "colonial discourse." They may be historically co-present with it and intervene in it, but can never be "read off" merely on the basis of their opposition to it. Anticolonialist discourse requires an alternative set of questions, techniques, and strategies in order to construct it.

Through this paper I shall move through forms of colonial discourse or descriptions of it, written from the late nineteenth century to the present. I have referred to specific historical texts in order to construct three theoretical problems which I consider crucial: in Temple's work the circulation of power as knowledge; in Said's the fixation/fetishization of stereotypical knowledge as power; and in Fanon's the circulation of power and knowledge in a binding of desire and pleasure.

The social Darwinist problematic of Charles Temple's *The Native Races and*

Their Rulers [1918] (1968) enacts the tension between "the free and continual circulation" that natural selection requires and the effects of colonial power which claims to assist natural selection by controlling racial degeneracy but, through that intervention, must necessarily impede free circulation. The colonial system then requires some justification other than mere material necessity; and if justification is understood as both vindication and correction, then we can see in this text a crucial adjustment in the exercise of colonial power. In the face of an ambitious native "nationalist" bourgeois, Temple's text marks the shift in the form of colonial government, from a juridical sovereign exercise of power as punitive and restrictive—as harbinger of death—to a disciplinary form of power.

Disciplinary power is exercised through indirection on the basis of a knowledge of the subject races as "abnormal." They are not merely degenerate and primitive but, Temple claims, they also require the "abnormality" of imperialist intervention to hasten the process of natural selection. If "normalization" can imply even the faint possibility of an absorption or incorporation of the subject races then, like mass rule at home, this must be resisted in the colonies. The natives are therefore "individualized," through the racist testimony of "science" and colonialist administrative wisdom, as having such divergent ethical and mental outlooks that integration or independence is deemed impossible. Thus marginalized or individualized, the colonial subject as bearer of racial typologies and racist stereotypes is reintroduced to the circulation of power as a "productive capacity" within that form of colonial government called "indirect rule."

The co-option of traditional elites into the colonial administration is then seen to be a way of harnessing the ambitious life-instinct of the natives. This sets up the native subject as a site of productive power, both subservient and always potentially seditious. What is increased is the visibility of the subject as an object of surveillance, tabulation, enumeration, and indeed, paranoia and fantasy. When the upward spiral of natural selection encounters differences of race, class, and gender as potentially contradictory and insurrectionary forces, whose mobility may fracture the closed circuit of natural selection, social Darwinism invokes what Temple calls "the decrees of all-seeing Providence." This agency of social control appeals in desperation to God instead of Nature to fix the colonized at that point in the social order from which colonial power will, in Foucault's specification, be able simultaneously to increase the subjected forces and to improve the force and efficacy of that which subjects them.

Colonial power produces the colonized as a fixed reality which is at once an "other" and yet entirely knowable and visible. It resembles a form of narrative in which the productivity and circulation of subjects and signs are bound in a reformed and recognizable totality. It employs a system of representation, a regime of truth, that is structurally similar to realism. And it is in order to intervene within that system of representation that Edward Said proposes a semiotic of "Orientalist" power, which in raising the problem of power as a question of narrative introduces a new topic in the territory of colonial discourse.

> Philosophically, then, the kind of language, thought, and vision that I have been calling Orientalism very generally is a form of radical realism; anyone employing Orientalism, which is the habit of dealing with questions, objects, qualities and regions deemed Oriental, will designate, name, point to, fix what he is talking or thinking about with a word or phrase, which is then considered either to have acquired, or more simply to be, reality. . . . The tense they employ is the timeless eternal; they convey an impression of repetition and strength. . . . For all these functions it is frequently enough to use the simple copula *is*. (Said 1978, 72)

But the syllogism, as Kristeva once said, is that form of Western rationalism that reduces heterogeneity to two-part order, so that the *copula* is the point at which this binding preserves the boundaries of sense for an entire tradition of philosophical thinking. Of this, too, Said is aware when he hints continually at a polarity or division at the very center of Orientalism (206). It is, on the one hand, a topic of learning, discovery, practice; on the other, it is the site of dreams, images, fantasies, myths, obsessions, and requirements. It is a static system of "synchronic essentialism," a knowledge of "signifiers of stability" such as the lexicographic and the encyclopedic. However, this site is continually under threat from diachronic forms of history and narrative, signs of instability. And, finally, this line of thinking is given a shape analogical to the dream-work, when Said refers explicitly to a distinction between "an unconscious positivity" which he terms *latent* Orientalism, and the stated knowledges and views about the Orient which he calls *manifest* Orientalism.

Where the originality of this account loses some of its interrogative power is in Said's inadequate engagement with alterity and ambivalence in the articulation of these two economies which threaten to split the very object of Orientalist discourse as a knowledge and the subject positioned therein. He contains this threat by introducing a binarism within the argument which, in initially setting up an opposition between these two discursive scenes, finally allows them to be correlated as a congruent system of representation that is unified through a political-ideological *intention* which, in his words, enables Europe to advance securely and *unmetaphorically* upon the Orient.

This seems to be a rather peremptory resolution to a problem posed with remarkable insight. It is compounded by a psychologistic reduction when, in describing Orientalism through the nineteenth century, Said identifies the *content* of

Orientalism as the unconscious repository of fantasy, imaginative writings, and essential ideas; and the *form* of manifest Orientalism as the historically and discursively determined, diachronic aspect.

To develop a point made above, the division/correlation structure of manifest and latent Orientalism leads to the effectivity of the concept of discourse being undermined by what I will call the polarities of intentionality. This is a problem fundamental to Said's use of the terms "power" and "discourse." The productivity of Foucault's concept of power/knowledge is its refusal of an epistemology which opposes form/content, ideology/science, essence/appearance. *Pouvoir/Savoir* places subjects in a relation of power and recognition that is not part of a symmetrical or dialectical relation—self/other, master/slave—which can then be subverted by being inverted. Subjects are always disproportionately placed in opposition or domination through the symbolic decentering of multiple power-relations which play the role of support as well as target or adversary. It becomes difficult, then, to conceive of the *historical* enunciations of colonial discourse without them being either functionally overdetermined or strategically elaborated or displaced by the *unconscious* scene of latent Orientalism. Equally, it is difficult to conceive of the process of subjectification as a placing *within* Orientalist or colonial discourse for the dominated subject without the dominant being strategically placed within it too. There is always, in Said, the suggestion that colonial power and discourse is possessed entirely by the colonizer, which is a historical and theoretical simplification. The terms in which Said's Orientalism is unified—which is, the intentionality and undirectionality of colonial power—also unifies the subject of colonial enunciation.

This is a result of Said's inadequate attention to representation as a concept that articulates the historical and fantasy (as the scene of desire) in the production of the "political" effects of discourse. He rightly rejects a notion of Orientalism as the misrepresentation of an Oriental essence. However, having introduced the concept of "discourse" he does not attend adequately to the problems it makes for the instrumentalist use of power/knowledge that he sometimes seems to require. This problem is summed up by his ready acceptance of the view that

> Representations are formations, or as Roland Barthes has said of all the operations of language, they are deformations. (Said 1978, 273)

This brings me to my second point, that the closure and coherence attributed to the unconscious pole of colonial discourse, and the unproblematized notion of the subject, restricts the effectivity of both power and knowledge. This makes it difficult to see how power could function productively both as incitement and interdiction. Nor would it be possible without the attribution of ambivalence to relations of power/knowledge to calculate the traumatic impact of the return of the oppressed—

those terrifying stereotypes of savagery, cannibalism, lust, and anarchy which are the signal points of identification and alienation, scenes of fear and desire, in colonial texts. It is precisely this function of the stereotype as phobia and fetish that, according to Fanon, threatens the closure of the racial/epidermal schema for the colonial subject and opens the royal road to colonial fantasy.

If Said's theory disavows that *mise-en-scène*, his metaphoric language somehow prefigures it. There is a forgotten, underdeveloped passage which, in cutting across the body of the text, articulates the question of power and desire that I now want to take up. It is a process that has the power to reorientate our representation and recognition of colonial "otherness."

> Altogether an internally structured archive is built up from the literature that belongs to these experiences. Out of this comes a restricted number of typical encapsulations: the journey, the history, the fable, the stereotype, the polemical confrontation. These are the lenses through which the Orient is experienced, and they shape the language, perception, and form of the encounter between East and West. What gives the immense number of encounters some unity, however, is the vacillation I was speaking about earlier. Something patently foreign and distant acquires, for one reason or another, a status more rather than less familiar. One tends to stop judging things either as completely novel or as completely well-known; a new median category emerges, a category that allows one to see new things, things seen for the first time, as versions of a previously known thing. In essence such a category is not so much a way of receiving new information as it is a method of controlling what seems to be a threat to some established view of things. . . . The threat is muted, familiar values impose themselves, and in the end the mind reduces the pressure upon it by accommodating things to itself as either "original" or "repetitious." . . . The Orient at large, therefore, vacillates between the West's contempt for what is familiar and its shivers of delight in— or fear of—novelty. (58–59)

What is this other scene of colonial discourse played out around the "median category?" What is this theory of encapsulation or fixation which moves between the recognition of cultural and racial difference and its disavowal, by affixing the unfamiliar to something established, in a form that is repetitious and vacillates between delight and fear? Is it not analogous to the Freudian fable of fetishism (and disavowal) that circulates within the discourse of colonial power, requiring the articulation of modes of differentiation—sexual and racial—as well as different modes of discourse—psychoanalytic and historical?

The strategic articulation of "co-ordinates of knowledge"—racial and sexual— and their inscription in the play of colonial power as modes of differentiation, defense, fixation, hierarchization, is a way of specifying colonial discourse which would be illuminated by reference to Foucault's poststructuralist concept of the *dispositif*, or apparatus. In displacing his earlier search for discursive regularity as *episteme,* Foucault stresses that the relations of knowledge and power within the apparatus are always a strategic response to an *urgent need* at a given historical moment—much as I suggested at the outset, that the force of colonial discourse as a theoretical and political intervention was the *need,* in our contemporary moment, to contest singularities of difference and to articulate modes of differentiation. Foucault writes:

> the apparatus is essentially of a strategic nature, which means assuming that it is a matter of a certain manipulation of relations of forces, either developing them in a particular direction, blocking them, stabilizing them, utilizing them, etc. The apparatus is thus always inscribed in a play of power, but it is always also linked to certain coordinates of knowledge which issue from it but, to an equal degree, condition it. This is what the apparatus consists in: strategies of relations of forces supporting and supported by, types of knowledge. (1980, 196)

In this spirit I argue for the reading of the stereotype in terms of fetishism. The myth of historical origination—racial purity, cultural priority—in relation to the colonial stereotype functions to "normalize" the multiple beliefs and split subjects that constitute colonial discourse as a consequence of its process of disavowal. The scene of fetishism functions similarly as, at once, a reactivation of the material of original fantasy—the anxiety of castration and sexual difference—as well as a normalization of that difference and disturbance in terms of the fetish object as the substitute for the mother's penis. Within the apparatus of colonial power, the discourses of sexuality and race relate in a process of *functional overdetermination*, "because each effect . . . enters into resonance or contradiction with the others and thereby calls for a re-adjustment or re-working of the heterogeneous elements that surface at various points" (195).

There is both a structural and functional justification for reading the racial stereotype of colonial discourse in terms of fetishism.[1] My rereading of Said establishes the *structural* link. Fetishism, as the disavowal of difference, is that repetitious scene around the problem of secondary castration. The recognition of sexual difference— as the precondition for the circulation of the chain of absence and presence in the realm of the symbolic—is disavowed by the fixation on an object that masks that

---

1. See Freud 1981, 345 ff.; for fetishism and "the Imaginary signifier," see Metz 1982, chap. 5. See also Neale 1979–80.

difference and restores an original presence. The functional link between the fixation of the fetish and the stereotype (or the stereotype as fetish) is even more relevant. For fetishism is always a "play" or vacillation between the archaic affirmation of whole-ness/similarity—in Freud's terms: "All men have penises"; in ours: "All men have the same skin/race/culture; and the anxiety associated with lack of difference"—again, for Freud: "Some do not have penises"; for us: "Some *do not* have the same skin/race/culture." Within discourse, the fetish represents the simultaneous play between metaphor as substitution (marking absence and difference) and metonymy (which contiguously registers the perceived lack). The fetish or stereotype gives access to an "identity" which is predicated as much on mastery and pleasure as it is on anxiety and defense, for it is a form of multiple and contradictory belief in its recognition of difference and disavowal of it. This conflict of pleasure/unpleasure, mastery/defense, knowledge/disavowal, absence/presence, has a fundamental significance for colonial discourse. For the scene of fetishism is also the scene of the reactivation and repetition of primal fantasy—the subject's desire for a pure origin that is always threatened by its division, for the subject must be gendered to be engendered, to be spoken. The stereotype, then, as the primary point of subjectification in colonial discourse, for both colonizer and colonized, is the scene of a similar fantasy and defense—the desire for an originality which is again threatened by the differences of race, color, and culture. My contention is splendidly caught in Fanon's title *Black Skin, White Masks* (1970), where the disavowal of difference turns the colonial subject into a misfit—a grotesque mimicry or "doubling" that threatens to split the soul and whole, undifferentiated skin of the ego. The stereotype is not a simplification because it is a false representation of a given reality. It is a simplification because it is an arrested, fixated form of representation that, in denying the play of difference (that the negation through the other permits), constitutes a problem for the *representation* of the subject in significations of psychic and social relations.

When Fanon talks of the positioning of the subject in the stereotyped discourse of colonialism, he gives further credence to my point. The legends, stories, histories, and anecdotes of a colonial culture offer the subject a primordial Either/Or (78–82). He is fixed in a consciousness of the body *either* as a solely negating activity *or* as a new kind of man, a new genus. What is denied the colonial subject, both as colonizer and colonized, is that form of negation which gives access to the recognition of difference in the symbolic. It is that possibility of difference and circulation which would liberate the signifier of skin/culture from the signifieds of racial typology, the analytics of blood, ideologies of racial and cultural dominance or degeneration. "Wherever he goes," Fanon despairs, "the Negro remains a Negro"—his race becomes the ineradicable sign of negative difference in colonial discourse. For the stereotype impedes the circulation and articulation of the signifier of "race" as anything other than its *fixity* as racism. We always already know that blacks are licentious, Asiatics duplicitous . . .

There are two "primal scenes" in Fanon's *Black Skin, White Masks*: two myths of the origin of the marking of the subject within the racist practices and discourses of a colonial culture. On one occasion a white girl fixes Fanon in look and word as she turns to identify with her mother. It is a scene which echoes endlessly through his essay "The Fact of Blackness": "Look, a Negro . . . Mama, *see* the Negro! I'm frightened. Frightened." "What else could it be for me," Fanon concludes, "but an amputation, an excision, a haemorrhage that splattered my whole body with black blood" (69). Equally, he stresses the primal moment when the child encounters racial and cultural stereotype in children's fictions, where white heroes and black demons are proffered as points of ideological and psychical identification. Such dramas are enacted *every day* in colonial societies, says Fanon, employing a theatrical metaphor—the scene—which emphasizes the visible—the seen. I want to play upon both these senses, which refer at once to the site of fantasy and desire and to the site of subjectification and power.

The drama underlying these dramatic "everyday" colonial scenes is not difficult to discern. In each of them the subject turns around the pivot of the "stereotype" to return to a point of total identification. The girl's gaze returns to her mother in the recognition and disavowal of the Negroid type; the black child turns away from himself, his race, in his total identification with the positivity of whiteness which is at once color and no color. In the act of disavowal and fixation the colonial subject is returned to the narcissism of the Imaginary and its identification of an ideal-ego that is white and whole. For what these primal scenes illustrate is that looking/hearing/reading as sites of subjectification in colonial discourse are evidence of the importance of the visual and auditory imaginary for the *histories* of societies (Metz 1982, 59–60).

My anatomy of colonial discourse remains incomplete until I locate the stereotype as an arrested, fetishistic mode of representation within its field of identification, which I have identified in my description of Fanon's primal scenes, as the Lacanian scheme of the Imaginary.[2] The Imaginary is the transformation that takes place in the subject at the formative mirror phase, when it assumes a discrete image which allows it to postulate a series of equivalences, samenesses, identities, between the objects of the surrounding world. However, this positioning is itself problematic, for the subject finds or recognizes itself through an image which is simultaneously alienating and hence potentially confrontational. This is the basis of the close relation between the two forms of identification complicit with the Imaginary—narcis-

2. For the best account of Lacan's concept of the Imaginary, see Rose 1981.

sism and aggressivity. It is precisely these two forms of "identification" that constitute the dominant strategy of colonial power exercised in relation to the stereotype which, as a form of multiple and contradictory belief, gives knowledge of difference and simultaneously disavows or masks it. Like the mirror-phase "the fullness" of the stereotype—its image *as* identity—is always threatened by "lack."

The construction of colonial discourse is then a complex articulation of the tropes of fetishism—metaphor and metonymy—and the forms of narcissistic and aggressive identification available to the Imaginary. Stereotypical racial discourse is then a four-term strategy. There is a tie-up between the metaphoric or masking function of the fetish and the narcissistic object-choice and an opposing alliance between the metonymic figuring of lack and the aggressive phase of the Imaginary. One has then a repertoire of conflictual positions that constitute the subject in colonial discourse. The taking up of any one position, within a specific discursive form, in a particular historical conjuncture, is then always problematic—the site of both fixity and fantasy. It provides a colonial identity that is played out—like all fantasies of originality and origination—in the face and space of the disruption and threat from the heterogeneity of other positions. As a form of splitting and multiple belief, the stereotype requires, for its successful signification, a continual and repetitive chain of other stereotypes. This is the process by which the metaphoric "masking" is inscribed on a lack which must then be concealed, that gives the stereotype both its fixity and its phantasmatic quality—the same old stories of the Negro's animality, the coolie's inscrutability, or the stupidity of the Irish which *must* be told (compulsively) again and afresh, and is differently gratifying and terrifying each time.

In any specific colonial discourse the metaphoric/narcissistic and the metonymic/aggressive positions will function simultaneously, but always strategically poised in relation to each other; similar to the moment of alienation which stands as a threat to Imaginary plenitude and "multiple belief" which threatens fetishistic disavowal. Caught in the Imaginary as they are, these shifting positionalities will never seriously threaten the dominant power relations, for they exist to exercise them pleasurably and productively. They will always pose the problem of difference as that between the preconstituted, "natural" poles of black and white with all its historical and ideological ramifications. The *knowledge of the construction* of that "opposition" will be denied the colonial subject. He is constructed within an apparatus of power which *contains,* in both senses of the word, an "other" knowledge—a knowledge that is arrested and fetishistic and circulates through colonial discourse as that limited form of otherness, that fixed form of difference, that I have called the stereotype.

My four-term strategy of the stereotype tries tentatively to provide a structure and a process for the "subject" of colonial discourse. I now want to take up the problem of discrimination as the political effect of such a discourse and relate it to the question of "race" and "skin." To that end it is important to remember that the multiple belief that accompanies fetishism does not only have disavowal value; it also has "knowledge value" and it is this that I shall now pursue. In calculating this knowledge value it is crucial to try to understand what Fanon means when he says that

> There is a quest for the Negro, the Negro is a demand, one cannot get along without him, he is needed, but only if he is made palatable in a certain way. Unfortunately the Negro knocks down the system and breaks the treaties. (1970, 114)

What this demand is, and how the native or Negro is made palatable requires that we acknowledge some significant differences between the general theory of fetishism and its specific uses for an understanding of racist discourse. First, the fetish of colonial discourse—what Fanon calls the epidermal schema—is not, like the sexual fetish, a secret. Skin, as the key signifier of cultural and racial difference in the stereotype, is the most visible of fetishes, recognized as common knowledge in a range of cultural, political, historical discourses, and plays a public part in the racial drama that is enacted every day in colonial societies. Second, it may be said that the sexual fetish is closely linked to the "good object"; it is the prop that makes the whole object desirable and lovable, facilitates sexual relations, and can even promote a form of happiness. The stereotype can also be seen as that particular "fixated" form of the colonial subject which *facilitates* colonial relations, and sets up a discursive form of racial and cultural opposition in terms of which colonial power is exercised. If it is claimed that the colonized are most often objects of hate, then we can reply with Freud that

> affection and hostility in the treatment of the fetish—which run parallel with the disavowal and acknowledgement of castration—are mixed in unequal proportions in different cases, so that the one or the other is more clearly recognizable. (1981, 357ff.)

What this statement recognizes is the wide range of the stereotype, from the loyal servant to Satan, from the loved to the hated, a shifting of subject positions in the circulation of colonial power which I tried to account for through the mobility of the metaphoric/narcissistic and metonymic/aggressive system of colonial discourse. What remains to be examined, however, is the construction of the signifier "skin/race" in those regimes of visibility and discursivity—fetishistic, scopic, imaginary—within which I have located the stereotypes. It is only on that basis that we can construct its "knowledge value," which will, I hope, enable us to see the place of fantasy in the exercise of colonial power.

My argument relies upon a particular reading of the problematic of representation which, Fanon suggests, is specific to the colonial situation. He writes:

> the originality of the colonial context is that the economic substructure is also a superstructure . . . you are rich because you are white, you are white because you are rich. This is why Marxist analysis should always be slightly stretched every time we have to do with the colonial problem. (1969, 31)

Fanon could either be seen as adhering to a simple reflectionist or determinist notion of cultural/social signification or, more interestingly, he could be read as taking an "antirepressionist" position (attacking the notion that ideology as miscognition, or misrepresentation, is the repression of the real). For our purposes I tend toward the latter reading, which then provides a visibility to the exercise of power, gives force to the argument that skin, as a signifier of discrimination, must be produced or processed as visible. As Abbot says, in a very different context:

> whereas repression banishes its object into the unconscious, forgets and attempts to forget the forgetting, discrimination must constantly invite its representations into consciousness, reinforcing the crucial recognition of difference which they embody and revitalizing them for the perception on which its effectivity depends. . . . It must sustain itself on the presence of the very difference which is also its object. (1979, 15–16)

What "authorizes" discrimination, Abbot continues, is the occlusion of the preconstruction or working-up of difference:

> this repression of production entails that the recognition of difference is procured in an innocence, as a "nature"; recognition is contrived as primary cognition, spontaneous effect of the "evidence of the visible." (16)

This is precisely the kind of recognition, as spontaneous and visible, that is attributed to the stereotype. The difference of the object of discrimination is at once visible and natural—color as the cultural/political sign of inferiority or degeneracy, skin as its natural "identity."

Although the "authority" of colonial discourse depends crucially on its location in narcissism and the Imaginary, my concept of stereotype-as-suture is a recognition of the *ambivalence* of that authority and those orders of identification. The role of fetishistic identification, in the construction of discriminatory knowledges that depend on the *presence of difference,* is to provide a process of splitting and multiple/contradictory belief at the point of enunciation and subjectification. It is this crucial splitting of the ego which is represented in Fanon's description of the construction of the colonial subject as effect of stereotypical discourse: the subject primordially fixed and yet triply split between the incongruent knowledges of body, race, ancestors. Assailed by the stereotype

> The corporeal schema crumbled, its place taken by a racial epidermal scheme. . . . It was no longer a question of being aware of my body in the third person but a triple person. . . . I was not given one, but two, three places. (Fanon 1970, 79)

This process is best understood in terms of the articulation of multiple belief that Freud proposes in the essay "Fetishism." It is a nonrepressive form of knowledge that allows for the possibility of simultaneously embracing two contradictory beliefs, one official and one secret, one archaic and one progressive, one that allows the myth of origins, the other that articulates difference and division. Its knowledge value lies in its orientation as a defense toward external reality, and provides, in Metz's words

> the lasting matrix, the effective prototype of all those splittings of belief which man will henceforth be capable of in the most varied domains, of all the infinitely complex unconscious and occasionally conscious interactions which he will allow himself between believing and not-believing. (1982, 70)

It is through this notion of splitting and multiple belief that, I believe, it becomes easier to see the bind of knowledge and fantasy, power and pleasure, that informs the particular regime of visibility deployed in colonial discourse. The visibility of the racial/colonial other is at once a *point* of identity—"Look at a Negro"—and at the same time a *problem* for the attempted closure within discourse. For the recognition of difference as "imaginary" points of identity and origin—such as black and white—is disturbed by the representation of splitting in the discourse. What I called the play between the metaphoric—narcissistic and metonymic—aggressive moments in colonial discourse—that four-part strategy of the stereotype—crucially recognizes the prefiguring of desire as a potentially conflictual, disturbing force in all those regimes of the "originary" that I have brought together. In the objectification of the scopic drive there is always the threatened return of the look; in the identification of the Imaginary relation there is always the alienating other (or mirror) which crucially returns its image to the subject; and in that form of substitution and fixation that is fetishism there is always the trace of loss, absence. To put it succinctly, the recognition and disavowal of "difference" is always disturbed by the question of its re-presentation or construction. The stereotype is, in fact, an impossible object. For that very reason, the exertions of the "official knowledges" of colonialism—pseudoscientific, typological, legal-administrative, eugenicist—are imbricated at the point of their production of meaning and power with the fantasy that dramatizes the impossible desire for a pure, undifferentiated origin. Not itself the object of desire but its setting; not an ascription of prior identities but their production in the syntax of the scenario of racist discourse; colonial fantasy plays a crucial part in those everyday scenes of subjectification in a colonial society that Fanon refers to repeatedly. Like fantasies of the origins of sexuality, the productions of colonial desire mark the discourse as

> a favoured spot for the most primitive defensive reactions such as turning against oneself, into an opposite, projection, negation. (Laplanche and Pontalis 1980, 318)

The problem of origin as the problematic of racist, stereotypical knowledge is a complex one and what I have said about its construction will come clear in this illustration from Fanon. Stereotyping is not the setting up of a false image which becomes the scapegoat of discriminatory practices. It is a much more ambivalent text of projection and introjection, metaphoric and metonymic strategies, displacement, overdetermination, guilt, aggressivity, the masking and splitting of "official" and fantasmatic knowledges to construct the positionalities and oppositionalities of racist discourse:

> My body was given back to me sprawled out, distorted, recoloured, clad in mourning in that white winter day. The Negro is an animal, the Negro is bad, the Negro is mean, the Negro is ugly; look, a nigger, it's cold, the nigger is shivering because he is cold, the little boy is trembling because he is afraid of the nigger, the nigger is shivering with cold, that cold that goes through your bones, the handsome little boy is trembling because he thinks that the nigger is quivering with rage, the little white boy throws himself into his mother's arms: Mama the nigger's going to eat me up. (Fanon 1970, 80)

It is the scenario of colonial fantasy which, in staging the ambivalence of desire, articulates the demand for the Negro which the Negro disrupts. For the stereotype is at once a substitute and a shadow. By acceding to the wildest fantasies (in the popular sense) of the colonizer, the stereotyped other reveals something of the fantasy (as desire, defense) of that position of mastery. For if "skin" in racist discourse is the visibility of darkness, and a prime signifier of the body and its social and cultural correlates, then we are bound to remember what Karl Abraham (1978) says in his seminal work on the scopic drive. The pleasure value of darkness is a withdrawal in order to know nothing of the external world. Its symbolic meaning, however, is thoroughly ambivalent. Darkness signifies at once birth and death; it is in all cases a desire to return to the fullness of the mother, a desire for an unbroken and undifferentiated line of vision and origin.

But surely there is another scene of colonial discourse, where the subverting "split" is recuperable within a strategy of social and political control. It is recognizably true that the chain of stereotypical signification is curiously mixed and split, polymorphous and perverse. The black is both savage (cannibal) and yet the most obedient and dignified of servants (the bearer of food); he is the embodiment of rampant sexuality and yet innocent as a child; he is mystical, primitive, simple-minded and yet the most worldly and accomplished liar, and manipulator of social forces. In each case what is being dramatized is a separation—*between* races, cultures, histories, *within* histories—a separation between *before* and *after* that repeats obsessively the mythical moment of disjunction. Despite the structural similarities with the play of need and desire in primal fantasies, the colonial fantasy does not try to cover up that moment of separation. It is more ambivalent. On the one hand, it proposes a teleology—under certain conditions of colonial domination and control the native is progressively reformable. On the other, however, it effectively displays the "separation," makes it more visible. It is the visibility of this separation which, in denying the colonized capacities of self-government, independence, Western modes of civility, lends authority to the official version and mission of colonial power. Colonial fantasy is the continual dramatization of emergence—of difference, freedom—as the beginning of a history which is repetitively denied. Such a denial is the clearly voiced demand of colonial discourse as the legitimization of a form of rule that is facilitated by the racist fetish. In concluding, I would like to develop a little further my working definition of colonial discourse given at the start of this paper.

Racist stereotypical discourse, in its colonial moment, inscribes a form of governmentality that is informed by a productive splitting in its constitution of knowledge and exercise of power. Some of its practices recognize the differences of race, culture, history as elaborated by stereotypical knowledges, racial theories, administrative colonial experience, and on that basis institutionalize a range of political and cultural ideologies that are prejudicial, discriminatory, vestigial, archaic, "mythical" and, crucially, are recognized as being so. By knowing the native population in these terms, discriminatory and authoritarian forms of political control are considered appropriate. The colonized population is then deemed to be both the cause and effect of the system, imprisoned in the circle of interpretation. What is visible is the *necessity* of such rule which is justified by those moralistic and normative ideologies of amelioration recognized as the "civilizing mission" or the "white man's burden." However, there coexists within the same apparatus of colonial power modern systems and sciences of government, progressive Western forms of social and economic organization which provide the manifest justification for the project of colonialism—an argument which, in part, impressed Karl Marx. It is on the site of this coexistence that strategies of hierarchization and marginalization are employed in the management of colonial societies. And if my deduction from Fanon about the peculiar visibility of colonial power is acceptable to you, then I would extend it to say that it is a form of governmentality in which the ideological space functions in more openly collaborative ways with political and economic exigencies. The barracks stand by the church which stands by the schoolroom; the cantonment stands hard by the "civil lines." Such visibility of the institutions and apparatuses of power is possible because the exercise of colonial power makes their *relationship* obscure, produces them as fetishes, spectacles of a naturalized racial preeminence. Only the seat of government is everywhere—alien and separate by that distance upon which surveillance depends for its strategies of objectification, normalization, and discipline.

Works Cited

Abbot, P. 1979. "On Authority." *Screen* (London) 20, no. 2.
Abraham, K. 1978. "Transformations of Scopophilia." In *Selected Papers in Psychoanalysis*. London.
Barker, F., et al., eds. 1985. *Europe and Its Others*. 2 vols. Colchester: University of Essex.
———. 1986. *Literature, Politics, and Theory*. London: Methuen.
Cousins, M. 1978. "The Logic of Deconstruction." *Oxford Literary Review* 3, no. 2.
Derrida, J. 1981. *Positions*. Chicago: University of Chicago Press.
Fanon, F. 1969. *The Wretched of the Earth*. Trans. Constance Farrington. Harmondsworth: Penguin.
———. 1970. *Black Skin, White Masks*. Trans. Charles Lam Markmann. London: Paladin.
Feuchtwang, S. 1980. "Socialist, Feminist, and Anti-Racist Struggles." *m/f* 4.
Foucault, M. 1980. "The Confession of the Flesh." In *Power/Knowledge*. Brighton: Harvester Press.
Freud, S. 1981. "Fetishism" (1927). In *On Sexuality*. Pelican Freud Library, no. 7. Harmondsworth: Penguin.
Gates, H. L., ed. 1984. *Black Literature and Literary Theory*. New York: Methuen.
Heath, S. 1975. "Film and System: Terms of Analysis." *Screen* (London) 16, nos. 1 and 2.
Laplanche, J., and J. B. Pontalis. 1980. "Phantasy (or Fantasy)." In *The Language of Psychoanalysis*. London.
Metz, C. 1982. "The Imaginary Signifier." Trans. in *Psychoanalysis and Cinema* by Ben Brewster. London.
Neale, S. 1979–80. "The Same Old Story: Stereotypes and Differences." *Screen Education* (London) 32–33.
" 'Race,' Writing, and Difference." 1985. *Critical Inquiry* 12, no. 1.
Rose, J. 1981. "The Imaginary." In *The Talking Cure: Essays in Psychoanalysis and Language*, ed. Colin MacCabe. New York: St. Martin's Press.
Said, E. 1978. *Orientalism*. New York: Pantheon Books.
———. 1979. *The Question of Palestine*. New York: Times Books.
Temple, C. [1918] 1968. *The Native Races and Their Rulers: Sketches and Studies of Official Life and Administrative Problems in Nigeria*. 2d ed. London: F. Cass.

Four

Black Cinemas, Film Theory, and Dependent Knowledge

Robert Crusz

The dominant tradition's seemingly recent discovery of "otherness" with regard to film practice and theory reveals the ideological hegemony of this tradition and ultimately, in relation to black cinemas, its underlying racism. This issue of *Screen,* devoted to other cinemas, reflects and carries on the hegemonic activity by providing, through its position of power, a space whereby "the process" can take place, "of securing the legitimacy and assent of the subordinated to their subordination" (Hall 1977, 388–89). By bringing other cinemas into its arena on its own terms to discuss, among other things, the relevance or otherwise of existing film theories to other practices, the hegemonic tradition continues to ensure its domination.

I do not intend reworking in depth the debates on the concepts of "ideology," Gramscian "hegemony," and "ideological cultural apparatuses" in order to substantiate my claim that current theoretical film journals are part of the ideological hegemonic activity: *Screen* readers are familiar with the concepts and the debates. Stuart Hallanalyzes and interrelates these concepts carefully (1977, 315–39). I will use sections of his argument to illustrate my point.

Within our specific social formation ideological hegemony is achieved through the consensus of "the agencies of the superstructures—the family, education system, the church, the media and cultural institutions, as well as the coercive side of the state—the law, the police, the army." Also, no one unified ruling class sustains this hegemony; rather it is supported by "a particular conjunctural alliance of class fractions: thus the content of dominant ideology will reflect this complex interior formation of the dominant classes" (Hall 1977, 333). In relation to black cinemas, theoretical and other film journals like *Screen, Undercut, Views, Framework, Sight and Sound* belong to this "complex interior formation" of the dominant, the "alliance of class fractions," and are part of the superstructures of the education system and the media and cultural institutions of a racist society.

Hegemony is not permanent; it has to be won and secured in history. There is no total incorporation of the dominated groups within the hegemonic structure. These groups retain their distinctive identities and their own specific ideological practices, yet they are contained, because, "when these subordinated classes are not strong or sufficiently organised to represent a 'counter hegemonic' force to the existing order, their own corporate structures and institutions can be used, by the dominant structure (hegemonized), as a means of enforcing their continued subordination." Hall cites the example of trade unions being used in this way—"confining its [the working class's] opposition within limits which the system can contain" (1977, 333). The ACTT's Workshop Declaration needs to be placed within this scenario as should useful discussions containing statements like

> Next are the workshops themselves and how they work: workers' collectives with people coming in with some training at that kind of artisanal level. Those ways of working are particularly good for people who have previously been disenfranchised—such as women and ethnic minorities—because a lot of it is actually building up confidence. (McCue 1984, 9)

The film union's recognition of workshops places oppositional voices in contained spaces first within its own hegemonic structure and then, through itself, within the wider structure. This containment is justified by claims that it is "particularly good" in order to build up "confidence." Why can't confidence be built within the mainstream? The answer to this will explain why the film industry is sexist and racist.

In order that a hegemonic structure can continue to dominate, it should achieve a "complementarity" between itself and the subordinate groups; i.e., given that the different subordinate groups are never completely immersed within the dominant structure and that struggle is always present, an "equilibrium" has to be reached "so that whatever are the concessions the ruling 'bloc' is required to make to win consent and legitimacy, its fundamental basis will not be overturned." The Workshop Declaration is one such concession. Special issues of theoretical film journals are another. What is more, dominant groups have to represent their particular interests as "general interests" in which all groups have an equal stake (Hall 1977, 334). Thus by restricted unionization black groups are involved in the class struggle. There is no problem for us here. But whether we will have an opportunity to effectively and successfully address racism in the labor movement remains to be seen. By publishing special issues on other cinemas, the dominant theoretical traditions make their particular concerns a matter of general interest in which all others have a stake. Whether regular debate on issues outside the paradigms of the dominant traditions and of particular interest to black filmmakers will be given space remains to be seen.

Hall identifies the mass media as "ideological apparatuses" and describes three crucial "cultural functions" of these "apparatuses." These functions could be attributed to other "cultural institutions" like theoretical film journals. The first function is

> the provision and the selective construction of social knowledge, of social imagery, through which we perceive the "worlds," the "lived realities" of others, and imaginarily reconstruct their lives and ours into some intelligible "world-of-the-whole," some "lived totality." (Hall 1977, 340–41)

In this special issue, *Screen* is involved in the "selective construction" of a "knowledge" about other cinemas in order to "perceive the 'worlds,' the 'lived realities'" of these cinemas and to reconstruct them into the totality of its particular concerns.

> In regions, classes and sub-classes, in cultures and sub-cultures, neighbourhoods and communities, interest groups and associative minorities, varieties of life-patterns are composed in bewildering complexity. . . . The second function of the modern media is to reflect and *reflect on* this plurality; to provide a constant inventory of the lexicons, life-styles and ideologies which are objectivated there. (Hall 1977, 341)

In their time dominant film theories have reflected and reflected on the pluralities of filmmaking and have provided an "inventory" of "the lexicons, life-styles and ideologies" of these practices. "Other cinemas" is just another addition to this inventory. But what is significant is that this inclusion of other cinemas in the dominant inventory legitimizes these cinemas theoretically and intellectually and makes them acceptable.

> The third function of the media . . . is to organize, orchestrate and bring together that which it has selectively represented and selectively classified.

Here, however fragmentarily and plurally, some degree of integration and cohesion, some imaginary coherence and unities must begin to be constructed. What has been made visible and classified begins to shake into an acknowledged order. . . . From this difficult and delicate negotiatory work, the problematic areas of consensus and consent begin to emerge. In the interplay of opinions, freely given and exchanged to which the idea of consensus always makes its ritual bow, *some voices* and opinions exhibit greater weight, resonance, defining and limiting power. (Hall 1977, 342)

The cultural and educational apparatuses like film journals are just some of the spaces where such voices exhibit their "weight," where "integration and cohesion" take place within and into an "acknowledged order." In relation to black film practices, these spaces are part of the process of a continuing colonial tradition where dominant forms of knowledge are preserved and disseminated. Journals like *Screen* are part of the complex non-neutral "technology" of the colonizers and part of the core, formative source of colonial knowledge which is transferred via the discourses of power to the periphery—the colonized. Hall's essay is limited to an economic and class analysis. It is necessary to look at domination and hegemony in relation to the colonial experience.

It was only after young British black people took to the streets to express their frustration that the cultural establishment, with its continuing colonial underpinnings, recognized British black filmmaking in any substantial way and provided opportunities for this sector to establish itself and expand into its various practices. The struggles, however, continue against the racist film institutions in all their large and small manifestations—mainstream industry, mainstream independents, the avant-gardes, the experimentalists, the workshops. The struggles go on for continuous funding, recognition, and legitimacy based on our terms as black filmmakers working with and for mainly black audiences. While the struggles continue on the financial and business levels, they are mirrored and paralleled on the practical and theoretical levels.

The technology of filmmaking has developed within the specific Euro-American context. As such it carries with it the particular history of that context. Linked to this particular technology are products, practices, and theories which have developed within a world view confined to Europe, both east and west, and to North America. Historically therefore, "particular technologies carry with them the scars of conflicts, compromises and particular social solutions reached by the particular society. Therefore, technology in general reflects the class relations of a particular society, the nature of its economic system, its patterns of conflict and conflict management" (Goonatilake 1984, 121) and also its racist representations and attitudes.

The Euro-American history and world view has misrepresented and marginalized black people. Therefore, when black people choose film as a means of earning a living, as a channel for political action, for our particular and specific aesthetic creations, for entertainment and for pleasure, we constantly have to work with and against a technology which is not neutral. This becomes more problematic when we, through the colonial relationship and being black in Britain today, are part of the same society and its particular technology while at the same time excluded, marginalized and made part of the problems of this society. Being simultaneously excluded and included presents spatial, relational, and psychological difficulties for black people conscious of this contradiction, but it helps us recognize the non-neutral technology for what it is—a "social gene" (Goonatilake 1984, 120) which on being transferred to another social context re-creates through positions of power and hegemony the social structures of its place of origin. This process is overt when cultural/technological "aid" packages like television hardware and software, in being transferred to Third World countries, become part of the process of neocolonialism. The process is covert when black filmmakers born and/or living and working in this country today, adopt film to articulate their relationships to and representations of the world they inhabit. It manifests itself in many forms, most of which are encompassed within the idea of "good professional practice." Such forms and practices are easily recognized as potential threats to black filmmaking, but are nevertheless consciously adopted by black filmmakers to create positions of power from which the dominant is engaged. Thus "good professional practices" are adopted and thrown back into the faces of the dominant.

In the theoretical field, however, the threats are not that easy to spot. As film technology has developed so has its theory within the particular world view. The body of theoretical knowledge now available has assumed the position of dominance along with the other cultural apparatuses of the particular society. As stated earlier this dominance is hegemonic in its maneuverings as fundamental core knowledge. Within the core, major philosophical problematics are discussed and major paradigms formed, while at the periphery where the dominated/colonized reside, the theoretical work undertaken is applied, imitative, repetitive, and confirmatory (Goonatilake 1984, esp. 15 and 110).

Thus black film theory, exposed to the dissemination of dominant knowledge through the ideological, educational, and cultural apparatuses of this particular society, finds itself using the language and conceptual tools of the dominant film theoretical traditions. Within the paradigms of these traditions (which were set without our participation) and with their tools of analysis, we have debated the Imaginary and the Symbolic, discussed narrative and discourse, studied realism and the positions of the subject, discussed representation and signification, looked at the politics of pleasure, desire, and sexuality, read our Brecht and Barthes, Heath and MacCabe,

Coward and Kristeva, analyzed aspects of the "look" and the "other," linked them to the colonial "look" and discourse, and studied our relationship to and reciprocity and collusion with that "look." The process continues, but so far it has resulted only in our knowing what we knew all along—our subjected and dominated position with special reference to colonialism.

It is true we have learned the mechanisms of that domination in detail (often through the most unnecessarily excruciating language) and are using it one way or another to challenge racism. But knowing the mechanisms and using the language appropriately only makes us participate in our own domination. We are therefore careful not to become privileged elites like the dependent intelligentsia of Third World countries molded on Western models. In seeking legitimacy, we seek it on our own terms, not on the hegemonic terms of the dominant. When we challenge the paradigms, as in the film *Territories* (directed by Isaac Julien, 1984),[1] the guardians of these paradigms become defensive and seek to slot our work into identifiable, legitimized categories. Thus *Territories* gets compared to, say, Godard or the avant-garde and doubts are cast as to whether it was made by a black filmmaker. At an open screening of films on black subjects,[2] the white section of the audience (those familiar with and practicing within the dominant theoretical and practical traditions) were desperate to slot black film work into *their* legitimate categories and keep the discussion within the dominant core theoretical knowledge. They wanted to know what we, the black filmmakers, were all about, where we were coming from and where we were going *within their paradigms*. Ultimately, whether one likes it or not, this is a racist attitude based on an allegiance to a dominant knowledge system and an expectation that the "colonized" should stay within the boundaries of this system.

Thus the problems for black filmmakers are many and complex. If we choose to work uncritically within the dominant traditions of practice and theory we face participating in our own subordination, misrepresentation, and marginalization. Working completely outside the system is naive and impossible. The very act of picking up a camera to negotiate our representations of our existence for ourselves together with our audiences is an acknowledgment and acceptance to a degree of our position *within* a total, continuing historical process specific to Western society—a process in which we, through inclusion/exclusion, played and continue to play a significant part. To work unproblematically outside film practice and theory would require total revolutionary change of the whole society and a repetition of the

1. Produced by Sankofa St. Martin's School of Art, 1984.
2. Part of a series of screenings/discussions on the subject "Power and Control" organized by Sankofa Film and Video, Ltd., 1984.

entire historical technical process of the discovery of photography and the moving image.

What is needed is a new theoretical practice developed with and through our audience, addressing issues specific to ourselves. This is done with an acute, immediate, and constant awareness of the dominant traditions always in the foreground—traditions not easy to ignore, too dominant to dismiss. But we have at least made a start at the revolutionary process by identifying the "existence of (their) rules, the facts of their meanings and the reality they embody" (Cartwright 1984, 59). With this awareness we undo their "rules," "meanings," and "realities" by making/remaking films for ourselves.[3]

> Our way to make it new is to make it again . . . and making it again is enough for us and certainly "almost us."

3. I have paraphrased the following quotation from photographer Richard Prince, "His way to make it new was to make it again . . . and making it again was enough for him and certainly, personally speaking, 'almost him' " (cited in Solomon-Godeau 1984, 99).

Works Cited

Cartwright, L. 1984. "The Front Line and Rear Guard." *Screen* (London) 25, no. 6 (November/December).

Goonatilake, S. 1984. *Aborted Discovery—Science and Creativity in the Third World.* London: Zed Press.

Hall, S. 1977. "Culture, the Media, and the Ideological Effect." In *Mass Communication and Society,* ed. J. Curran et al. London: Open University.

McCue, M. 1984. " 'Training' the Independents." *Screen* (London) 25, no. 6 (November/December).

Solomon-Godeau, A. 1984. "Winning the Game When the Rules Have Been Changed: Art Photography and Postmodernism." *Screen* (London) 25, no. 6 (November/December).

Five

Minimal Selves

Stuart Hall

A few adjectival thoughts only . . .

Thinking about my own sense of identity, I realize that it has always depended on the fact of being a *migrant,* on the *difference* from the rest of you. So one of the fascinating things about this discussion is to find myself centered at last. Now that, in the postmodern age, you all feel so dispersed, I become centered. What I've thought of as dispersed and fragmented comes, paradoxically, to be *the* representative modern experience! This is "coming home" with a vengeance! Most of it I much enjoy—welcome to migranthood. It also makes me understand something about identity which has been puzzling me in the last three years.

I've been puzzled by the fact that young black people in London today are marginalized, fragmented, unenfranchised, disadvantaged, and dispersed. And yet, they look as if they own the territory. Somehow, they too, in spite of everything, are centered, in place: without much material support, it's true, but nevertheless, they occupy a new kind of space at the center. And I've wondered again and again: what is it about that long discovery-rediscovery of identity among blacks in this migrant situation which allows them to lay a kind of claim to certain parts of the earth which aren't theirs, with quite that certainty? I do feel a sense of—dare I say—envy surrounding them. Envy is a very funny thing for the British to feel at this moment in time—to want to be black! Yet I feel some of you surreptitiously moving toward that marginal identity. I welcome you to that, too.

Now the question is: is this centering of marginality really *the* representative postmodern experience? I was given the title "the minimal self." I know the discourses which have theoretically produced that concept of "minimal self." But my experience now is that what the discourse of the postmodern has produced is not something new but a kind of recognition of where identity always was at. It is in that sense that I want to redefine the general feeling which more and more people seem to have about themselves—that they are all, in some way, *recently migrated,* if I can coin that phrase.

The classic questions which every migrant faces are twofold: "Why are you here?" and "When are you going back home?" No migrant ever knows the answer to the second question until asked. Only then does she or he know that really, in the deep sense, she/he's never going back. Migration is a one-way trip. There is no "home" to go back to. There never was. But "why are you here?" is also a really interesting question, which I've never been able to find a proper answer to either. I know the reasons one is supposed to give: "for education," "for the childrens' sake," "for a better life, more opportunities," "to enlarge the mind," etc. The truth is, I am here because it's where my family is not. I really came here to get away from my mother. Isn't that the universal story of life? One is where one is to try and get away from somewhere else. That was the story which I could never tell anybody about myself. So I had to find other stories, other fictions, which were more authentic or, at any rate, more acceptable, in place of the Big Story of the endless evasion of patriarchal family life. Who I am—the "real" me—was formed in relation to a whole set of other narratives. I was aware of the fact that identity is an invention from the very beginning, long before I understood any of this theoretically. Identity is formed at the unstable point where the "unspeakable" stories of subjectivity meet the narratives of history, of a culture. And since he/she is positioned in relation to cultured narratives which have been profoundly expropriated, the colonized subject is always "somewhere else:" doubly marginalized, displaced always *other* than where he or she is, or is able to speak from.

It wasn't a joke when I said that I migrated in order to get away from my family. I did. The problem, one discovers, is that since one's family is always already "in here," there is no way in which you can actually leave them. Of course, sooner or later, they recede in memory, or even in life. But these are not the "burials" that really matter. I wish they were still around, so that I didn't have to carry them around, locked up somewhere in my head, from which there is no migration. So from the first, in relation to them, and then to all the other symbolic "others," I certainly was always aware of the self as only constituted in that kind of absent-present contestation with something else, with some other "real me," which is and isn't there.

If you live, as I've lived, in Jamaica, in a lower-middle-class family that was trying to be a middle-class Jamaican family trying to be an upper-middle-class Jamaican family trying to be an English Victorian family . . . I mean the notion of displacement as a place of "identity" is a concept you learn to live with, long before you are able to spell it. Living with, living through difference. I remember the occasion when I returned to Jamaica on a visit sometime in the early 1960s, after the first wave of migration to England, my mother said to me: "Hope they don't think you are one of those immigrants over there!" And of course, at that point I knew for the first time I was an immigrant. Suddenly in relation to that narrative of migration, one version of the "real me" came into view. I said: "Of course, I'm an immigrant. What do you think I am?" And she said in that classic Jamaican middle-class way, "Well, I hope the people over there will shove all the immigrants off the long end of a short pier." (They've been shoving ever since.)

The trouble is that the instant one learns to be "an immigrant," one recognizes one can't be an immigrant any longer: it isn't a tenable place to be. I, then, went through the long, important, political education of discovering that I am "black." Constituting oneself as "black" is another recognition of self through difference: certain clear polarities and extremities against which one tries to define oneself. We constantly underestimate the importance, to certain crucial political things that have happened in the world, of this ability of people to constitute themselves, psychically, in the black identity. It has long been thought that this is really a simple process: a recognition—a resolution of irresolutions, a coming to rest in some place which was always there waiting for one. The "real me" at last!

The fact is "black" has never been just there either. It has always been an unstable identity, psychically, culturally, and politically. It, too, is a narrative, a story, a history. Something constructed, told, spoken, not simply found. People now speak of the society I come from in totally unrecognizable ways. Of course Jamaica is a black society, they say. In reality it is a society of black and brown people who lived for three or four hundred years without ever being able to speak of themselves as "black." Black is an identity which had to be learned and could only be learned in a certain moment. In Jamaica that moment is the 1970s. So the notion that identity is a simple—if I can use the metaphor—black or white question, has never been the experience of black people, at least in the diaspora. These are "imaginary communities"—and not a bit the less real because they are also symbolic. Where else could the dialogue of identity between subjectivity and culture take place?

Despite its fragmentations and displacements, then, "the self" does relate to a real set of histories. But what are the "real histories" to which so many at this conference have "owned up"? How new is this new condition? It does seem that more and more people now recognize themselves in the narratives of displacement. But the narratives of displacement have certain conditions of existence, real histories in the contemporary world, which are not only or exclusively psychical, not simply "journeys of the mind." What is that special moment? Is it simply the recognition of a general condition of fragmentation at the end of the twentieth century?

It may be true that the self is always, in a sense, a fiction, just as the kinds of "closures" which are required to create communities of identification—nation, ethnic group, families, sexualities, etc.—are arbitrary closures; and the forms of political action, whether movements, or parties, or classes, those too, are temporary, partial, arbitrary. I believe it is an immensely important gain when one recognizes that all identity is constructed across difference and begins to live with the politics of difference. But doesn't the acceptance of the fictional or narrative status of identity in relation to the world also require as a necessity, its opposite—the moment of arbitrary closure? Is it possible for there to be action or identity in the world without arbitrary closure—what one might call the necessity to meaning of the end of the sentence? Potentially, discourse is endless: the infinite semiosis of meaning. But to say anything at all in particular, you do have to stop talking. Of course, every full stop is provisional. The next sentence will take nearly all of it back. So what is this "ending"? It's a kind of stake, a kind of wager. It says, "I need to say something, something . . . just now." It is not forever, not totally universally true. It is not underpinned by any infinite guarantees. But just now, this is what I mean; this is who I am. At a certain point, in a certain discourse we call these unfinished closures, "the self," "society," "politics," etc. Full stop. OK. There really (as they say) is no full stop of that kind. Politics, without the arbitrary interposition of power in language, the cut of ideology, the positioning, the crossing of lines, the rupture, is impossible. I don't understand political action without that moment. I don't see where it comes from. I don't see how it is possible. All the social movements which have tried to transform society and have required the constitution of new subjectivities have had to accept the necessarily fictional, but also the fictional necessity, of the arbitrary closure which is not the end, but which makes both politics and identity possible.

Now I perfectly recognize that this recognition of difference, of the impossibility of "identity" in its fully unified meaning, does, of course, transform our sense of what politics is about. It transforms the nature of political commitment. Hundred-and-one percent commitment is no longer possible. But the politics of infinitely advancing while looking over the shoulder is a very dangerous exercise. You tend to fall into a hole. Is it possible, acknowledging the discourse of self-reflexivity, to constitute a *politics* in the recognition of the necessarily fictional nature of the modern self, and the necessary arbitrariness of the closure around the imaginary communities in relation to which we are constantly in the process of becoming "selves"?

Looking at new conceptions of identity requires us also to look at redefinitions of the forms of politics which follow from that: the politics of difference, the politics of self-reflexivity, a politics that is open to contingency but still able to act. The politics of infinite dispersal is the politics of no action at all; and one can get into that from the best of all possible motives (i.e., from the highest of all possible intellectual abstractions). So one has to reckon with the consequences of where that absolutist discourse of postmodernism is pushing one. Now, it seems to me that it is possible to think about the nature of new political identities which isn't founded on the notion of some absolute, integral self and which clearly can't arise from some fully closed narrative of the self, a politics which accepts the "no necessary or essential correspondence" of anything with anything. And there has to be *a politics of articulation*—politics as a hegemonic project.

I also believe that out there other identities *do* matter. They're not the same as my inner space, but I'm in some relationship, some dialogue, with them. They are points of resistance to the solipcism of much postmodernist discourse. I have to deal with them, somehow. And all of that constitutes, yes, a politics, in the general sense, a politics of constituting "unities"-in-difference. I think that is a new conception of politics, rooted in a new conception of the self, of identity. But I do think, theoretically and intellectually, it requires us to begin, not only to speak the language of dispersal, but also the language of, as it were, contingent closures of articulation.

You see, I don't think it's true that we've been driven back to a definition of identity as the "minimal self." Yes, it's true that the "grand narratives" which constituted the language of the self as an integral entity don't hold. But actually, you know, it isn't just the "minimal selves" stalking out there with absolutely no relation to one another. Let's think about the question of nation and nationalism. One is aware of the degree to which nationalism was/is constituted as one of those major poles or terrains of articulation of the self. I think it is very important the way in which some people now (and I think particularly of the colonized subject) begin to reach for a new conception of ethnicity as a kind of counter to the old discourses of nationalism or national identity.

Now one knows these are dangerously overlapping terrains. All the same they are not identical. Ethnicity *can* be a constitutive element in the most viciously regressive kind of nationalism or national identity. But in our times, as an imaginary community, it is also beginning to carry some other meanings, and to define a new space for identity. It insists on difference—on the fact that every identity is placed, positioned, in a culture, a language, a history. Every statement comes from somewhere, from somebody in particular. It insists on specificity, on conjuncture. But it is not necessarily armor-plated against other identities. It is not tied to fixed, permanent, unalterable oppositions. It is not wholly defined by exclusion.

I don't want to present this new ethnicity as a powerless, perfect universe. Like all terrains of identification, it has dimensions of power in it. But it isn't quite so framed by those extremities of power and aggression, violence and mobilization, as the older forms of nationalism. The slow contradictory movement from "nationalism" to "ethnicity" as a source of identities is part of a new politics. It is also part of the "decline of the West"—that immense process of historical relativization which is just beginning to make the British, at least, feel just marginally "marginal."

Six

Digging for Britain:
An Excavation in
Seven Parts

Dick Hebdige

We want . . . a nation at ease with itself.
                                    John Major

A national culture is not a folk-lore, nor an abstract populism that believes it can discover a people's true nature. A national culture is the whole body of efforts made by a people in the sphere of thought to describe, justify and praise the action through which that people has created itself and keeps itself in existence.
                                    Frantz Fanon

Perhaps, instead of thinking of identity as an accomplished fact, which the new cultural practices then represent, we should think, instead, of identity as a "production" which is never complete, always in process, and always constituted with, not outside, representation.
                                    Stuart Hall

The essay entitled "Digging for Britain" (elsewhere referred to as DFB) was first published in the catalog for *The British Edge*, an exhibition and events program, mounted in the autumn of 1987 at the Institute of Contemporary Art, Boston, Massachusetts.[1] DFB looks at how different, often contradictory myths of "Britishness" are constructed, lived, and represented in contemporary British society, how they circulate as sounds and images, signs and narratives in popular culture, and how they themselves are regularly used in various combinations to "interpellate" (call up and hold in place) different "imaginary communities" (Anderson 1983) round the larger image of the

1. The ICA program aimed to showcase innovative new work in contemporary British art and culture and included gallery installations by artists Tim Head, Hannah Collins, David Mach, Mary Kelly, Victor Burin, Edward Allinton, and Narrative Architecture Today (NATO); screenings of independent film and video (including work by Derek Jarman, Sally Potter, George Barber, and Isaac Julien); a series of music events at a local nightclub (performances by Culture Smiley, Mark Stewart and the Mafia, Wire, and the Wolfgang Press); and lectures by visiting artists and critics.

120

nation or the "national interest." The Thatcher years saw a particular investment in a set of images and myths designed to "put the 'Great' back into Great Britain again" (to quote a 1980s Tory Party campaign slogan). The ideas of British "grit" and rugged island independence, of Britain as a nation of "hardworking, home-loving ordinary people" were regularly invoked to secure popular support for the Thatcherite project of "regressive modernization" (Hall and Jacques 1985). This project entailed the selective appropriation of elements of national "heritage" (e.g., Victorian entrepreneurial values) which were summoned up to lay to rest the more recent ghosts of postwar consensus politics, welfarism, and 1960s libertarianism while, at the same time, selected British institutions (e.g., local government, the health service, education) were opened up to "free market forces."

DFB was written when that project was beginning to appear immune to effective opposition, when Thatcher herself, about to embark on a third term in office, looked virtually invincible. In other words, it was written (just) before Black Monday in October 1987, when the value of shares held on the London stock exchange suffered a sudden, massive drop, before the recession which presaged the demise (or at least mutation) of the legendary power-dressing yuppie. It was written before the art market crash and the fall of design entrepreneurs like George Davies and Terence Conran, before what the *Guardian,* reporting on the "spectacularly messy collapse" in September 1990 of the Michael Peters Design Group (responsible for styling Bang and Olufson TV sets, Nat West reports, the new Heinz baked beans label, Smile stamps, the Powergen logo, the Tory Torch of Freedom logo), described as "the growing line of fallen 1980s icons from the polluting of Perrier and fall of filofax to the slump of the Saatchis" (*Guardian,* 10 September 1990). DFB was written before the "caring" 1990s and another (Gulf) War, before incessant skiing trips together with another increase in the money awarded the Royal Family precipitated, for a few months in 1991, an alleged decline in their popularity at home, unrivaled in the second Elizabethan age. It was written, finally, long before the grumbling anti-European animus of the Bruges group conspired at last with soaring interest rates, high inflation, and the poll tax to get Mrs. Thatcher ousted from office at the hands of her own party in mid-November 1990. There is a sense in which DFB reads like a text rescued from a lost world. In a way the problem of unplanned obsolescence dogged the essay from day one and the limited generalizability of the material and insights contained therein indicates, perhaps, how much of enduring value may be lost to sociology in an "excavation" of popular culture which substitutes a "fascination" with contingent, surface forms for the traditional toils of the "depth model" and deep structural analysis.

It is, then, not the purpose of these remarks to make any claims for the intrinsic value of the essay, still less to present it as an exemplar of what postmodernism can do for the study of popular culture. On the contrary, it may well serve to deter those who might otherwise be tempted to experiment with modes of data presentation. Certainly parts of the essay look to me now—as they will, no doubt, to any future readers—as portentous, dated, and overdressed as the rock music video clips discussed inside them. And no matter how many arguments are produced for the aestheticization of theory, such arguments fail to make writing that at times resembles the verbal equivalent of dry ice in an old Ultravox video any more acceptable or easy to read. Instead of seeking to recover or redeem the original intentions, the aims of this discussion are threefold: (1) to situate the essay in some kind of historical and epistemological context; (2) to consider some of the problems posed by its interpretive and presentational "take" on contemporary cultural issues; and (3) to explicate what I regard to be the key assumptions and positions which lie, for the most part buried and unstated, in both the essay and the strategy which "speaks" it.

In the first instance, the original (U.S. public arts) context for which DFB was written accounts for some, at least, of the essay's substantive concerns—for example, the references to British heritage and English romanticism, the focus on contemporary British design and, specifically, on the mediated aesthetics of U.K. youth culture in the 1980s. It explains perhaps why much of the "popular culture" examined here (documentary and independent film and video, avant-garde design, fine art, Indi pop, etc.) hardly seems to qualify as "popular" at all. That context also helps to explain (if not to excuse) the peculiarities of style and presentation. I opted in the essay for a polyvocal, image-centered approach partly because I knew from experience that such an approach would be more amenable than a conventionally argued "thesis" to the kind of mixed media presentation—incorporating video, audiotape, slides, and "live" commentary—I wanted to give in lieu of the critic's conventional "paper" in the lecture series accompanying the exhibition. Of course, the transgressions of academic codes of detachment, consistent "voice," and so on were not just expedient but rather formed part of that more general questioning of the established forms and functions of institutionalized critique identified by the late 1980s with postmodernism.

A postmodern (or alternatively "New Times") (Hall and Jacques 1990) problematic drew the essay together at another level round a number of themes: the nation as "imaginary community," the decline of national sovereignty and national autonomy, the contradictory dynamics of globalization and localization, the imbrication of culture, technology, and economics, the place of consumption in the construction of social identities, the reversibility of center-margin oppositions, the stress on fragmentation and difference, surface and style, the strategic invocation of memory and the past, the emergence of "new (black British) ethnicities." Needless to say, many of these issues have been more fully elaborated and more competently theorized elsewhere and by others, not least in the interval since the original publication.

It is worth reviewing briefly some of the theoretical advances accomplished in recent years round at least one of the essay's central points of focus—the ethnicity/identity axis. The last few years have seen an explosion of discourse round cultural identity, an explosion which Kobena Mercer, through a combination of astute social-historical/political analysis and a sustained deconstruction of "the *trope* of race," links suggestively to the "crisis of political agency" afflicting the left in the post-1968 period—a crisis which Mercer argues became particularly acute in the Thatcher era.[2] Drawing on the insights of, among others, Gramsci, Laclau, and Mouffe, Mercer confronts the full implications of a "relational" view of both identity *and* hegemonic struggle without retreating back into either "ethnic absolutism" or the utopian rhetoric of "rainbow alliance(s)."[3] Instead he concentrates on the sheer *difficulty* of "learning to live with difference," on the ambivalent potentialities of a "politics of identity" in postmodern, postindustrial, postcolonial societies like the contemporary U.K.—a politics of identity which he contrasts with the emancipatory and essentialist "identity politics" left over from the "counterculture" of the 1960s. In much the same vein and working with a similar set of critical resources (here in the context of an analysis of Caribbean hybridity), Stuart Hall (1991) has usefully distinguished two influential though not entirely commensurable models of identity which operate across the blurred boundaries of cultural studies and cultural politics today. The first defines cultural identity in terms of one shared culture rooted in, and guaranteed by, a common historical experience. In this version, the

> "oneness," underlying all the other, more superficial differences, is the truth, the essence, of "Caribbeanness" of the black experience. It is this identity which a Caribbean or black diaspora must discover, excavate, bring to light and express through . . . representation.

By way of contrast, the second model presents identity as an always open-ended process of becoming, conditioned by the "positions of enunciation" available at any one moment to historically and socially situated subjects. Here identity is theorized as

2. Kobena Mercer in Grossberg et al. 1992 and in Rutherford 1991. See also Gramsci 1972; Laclau and Mouffe 1985; and Laclau 1991.
3. See Paul Gilroy in Grossberg et al. 1992 for an impressive critique of the uses to which the "trope of race" has been put in Anglo-American cultural studies. Gilroy's essay takes a longer historical view than Mercer's and includes an examination of the metaphors of migration rooted in the experience and memory of slavery.

constituted not outside but within representation . . . not as a second-hand mirror held up to reflect what already exists, but as that form of representation which is able to constitute us as new kinds of subjects, and thereby enables us to discover places from which to speak.

These contributions both clarify and complexify the issues at stake in any discussion of national or ethnic identity without closing off in advance the strategies and choices likely to emerge from such discussion. In comparison, the "Digging for Britain" piece may appear to readers in the 1990s as both too simple-minded, too limited in terms of its political imagination, and too elaborate, too stuffed with irrelevant detail. As the title, perhaps, suggests, it straddles the two versions of identity distinguished by Hall and remains half stuck inside an earlier set of questions (concerning roots and authenticity, the location of the *real* subcultural resistance to official, i.e., ideological, "lies"), and half aware that there are other questions to be framed once the decision is made to confront head on the challenge of the contingent character of human agency and historical change. Unfortunately, all too often, the old questions win through. At certain key points in DFB, cultural politics threaten to degenerate into a Manichaean opposition between rebellious goodies and Establishment baddies, as Lawrence Grossberg (1988) has pointed out in his critique of the essay:

> Power, however dispersed, is always articulated [in DFB] into a struggle between the popular—represented by London's street-styled and economically marginalized male youth and the [evil] other of Thatcherism and official culture. Culture is differentiated according to a single dichotomous vision of contemporary Britain and of the possibilities of British identity. . . . There is an assumed necessary correspondence between social position, lived experience, cultural practice and political significance.

Such a reductive view of what Grossberg more adequately figures as the "continuous 'war of position' dispersed across the entire terrain of social and cultural life" suggests, as he indicates in his critique, that the more urgent lessons of postmodernism have hardly been assimilated here. Nonetheless, while DFB may look out of place, it's clear enough where it *does* fit in those debates on popular culture, "ethnicity," and national identity which constitute some of the most powerful vectors in (British) cultural studies today.

But the form of the essay is, as they used to say, "something else." Justifications for a "narrative poetics" within the social sciences have been put forward intermittently since the earliest attempts to legitimate and codify qualitative method. The recent work of Clifford, Marcus, and others (Clifford and Marcus 1986; Clifford 1988) which seeks to deconstruct anthropology's colonial inheritance and to integrate "the poetics and politics of ethnography" embodies a thorough investigation of the relevant issues, especially when read alongside Clifford Geertz's powerful defense (1988) of the anthropological project. Closer to home, the confidence with which the critic can pronounce from a safe distance on the "meaning" of contemporary cultural "forms" has been shaken for at least two decades now by the "discursive turn" in cultural studies,[4] taken to accommodate the now-familiar series of European theory imports (semiotics, poststructuralism, etc.). The challenge to the truth claims of what Mercer (1992) calls the "Big Picture" theories like Marxism has been highlighted over the same period by the "acknowledgement of the *plural* sources of antagonism" which heralded the arrival of "new" social movements and new political demands. And the steady stream of criticism which, since the late 1950s, sought to promote the academic study of popular culture has turned into a flood thirty years on as the key concepts used to define the "postmodern condition"—eclecticism (Lyotard), simulation (Baudrillard), indifference (Grossberg), dedifferentiation (Lash), recoding (Foster), pastiche (Jameson), weak thought (Vattimo), etc.—have begun to circulate and, in the process, to accelerate the "implosion" (Baudrillard) of the analytical hierarchies and binary oppositions (base v. superstructure; high v. low; minority v. mass) which used to underwrite the study of contemporary culture in humanities and social science departments in past decades.

It is not just that, as Steven Connor (1989) puts it, cultural critics today "unabashedly bring to bear on [popular culture] the same degree of theoretical sophistication as they would bring to any high cultural artefact." As Connor himself goes on to indicate in his comprehensive review of postmodernist culture, for many of us this expansion of both the legitimated field of study and the "means of dissemination" (e.g., audiovisual technologies) modifies the terms of critical engagement in such a way and to such an extent that the old contract governing the relations between readers and texts, between audiences, critics, and their objects of study have to be radically redrawn. To take just one example, the postmodern pedagogy of people like Gregory Ulmer, Gavriel Salomon, and Genevieve Jacquinot builds on the work, of among others, Barthes, Derrida, and Walter Ong (see Parr 1991; Ulmer 1985, 1989; Salomon 1981; Hebdige 1991), takes implosion as a starting point rather than a source of lamentation, and seeks to "provide an educational discourse for an age of video"—one which Ulmer suggests should prioritize "a shift away from the exclusive domination of mind . . . to a mode that includes the body" (Ulmer 1985, 1989). Elsewhere, in an attempt to respond constructively to the new conditions under which signs, information, knowledges circulate today, I have argued (Hebdige 1988) that there are positive benefits to be derived from "the splintering of the masterly overview and the totalizing aspiration" and that the cultivation of a more relaxed

4. See Stuart Hall in Grossberg et al. 1992 for an account of these accommodations.

("critical but credulous") disposition on the part of the critic is not incompatible with either rigor or responsibility in an epoch characterized by Barbara Hernnstein Smith (1988) as "the age of value without truth-value." If the "price paid by a powerful rationality is a terrific limitation in the object it manages to see and talk about" (G. Vattimo quoted in Chambers 1990), then the proliferation of objects and our possible relations to them and with them promised in postmodern philosophy and postmodernist critical practice might also license "a productive blurring of the line between fiction and critique, a blurring, too, of origins and roles in such a way that no single author can lord it over the world of the text (or, it goes without saying, the text of the world)" (Hebdige 1988).

All these factors, pressures, and decentering moves helped in different ways to determine the style of presentation chosen for the "Digging" essay. I set out to suspend a "constellation" of ideas and images of British identity in a "textile" web of associations which would in turn, I hoped, be more flexible, more open-ended, more *dialogical,* to use Mikhail Bakhtin's term, than the conceptual frameworks generally preferred in academic or analytical work on contemporary culture. The essay was, in this way, an attempt, following Walter Benjamin's famous analogy, to "excavate" rather than to explicate the contested ground of British cultural identity in the late 1980s via a series of competing and contingently related images and narratives of nation. Those images and narratives had to be plural enough to demonstrate that, as Bruce Ferguson (1991) puts it, "the nation is an impossible name, an incorrigible sign," that "repressions [are] necessary to produce a unified image," and that there is a cost that accrues from that repression.

This last point leads us back to the conjunctural analysis of the crisis of the Thatcherite formation with which I opened these remarks because it is somewhere here in the gap between the image, the act of utterance, and the repression which makes them both possible that the essay's stylistic "strangeness" and the substantive issue of identity (and difference) come together. To sum up: instead of laying out "arguments" in a more or less linear fashion, the idea was to subject hegemonic constructions of "Britishness" and "national heritage," specifically those foregrounded in Thatcherism, to a kind of immanent critique by using anecdotes, metaphors, collage, and quotation in ways that would expose to view the edgy ambivalence of the figure of the "British edge" itself. For a moment's reflection reveals at least two opposed "readings" of that metaphor (which is presumably why the curators chose it as a title in the first place): (1) Britain's putative "edge" over its competitors in what were, at the time of writing in late 1987, the still burgeoning advertising, marketing, and design sectors, the British "lead" in certain areas of finance, retail, and the culture industries (e.g., the British "invasion" of American MTV in the mid 1980s); and (2) the British "edge" as in the repressed or excluded margin, the unincorporated remainder automatically produced in exclusive definitions of nationhood and national belonging, e.g., the threatening others alluded to in Powell's "rivers of blood" speech in 1968 (Mercer 1992) or in Thatcher's "enemies within" speech. To turn the metaphor one last time, it is tempting to suggest that the Thatcherite bloc, centered at the point where these two lines of antagonism intersect, was torn apart in late 1990 by spiraling inflation and interest rates and global recession which removed the first "edge" altogether and by the Ridley-Thatcher "wrecking" stance on 1992 which left Britain (at least the increasingly centralized province of "little England") hanging off the edge of the new federal Europe.

The text of "Digging for Britain: An Excavation in Seven Parts" follows. Its combined notes and references are reproduced at the end of the essay, preceding the list of works cited in this introduction.

> Dig! Dig! Dig! And your muscles will grow big.
> Keep on pushing in the spade!
> Never mind the worms
> Just ignore the squirms
> And when your back aches laugh with glee
> And keep on diggin'
> Till we give our foes a wiggin
> Dig! Dig! Dig! to Victory.
> (Ministry of Food jingle to promote the 1943 Home Front
> nutritional self-sufficiency campaign, "Digging for Victory")

> . . . true, for successful excavators, a plan is needed. Yet no less indispensable is the cautious probing of the space in the dark loam, and it is to cheat oneself of the richest prize to preserve as a record merely the inventory of one's own discoveries, and not this dark joy of the place of the finding itself. Fruitless searching is as much a part of this as succeeding, and consequently remembrance must not proceed in the manner of a narrative or still less that of report, but must, in the strictest epic and rhapsodic manner, assay its spade in ever-new places, and in the old ones delve to ever deeper layers.
> (Walter Benjamin, "A Berlin Chronicle," from *One Way Street*, 1940)

To write in general terms about the "British edge" is fraught with risk. When words like "nation," "culture," and "identity" are placed together, historiography has a tendency to degenerate into fairy tale and narrative; multi- and multiply contested traditions to congeal into *the* singular "Great Tradition," a set of lifeless monuments authored by "Great Men." Walter Benjamin's metaphor of "excavation" provides an alternative model of history writing. His preferred methods for drawing up the stuff of history to the surface through an attention precisely to the detail are well known—his reasoned preference for pastiche, quotation, aphorism over linear "reconstructions"; his preference, too, for "exhibiting" the relations in which particular phenomena are embedded rather than "explaining" their imagined origins. Benjamin was always reluctant to subsume individual phenomena under general concepts and advocated that the writer should cultivate a sensitivity both to the uniqueness, importance, and complexity of individual detail ("the fragment is the gateway to the whole") and to the invisible networks of relations—what he called the "constellations"—in which they were embedded, drawn together, and made meaningful. He felt himself drawn irresistibly by the incandescence of the particular, drawn back again and again to "this dark joy of the place of the finding itself."

Taking Benjamin's metaphor and his method as a model in this essay, I shall try to dig for Britain—to explore some of the rich, heterogeneous (and contradictory) connotations surrounding terms like "national identity," "British culture," the "British edge," and to sift through the relics that are turned up as we cut back and forth between different geological strata, different points in time. Some "places" will possess a particular intensity and power (1940, time of war; 1977, time of punk; 1987, time of writing)—they provide the temporal coordinates through which the excavation can be guided and directed. This dig has been undertaken not as an attempt to recover some lost substantial unity ("England, My England"): the fragments dispersed throughout the different layers are unlikely to be parts of the same, single object. Instead it will be conducted in the spirit of the seance as a convocation of bits and pieces of the past (the national past, the personal past), as a procession, first and foremost, of images of Britain, for as Benjamin puts it: "To articulate the past historically does not mean to recognize it 'the way it really was' (Ranke). It means to seize hold of a memory as it flashes up at a moment of danger."[1]

England, Your Englands

The year 1940 was one such moment. In his essay "England, Your England," George Orwell sought to capture the English "character" in a series of vivid, fragmentary insights:

> One has only to look at their methods of town-planning and water-supply, their obstinate clinging to everything that is out of date and a nuisance, a spelling system that defies analysis and a system of weights and measures that is intelligible only to the compilers of arithmetic books, to see how little they care about mere efficiency. . . . Another English characteristic . . . is the addiction to hobbies and spare-time occupations, the *privateness* of En-

glish life. We are a nation of flower lovers[,] . . . of stamp-collectors, pigeon-fanciers, amateur carpenters, coupon-snippers, darts-players, crossword-puzzle fans. All the culture that is most truly native centres round things which even when they are communal are not official—the pub, the football match, the back garden, the fireside, and the "nice cup of tea." The liberty of the individual is still believed in, almost as in the nineteenth century. But this has nothing to do with economic liberty, the right to exploit others for profit. It is the liberty to have a home of your own, to do what you like in your spare time, to choose your own amusements instead of having them chosen from above. . . . it is obvious, of course, that even this purely private liberty is a lost cause. Like all other modern peoples, the English are in the process of being numbered, labelled, conscripted, "co-ordinated." But the pull of their impulses is in the other direction, and the kind of regimentation that can be imposed on them will be modified in consequence.[2]

Orwell's passionate and controversial eulogy to the "ordinariness" of the "British working people" was written in the aftermath of Dunkirk, just before the bombs began to rain on Britain's cities. The portrait, even now, can strike a chord. It is conditioned by Orwell's almost palpable affection for the ordinary and the unremarkable wherever he encountered them surviving against all the odds, although the poignancy of that emotion was no doubt heightened for Orwell, writing in 1940, with the Germans apparently about to invade. Many of the defining qualities of that Britishness—more accurately, that Englishness—which Orwell singles out in contrast to the cold "realism," the mindless mass somnabulism of the "truly modern men, the Nazis and the Fascists" could be used to trace out the eccentric contours of the "national character" today: the "privateness," the hobbies, the insular, parochial preoccupations. Such is the nature of national stereotypes. They are infinitely flexible forms of wishful thinking. The quest for a German or Japanese "essence," a wild, sadistic, wayward gene "responsible" for Auschwitz or the River Kwai is surely, we know now, futile. No such gene, no such essence exists: those of us *Schuldig geboren,* born guilty and born late, find it hard to place much faith in the authority of words like "race," in the permanence or plausibility of single definitions of "destiny" or "nation."

For much has changed in England in 1987 after over forty years of imperial decay, industrial disaster, the ill-directed lurch and stumble of a hotch-potch mixed economy, after the bungle of Suez, the tatty dumbshow of the King's Road, and the "swinging sixties," after the Stones and the yuppies and the Sex Pistols, after soccer hooliganism and the massacre at the Heysel football stadium in 1984, above all, after eight years of Mrs. Thatcher's iron tillage, the soil of nation and the "British character" are barely recognizable. The ground is still more or less the same—Orwell would no doubt have identified the various mineral constituents: the granitelike persistence of social class, the rocklike insularity, the bloody minded sticking to feet and yards and inches when the rest of the world has long ago gone metric. But though the ground remains the same, the landscape has transformed: all changed . . . changed utterly.

In 1940, it was still possible in times of crisis to call up in both senses—to enlist for national service and to interpellate as loyal subjects of the Crown—a more or less (racially and, in the broadest sense, culturally) homogeneous "community" of "decent, fair-minded" Britons.[3] (A larger "commonwealth" was called up, too, beyond national and racial boundaries.) A British nation could be forged, despite the persistence of the deepest class divisions in the Western world ("England is the most class-ridden country under the sun," said Orwell). A community of interest could be welded together around words like "liberty," "democracy," "natural justice," around what Thomas Carlyle once called a native "hatred of disorder, a hatred of injustice which is the worst disorder."[4] This mythical but mobilizable nation (mobilizable indeed because mythical)—the sentimental heart of a vast financial and commercial cartel called the British Empire—has been replaced in the 1980s by Mrs. Thatcher's vision of a "property-owning democracy" and an "enterprise culture," a dream which is no more real, no more imaginary, and perhaps, in the long run, no less politically effective than that other, earlier, picture-postcard construction of the decent, jackboot-hating British type. Mrs. Thatcher's nation is composed of different stuff. It is populated by a different "people." It is full of early risers and hard workers who can think for themselves without big bully trade unions ("Rise early, work late, strike oil—that's the only strike worth having!" was an early 1980s Thatcher slogan). Mrs. Thatcher's nation comprises, most of all, family people mortgaged and industrious, an army of smiling shop assistants led by intrepid "go-getters" pulled up by their bootstraps from the ranks. Its higher echelons are occupied not by "faceless bureaucrats" or a faded, fopperish gentry but by a hard-eyed meritocracy of "self-made businessfolk" toiling seven days a week in the burgeoning service, finance, and communications sectors—a people with a portfolio of shares under its arm (this, after all, to use another Thatcher catchphrase, is "popular capitalism")—shares acquired in the recent flotations on the stock market of formerly nationalized industries: British Telecom, North Sea Oil, British Gas, British Airways.

Against this nation (for identities require differences) are ranked the "enemies without and within": outside the gates, the swarthy terrorists, the PLO and IRA, the "Argies" and the Reds; inside, sliding like an asp across Britannia's milk-white bosom, the trade unions, the agitators, the wastrels, the "scroungers," the "moaning minnies," the "do-gooders," and the "loony Left," the unassimilable ethnic minorities too insignificant in number to be worth courting for a vote, the out of work "who simply don't want to work."[5]

The New Albion—U.K. Inc.—was declared officially open for business one morning in October 1986 on the day of the so-called Big Bang when, as a part of the general process of institutional overhaul, "rationalization," and removal of controls on the free play of market forces—a process which Mrs. Thatcher has recently dubbed her "cultural revolution"—the City of London abolished the traditional demarcation between jobbers and brokers. On that day British share dealing went "online," and the stock exchange was thrown wide open to the international markets of a world *sans frontières, sans temps*—where money circulates three months in advance around commodities which may never exist in the real world but which function as signs in a game called the "futures market," in a placeless world of capital cities where nations exist only as currency prices, where dealers hang all day on the end of a telephone wire with one eye on the visual display unit of a computer terminal, in a timeless world where fortunes can be made and blipped away again in a fraction of a nanosecond.

And in the meantime, down on planet Earth, the British bobby, that no less mythical embodiment of mild English manners, courtesy, and common sense—a figure that Orwell, himself a sometime member of the Imperial Indian Police, would certainly have recognized—has been replaced by a growing army of specially trained, highly paid, frequently armed professionals deploying, in the routine policing of industrial disputes and multiracial riots on the mainland, surveillance and crowd control techniques perfected in the war in Northern Ireland.

For nations and identities are delicate, resilient things. Neither purely organic nor directly imposed, neither simply invented nor stumbled upon, they are substantial apparitions. And national identities especially so. They are, in essence, multiply contested invocations, snatched attempts to solve what Patrick Wright calls the vexed "question of historicity, of cultural authenticity and security in the face of change."[6]

Visions of the Daughters of Albion (*Spare Time,* 1939)

I load the video machine with a cassette of a 1939 documentary film. (It is sometimes claimed that Britain has the highest per capita ownership of VCRs in the world.) The film, directed by Humphrey Jennings, is called *Spare Time*. It is permeated with the kind of openly avowed curiosity about and affection for the "British working people" that gave so much of the documentary output of that decade from the photo weeklies to the English journeys of Priestley and Orwell to the work of Tom Harrisson's *Mass Observation Unit* its peculiar flavor—at once pungent and cloying—that unmistakable mixture of the patronizing, the heartfelt, and the voyeuristic which speaks not just of *times* past but of a superseded social order—a disintegrated or, at the very least, severely damaged caste.[7] All this is tempered, in this particular case, by Jennings's surrealist eye, the gentle, probing lyricism which makes his films so memorable.

Over footage of flickering industrial landscapes, a voice addresses the world in the clipped patrician accent which is the trademark of the films produced under the aegis of John Grierson at the Empire Marketing Board and the GPO: "This is a film about the way people spend their spare time in three separate industries: steel, cotton, and coal. Between work and sleep comes the time we call our own. What do we do with it?" Orwell's England of hobbyists, darts-players, brass-band enthusiasts, pigeon-fanciers, and ballroom dancers rolls by on a gray stream of images and old popular music. In the center of this stream, for me at least, a stone, a startling *punctum,* an interruption of the flow.[8]

The section on cotton opens onto a dingy recreation ground flanked by the squat terraced houses typical of northern industrial towns before the war. Out of the damp, freckly fog produced through the unfortunate conjunction of the original atmospheric conditions and deteriorated film stock, a little troupe of child kazoo-players marches grimly into frame led by a bandleader waving a short baton. The camera closes in on an adolescent boy, his long pale face bereft of any vestige of expression beyond the hideous, awkward *consciousness* of adolescence (this is long before adolescence had acquired its mystique, long before James Dean and *Catcher in the Rye*).

The boy holds up an illegible placard, and our attention is directed to the baton bearer. Dressed like his charges in a tailored mock-military uniform with billowing sleeves and pinched-in cuffs made of Widow Twankey satin,[9] he turns his back to the camera to oversee the raising of Albion: a little girl in a cut-down sheet wearing a miniature fireman's helmet is hoisted aloft by four stern-faced boys.

The band strikes up with "Rule Britannia." The little symbol stands for a moment facing the camera, wobbling slightly on her boards, Britannia's shield (a round cake-tin lid with a Union Jack painted on it) on one arm, an aluminium foil trident in the other. A row of dark chimney pots frames her burnished head as a flag flaps softly in the foreground and the conductor's arms wave off and into the opening bars of the battle hymn with the crisp, fluttering movements popularized by Geraldo, Joe Loss, and all the other 1930s dance band leaders. A tiny tot—younger than the others—the band mascot?—grimaces at the camera, her satin cap cocked at a cute angle like Shirley Temple on *The Good Ship Lollipop.* The kazoos pipe out the marching song of the British Empire: "Rule Britannia."

Played as the composer no doubt intended it to be played by a military brass band, the song is redolent of stone lions and solemn state occasions. It is a paean to the indomitable British spirit. It celebrates the fierce defense of individual liberty conjured up by the Magna Carta, enshrined (or so the story goes) in British law. Its lyrics commemorate nine hundred years of freedom from foreign dictatorships ("Britons never, never, never shall be slaves"); the bullish, bulldoggish (soon to be Churchillian) independence of a rugged island race. It reiterates the pledge to retain naval supremacy at all costs: "Britannia rules the waves."

All this pomp and circumstance, all this history made suddenly bizarre, domesticated, brought down to size by a group of children blowing in unison into the manufactured equivalent of a tissue paper and comb. With grave inscrutable expressions, a row of girls, swaying slightly in time to the music, blows little trills at the end of each line (at one point "Rule Britannia" threatens to merge imperceptibly with the old music hall favorite "I'm Forever Blowing Bubbles"). With the gravity born of concentration, the children are decorating, embellishing the original tune. They are "yiddling"—jazzing up the authorized version. The kazoo band is embroidering its own gaudy motifs on the red, white, and blue—motifs woven out of the bandleader's imagination, but derived in essence from Hollywood, from Busby Berkeley musicals, from photographs of American marching bands, from the stylistic flourishes of American popular songs, from the group dynamics of *Snow White and the Seven Dwarfs*. The New Jerusalem is here proclaimed among England's dark satanic mills in warbling glissandi by a shining host of pinched-faced seraphim. The Countenance Divine which shines forth upon the assembled throng from behind the bandleader's shoulder is—unmistakably—Walt Disney's.

The original motivation for this patriotic display—a motivation which is anyway obscured by the English drizzle, by the blank delivery and the deadpan expressions, by the passage of time and the images blurred by that passage—doesn't really matter. The question of a satirical intention, as far as Humphrey Jennings is concerned, is neither here nor there (though we can surely discount such an intention on the part of the band itself). The solemn observance of Empire Day in the schools even of my childhood in the 1950s, and the provenance of the "organized youth," the patriotic aftermath of the British forces' derring-do at Mafeking and Bloemfontein,[10] would seem to indicate that this is a straightforward affirmation of loyalty to the Crown, an oath of fealty, albeit one expressed in the "Americanized" accent so typical of a certain kind of British popular culture then as now. The intention is obscure, perhaps irrelevant.

But the kitsch—of course—the pathos, makes us smile. Fifty years on, the performance evokes a "tender feeling."[11] We are moved by the campy contrast between what we see and what we hear, between all that visible effort (the uniforms, the military postures, the needle-browed concentration) and what it actually achieves—the funny strangulated noise that crackles on the soundtrack. We are moved by the sad-sweet innocence, the quaintness of which is compounded by age—by *our* age (these grave little children), by the age in which we live (these ancient children), in a cotton town before the war, before Hiroshima, before the ignominious bundling off the stage of history of the straight-backed British Empire, before the "birth of the teen-ager" and the final death throes of King Cotton, before, above all, the treachery of video (treacherous, this taking out of time of the original event, the original film watched at a distance on my Japanese Sony TV, paused, re-viewed on fast-forward fifty years on in the middle of the 1980s and another recession).

Whatever the intention, a transformation has nonetheless occurred.

> In this casual comedy, the monarch too has resigned his part.
> He, too, has been changed in his turn.
> All changed, changed utterly.
> A terrible beauty is born:
> His Majesty, King George VI, is wearing Mickey Mouse ears.[12]

Auguries of Innocence (Sounding Out New Britains)

Albion: Britain (Pliny) from Latin: *albus,* white, the allusion being to the white cliffs of Dover.

> Keep our Empire undismembered
> Guide our Forces by Thy Hand,
> Gallant blacks from far Jamaica,
> Honduras and Togoland;
> Protect them Lord in all their fights,
> And, even more, protect the whites.
>
> Think of what our Nation stands for,
> Books from Boots and country lanes,
> Free speech, free passes, class distinction
> Democracy and proper drains.
> Lord, put beneath Thy special care
> One-eighty-nine Cadogan Square.
> > (John Betjeman, "In Westminster
> > Abbey," 1940)

I have spoken all the while of "the nation", "England", as though 45 mil-lion souls could somehow be treated as a unit. But is not England notor-iously two nations, the rich and the poor? Dare one pretend that there is anything in common between people with 100,000 pounds a year and people with one pound a week? And even Welsh and Scottish readers are likely to have been offended because I have used the word "England" more often than "Britain", as though the whole population dwelled in London and the Home Counties and neither north nor west possessed a culture of its own. . . . A Scotsman, for instance, does not thank you if you call him an Englishman. You can see the hesitation we feel on this point by the fact that we call our islands by no less than six different names: England, Britain, Great Britain, the British Isles, the United Kingdom and, in very exalted moments, Albion. (George Orwell, "England, Your England," 1940)

Those whom the gods wish to destroy they first make mad. We must be mad, literally mad, to be permitting the annual inflow of some 50,000 dependents, who are for the most part the material of the future growth of the immigrant-descended population. It is like watching a nation busily engaged in heaping up its own funeral pyre. So insane are we that we actually permit unmarried persons to immigrate for the purpose of founding a family with spouses and fiancées whom they have never seen. As I look ahead, I am filled with foreboding. Like the Roman, I seem to see "the River Tiber foaming with much blood." That tragic and intractable phenomenon which we watch with horror on the other side of the Atlantic, but which there is interwoven with the history and existence of the States itself, is coming upon us here by our own volition and neglect. (Enoch Powell, Birmingham Address, 20 April 1968)

The West Indian or Asian does not by being born in England become an Englishman. In law he is a United Kingdom citizen, by birth in fact he is a West Indian or Asian still. (Enoch Powell, speech to the London Rotary Club, Eastbourne, November 1968)

The question mark which hangs over the "united" in United Kingdom has been highlighted in the postwar period through that process of entropy which Tom Nairn has dubbed "the break-up of Britain." In Nairn's account, the dominance of England (the "incubator of capitalism")—of English rule and Westminster—within the British Isles has been challenged by the emergence in the 1970s of Welsh and Scottish nationalism (in the latter case fuelled by North Sea oil), by the deliberate accentuation of Celtic "differentiae" and the resuscitation of the formerly "dead" or "dying" Gaelic languages, by the "Troubles" in Northern Ireland, and the controversy surrounding Britain's membership of the European community.[13]

In the ten years or so since Nairn's book was first published, the stark division between the prosperous south and the deindustrialized, impoverished north—made most bitterly apparent in the year-long miners' strikes—has been stretched and deepened into a gulf during the Thatcher years. And Enoch Powell's brooding rhetoric condemning the "betrayal of the nation" by Westminster, the "swamping" of British singularity by successive waves of alien (i.e., non-European) immigration, threads darkly underneath the public discourse of national decline—a stream of oratory flowing "like the River Tiber foaming with much blood," it soaks through to the surface of the speeches made on the appropriate occasions—in the wake of a riot, on the eve of an election—by right-minded politicians to color their pronouncements on the "crisis," "national identity," endangered "birthright."

But there are, of course, other stories, other histories. On the other side of the imperialist imaginary, beyond the nostalgia for the stable and the fixed, new identities, new communities are being formed which can't be reduced to the old frameworks of class or returned to the social and ideological locations guaranteed by traditional party politics in Britain.

"The place of the finding itself" can be quite to one side of the center, in an overlooked corner or right beneath our feet in, for instance, the domain of the "trivial" and the "popular."

To strike the spade again into some already well-turned soil, punk has often been cited as a terminus or starting point in chronological accounts of the relationship between postwar British popular music, popular culture, and design. The auguries—the visual and aural "noise" that signaled punk's arrival—have been interpreted and reinterpreted. They have been "read" as a direct reflection or expression of adolescent anomie, unemployment, "identity crisis" (dole queue rock); as symptoms of a further decline in traditional familial values, a collapse of social, sexual, and sartorial norms, as prognostics of the "death of meaning" or the "waning of affect" (Fredric Jameson); as evidence of the Art School's influence on the British pop scene (Simon Frith), as an ironic commentary on the rhetoric of crisis (clothes for Britain to go down the drain in—what Phil Cohen calls "Storm and Dress Theory"), as a deconstruction of the languages of rock and teen rebellion (Dave Laing), as critical modernism for the masses (Greil Marcus, Iain Chambers), as the inspired creation—through bricolage, parody, and dreamwork—of a cohort of entrepreneurs, musicians, designers, and stylists, as a disaffected "subculture's" "resistance" to the lies of consensus politics (Dick Hebdige).[14] On the one hand, the lyrics and the looks of punk music and fashions topicalized the themes of "youth unemployment," "urban crisis," "national decline"—themes which were generalized as the recession deepened during the next decade, especially when the pressure points in the inner cities erupted in the youth riots of 1981 and 1985. On the other hand, punk's visual and musical hyperboles helped to boost the British textile and design industries, put Britain (or at least London) back on the international fashion map, led to a (temporary) boom in independent record production, and marked the beginning of a long-term (re)visualization of popular music which spread from poster and record sleeve design to the massive investment in video promotions which was to pave the way for the "second British invasion" of the U.S. charts after MTV was set up in the early 1980s.

But punk also inaugurated in earnest the long retreat from the phallocentric codes of "cock rock" and the rediscovery of other (more or less marginalized) musics—bebop, cool jazz, swing, R & B, salsa, reggae, funk, blues, and the 1940s/1950s "torch singing."[15] It marked the beginning of a long-term questioning of the mythologies of technique, originality, genre boundaries, and authorship in pop and rock which was eventually to lead to the invention of new musics—electro pop, MC reggae, rap, jazz funk, etc. These new or transfigured musical languages have been used by performers and "fans" alike to contest the given constructions of masculinity and femininity available within the wider culture and to articulate less monotonously phallic and/or heterosexual structures of desire (e.g., the music and performance styles of the Slits, the Au Pairs, Carmen, Sade, Alison Moyet, Culture Club, Bronski Beat, the Communards, Frankie Goes to Hollywood, the Smiths).

A moratorium was also held in British punk on questions of race, ethnicity, nation. Not only did this involve refusals of the ideal of a *united* nation in songs like "White Riot" (the Clash) and "Anarchy in the U.K." (the Sex Pistols) and the negative "white noise" of hardcore and later Oi (early 1980s neoskinhead "music"). There were also attempts actively to erode internal racial-ethnic divisions in Britain and within the punk movement itself, both through explicit interventions like Rock Against Racism (RAR) and Two Tone and through the creation of hybrid musics which integrated or spliced together black and white musical forms. RAR—set up by music journalists, designers, performers, record business personnel—together with the Anti-Nazi League—a broad, nonaligned pressure group headed by political, sports, and show business figures—set out to mobilize a popular front against the threatened resurgence in the late 1970s of racist political parties like the National Front (NF). Using the demotic forms of the rock concert, the poster, the magazine (*Temporary Hoarding*), and the slogan (e.g., NF = No Fun), RAR activists sought to shift the emergent structure of feeling inscribed within punk away from the nihilism and racism of some elements in punk itself toward the left-libertarian multiculturalism which was being simultaneously promoted by the *New Musical Express*—at that time Britain's leading music paper.[16]

Less overtly "political" and interventionist in tone, less didactic in character, Two Tone was a loose confederation of music groups (the Specials, the Beat, the Selector, Madness) from diverse racial-ethnic backgrounds who set out to produce a fusion of white (punk) and black (reggae) British musical traditions by developing a contemporary version of 1960s Jamaican ska (a forerunner of reggae). This transmogrified ska—more congenial, accessible, and easily danced to than punk, less exclusive, separatist, and turned in upon itself than "heavy" roots reggae—provided a vehicle designed literally to move the audience through dance into a new kind of British territory, a new multicultural space, an organic bonding of signs and bodies. Here, through the forging of a series of formal and informal, aesthetic and experiential "fits," an affective alliance was offered as the ground on which organic solidarity could develop between disaffected black and white youths—a solidarity the authenticity of which was guaranteed by the "rootedness" of the Two Tone musicians themselves in the Ghost Town of the inner city.

This forging of affective alliances through the invocation of a specific mix of signs and rhythms has always functioned as a vital strategy within black music, creating, as Paul Gilroy has forcefully argued in *There Ain't No Black in the Union Jack,* a diasporan identity among the black urban dispossessed, an identity which can be mobilized to abolish geographical distances and the systematic mystification of a shared history and common interests. In Britain, from the 1960s onward, reggae music, transmitted through channels embedded deep in the black community, has offered a powerful bass line against "Babylon pressure." The sound systems— the mobile reggae discos with their own deejays, emcees ("microphone chanters"), their "specials" and "dub plates" (specially recorded rhythms "owned" by the system), their own local followings—are networks of live wires and speakers. They call up (assemble and service) particular "communities" wherever they are plugged in and played. Hip-hop, funk, and "wild style" have functioned in a similar way in the 1980s. These forms and the cultural and commercial institutions which support them have worked to forge a community beyond the constricting "arboreal" logic of race and "roots."[17]

The affective alliances created through rap and hip-hop—through what might sound on first hearing like a deconstructed (schizophrenic/schizogenic) collage of broken, stuttering, and fragmented noise—binds together black and white youths historically and geographically dispersed, dispossessed, divided against each other as the modern Western empires implode into their metropolitan centers, Afrika Bambaata's Zulu Nation (a British chapter was formed in 1984 under the auspices of MC Spyrock at WLR, a London pirate radio station) is rapped up in a tradition which valorizes verbal and physical dexterity and which is, according to Bambaata and James Brown, overtly pledged to the sublimation of fight into dance, of conflict into contest, of desperation into style and a sense of self-respect.[18] The definite contours of race—the topography of skin—begin to be rubbed away in the mosaic—the musics and found sounds of Bambaata, who dissolves continents and categories as he mixes punk with funk, a snatch of a Monkees' melody with a quote from Beethoven, a Keith Richards's guitar riff, the theme from *The Munsters* or *The Pink Panther,* centering these sounds around a solid bass line laid down originally by Chic, the U.S. disco band. The earthbound logic of "national" and "ethnic" cultures is further disordered by the tape-deck tourism of Malcolm McLaren, who fuses opera and rap, Zulu, Latin, and Burundi rhythms of Appalachian hillbilly music. As rhythms, melodies, and harmonies are borrowed, worked with, quoted, and returned to the airwaves, new connections are made, new "communités" made possible both within and beyond the confines of race and nation.

Now with that fusion of Indian and Pakistani folk forms and Western popular music sometimes referred to as "Indi pop," a novel British-Asian (more accurately, British–South Asian) cultural identity has begun to form and find its voice—an identity uniquely adapted to local conditions, attuned to the diverse, often conflicting experiences of parents who emigrated from the subcontinent and from Kenya and Uganda in the 1960s and their children born and brought up in Britain. The answer once again is in the mix—the blend in Bangra music of Punjabi rhythms, the electronic instrumentation and production values of the Western popular music industry, and performance styles gleaned partly from domestic video viewings of imported Indian musicals, partly from the onstage poses of Western "stars" like Boy George, Madonna, Elvis Presley. Bangra and Indi pop, the vibrant trademarks of a growing number of second-generation British Asians, are played across the gaps and tensions not just between the "home" and the "host culture," with their different languages, behavioral norms, belief systems, and cuisines, not just between *two* cultures (the "traditional" East, the "permissive" or "progressive" West), but between many *different* South Asian cultures, between the multiple boundaries which for centuries have marked off different religions, castes, ethnic traditions within a "community" which appears homogeneous only when viewed from the outside.

If, as Prabhu Guptara has recently put it, the place called "India" is a British creation, if "Kashmir in the north, Kerela in the south, Gujarat in the west, and Mizoram in the east have nothing in common except that they were all conquered by the British at some stage and made independent together," [19] if the concept of "nation" seems meaningless when applied to a vast expanse of territory whose people, according to the last census, speak more than a thousand different languages, then a new pan-Asian/British community is being brought together *in the face of* the increasingly racist proscriptions which have motivated official definitions of British citizenship and British culture for centuries—explicitly so since the 1960s, when Enoch Powell made his ominous intervention in the politics of race in Britain—proscriptions which have found their way directly onto the statute book in the form of racist legislation like the Nationality Act of 1981.

As Tamil refugees strip on the tarmac at Heathrow Airport in protest at the threat of deportation, as visa restrictions determine entry to Britain on the grounds of race and consign black and brown peoples to second-class status within the Commonwealth, as Bengali residents are subjected to routine racist attacks on the streets and housing estates of east London and Bradford, a brighter blurring of the old divisive ethnic and religious lines which set, for instance, Muslim against Hindu, Hindu against Sikh, seems about to occur in the dance halls and ballrooms of Britain's cities hired out for Bangra nights by Asian promoters and attended by contingents from most of the major "Asian" communities now established in Britain. Another new territory is opened up here: a positive assertion of another nonwhite *British* presence.

The miscegenation of sounds and images originating in quite separate ethnic contexts heralds the emergence, then, of new native styles, incipient social identities. In the mid-1980s, in fast-style reggae (reggae's response to the call of black American rap), a new generation of young black British MCs like Culture Smiley, Lady Di, Lorna Gee, and Tipper Irie began talking their way beyond "Africa" and the retrospective destiny of Rasta into a new British space, affirming hybrid identities formed out of the conjunction of Caribbean and indigenous traditions, forms, and idioms. In Culture Smiley's, "Cockney Translation" (1984), for instance, the dense and overgrown interiors, the echoing spaces, and weird effects of dub reggae have been flattened down beneath the light, tight beat pushed out by a drum machine. Over this rhythm punctuated by gleeful snatches of brass, Culture Smiley (David Emmanuel) reels off the rap, alternating lines of cockney rhyming patter and Caribbean patois, exchanging identities like masks:

> 11, 10, 9, 8, 7, 6, 5, 4, 3, 2, 1
> It's Culture Smiley with the mike in a me hand
> Me come to teach you right and not the wrong
> In a de Cockney translation.
>
> Cockney have names like Terry, Arthur and Del-Boy
> We have names like Winston, Lloyd and Leroy,
> We bawl out YOW! While cockneys say Oi!
> What Cockney calla Jacks, we call a Blue Bwoy
> Say Cockney have mates while we have spar
> Cockney live in a drum while we live in a yard
> Rope chain and choparita me say, cockney call tom
> Say cockney say Old Bill, We say dutty Babylon
> In a de cockney translation
> In a de cockney translation.
>
> ("Cockney Translation," 1984)

For young blacks in Britain in the wake of the riots in Brixton and at Broadwater Farm, liable to negative coverage in the press and on TV (where they figure predominantly as victims, culprits, unemployment figures, "immigration" figures), subject to aggressive and intensive policing, such a blatant assertion of the right to be a black Londoner, to be both black and British, has political bite—this is an identity traced out along a special jagged kind of "British edge."

The "casual" style of dress which since the early to mid-1980s has functioned as a uniform for "streetwise" inner-city youth of whatever ethnic origin represents a similar appropriation—this time of the signs of "quality," "distinction," (international) "class." The various combinations of expensive designer label sportswear (Sergio Tacchini tracksuits, Adidas running shoes, Lacoste and Christian Dior shirts, etc.) are at once a repudiation of the rhetoric of wasted youth and of subcultural "costume" for "good (classical) clothes." The casual fashions euphemize the joblessness or irregular employment by converting "casual" work in the "black economy" into a comfortable and affluent "casual *style.*" They swap enforced "idleness" for a "life of leisure." The casual style asserts the right to be relaxed, at *home* on Britain's windy streets instead of yearning back to an imaginary homeland in Africa, the Caribbean, India, Pakistan, Cyprus, "Albion." The casual look displaces attention away from the question of ethnic origin onto the question of how to build affinities on a shared cultural and aesthetic ground. It is focused on a set of common preferences rooted in the experience of the contemporary realities of city life. A community of taste can thus be formed that smudges ethnic lines. In the culture of the "casuals" of the British (or is it just the English?) inner city in the 1980s, the question of roots and "breeding"—of where a person "comes from"—fades into insignificance before the altogether more *soluble* question of the pedigree of his or her clothes (designer label roots).

This is the generation which in the different (though by no means unrelated) institutional sites of independent film and video production—funded by organizations like the British Film Institute, Channel 4, and the Left-led inner-city education authorities—is finding a distinctive voice and vision for black Britons—a vision and a voice which challenge the established fixings of both "black politics" and "black film." Young black intellectuals working together in the new film and video collectives (e.g., SANKOFA, CEDDO, the Black Audiovisual Collective) are disrupting the image flow, smudging the line which separates the two dominant image strands of the black communities which are relayed through the British press and TV—troublesome blacks (the riots) and fun-loving blacks (the grinning dance of carnival). In films like *Handsworth Songs* and *Territories,* the filmmakers use everything at their disposal—the words of Fanon, Foucault, C. L. R. James, TV news footage, didactic voice-over, interviews and found sound, the dislocated ghostly echoes of dub reggae, the scattergun of rap—in order to assert the fact of difference, to articulate new relations to the body, subjectivity, politics, to make fresh connections between another set of bodies, another set of histories—to open up the "territories of race[,] . . . of class . . . or sexuality."[20] Deconstruction here takes a different turn as it moves outside the gallery, the academy, the library to mobilize the *crucial* forms of lived experience and resistance embedded in the streets, the shops, and clubs of urban life. Deconstruction here is *used* publicly to cut across the categories of "body" and "critique," the "intellectual" and the "masses," "Them" and "Us," to bring into being a new eroticized body of critique, a sensuous and pointed logic—and to bring it to *bear* on the situation, to make the crisis *speak.*

Curses, says the Proverb, are like chickens, they return always home. (Thomas Carlyle, "The Irish," 1839)

For the British Empire has folded in upon itself and the chickens have come home. And as the pressure in the cities continues to mount, the old unities have shattered: the ideal of a national culture transcending its regional components and of a racially proscribed "British" identity consistent and unchanging from one decade to the next—these fantasies have started cracking at the seams. More and more people are growing up feeling, to use Colin MacInnes's phrase, "english half-english."

> There's no such thing as "England" any more . . . welcome to India brothers! This is the Caribbean! . . . Nigeria! . . . There is no England, man. This is what is coming. Balsall Heath is the centre of the melting pot, 'cos all I ever see when I go out is half-Arab, half-Pakistani, half-Jamaican, half-Scottish, half-Irish, I know 'cos I am (half-Scottish/half-Irish) . . . who am I? . . . Tell me who do I belong to? They criticize me, the good old England. Alright, where do I belong? You know I was brought up with blacks, Pakistanis, Africans, Asians, everything, you name it . . . who do I belong to? . . . I'm just a broad person. The earth is mine. . . . you know we was not born in Jamaica. . . . we was not born in "England." We were born here, man. It's our right. That's the way I see it. That's the way I deal with it. (Jo Jo, a white reggae fan, interviewed in Birmingham's Balsall Heath, one of the oldest areas of black settlement in Britain)[21]

America A Prophecy (Levi Jeans, Coca Cola, Men from Mars)

I switch from video to broadcast TV: on *Dallas*, J.R. is about to be shot in the back. Later on I might catch an episode of *Hill Street Blues* or *St. Elsewhere*, a news item on Irangate or the sudden death of Andy Warhol, or a situation comedy like *Cheers* or *Taxi*.

It was estimated as long ago as 1973 that 50 percent of the world's screen time was taken up with American films and that American-made programs accounted for more than 20 percent of total TV transmission time in Western Europe, that 20–25 percent of British manufacturing output was American controlled and that eight of the leading advertising agencies in the U.K. were owned by American companies.[22] Developments in broadcasting in the last fifteen years—developments which range from deregulation and the privatization of national TV networks to the rise of cable and satellite technologies and the growth of multinational communication conglomerates—have undoubtedly led to increased American penetration of international image markets (though the Japanese are beginning to fight back, apparently, with cartoons pitched at Southeast Asian markets). In 1984, Armand Mattelart, Michele Mattelart, and Xavier Delcourt in their book *International Image Markets* estimated that by 1982 over 80 percent of all imported programs shown on Italian TV were American, that the distribution of Latin American films had actually declined in Spanish-speaking countries since the 1970s, that 61 percent of the feature films programmed on Spanish TV were American in origin, that between 1975 and 1980 Britain lost half its internal market in film to U.S.-based companies, and that national production fell from 41 to 20 percent. A brief boom in mainstream British film production in the early 1980s was halted due to a lack of adequate capitalization and the removal by the chancellor of a "favorable tax environment" for the industry. As a result, another cohort of British filmmakers have "defected" to Hollywood.

The shared language, the strategic links and military commitments within the NATO alliance, and the common cultural and historical heritage binding Britain to the States seem likely further to accentuate these trends in future years. In 1986 the spacious, centrally located, newly opened Boilerhouse Gallery in the Victoria and Albert Museum in South Kensington was given over to an exhibition (sponsored by the Conran Foundation) celebrating a hundred years of Coca Cola, entitled *Coca Cola: Designing a Megabrand*.

I switch to Channel 4 and tune in to an old *Twilight Zone* double bill. The first *Twilight Zone* story concerns a man who travels back and forth in time. . . .

There is a break for ads. The gleaming flank of a chrome-encrusted car glides up to the entrance of a "typical" age-of-affluence U.S. laundromat as Marvin Gaye's voice opens out into the refrain from the mid-1960s Motown hit "I Heard It through the Grapevine." We are back in the pastiche (timeless) 1950s of the latest string of Levi TV ads made for the British style and fashion-conscious *Face*-reading market(s) where, in the Old Edward Hopper Laundromat on 501 Street, a 1980s hunk with a Tony Curtis hairstyle (Nick Kamen, model-turned-pop-star-pin-up) strips off his T-shirt and his jeans before placing them in a "classical" front-loading washing machine (baring his boxer shorts in the process), and sitting down in a nonchalant narcissistic daze on the laundromat bench alongside a cast of 1950s "American" stereotypes who could serve as stand-ins for the figures in a Duane Hanson exhibition (giggling pony-tailed bobby-soxers, chewing fat guy with hamburger, mortified bluestocking with glasses, etc.).

The Levi logo fades and we are back into the second story from the *Twilight Zone*. In this episode a three-armed Martian, a scout for an invading force, is prevented from taking over a small American town by the owner of a soda fountain who removes his cap in the final shot to reveal a third eye in the middle of his forehead—Venus has already invaded.

The Proverbs of Hell (British Designers on Design)

Without Contraries there is no progression. Attraction and Repulsion, Reason and Energy, Love and Hate, are necessary to Human existence.

From these contraries spring what the religious call Good and Evil. Good is the passive that obeys Reason. Evil is the active spring from Energy. Good is Heaven. Evil is Hell.

As I was walking among the fires of hell, delighted with the enjoyments of Genius; which to Angels look like torment and insanity, I collected some of their Proverbs; thinking that as the sayings used in a nation, mark its character, so the Proverbs of Hell, shew the nature of Infernal wisdom.

(William Blake, *The Marriage of Heaven and Hell*, 1793)

The Proverbs

If people can't make a stand, they can at least wear one. (Katherine Hamnett, fashion designer, on her designer-slogan T-shirts)

Destroy, Disorder, and Disorientate. (The 3-D label of fashion designers John Richmond and Marie Cornejo; the woven labels also include quotes from the work of the Italian Marxist theorist Antonio Gramsci)

Cash from Chaos. (Malcolm McLaren, sound designer, concept and product packager, 1979)

What's interesting about England right now is that there's a definite movement to get involved with the Third World: to wear an African dress, and put it with a Dominican hat, throw in some Peruvian beads and wear make-up like one of the tribes in New Guinea—simply because we have to go even further to demonstrate that we want to get out of this island mentality, this village we live in, and relate ourselves to those taboos and magical things we believe we've lost. (Malcolm McLaren, interviewed in the *Face,* 1983)

You can't touch the foundation of the Establishment. It changes its clothes as fast as you can cut them up. If you are a radical, it's only a matter of time before you are automatically accepted—that's provided you don't go bankrupt. (Neville Brody, typographer, graphic artist, record sleeve and magazine designer, 1986)

We have put together a design environment for Duran Duran. . . . To us Duran Duran are ICI or Kodak. (Malcolm Garrett of Assorted Images, record sleeve designer, 1985)

Barbie takes a trip round nature's cosmic curves. (Title of the 1985 fashion collection of Bodymap [Steve Stewart and David Hollah], with textiles based on computer graphics courtesy of Hilde Smith, self-styled "surface-pattern designer")

. . . Sometimes it's just tacky parody. (Vivienne Westwood, fashion designer, on "Street Fashion")

Although it's a Fourth-World economy, it's a first-rate culture. (Daniel Weill, "product" designer, on Britain, 1986)[23]

Jerusalem: Emanations of the Giant Albion (Of Piracy and Jungloid Roots)

> Tyger Tyger burning bright,
> In the forests of the night;
> What immortal hand or eye,
> Could frame thy fearful symmetry?
>
> When the stars threw down their spears
> And water'd heaven with their tears:
> Did he smile his work to see?
> Did he who made the Lamb make thee?
> (William Blake, "The Tyger," 1794)

The British edge is in fashion, in record work, it's not in fine art, it's not in film. British film hasn't progressed in the last twenty years. If they change the formula it doesn't sell. The British edge is in TV commercials and pop videos—in the really upmarket promos for established acts and the really cheap ones where they go for maximum impact with special effects and animation. The Americans come back now and then with a killer. They've got exceptional talent there but it's in smaller numbers than in Britain. Design is run like a business there and they do know how to run it. It's not like that in Britain. Design is not what I'd call an adult business over here. It's not taken seriously. But the standards are higher here than in the States, the general level of the work, the energy, the ideas, the willingness to risk. I honestly believe you could group a pile of (design) people together in London and they would kill anybody. (Dave Richardson, founder of Shoot That Tiger design agency)

In 1982, Margaret Thatcher presided over a series of seminars held at Downing Street devoted to the subject of British design. Four years later, for the first time in British business history, a handful of the largest design practices went public on the stock market. Interior designers Sir Terence Conran and Rodney Fitch, the advertising magnates Saatchi and Saatchi, and the fashion designer Stephen Marks are now among the hundred richest people in the U.K., beneficiaries in large part of the decade-long retail boom for which they are also partially—directly or indirectly—responsible.[24] The phenomenal growth rates enjoyed by these companies (a symptom of the 1980s "takeover fever" that has gripped the business community from New York to London, from Boessky to Sanders) may or may not be reliable indicators of the long-term financial viability of large-scale design practices in Britain. We can only wait and see. But as the vaunted transformation of the British high street proceeds apace, there are signs of a slight faltering of momentum—the queue of mega-clients is shortening as the corporate giants and nationwide chain stores receive their total image overhauls. Growth at the top end can also lead to the imposition of monolithic house-styles which stifle diversity. All too often the packaging of product lines descends into designer cliché. All too often the "revolution" in shop interiors means the installation of standardized fittings: the creation of the "Americanized" postmodern space that Jameson describes in which consumers drift like the zombies in George Romero's *Dawn of the Dead* from atrium through galleria to the shop-within-a-shop. The refurbished Debenhams in London's Oxford Street or the recently opened Dôme cocktail bar in Islington could be sited in any capital city anywhere in the Western world. The effacement of regional differentiae beneath the hyper-deluxe chic which has become synonymous in some quarters with the very word "design" forms part of that englobement of the real by uniform "solutions" underpinned by uniform exchange values, part of the urgent onward march of commodification into every corner of civil society which Marx discerned a century ago as he sat in the British Museum in the heart of London writing *Capital*.

But "development" itself is fraught with contradictions. It can meander as it marches and—once again—in British design it is in the margins, not the mainstreams, in the "ephemeral" areas of graphics, fashion, music, and video production, the experimental work in interiors, in the product prototypes and Heath Robinson-like follies of subindustrial design that the crucial "edge" in British design culture is most startlingly encountered.

In the years at least since punk there is in the more vivid output of the smaller studios a shared reliance in the design process on intuition, serendipity, obsession, a parody of "English" empirical method—a working-out from the material rather than working-down from some pregiven master plan. From Vivienne Westwood's Appalachian Buffalo Girl fashions, her outlaw, pirate, and witch couture, to Jamie Reid's situationist-inspired graphics, from Hilde Smith's computer-simulating textile designs to Neville Brody's trademark typefaces and Nigel Coates's dreamlike "narrative" interiors, from the "Mad Max of product design" (Ron Arad) to the "King of the Cubist kitchen conversation" (Michael Graves), we find the same blurring of the lines between genres and categories, high and low forms, fine art and popular culture, pure and applied arts, the same questioning of the functions and formulas of design, the same impatience with fixity, with the established wisdoms and certainties of art and design lore. And always there is an absence of straight lines linking cause to effect: the logic of catastrophe and surprise is everywhere paramount. On the pages of stylezines like *The Face* and *I-D,* the "laws" of layout and "good" typography are laid waste as grids are abandoned, as color bars and registration marks—the invisible "backstage" tools of conventional design practice—are brought forward and incorporated into the final design, as photographs are stretched and blurred and "swished" across the glass of the photocopy machine, as incommensurable typefaces are mixed and new, scarcely legible ones invented. In the clothes of Westwood and Bodymap, classical scale and structure are collapsed into outlandish, asymmetrical shapes. The rules of couture and modernist functionalism are systematically broken as holes and gashes interrupt the "line," as silks and man-made fibers fight it out on the happy battlefield of the restructured body. In the record sleeve designs of the late Barney Bubbles, and of the newer studios—XL, Assorted iMaGes, Shoot That Tiger, Town & Country Planning—every available image source is raided, from the authorized histories of art and design to comic books and car manual illustrations, from Renaissance perspective to the grotesque, from the Bauhaus to Walt Disney, from Rodchenko and Lissitsky to de Stijl, from Spencer's *Pioneers of Modern Typography* to socialist realism to Hollywood and beyond.

The vision is hallucinogenic and excessive. Disturbingly, there is plenty of evidence of formal education of one kind or another, evidence of what the French sociologist Pierre Bourdieu calls "cultural capital," but there is nothing scholarly or bookish about the way this knowledge is held and deployed. In fact there is something decidedly unhinged about it. Britannia here appears as a psychotic bag lady shuffling through a ruined city muttering to herself, her bags stuffed with old books, rusting heirlooms, priceless paintings.

The British edge is "ex-centric" in a very "English" way. It is quite unlike its Milanese equivalent. The genius of Italian design stems from the ease of access enjoyed by Italian designers to what is, perhaps, the richest visual heritage in western Europe, from a culture steeped in a tradition of "extravagant" expenditure and overt displays of solvency that goes back to the Medicis if not to Imperial Rome. ("Italy [has] a different mentality as a country, it's used to a weak currency and that's encouraged the idea that money should be spent and enjoyed"—Lynne Wilson, British designer resident in Milan, quoted in *Street Style: British Design in the 1980s.*) Italian designers can draw on a vast reserve of artisanal and craft skills which have survived into the late twentieth century because industrialization in Italy came comparatively late and because, outside the major cities, large-scale industrial production is only precariously established and has left the infrastructure of small craft workshops relatively untouched. (When Bertolucci sought to recreate the emperor's palace in Peking for his recent film, *The Last Emperor,* he had to fly in the craftsmen from Florence and Siena to do the necessary restorations because the appropriate native skills and specialist knowledge had been wiped out during the Cultural Revolution.)

No such advantages are there to be exploited by the designer working in Britain, the land of Oliver Cromwell, Samuel Arkwright, James Watt, and the "threadbare ethic" where the early lead in industrial output effectively destroyed the craft base (the post-1960s Anglo-craft "revival" is still tinged with a nostalgia for the rustic and the anti-urban which has roots stretching back via the ruralistic painters and the hippies to Cobbett and Constable). And in Britain the designer has to contend with the obdurate lingering residues of an Anglo-Saxon puritanism that can still dictate that furniture, for instance, should come thirty-seventh in the list of the average English person's spending priorities, according to McDermott in *Street Style*. So NATO (Narrative Architecture Today) and Ron Arad are not like Memphis, the Italian design group who work with vernacular 1950s formica motifs which they "redeem" by "elevating" the color scheme (from lurid primaries to "tasteful" pastels) and the materials used (mixing plastic and marble, etc.).

There isn't the same sense of archness, the same relaxed bending of the rules, the same *disciplined* (controlled) use of metaphor and irony—the hallmarks which distinguish 'quality' Milanese design—in the work of Arad and Coates, Fred Baier and Daniel Weill (for disciplined metaphor, e.g., Memphis = ancient Egyptian capital [primitivism + the cradle of classical Western civilization] *and* the hometown of Elvis Presley [primitivism + the cradle of postwar Western civilization]). Logic figures only as a half-remembered ghost in the soft machine of British avant-garde design—the connections for the most part are somatic. Everyday objects suffer a sea change as contraries are merged, forms and functions transposed to produce the kinds of thing we encounter during sleep: a classless class of impractical, impossible objects—deflated plastic chairs, a hi-fi system encased in blocks of broken concrete (Arad), spindly 1950s bentwood furniture upholstered in wetsuit rubber (Baier), a Radio Bag comprising functioning components suspended in a transparent plastic bag with flexible PVC speakers (Weill). The authority and linearity of history, the exteriority of tradition give way to personalized reverie and remembrance: in Nigel Coates's interiors, decay is designed in as a resonant factor. In his design for the Metropole restaurant in Tokyo in 1986, for instance, he created a dreamscape of "europe," a "europe" half-forgotten, half-destroyed. Beneath a ceiling festooned like a pirate ship or ship of fools with billowing drapes he integrated found objects and contemporary features, an embassy flagpole, a revolving globe, classical statuary, old clocks, specially commissioned murals, doors taken from an old London hotel. Empty space is used here as a landing pad for ghostly presences: a seance is convened of auratic objects which bear with them the traces of their earlier contexts and uses, their other, former lives.

For the past is inescapable. It runs like Carlyle's chickens always *home,* back into the present moment. The world of culture as seen from the British edge is the "civilized world" viewed at twilight from the other side of the British Empire, from the wild side of sobriety, order, and the "rational." It is civilization viewed from a tropic, a jungloid place where nothing quite adds up any more. Frith and Horne may be right: the vitality and unpredictability of British pop culture may say more about the British higher education system than it does in any direct way about the class system, the mythological "streets," or some general zeitgeist of the past. It may, as Frith and Horne suggest in *Art into Pop,* stem from the sudden mind-boggling exposure of untrained youth to Big Ideas in the ramshackle hothouse of the Great British art school rather than from the mysteriously authored emanations of Blake's "Great Albion."

It's in the interlinked fields of music and fashion that the "killing combination" of piracy and jungloid roots in the production of British popular culture has attracted most attention and interest internationally. While the popular music business has always relied on the profitable alignment of "attractive" or "arresting" sounds and images, there has, in the last few decades, been an investment on an unprecedented scale in the development of audiovisual technologies and marketing techniques designed to make such an alignment more profitable and secure. Britain is the home of the pop video, and the pop video is an undecidable (ideal) commodity: neither "pure entertainment" nor "straightforward promotion," it is a commodity in its own right (i.e., it's sold in shops), designed to sell another commodity (the band, the clothes, the image, the attitudes they're designed to "represent"), to "tell," often through nonlinear narrational devices, an image, not a story—the image of the group. Ideally from a marketing viewpoint, pop video turns in such a way that the image and the sound, the video and the record chase after each other (i.e., sell each other) in a double helix which seems to promise cash for all concerned. Furthermore it functions as raw material for broadcast (e.g., MTV). There is no doubt a tangled, contradictory dynamic dictating the leap into music visualization, but the more immediate economic pressures seem clear enough: the decline in record sales worldwide, the fragmentation of markets, the collapse of any kind of unitary youth market.

The postpunk fragmentation of music markets, the displacement of attention (and energy and capital resources) away from the constructed sound to the constructed look (especially pronounced in the last few years with the decline in new musical ideas on the British pop and rock scenes), and the creation of more flexible, aggressive, and ingenious marketing strategies—these trends are perhaps most advanced in Britain. The "postmodern" implications of these developments have been explored suggestively at length elsewhere.[25] To sum up, it is argued that as vinyl begins competing with less palpably *material* audio technologies (CD, audiotape, etc., and in the latter case, less controllable ones) and as the studio takes over from the stage as the primary production site, sound recording is freed from the moral obligation of (high) "fidelity" to "live" (where the living human voice and instrumental virtuosity convey "presence," where the proscenium arch and the spotlit stage confer a priestlike authority on the performer). Sound itself is freed from the restrictions of time and the contiguous magic of the single session—as the music is broken down into independently recorded sections, assembled on a multitrack mixer, stretched and "sculptured" by audio engineers. Sound begins to lose its priority, becoming just one designed element in a totally designed package composed of both aural signals and visual signs, "concepts," postures, "lifestyles." The record—the thing itself—the hard, black, brittle vinyl, the circle of frozen sounds—dematerializes. It melts and bends in the era of the floppy disc and the flexi-disc, the tape deck and the personalized portable stereo. And it is *rematerialized* (1) as image, as a "bag" (record sleeve), a video, magazine advertisements, TV commercials, point-of-sale 3-D installations, a "picture disc" (on a picture disc, a star's face is inscribed on the record itself); and (2) as an image-thing-to-be-identified-with-and-identified-by (the record-as-thing now has what record executives call "cultural utility": it has an "expressive" value in the first instance, not in the last [subcultural] moment of "appropriation" [i.e., the "expressive" component—the mark of difference that signals the "sub" in subculture—is designed in, not projected in by people on "the street"]). "It says who you are—like fashion shoes, a Big Mac, or a Sony Walkman" (Paul Walton). The apotheosis of this process of de- and rematerialization occurs in hip-hop, where the "finished product" is opened up again and the record-object is turned into a percussive instrument to be handled, "scratched," and mixed with quotes from other records by the hip-hop dee-jays who skip between multiple turntables to produce fresh "one off" aural compositions "live." (A similar "deconsecration" of the finished product occurs in reggae in "versioning," which has been institutionalized in popular music in the form of dub club and guest "mixes," and nine- and twelve-inch versions of the same record.)

New job categories have been created within the British music/fashion/video industries to accommodate and facilitate these changes. "Concept packagers" and "style and image engineers" work alongside "sound designers" to unleash sound-and-image kits on a primed and stimulated market.

The selling of Frankie Goes to Hollywood marks out one kind of limit to promotion. This was state-of-the-art music business packaging: a detective story (the mystery: who or what is/are "Frankie"?) which unfolded in a series of tantalizing stages: (1) preplanned orchestration of media interest/outrage; (2) selection of key signifiers (leather, S & M, "the gay club," boxy suits, Holly's face, "hardcore" amyl nitrate disco rhythms); (3) mobilization of "shock" and "censure" (record and video BBC bannings); (4) remixing of the original cut in new formats (several twelve-inch versions of the same number, each reissued in a different [collectible] "bag"); (5) promotion of the ethos of promotion-for-promotion's sake, packaging as art. The *Welcome to the Pleasure Dome* album (1984) came complete with quotations from Coleridge, Baudelaire, Barthes, and Nietzsche. An advertising mock-up on the inner sleeve of the foldout cover offered, in addition, Baudelaire socks and Nietzsche T-shirts available by mail order.

But any notional benefits derived from native packaging and promotional expertise are overshadowed by Britain's poor industrial performance. London in the 1980s may qualify as one of the world's leading advertising and media production centers (hosting, for example, the two principal international TV news agencies, WTN and Visnews), but Britain remains unable to compete with its industrial competitors in the design and construction of communications hardware. Britain's long-lost manufacturing edge (forfeited a century ago to Germany and the U.S.) has been even further eroded in the postwar years. Explanations for Britain's postimperial, postindustrial decline are, of course, various through the well-worn metaphors of illness and old age—metaphors which first gained a wide currency in the "angry" 1950s continue to naturalize and strengthen perceptions of national decline.[26]

It is often claimed, for instance, that native traditions of workmanship have been finished off in the past three decades by the "British disease" (which is variously diagnosed as overcautious patterns of business investment; undercapitalized industry and research; inefficient, short-sighted management; decrepit plant and work practices; a non–vocationally-oriented education system; and/or a "lazy," "greedy," untrained, or—alternatively—inappropriately trained, workforce). What survived of native manufacturing after the prewar depression, German bombing, and a combination of the ailments listed above has been further decimated by the "hollowing out" of the industrial base as investments are shifted into the finance and service sectors, as research and development are moved overseas, as British "manufacturing" comes increasingly to turn on the assembly of prepackaged components produced at low cost for low wages in Taiwan, Japan, or South Korea.[27] In this elegy to England's lost prestige and power, Britain "colonized," in the words of Tony Benn, by "the Common Market, the Pentagon, the IMF and the multinationals"[28] becomes just one more staging post on the circuits (of money, resources, goods, and services) owned, organized, and overseen from elsewhere.

The Sick Rose ("The Queen Is Dead," 1986)

> O Rose thou art sick.
> The invisible worm,
> That flies in the night
> In the howling storm:
>
> Has found out thy bed
> Of crimson joy:
> And his dark secret love
> Does thy life destroy.
>
> (William Blake, "The Sick Rose," 1794)

I push the eject button, take out the *Spare Time* tape, and load in Derek Jarman's video promo for the Smiths, "The Queen Is Dead," made in 1986. The tape opens with old black-and-white footage of a cathedral spire. It seems a lot has changed in fifty years, not least the consciousness of time itself: the past has become a reservoir of signifiers to be tapped, consumed, recycled like the London water supply. On the soundtrack a chorus of young voices sings lines from some forgotten (playground?) song. The cathedral image is replaced by color film of a group of unkempt children, blinking in the sunlight. As the drums crash into the opening bars of "The Queen Is Dead," the camera is bundled along behind a young "boy" dressed in the archaic costume of a 1950s childhood, the short trousers, and "short back and sides" haircut designed to mark the "hims" off from the "hers". . . . The hairstyle, humiliating sign—in the sideburned 1950s of *my* youth—of the impotence of little boys to resist the will of parents, teachers, barbers—is now in the late 1980s eminently fashionable with young people of both genders (nowadays it functions to detach "youth" from its fixings in the "swinging," "liberated," sexed and "sex mad" 1960s).[29]

In a series of jump cuts synchronized to the beat of the drums, we see the "boy" spray-painting the song's title along the broken wall that marks the boundary of an abandoned industrial estate. A close-up reveals that the "boy" is a young woman, and as the 4/4 rock beat calls the (camera) shots we are taken on a ride at breakneck speed through a disorienting image-montage: rings of fire alternate with a spiraling red rose, a yellow sunflower, a child's xylophone, a red guitar that spins in the center of the frame. A man, stripped to the waist, cracks eggs on his head; a woman, stripped to the waist, walks toward a tower block and unfurls a Union Jack in its shadow. Image is laid upon image in a series of superimpositions so dense and excessive that the single lines of (cinematic) narrative—the this-then-this-then-this of plot and story—dissolve into the synchronicities of video and computer-generated effects. Metonymy and repetition impose instead a different kind of order: a royal crown revolves across the screen over a still of Buckingham Palace. Postcard shots of Westminster Bridge and the Houses of Parliament frame a filmed sequence of a quiet suburban street, its mock-Tudor frontages bathed in bright sunlight. This sequence in turn is laid against a rapid black-and-white collage of sharp images of office blocks. Skyscrapered modernity, the International Style, and "zany" 1960s poses clash against the cozy pebble-dash of the typically English semidetached home—the suburban Betjeman "cottage" of the 1930s-built commuter belts that still encircle London.

Through it all, a single image-figure dances: the statue of Eros detached by some editor's scissors from its moorings in the granite steps at Piccadilly Circus. It flies across the image flow, this emblem of desire, appearing at different points as photographed monument, as free "floating signifier," as the mascot perched on the bonnet of a Rolls-Royce car, as a parodic incarnation of one of Yeats's "cocks of Hades" in the image of a crouching, crowing boy dressed in chicken-feather wings.[30] As the singer's voice loops crazily round the helter-skelter lyrics, a row of little girls, rescued from some ancient 1930s film clip, dance in a line, their identical dresses with neat velvet collars, their uniformly bobbed hair swaying to the beat. "Blood-begotten spirits," they dance, these ancient children, round and round the rings of fire, dying, as the tape turns, "into a dance," into "an agony of flame that cannot singe a sleeve"; "So ashamed to discover," (wails Morrissey, the "vocalist"), "That I'm the eighteenth pale descendant of some old queen or other."

What I'm watching here is a different kind of royal wedding video: the marriage of two queens—Widow Twankey, the traditional pantomime dame, and Queen Elizabeth II—and with this merger, this blending-in of "high" and "low," the reconciliation of all contraries in magic, the fusion of the sexes in the image of the superhuman form of Eros.

> Before me floats an image, man or shade,
> Shade more than man, more image than a shade;
> . . . I hail the superhuman,
> I call it death-in-life and life-in-death

wrote William Butler Yeats—Dublin-born and schooled in London—as he sailed off to Byzantium.

> God save the Queen
> She ain't a human being.
> There ain't no future in England's dreaming

sang London-Irish John Lydon (Johnny Rotten of the Sex Pistols) forty years later, as he sailed off for Hollywood (via New York City).

The allegory on which both song and video (and Sex Pistol song) are based is as transparent as it is clichéd. The same allegory has been set to work repeatedly in the postwar British cinema in the "grotesque (sur)realism" of films like *The Ruling Class, O Lucky Man!, Britannia Hospital*, and Jarman's own feature, *Jubilee*.[31] The allegorizing is "camp," the debunking intention self-consciously "critical" and "anti-patriotic." It sets out to expose the vanity of national pretensions to either "unity" or "greatness" by celebrating the repressed or excluded social, sexual, and semantic margins—the bits that do not fit into the preferred narratives of Englishness. In this "end-of-England" allegory the signifiers of national pride, consensus, and heritage are decomposed and ironized. Eros substitutes for logos, "crisis" for "homeland." Here among the "liberal," "Left" or "nonaligned," "anarchic," or just plain "alienated" British arts intelligentsia, the queen indeed is dead: a victim of deconstruction along with the mythically unified "straight and narrow" community she notionally represents.[32]

And yet, twenty years after the collapse of the British Empire, the queen is still head of state in eighteen countries. And if *popularity* and media-generated interest are anything to go by, then the queen, the royal family, the office of the monarchy itself, and the order and continuity it supposedly guarantees and represents are very much alive in 1987. Fifty years after the Abdication Crisis, popular support for and interest in the monarchy has probably never been stronger in Great Britain, the republican impulse never so weak. It is, for instance, a significant and telling irony that one of the factors contributing to EMI's decision to terminate their contract with the Sex Pistols in 1977 was the response of the women workers at the record pressing plant, shocked and offended by Jamie Reid's "customized" version of Sir Cecil Beaton's famous portrait of the queen emblazoned on the cover of the "No Future" single. The women refused to pack vinyl in a sleeve consisting of an image of Elizabeth II with her eyes and mouth striped out with the black bars which conventionally connote criminal anonymity. In prophetic anticipation of the born-again royalism of the British working class in the 1980s, the gut reaction against art school punk and antimonarchist visual "noise" came from the shopfloor rather than—as the Sex Pistols' publicists would have it—from the offices of the fusty old "Establishment."

During this decade we have had two royal weddings watched "live" via satellite by millions worldwide.

> "The Royals" is the longest-running soap opera in Britain. . . . We have become just as intimate with the doings of the folk from Buckingham Palace as we have with the folk from Southfork Ranch.[33]

In 1982, all the queen's forces and all the queen's men—the special police unit guarding Buckingham Palace, headed at the time by Commander Michael Trestrail (who in another "scandal" was forced to resign the same summer over revelations concerning his relationship with a male prostitute)—failed to prevent a mentally disturbed commoner called Michael Fagan from breaking into the queen's bedroom one spring morning intent on talking through his domestic problems with Her Majesty.

No more poignant indication of the charmed life of the monarchy in 1980s England could be found than in this strange, pathetic meeting in the gray-lit dawn between a fifty-six-year-old woman caught between her dreams and great affairs of state and her distressed, dishevelled subject. At around 7:00 A.M., Her Majesty's eyes opened to see, silhouetted at the window, the diminutive figure of Mr. Fagan, who sat unshaven on the edge of the bed, asking in a north London accent not for a fortune in jewels or the release of imprisoned terrorists, not for a united Ireland, a change in England's obsolete licensing laws, or a helicopter to the airport, not even for a date with Jody Foster, but for a "bit of a chat" and a "light" for his "fag."

The centuries of sporting links between landed aristocrats and the "criminal classes," the centuries which saw the maturation of what Gareth Stedman Jones has called that "affinity of outlook between the 'top and bottom drawer' against the 'kill joys' in between"[34] the forces, contradictions, and chances that have combined to produce the uniquely *British* compromise, that affective alliance between what Malcolm McLaren calls "a corrupt and faded aristocracy" and a "brutalized proletariat" converge in the crepuscular dawn of the morning above the bed in a room in the queen's largest London residence.

In March 1987 Michael Shea, the queen's secretary for the past nine years, resigned. (He had been brought over from the British Information Service in New York after his "brilliant" handling of the Royal Bicentennial Tour.) More than any other individual, Shea is probably responsible for the buoyant state of the monarchy in Britain today. He was the man who modernized the royal image, who "professionalized" media access (giving the go-ahead for relaxed *vérité*-style documentaries, cozy fireside chats between royals and TV "personalities"). He was the man who stage-managed "state occasions" for the benefit of the cameras, who allegedly leaked news of the controversial rift between Buckingham Palace and Downing Street, and who once in an indiscreet moment disclosed to a Canadian journalist that the queen's nickname among palace staff was "Miss Piggy" (from *The Muppet Show*). In March, Shea left the royal service to take up a PR job with the Anglo-American multinational conglomerate Hanson Trust, for three times his former salary.[35]

It would be fitting, as Mr. Shea ascends the steps of Concorde to take up his new job, for the surviving members of the original Lancashire cotton-mill kazoo band to be reassembled on the tarmac to pipe him out with an appropriate medley of mid-Atlantic tunes: Walt Disney's "When You Wish upon a Star," perhaps, or William Blake's "Jerusalem," played not as Blake himself intended, as a battle cry, a ringing call to build the Holy City here and now on England's "green and pleasant land," but as a hymn to resignation, a looney toon, a lullaby to Britain.

Notes and References

This essay was first commissioned by the Institute of Contemporary Art, Boston, Massachusetts, USA. The author wishes to acknowledge the support offered by the Institute for this work.

1. Walter Benjamin (1973) "Theses on the Philosophy of History," *Illuminations*, London: Fontana, 255.

2. George Orwell, "England, Your England" [itself a parodic reference to D. H. Lawrence's "England, My England"], in F. Kermode et al., eds. (1973) *The Oxford Anthology of English Literature, Vol. 2: 1880–The Present*, Oxford: Oxford University Press, 2143.

3. For the debate on populism and nationalism in Britain, see, for instance, S. Hall and M. Jacques (1983) *The Politics of Thatcherism*, London: Lawrence and Wishart, with *Marxism Today;* J. Donald et al., eds. (1984) *Formations of Nation and People*, London: Routledge and Kegan Paul; M. Langlan and B. Schwartz, eds. (1985) *Crises in the British State, 1880–1930*, London: Hutchinson; B. Schwartz, "Conservatism, Nationalism, and Imperialism," in J. Donald and S. Hall, eds. (1986) *Politics and Ideology*, Milton Keynes: Open University Press; Martin Wiener (1985) *English Culture and the Decline of the Industrial Spirit*, Harmondsworth: Penguin; Benedict Anderson (1983) *Imagined Communities*, London: Verso.

Since I wrote this essay, the critical literature on national and ethnic cultural identity has been greatly expanded. See, among others, D. Morley and K. Robbins (1989) "Spaces of Identity," *Screen* 30, no. 4 (autumn), and (1990) "No Place Like *Heimat:* Images of Home(land) in European Culture," *New Formations* 12 (winter); and I. Chambers (1990) *Border Dialogues*, London: Comedia/Routledge, which not only provides an overview of recent debates on "Englishness" but also offers in its probing of the "ground" of postmodernity a more lucid and concise rationale for the eccentric form of this present essay than I could myself provide. Also there is a great deal of recently published, critically innovative, and politically suggestive work which sets out to deconstruct colonial discourse and the tropes of "race." See, for instance, Gayatri Chakravorty Spivak (1987) *In Other Worlds*, London: Methuen, and (1990) *The Post-Colonial Critic: Interviews, Strategies, Dialogues*, London: Routledge; H. K. Bhabha (1990) *Nation and Narration*, London: Routledge, and (1994) *The Location of Culture*, London: Routledge; also K. Mercer (1987) "Black Hair Style/Politics," *New Formations* 3, and "'1968': Periodizing Postmodern Politics and Identity," in L. Grossberg et al., eds. (1992) *Cultural Studies*, London: Routledge. Also Paul Gilroy (1987) *There Ain't No Black in the Union Jack*, London: Hutchinson, and "Cultural Studies and Ethnic Absolutism," in L. Grossberg et al., eds. (1992) *Cultural Studies*, London: Routledge. Finally, D. Webster (1988) *Looka Yonder*, London: Comedia/Routledge is wholeheartedly recommended for its scholarly and readable exploration of the impact of the "imaginary America of populist culture" on British and European taste formations and cultural identities.

4. Thomas Carlyle (1839) "The Irish," in *Chartism*, London: Chapman and Hall, 1858.

5. The phrase "enemies within" was first used by Thatcher during the miners' strike in 1984 to distinguish internal from external threats to national security. All the other terms which appear in quotation marks elsewhere in this sentence—"scroungers," etc.—are taken from "Thatcherite discourse" (i.e., either from personal statements made by the prime minister or from Thatcherite press editorials, publicity campaigns, etc.).

6. P. Wright (1987) *On Living in an Old Country: The National Past in Contemporary Britain*, London: Verso.

7. See, for example, J. B. Priestley (1934) *An English Journey,* London: Heinemann and Victor Gollancz; G. Orwell (1937) *The Road to Wigan Pier,* London: Victor Gollancz; Tom Harrisson (1978) *Living through the Blitz,* Harmondsworth: Penguin; A. Calder and D. Sheridan, eds. (1985) *Speak for Yourself: Mass Observation Anthology, 1937–1949,* Oxford: Oxford University Press; M. Jennings, ed. (1982) *Humphrey Jennings: Filmmaker, Painter, Poet,* London: BFI; F. Hardy, ed. (1946) *Grierson on Documentary,* London: Faber and Faber.

8. For the distinction between *studium* and *punctum,* see R. Barthes (1981) *Camera Lucida,* New York: Hill and Wang: "The *studium* is that very field of unconcerned desire . . . of inconsequential taste. . . . [That element of the photograph] which will disturb the *studium* I shall call . . . the *punctum* for punctum is also: sting, speck, cut, little hole—and also a cast of the dice. A photograph's *punctum* is that accident which pricks me (but also bruises me, is poignant to me)." Barthes develops a similar topology of reader-text "intensities" with regard to film in "The Third Meaning," in S. Heath, ed. (1977) *Image-Music-Text,* London: Fontana.

9. Widow Twankey is a pantomime "dame," traditionally played as a comic grotesque by a female impersonator. For the history of cross-dressing in pantomime and elsewhere, see P. Ackroyd (1979) *Dressing Up: Transvestism and Drag: The History of an Obsession,* London: Thames and Hudson.

10. The Boy Scout movement was formed by Baden-Powell after the Boer War. The poor physical condition and listlessness of young urban working-class recruits to the forces was regarded as a factor in the British defeat and as a long-term threat to the survival and strength of the Nation, the Empire, hence the "race." See, for instance, R. S. S. Baden-Powell (1909) *Scouting for Boys: A Handbook for Instruction in Good Citizenship,* London: Scout Association; J. Springhall (1974) *Coming of Age: Adolescence in Britain, 1860–1960,* London: Gill and Macmillan; G. Pearson (1983) *Hooligan: A Haunt of Respectable Fears,* London: Macmillan; M. Blanch (1979) "Imperialism, Nationalism, and Organized Youth," in J. Clarke et al., eds., *Working-Class Culture: Studies in History and Theory,* London: Hutchinson.

11. "Camp taste is, above all, a mode of enjoyment, of appreciation—not judgement. . . . Camp taste is a kind of love, love for human nature. It relishes rather than judges the little triumphs and awkward intensities of 'character.' . . . Camp taste identifies with what it is enjoying. People who share this sensibility are not laughing at the thing they label as 'camp,' they're enjoying it. Camp is a tender feeling" (S. Sontag [1966] "Notes on Camp," *Against Interpretation,* New York: Farrar, Straus and Giroux, 291–92).

12. These lines are a travesty of the following lines from W. B. Yeats's poem "Easter 1916," written in September 1916 to honor what Maude Gonne called the "tragic dignity" of the martyrs of the failed rebellion of 24–29 April, organized in Dublin against the English by the Irish Republican Brotherhood:

> This other man I had dreamed
> A drunken, vainglorious lout.
> He had done most bitter wrong

> To some who are near my heart.
> Yet I number him in the song;
> He, too, has resigned his part
> In the casual comedy;
> He, too, has been changed in his turn.
> Transformed utterly:
> A terrible beauty is born.

The original reference is to Major John MacBride, estranged husband of Maude Gonne, hence—as far, at least, as Yeats was concerned—a former rival in love.

13. T. Nairn (1977) *The Break-Up of Britain: Crisis and Neo-nationalism*, London: Verso.

14. For instance, F. Jameson (1984) "Postmodernism or the Cultural Logic of Late Capital," *New Left Review* 146 (July–August); S. Frith (1983) *Sound Effects: Youth, Leisure, and the Politics of Rock*, London: Constable, and Frith with H. Horne (1986) *Art into Pop*, London: Methuen; G. Marcus (1989) *Lipstick Traces: A Secret History of the Twentieth Century*, London: Secker and Warburg; I. Chambers (1985) *Popular Culture: The Metropolitan Experience*, London: Methuen; D. Laing (1985) *One Chord Wonders*, Milton Keynes: Open University Press; D. Hebdige (1979) *Subculture: The Meaning of Style*, London: Methuen.

15. See S. Frith and A. McRobbie (1978–79) "Rock and Sexuality," *Screen Education* 29 for the distinction between "cock rock" and "teenybop."

16. See P. Gilroy (1987) *There Ain't No Black in the Union Jack*, London: Hutchinson; D. Widgery (1986) *Beating Time: Riot 'n' Race 'n' Rock 'n' Roll*, London: Chatto and Windus; D. Hebdige (1987) *Cut 'n' Mix: Culture, Identity, and Caribbean Music*, London: Comedia/Routledge, and (1988) *Hiding in the Light: On Images and Things*, London: Comedia/Routledge (this section includes passages drawn directly from this last book, 212–15).

17. I have tried to develop these arguments further in two articles: (1989) "After the Masses," *Marxism Today* (January), reprinted in S. Hall and M. Jacques, eds. (1990) *New Times: The Changing Face of Politics in the 1990s*, London: Lawrence and Wishart, with *Marxism Today;* and (1990) "Fax to the Future," *Marxism Today* (January).

18. See D. Toop (1984) *The Rap Attack: African Jive to New York Hip Hop*, London: Pluto.

19. Prabhu Guptara (1987) "Look Who's Winning the Glittering English Prizes," *Evening Standard* (2 February).

20. See SANKOFA Black Film and Video Collective (1985) *Territories*, directed by I. Julien. But see also *The Passion of Remembrance* (1987), *Looking for Langston* (1990), and *Young Soul Rebels* (1991) by the same director; also the Black Audio Film Collective's *Expeditions* (1983) and *Handsworth Songs* (1985). For parallel developments in fine arts, see, for example (1989) "The Other Story: AfroAsian Artists in Postwar Britain," *Third Text* 8/9 (autumn/winter). For debates around the new black British films, their relations in both popular cinema and "new ethnicities," see K. Mercer, ed. (1988) *Black Film, British Cinema*, London: Institute of Contemporary Arts, especially the essays by Mercer, Hall, Williamson, and—for sharply distinguished responses to the new Black avant garde—the

exchanges between Rushdie, Hall, and Howe. For a further critique of the place of black experimental film within both modernism and black "vernacular" culture, see P. Gilroy (1989) "Cruciality and the Frog's Perspective: An Agenda of Difficulties for the Black Arts Movement in Britain," *Art and Text* 32 (autumn). See also the work by Cornel West both on black British cinema and the work of Spike Lee.

21. See S. Jones (1987) *White Youth and Jamaican Popular Culture,* Basingstoke: Macmillan.

22. See C. W. E. Bigsby, ed. (1975) *Superculture: American Popular Culture and Europe,* Bowling Green, Ky.: Bowling Green University Press.

23. Most of the "proverbs" have been taken from C. McDermott (1987) *Street Style: British Design in the 1980s,* London: Design Council.

24. See C. McDermott (1987) *Street Style: British Design in the 1980s,* London: Design Council; and J. Thackara and S. Jane (1986) *New British Design,* London: Thames and Hudson.

25. See, for instance, I. Chambers (1985) *Popular Culture: The Metropolitan Experience,* London: Methuen, and (1990) *Border Dialogues,* London: Comedia/Routledge, also (1987) "The Obscured Metropolis," *Cultural Studies* (London), no. 1 (January).

26. Listen, for instance, to Jimmy Porter in J. Osborne (1956) *Look Back in Anger,* or read the tirades delivered by Osborne, Lindsay Anderson, and Kenneth Tynan against English conservatism, antimodernism, and colonial atavism (e.g., the Suez debacle) published in their (1957) *Declaration,* London: MacGibbon and Kee.

27. These loosely and polemically argued points bear little relation to the more ambitiously (and competently) theorized analyses of "post-Fordism" and "disorganized capitalism" developed by Robin Murray, Scott Lash, and John Urry. For examples of this work, see, for instance, S. Hall and M. Jacques, eds. (1990) *New Times: The Changing Face of Politics in the 1990s,* London: Lawrence and Wishart. See also P. Hirst's critique of "post-Fordism" in the same volume. In addition, see R. Murray (1988) "Life after Henry Ford," *Marxism Today* (October); S. Lash and J. Urry (1987) *The End of Organized Capitalism,* Cambridge: Polity Press. Further, see D. Harvey (1989) *The Condition of Postmodernity,* Oxford: Basil Blackwell, for a comprehensive account of "flexible accumulation" and the spatial implications of the new modes of capitalist finance, production, distribution, and exchange. Also, see debates in *Marxism Today* on the political dimensions of the new "global-local nexus"; E. Soja (1989) *Postmodern Geographies,* London: Verso; D. Massey (1984) *Spatial Divisions of Labour: Social Structures and the Geography of Production,* London: Macmillan, and (1989) "Subjects in Space," *New Formations* 11 (summer).

28. T. Benn (1981) "Britain Is a Colony," *New Socialist* 1 (October). For a critique of hard left anti-Americanism, see especially D. Webster (1988) *Looka Yonder,* London: Comedia/Routledge, chap. 7 and conclusion.

29. Another historical irony: 1960s styles are again back in fashion in the "rave" culture of the early 1990s. Many of the angst-ridden white "indie" bands who modeled their image and vocal style on Morrissey and the Smiths switched in the late 1980s/early 1990s to the black-influenced "dance music" styles derived from black American house music and the so-called Manchester sound.

30. The reference comes from W. B. Yeats's poem "Byzantium" (1930), which builds on the earlier poem "Sailing to Byzantium." Yeats's late romanticism, his interest in the esoteric tradition, in the occult image of the "gyre" and the "shade," "dreaming back" or unwinding its natural life through an unraveling swathe of images, all seem apposite here. The fascination with the textures of "Englishness," the Proustian attention to conjuring up (or with) the past, the preciosity and mysticism evident in the output of both Jarman and Morrissey all suggest that they might qualify for membership of an English equivalent of Yeats's "Celtic Twilight" circle. The "evocation" of Jarman's film I attempt here "diverts" lines taken from stanzas 2 to 4 of that poem, especially the fourth:

> At midnight on the Emperor's pavement flit
> Flames that no faggot feeds, nor steel has lit,
> Nor storm disturbs, flames begotten of flame,
> Where blood-begotten spirits come
> And all complexities of fury leave,
> Dying into a dance,
> An agony of trance,
> An agony of flame that cannot singe a sleeve.

31. Certain of the more recent crop of British movies (e.g., Jarman's own *The Last of England* as well as *Business as Usual, Eat the Rich, Empire State,* and *Sammy and Rosie Get Laid,* most of which were released after this text was first published) extend the same basic imagery and build upon the same allegory. They all evoke the "sense of an ending" (of the truth-value or plausibility) of the dominant national myths.

32. I want to distinguish my attempt to characterize the "antinationalist," "antinormative" political and aesthetic tendencies in recent independent British films from the kind of vitriolic dismissal meted out by a right-wing historian like Norman Stone, who, in the *Sunday Times,* 10 January 1988, wrote off all the films mentioned in the previous note (along with *My Beautiful Laundrette*) as "tawdry, ragged, rancidly provincial . . . semi-educated ambitious mediocrities (which were) overcompeting in a declining market, suffering from bouts of muddled creativity, waiting in line to catch public or semi-public money while dreaming of revolting sensationalism." I direct my criticisms exclusively at the institutionalized nature of the "symbolism" employed in many of these films, at the overpolarized vision of cultural and political conflict encoded therein, and the likely impact of both these "predictabilities" on the extent and degree of genuine audience "engagement" with the "issues" supposedly raised within the films. For the rest, I am aware that most of Stone's comments ("tawdry . . . provincial . . . muddled . . . sensational," etc.) could (and no doubt would) be applied with equal venom to this essay.

33. R. Coward (1984) "The Royals," in *Female Desire,* London: Paladin.

34. Gareth Stedman Jones (1982) "Working-class Culture and Working-class Politics in London, 1870–1890: Notes on the Remaking of a Working Class," in B. Waites, ed., *Popular Culture: Past and Present,* London: Croom Helm.

35. For the extent of routine collusion/alignment of interests between Buckingham Palace

and the media during the royal wedding, see, for instance, D. Dayan and E. Katz (1985) "Electronic Ceremonies," in M. Blonsky (ed.) *On Signs,* Oxford: Basil Blackwell. On 20 July 1986 a report appeared in the *Sunday Times* that the queen was concerned about the Thatcher government's socially divisive policies, its handling of the miners' strike, and the implications for the future of the Commonwealth of the government's refusal to impose sanctions on South Africa. Hugo Young points out in his book on Thatcher (1989) *One of Us,* London: Macmillan, that "this story turned out, on inspection, to be almost entirely false" and that the telling differences between the two women were primarily ones "of style and feel" rather than substantive opinion. Toward the end of her reign, Mrs. Thatcher proclaimed her identity of outlook with the monarch by adopting the "royal We," so that when her daughter-in-law gave birth to an heir in 1989, Thatcher announced the transformation in her status with the words, "We are a grandmother."

Works Cited

Anderson, B. 1983. *Imagined Communities: Reflections on the Origin and Spread of Nationalism.* London: Verso. Rev. ed., London: Verso, 1991.

Chambers, I. 1990. *Border Dialogues.* London: Routledge.

Clifford, J. 1988. *The Predicament of Culture: Twentieth-Century Ethnography, Literature, and Art.* Cambridge: Harvard University Press.

Clifford, J., and G. Marcus, eds. 1986. *Writing Culture: The Poetics and Politics of Ethnography.* Berkeley: University of California Press.

Connor, S. 1989. *Postmodernist Culture: An Introduction to Theories of the Contemporary.* Oxford: Basil Blackwell.

Ferguson, B. 1991. "Un-natural Acts and Tongue Ties." In *Un-natural Traces: Contemporary Art from Canada.* London: Barbican Art Gallery.

Geertz, C. 1988. *Works and Lives: The Anthropologist as Author.* Stanford: Stanford University Press.

Gilroy, P. 1992. "Cultural Studies and Ethnic Absolutism." In *Cultural Studies,* ed. L. Grossberg et al. London: Routledge.

Gramsci, A. 1972. *The Prison Notebooks.* London: Lawrence and Wishart.

Grossberg, L. 1988. *It's a Sin: Essays on Postmodernism, Politics, and Culture.* Sydney: Institute of Fine Art, University of Sydney.

Grossberg, L., et al., eds. 1992. *Cultural Studies.* London: Routledge.

Hall, S. 1990. "Cultural Identity and Diaspora." In *Identity,* ed. J. Rutherford. London: Lawrence and Wishart.

———. 1992. "Cultural Studies and Its Theoretical Legacies." In *Cultural Studies,* ed. L. Grossberg et al. London: Routledge.

Hall, S., and M. Jacques, eds. 1985. *The Politics of Thatcherism.* London: Lawrence and Wishart, in conjunction with *Marxism Today.*

———. 1990. *New Times: The Changing Face of Politics in the 1990s.* London: Lawrence and Wishart, in conjunction with *Marxism Today.*

Hebdige, D. 1988. *Hiding in the Light: On Images and Things.* London: Routledge/Comedia.
———. 1991. "What Is Soul?" In *Video Icons and Values,* ed. A. M. Olson et al. Albany: State University of New York.
Laclau, E. 1991. *New Reflections on the Revolution of Our Time.* London: Verso.
Laclau, E., and C. Mouffe. 1985. *Hegemony and Socialist Strategy.* London: Verso.
Mercer, K. 1990. "Welcome to the Jungle: Identity and Diversity in Postmodern Politics." In *Identity,* ed. J. Rutherford. London: Lawrence and Wishart.
Mercer, K. 1992. "'1968': Periodizing Postmodern Politics and Identity," in *Cultural Studies,* ed. L. Grossberg et al. London: Routledge.
Olson, A. M., et al., eds. 1991. *Video Icons and Values.* Albany: State University of New York.
Parr, C., and D. Parr. 1991. "Afterword: Beyond Lamentation." In *Video Icons and Values,* ed. A. M. Olson et al. Albany: State University of New York.
Rutherford, J., ed. 1990. *Identity.* London: Lawrence and Wishart.
Salomon, G. 1981. *Communication and Education: Social and Psychological Interactions.* London: Sage.
Smith, B. H. 1988. "Value without Truth-Value." In *Life after Postmodernism,* ed. J. Fekete. Basingstoke: Macmillan.
Ulmer, G. 1985. *Applied Grammatology: Post(e)-Pedagogy from Jacques Derrida to Joseph Beuys.* Baltimore: Johns Hopkins University Press.
Ulmer, G. 1989. *Teletheory.* London: Routledge.

Seven

New Ethnicities

Stuart Hall

I have centered my remarks on an attempt to identify and characterize a significant shift that has been going on (and is still going on) in black cultural politics. This shift is not definitive, in the sense that there are two clearly discernible phases—one in the past which is now over and the new one which is beginning—which we can neatly counterpose to one another. Rather, they are two phases of the same movement, which constantly overlap and interweave. Both are framed by the same historical conjuncture and both are rooted in the politics of antiracism and the postwar black experience in Britain. Nevertheless I think we can identify two different "moments" and that the difference between them is significant.

It is difficult to characterize these precisely, but I would say that the first moment was grounded in a particular political and cultural analysis. Politically, this is the moment when the term "black" was coined as a way of referencing the common experience of racism and marginalization in Britain and came to provide the organizing category of a new politics of resistance, among groups and communities with, in fact, very different histories, traditions, and ethnic identities. In this moment, polit-

163

ically speaking, "The Black Experience," as a singular and unifying framework based on the building up of identity across ethnic and cultural difference between the different communities, became "hegemonic" over other ethnic/racial identities—though the latter did not, of course, disappear. Culturally, this analysis formulated itself in terms of a critique of the way blacks were positioned as the unspoken and invisible "other" of predominantly white aesthetic and cultural discourses.

This analysis was predicated on the marginalization of the black experience in British culture; not fortuitously occurring at the margins, but placed, positioned at the margins, as the consequence of a set of quite specific political and cultural practices which regulated, governed, and "normalized" the representational and discursive spaces of English society. These formed the conditions of existence of a cultural politics designed to challenge, resist, and, where possible, transform the dominant regimes of representation—first in music and style, later in literary, visual, and cinematic forms. In these spaces blacks have typically been the objects, but rarely the subjects, of the practices of representation. The struggle to come into representation was predicated on a critique of the degree of fetishization, objectification, and negative figuration which are so much a feature of the representation of the black subject. There was a concern not simply with the absence or marginality of the black experience but with its simplification and its stereotypical character.

The cultural politics and strategies which developed around this critique had many facets, but its two principal objects were, first, the question of *access* to the rights to representation by black artists and black cultural workers themselves. Second, the *contestation* of the marginality, the stereotypical quality, and the fetishized nature of images of blacks, by the counterposition of a "positive" black imagery. These strategies were principally addressed to changing what I would call the "relations of representation."

I have a distinct sense that in the recent period we are entering a new phase. But we need to be absolutely clear what we mean by a "new" phase because, as soon as you talk of a new phase, people instantly imagine that what is entailed is the *substitution* of one kind of politics for another. I am quite distinctly *not* talking about a shift in those terms. Politics does not necessarily proceed by way of a set of oppositions and reversals of this kind, though some groups and individuals are anxious to "stage" the question in this way. The original critique of the predominant relations of race and representation and the politics which developed around it have not and cannot possibly disappear while the conditions which gave rise to it—cultural racism in its Dewesbury form—not only persist but positively flourish under Thatcherism.[1] There is no sense in which a new phase in black cultural politics could

1. The Yorkshire town of Dewesbury became the focus of national attention when white parents withdrew their children from a local school with predominantly Asian pupils on the

replace the earlier one. Nevertheless it is true that as the struggle moves forward and assumes new forms, it does to some degree *displace,* reorganize, and reposition the different cultural strategies in relation to one another. If this can be conceived in terms of the "burden of representation," I would put the point in this form: that black artists and cultural workers now have to struggle, not on one, but on *two* fronts. The problem is, how to characterize this shift—if indeed, we agree that such a shift has taken or is taking place—and if the language of binary oppositions and substitutions will no longer suffice. The characterization that I would offer is tentative, proposed mainly to try to clarify some of the issues involved, rather than to preempt them.

The shift is best thought of in terms of a change from a struggle over the relations of representation to a politics of representation itself. It would be useful to separate out such a "politics of representation" into its different elements. We all now use the word "representation," but, as we know, it is an extremely slippery customer. It can be used, on the one hand, simply as another way of talking about how one images a reality that exists "outside" the means by which things are represented: a conception grounded in a mimetic theory of representation. On the other hand, the term can also stand for a very radical displacement of that unproblematic notion of the concept of representation. My own view is that events, relations, structures do have conditions of existence and real effects outside the sphere of the discursive; but only within the discursive, and subject to its specific conditions, limits, and modalities, do they have or can they be constructed within meaning. Thus, while not wanting to expand the territorial claims of the discursive infinitely, how things are represented and the "machineries" and regimes of representation in a culture do play a *constitutive,* and not merely a reflexive, after-the-event, role. This gives questions of culture and ideology, and the scenarios of representation—subjectivity, identity, politics—a formative, not merely an expressive, place in the constitution of social and political life. I think it is the move toward this second sense of representation which is taking place and which is transforming the politics of representation in black culture.

This is a complex issue. First, it is the effect of a theoretical encounter between black cultural politics and the discourses of a Eurocentric, largely white, critical cultural theory which in recent years has focused so much analysis on the politics of representation. This is always an extremely difficult, if not dangerous, encounter. (I think particularly of black people encountering the discourses of poststructuralism, postmodernism, psychoanalysis, and feminism.) Second, it marks what I can only call "the end of innocence," or the end of the innocent notion of the essential black

---

grounds that "English" culture was no longer taught on the curriculum. The contestation of multicultural education from the right also underpinned the controversies around the Bradford headmaster Ray Honeyford. See Gordon 1987.

subject. Here again, the end of the essential black subject is something which people are increasingly debating, but they may not have fully reckoned with its political consequences. What is at issue here is the recognition of the extraordinary diversity of subjective positions, social experiences, and cultural identities which compose the category "black"; that is, the recognition that "black" is essentially a politically and culturally *constructed* category, which cannot be grounded in a set of fixed trans-cultural or transcendental racial categories and which therefore has no guarantees in Nature. What this brings into play is the recognition of the immense diversity and differentiation of the historical and cultural experience of black subjects. This inevitably entails a weakening or fading of the notion that "race" or some composite notion of race around the term "black" will either guarantee the effectivity of any cultural practice or determine in any final sense its aesthetic value.

We should put this as plainly as possible. Films are not necessarily good because black people make them. They are not necessarily "right-on" by virtue of the fact that they deal with the black experience. Once you enter the politics of the end of the essential black subject you are plunged headlong into the maelstrom of a continuously contingent, unguaranteed, political argument and debate: a critical politics, a politics of criticism. You can no longer conduct black politics through the strategy of a simple set of reversals, putting in the place of the bad old essential white subject, the new essentially good black subject. Now, that formulation may seem to threaten the collapse of an entire political world. Alternatively, it may be greeted with extraordinary relief at the passing away of what at one time seemed to be a necessary fiction. Namely, either that all black people are good or indeed that all black people are *the same*. After all, it is one of the predicates of racism that "you can't tell the difference because they all look the same." This does not make it any easier to conceive of how a politics can be constructed which works with and through difference, which is able to build those forms of solidarity and identification which make common struggle and resistance possible but without suppressing the real heterogeneity of interests and identities, and which can effectively draw the political boundary lines without which political contestation is impossible, without fixing those boundaries for eternity. It entails the movement in black politics from what Gramsci called the "war of maneuver" to the "war of position"—the struggle around positionalities. But the difficulty of conceptualizing such a politics (and the temptation to slip into a sort of endlessly sliding discursive liberal-pluralism) does not absolve us of the task of developing such a politics.

The end of the essential black subject also entails a recognition that the central issues of race always appear historically in articulation, in a formation, with other categories and divisions and are constantly crossed and recrossed by the categories of class, of gender, and ethnicity. (I make a distinction here between race and ethnicity to which I shall return.) To me, films like *Territories, Passion of Re-membrance, My Beautiful Laundrette,* and *Sammy and Rosie Get Laid,* for exam-ple, make it perfectly clear that this shift has been engaged, and that the question of the black subject cannot be represented without reference to the dimensions of class, gender, sexuality, and ethnicity.

Difference and Contestation

A further consequence of this politics of representation is the slow recognition of the deep ambivalence of identification and desire. We think about identification usu-ally as a simple process, structured around fixed "selves" which we either are or are not. The play of identity and difference which constructs racism is powered not only by the positioning of blacks as the inferior species but also, and at the same time, by an inexpressible envy and desire; and this is something the recognition of which fun-damentally *displaces* many of our hitherto stable political categories, since it implies a process of identification and otherness which is more complex than we had hith-erto imagined.

Racism, of course, operates by constructing impassable symbolic boundaries be-tween racially constituted categories, and its typically binary system of representa-tion constantly marks and attempts to fix and naturalize the difference between belongingness and otherness. Along this frontier there arises what Gayatri Spivak (1987) calls the "epistemic violence" of the discourses of the other—of imperialism, the colonized, orientalism, the exotic, the primitive, the anthropological, and the folkloric. Consequently the discourse of antiracism had often been founded on a strategy of reversal and inversion, turning the "Manichaean aesthetic" of colonial discourse upside down. However, as Fanon constantly reminded us, the epistemic violence is both outside and inside, and operates by a process of splitting on both sides of the division—in here as well as out there. That is why it is a question, not only of "black-skin, white-skin" but of *Black Skin, White Masks*—the internaliza-tion of the self-as-other. Just as masculinity always constructs femininity as dou-ble—simultaneously Madonna and Whore—so racism constructs the black subject: noble savage and violent avenger. And in the doubling, fear and desire double for one another and play across the structures of otherness, complicating its politics.

Recently I've read several articles about the photographic text of Robert Map-plethorpe—especially his inscription of the nude, black male—all written by black critics or cultural practitioners.[2] These essays properly begin by identifying in Mapplethorpe's work the tropes of fetishization, the fragmentation of the black image, and its objectification, as the forms of their appropriation within the white,

2. Mercer 1987 and various articles in Bailey 1986, an issue on "black experience."

gay gaze. But, as I read, I know that something else is going on as well in both the production and the reading of those texts. The continuous circling around Mapplethorpe's work is not exhausted by being able to place him as the white fetishistic gay photographer; and this is because it is also marked by the surreptitious return of desire—that deep ambivalence of identification which makes the categories in which we have previously thought and argued about black cultural politics and the black cultural text extremely problematic. This brings to the surface the unwelcome fact that a great deal of black politics, constructed, addressed, and developed directly in relation to questions of race and ethnicity, has been predicated on the assumption that the categories of gender and sexuality would stay the same and remain fixed and secured. What the new politics of representation does is to put that into question, crossing the questions of racism irrevocably with questions of sexuality. That is what is so disturbing, finally, to many of our settled political habits about *Passion of Remembrance*. This double fracturing entails a different kind of politics because, as we know, black radical politics has frequently been stabilized around particular conceptions of black masculinity, which are only now being put into question by black women and black gay men. At certain points, black politics has also been underpinned by a deep absence or more typically an evasive silence with reference to class.

Another element inscribed in the new politics of representation has to do with the question of ethnicity. I am familiar with all the dangers of "ethnicity" as a concept and have written myself about the fact that ethnicity, in the form of a culturally constructed sense of Englishness and a particularly closed, exclusive, and regressive form of English national identity, is one of the core characteristics of British racism today (Hall 1978). I am also well aware that the politics of antiracism has often constructed itself in terms of a contestation of "multiethnicity" or "multiculturalism." On the other hand, as the politics of representation around the black subject shifts, I think we will begin to see a renewed contestation over the meaning of the term "ethnicity" itself.

If the black subject and black experience are not stabilized by Nature or by some other essential guarantee, then it must be the case that they are constructed historically, culturally, politically—and the concept which refers to this is "ethnicity." The term "ethnicity" acknowledges the place of history, language, and culture in the construction of subjectivity and identity, as well as the fact that all discourse is placed, positioned, situated, and all knowledge is contextual. Representation is possible only because enunciation is always produced within codes which have a history, a position within the discursive formations of a particular space and time. The displacement of the "centered" discourses of the West entails putting in question its universalist character and its transcendental claims to speak for everyone, while being itself everywhere and nowhere. The fact that this grounding of ethnicity in difference was deployed, in the discourse of racism, as a means of disavowing the realities of racism and repression does not mean that we can permit the term to be permanently colonized. That appropriation will have to be contested, the term disarticulated from its position in the discourse of "multiculturalism" and transcoded, just as we previously had to recuperate the term "black" from its place in a system of negative equivalences. The new politics of representation therefore also sets in motion an ideological contestation around the term "ethnicity." But in order to pursue that movement further, we will have to retheorize the concept of "difference."

It seems to me that, in the various practices and discourses of black cultural production, we are beginning to see constructions of just such a new conception of ethnicity: a new cultural politics which engages rather than suppresses difference and which depends, in part, on the cultural construction of new ethnic identities. Difference, like representation, is also a slippery, and therefore contested, concept. There is the "difference" which makes a radical and unbridgeable separation; and there is a "difference" which is positional, conditional, and conjunctural, closer to Derrida's notion of *différance,* though if we are concerned to maintain a politics it cannot be defined exclusively in terms of an infinite sliding of the signifier. We still have a great deal of work to do to *decouple* ethnicity, as it functions in the dominant discourse, from its equivalence with nationalism, imperialism, racism, and the state, which are the points of attachment around which a distinctive British or, more accurately, English ethnicity have been constructed. Nevertheless, I think such a project is not only possible but necessary. Indeed, this decoupling of ethnicity from the violence of the state is implicit in some of the new forms of cultural practice that are going on in films like *Passion* and *Handsworth Songs.* We are beginning to think about how to represent a noncoercive and a more diverse conception of ethnicity, to set against the embattled, hegemonic conception of "Englishness" which, under Thatcherism, stabilizes so much of the dominant political and cultural discourses, and which, because it is hegemonic, does not represent itself as an ethnicity at all.

This marks a real shift in the point of contestation, since it is no longer only between antiracism and multiculturalism but *inside* the notion of ethnicity itself. What is involved is the splitting of the notion of ethnicity between, on the one hand, the dominant notion which connects it to nation and "race" and, on the other hand, what I think is the beginning of a positive conception of the ethnicity of the margins, of the periphery. That is to say, a recognition that we all speak from a particular place, out of a particular history, out of a particular experience, a particular culture, without being contained by that position as "ethnic artists" or filmmakers. We are all, in that sense, *ethnically* located and our ethnic identities are crucial to our subjective sense of who we are. But this is also a recognition that this is not an ethnicity which is doomed to survive, as Englishness was, only by marginalizing, dispossessing, displacing, and forgetting other ethnicities. This precisely is the politics of ethnicity predicated on difference and diversity.

The final point which I think is entailed in this new politics of representation has to do with an awareness of the black experience as a *diaspora* experience, and the consequences which this carries for the process of unsettling, recombination, hybridization, and "cut-and-mix"—in short, the process of cultural *diasporaization* (to coin an ugly term) which it implies. In the case of the young black British films and filmmakers under discussion, the diaspora experience is certainly profoundly fed and nourished by, for example, the emergence of Third World cinema; by the African experience; the connection with Afro-Caribbean experience; and the deep inheritance of complex systems of representation and aesthetic traditions from Asian and African culture. But, in spite of these rich cultural "roots," the new cultural politics is operating on new and quite distinct ground—specifically, contestation over what it means to be "British." The relation of this cultural politics to the past, to its different "roots," is profound, but complex. It cannot be simple or unmediated. It is (as a film like *Dreaming Rivers* reminds us) complexly mediated and transformed by memory, fantasy, and desire. Or, as even an explicitly political film like *Handsworth Songs* clearly suggests, the relation is intertextual—mediated, through a variety of other "texts." There can, therefore, be no simple "return" or "recovery" of the ancestral past which is not reexperienced through the categories of the present: no base for creative enunciation in a simple reproduction of traditional forms which are not transformed by the technologies and the identities of the present. This is something that was signaled as early as a film like *Blacks Britannica* and as recently as Paul Gilroy's important book *There Ain't No Black in the Union Jack* ([1987] 1991). Fifteen years ago we didn't care, or at least I didn't care, whether there was any black in the Union Jack. Now not only do we care, we *must*.

This last point suggests that we are also approaching what I would call the end of a certain critical innocence in black cultural politics. And here, it might be appropriate to refer, glancingly, to the debate between Salman Rushdie and myself in the *Guardian* some months ago. The debate was not about whether *Handsworth Songs* or *The Passion of Remembrance* were great films or not, because, in the light of what I have said, once you enter this particular problematic, the question of what good films are, which parts of them are good and why, is open to the politics of criticism. Once you abandon essential categories, there is no place to go apart from the politics of criticism and to enter the politics of criticism in black culture is to grow up, to leave the age of critical innocence.

It was not Salman Rushdie's particular judgment that I was contesting, so much as the mode in which he addressed the films. He seemed to me to be addressing them as if from the stable, well-established critical criteria of a *Guardian* reviewer. I was trying, perhaps unsuccessfully, to say that I thought this an inadequate basis for a political criticism and one which overlooked precisely the signs of innovation, and the constraints under which these filmmakers were operating. It is difficult to define what an alternative mode of address would be. I certainly didn't want Salman Rushdie to say he thought the films were good because they were black. But I also didn't want him to say that he thought they weren't good because "we creative artists all know what good films are," since I no longer believe we can resolve the questions of aesthetic value by the use of these transcendental, canonical cultural categories. I think there *is* another position, one which locates itself *inside* a continuous struggle and politics around black representation, but which then is able to open up a continuous critical discourse about themes, about the forms of representation, the subjects of representation, above all, the regimes of representation. I thought it was important, at that point, to intervene to try to get that mode of critical address right, in relation to the new black filmmaking. It is extremely tricky, as I know, because as it happens, in intervening, I got the mode of address wrong too! I failed to communicate the fact that, in relation to his *Guardian* article, I thought Salman was hopelessly wrong about *Handsworth Songs,* which does not in any way diminish my judgment about the stature of *Midnight's Children*. I regret that I couldn't get it right, exactly, because the politics of criticism has to be able to get both things right.

Such a politics of criticism has to be able to say (just to give one example) why *My Beautiful Laundrette* is one of the most riveting and important films produced by a black writer in recent years and precisely for the reason that made it so controversial: its refusal to represent the black experience in Britain as monolithic, self-contained, sexually stabilized, and always "right-on"—in a word, always and only "positive," or what Hanif Kureishi has called "cheering fictions": "the writer as public relations officer, as hired liar. If there is to be a serious attempt to understand Britain today, with its mix of races and colours, its hysteria and despair, then, writing about it has to be complex. It can't apologise or idealize. It can't sentimentalize and it can't represent only one group as having a monopoly on virtue" (Kureishi 1985). *Laundrette* is important particularly in terms of its control, of knowing what it is doing, as the text crosses those frontiers between gender, race, ethnicity, sexuality, and class. *Sammy and Rosie* is also a bold and adventurous film, though in some ways less coherent, not so sure of where it is going, overdriven by an almost uncontrollable, cool anger. One needs to be able to offer that as a critical judgment and to argue it through, to have one's mind changed, without undermining one's essential commitment to the project of the politics of black representation.

Works Cited

Bailey, D. 1986. *Ten.8* (Birmingham) no. 22.

Gilroy, P. 1991. *There Ain't No Black in the Union Jack.* London: Hutchison, 1987. Reprint, Chicago: University of Chicago Press.

Gordon, P. 1987. "The New Right, Race, and Education." *Race and Class* (London) 29, no. 3 (winter).

Hall, S. 1978. "Racism and Reaction." *Five Views on Multi-Racial Britain.* London: Commission for Racial Equality.

Kureishi, H. 1985. "Dirty Washing." *Time Out* (London), 14–20 November.

Mercer, K. 1987. "Imagining the Black Man's Sex." In *Photography/Politics: Two,* ed. P. Holland et al. London: Comedia/Methuen.

Spivak, G. 1987. *In Other Worlds: Essays in Cultural Politics.* London: Methuen.

Eight

Two Kinds of Otherness: Black Film and the Avant-Garde

Judith Williamson

This was a talk given at the "Black Film, British Cinema" conference organized by Kobena Mercer with Erica Carter at the Institute of Contemporary Arts, London, in February 1988. The conference drew a wide range of black and Asian filmmakers and cultural critics, and those involved in oppositional filmmaking generally; it was an informal and productive event, mainly because the atmosphere was easy enough to allow the raising of questions which, if they had been asked before, had certainly not been asked very publicly or loudly within this milieu. In my recollection of the day, Stuart Hall was a key figure in moving the discussion toward these hitherto undebated areas, and my contribution to it started from the point at which he had suggested that "films are not necessarily good because black people make them. They are not necessarily 'right-on' by virtue of the fact that they deal with the black experience."

. . .

I'm going to start from where Stuart Hall finished off. When he was talking about the possibility of a criticism that would neither hold up certain independent films quite uncritically as being "right-on," nor criticize them from a mainstream position—that's really what I've been trying to do over the last few years on the *New Statesman*. And I want to talk, not only about criticism, but about the kinds of forms available for filmmakers engaging in oppositional practice, and the way our notions of those forms cross with issues of race to produce a sort of doubly other cinema. Finally, I want to try and resuscitate the question of class, which recently seems to have been dropping right out of the race-gender-class trilogy.

I'm also starting from my own position as a critic because part of what I try to do in my work is to engage with mainstream criticism. In practice that means, for example, that in doing a critique of *Sammy and Rosie Get Laid,* a film I really didn't like, I had to spend about a third of my column engaging with Norman Stone's reactionary attack on it and carrying on that debate with other critics while trying to criticize the film as well. I think that's the kind of thing Stuart was talking about and it's quite a difficult thing to balance.

But I'd like to make a distinction between mainstream criticism and mainstream cinema. This is really quite important. While I would say I'm totally hostile to mainstream critics and the kinds of assumptions underlying almost all the cinema criticism in the national press today, I don't feel the same extreme opposition to all forms of mainstream cinema. And I think it's important *not* to collapse together, as the oppositional movement often has done, a cinematic—i.e., filmmaking—practice and a critical practice. It's become a sort of tenet of the oppositional area of cultural politics we all move in (and not only in film) that practice and criticism go hand in hand, until they're almost seen as the same. This collapsing together—which is part of that whole seventies idea of theoretical-practice-as-part-of-practice—has, I think, to some extent gone past its useful point. Because, as I said, it's important to me to be able to attack mainstream critics but not always to sweep out everything within mainstream cinema at the same time—certainly not to sweep out the mainstream cinema *audience,* which is what I mean when I talk about class in this context.

I'll come back to that point, but for now I'm setting up this slightly unfashionable dichotomy between filmmaking practice and criticism or theory because I want to consider the effects of their elision on the kind of oppositional area that most of us work in. I was educated as a Marxist to understand the relation between theory and practice as a dialectical relationship, where theory isn't a blueprint for action but, almost the reverse, an attempt to find translatable patterns in what *has* happened, translatable in that they can be used to help understand other situations and prevent repeating mistakes. So, as I see it, theory isn't so much a set of guidelines for what to do, but a sort of stocktaking where you try to get to grips with a situation. I'm saying this because most of us feel the pinch of certain orthodoxies that have grown up around what you could very loosely call "*Screen* theory," and people are now working in an area where oppositional cultural theory sometimes feels every bit as rigid as the orthodoxies of the dominant cinematic practice we're meant to be against.

I'm not saying I disagree with oppositional theories, in fact, I'm one of the people who are always going around saying they should be *more* oppositional, but I'm trying to diagnose something about the atmosphere in the field of independent, oppositional filmmaking within which the new work from black filmmakers here is broadly located. I do believe our fear of criticism from one another is sometimes stronger than our engagement with those people "out there" who we don't actually know, but who are, in fact, the readers or viewers of our work. This fear and the anxiety that goes with it have crippling results for filmmakers and critics alike. And what happens when people can't make or take criticism openly on a professional level is that it goes underground and becomes far more snide, which in turn fuels people's fear of being criticized, and so on and so on.

This is probably the moment for me to say something which I think has to be said, which is that, while I don't feel uncomfortable about it, there are problems with being a white critic speaking at something like this and writing about black film practice. Without wanting to make too crude an analogy or simply superimpose race and gender, I know I have spent years personally complaining about male critics edging in and intervening within feminist debates about film and I am aware that I could be in a similar position here. I'm saying this not as an apology—since I was invited to speak at this event—but because it isn't often discussed and there seems to be enormous embarrassment around this area. I've found—at a pragmatic level of noticing what people say in private and comparing it with what they will say or write in public—that there is a reluctance by white critics to make criticisms of films by black filmmakers because they feel (sometimes quite rightly) not qualified to do so, or, to put it more bluntly, they are afraid of appearing racist.

On the one hand, I think it's quite right that white critics should hesitate when they are confronted with films coming out of a different experience from their own. But on the other hand, there are, to continue being blunt, problems with being a white critic in a different way because it makes criticisms which may have some substance more easily dismissible. Kobena Mercer has written in a paper on the aesthetics of black independent film in Britain that white critics' and audiences' perception of the "influence of Euro-American avant-garde cinema and film theory" on works like *Passion of Remembrance* and *Handsworth Songs* "suggests an underlying anxiety to pin down and categorize a practice that upsets and disrupts fixed expectations and normative assumptions about what 'black' films should look like" (Mercer 1988). Nevertheless, most of the filmmakers at this conference whose work we're discussing learnt their craft—frequently at art school—within the Euro-American independent film tradition. I'm raising this particular piece of argument because it preempts my main point, which deals precisely with this issue, the place of avant-garde cinema, or rather, of these films within that place. The issue of theory I've already tried to deal with a bit. Anyway, whatever the status of my perceptions are as a white critic, I just think the point had to be raised and it would be a strange day if nobody said it. So I'm saying it.

Coming back to what I would call oppositional criticism, the one loosely based around *Screen* or which operates in the area of developing critical practice that Stuart Hall was outlining—within this sphere there is another kind of good/bad dichotomy alongside the one he described. And I'm glad he was the person that said it: a film made by a black filmmaker is not "good" automatically because the director is black any more than a film made by a woman is good because it's made by a woman. Basically he's saying goodbye to the simplistic black-film-good/white-film-bad dichotomy in favor of a more complex way of understanding the politics of ethnicity. Of course, just saying it doesn't change things overnight and I think it will be some time before those black films which are especially in the limelight at the moment lose their aura of untouchability. Apart from making the critic's job more difficult, that aura must in many ways be a burden to the filmmakers, who have to be constantly producing showpieces and be on show themselves—a position which in my experience never helped anyone to develop their work, and which reflects somewhat dubiously on the film culture that makes such demands. Those demands are, in a sense, a part of that polarity Stuart described, and in the long run I think it will be the highly pressurized, young black filmmakers who benefit most from his attempt to dismantle this simple equation of black filmmaking with "right-on" filmmaking, an equation which keeps it locked in a particular kind of otherness.

For besides that good/bad orthodoxy centered on race which Stuart described, there is another kind of orthodoxy within this critical arena, another good/bad dichotomy which, to parody it rather crudely, says, realist, narrative, mainstream cinema: bad; non-narrative, difficult, even boring, oppositional cinema: good. We must all be familiar with this, and whether or not one agrees with that formulation it has had a great influence on the kinds of positions people can take up as filmmakers or critics. Pursuing my analogy with Stuart's point: there's another other that I want to tackle from my position as film critic, which is the avant-garde as the other of Hollywood cinema.

We've all become adept at handling this term: as women and feminists we have become skilled at understanding our position as "other" to male culture, and the whole black political movement has for years put forward very highly developed theories and perceptions of how the black functions as "other" to white culture and so on. Within film criticism I'm constantly confronted with the avant-garde or the "difficult" as the "other" of Hollywood or mainstream cinema and I think this otherness is just as problematic a relationship, just as much inscribed within what it's supposed to be different from.

I'm only going to invoke one theorist in this talk, but I think the work of the French writer Pierre Bourdieu (1984) is really useful in theorizing the way that the place of the avant-garde in art or film as the oppositional or the difficult is one that's actually written into and circumscribed by the culture to which it's meant to be opposed. I'm not trying to be all gloomy and suggest that one can never do anything different or oppositional or make new forms that will push people's perceptions beyond the usual—far from it; I just think that to be productively oppositional, the place occupied by the avant-garde as the structured-in-opposite of the mainstream is something we have to be aware of.

Of course, the concept of Third Cinema was developed exactly in order to avoid that mainstream/avant-garde dichotomy, in recognition of the fact that neither side of it is inherently oppositional or politicized, or, to put it differently, that the whole polarity can still be completely contained within First World and colonialist culture. The concept of Third Cinema also presupposes a different constituency, an audience which is neither necessarily the predominantly white, mainstream cinema audience nor the (also predominantly white) avant-garde, cinémathèque audience. But I don't quite know where that gets us in this context, which is, frankly, closer to the avant-garde than anything else. Looking around the room I see lots of people who were at the Third Cinema conference in Edinburgh, where battles were raging about what black cinema was and whether a straightforward narrative film could be a truly oppositional form of filmmaking. I'm dragging that argument back into *this* conference because the filmmakers that Kobena Mercer describes in his article as drawing on a strong Third World inheritance were actually, at that event, arguing *against* various African and also black U.S. filmmakers who advocated what I would call fairly un-avant-garde but politically strident work. The key debate about the possibility or the concept of a black aesthetic or a specifically black form of filmmaking is one that's central here; because if there *isn't* such an aesthetic, then black filmmakers are faced with precisely the problem that confronts all filmmakers, in that rather inhibiting context I set out to describe—which is how to pitch your work. And related to that, although it's not always within the filmmakers' control, is dealing with how your work is taken up.

And that's where my point about the avant-garde comes in. It is particularly striking that the black British work that's been taken up most widely in the world of theory, been most written about, and also picked up at festivals, on tours, and so on, is the work that fits most obviously into that category avant-garde. This isn't a criticism of the work and it isn't necessarily the work's "fault," so to speak. But, again on a level entirely to do with personal observation, the reception in somewhere like

New York of Black Audio's and Sankofa's work has as much to do with its being formally inventive and, for lack of a better term, avant-garde, as to do with its being black, or rather, it's to do with the combination of the two.

What I'm saying is not a criticism but an observation; I think it's helpful to make it because the formal properties of those films have somehow, in most of the critical discourse surrounding them, been subsumed into their "blackness." Yet, say, a Ceddo production like *The People's Account* is just as "black." Coco Fusco has said quite rightly that it's easier to import one's others than to confront them at home. And I would add that it's sometimes easier to confront the political other—the other of ethnicity and, in the case, say, of *Passion,* sexuality—when it occupies the space of other in that cinematic dichotomy I was trying to describe. Coco's monograph on the work of Black Audio and Sankofa (for whom she's arranged a tour in New York) is called *Young, British, and Black.*[1] But, more accurately, it should be called "Young, British, Black, and Avant-garde," for this is what distinguishes the work she has chosen to tour from that of other equally young, equally British, and equally black filmmakers.

Now I too, like Coco, find the work of these particular groups especially interesting, and that's precisely because I *am* interested in finding new forms and experimenting: with documentary (*Handsworth Songs*) and with narrative (*Passion of Remembrance*). All I'm saying is that we should be clear that black filmmaking and experimental filmmaking are not automatically the same thing. I'm hardly the best person to sound off at a black cinema conference on whether or not there *is* the possibility of a black cinema (though I've always understood that question, in other contexts, as one of audience rather than aesthetics—I'll come back to this). But truly, I don't see how there can be such a thing as a homogeneous black aesthetic, as became clear in the disagreements at Edinburgh. Or again, using an analogy with feminist debates, where I feel better qualified to make definite pronouncements: during the seventies those of us involved in feminist discussions about cinema were endlessly having these fights about "Is there a women's cinema" (my answer is "yes, if it's one that women watch") and "Is there a feminist or female (which I know aren't the same thing) aesthetic"—to which I would be inclined to say "no."

I remember a particular debate that took place at the London Film-Makers' Co-op, about whether, if a woman was behind the camera, you would avoid having the voyeuristic gaze analyzed by Laura Mulvey (1975) as the male look at the female object. There were actual rows about whether or not it was wrong to have a man behind the camera even if a woman was directing. Of course it may be a hassle for

1. This was also the title of the touring exhibition itself, curated by Coco Fusco, produced by Ada Griffin, and presented by Third World Newsreel, New York, May 1988.

quite other reasons to have a man behind the camera, but I don't think there is anything essential to gender or race about either a gaze or an aesthetic.

There *is* a *cultural* dimension to it, but then that brings us exactly back to cultural forms and how to use them. I've made this detour into feminist territory because when someone asked in the last session "Can a white person make a Third Cinema film?" my instinct was to answer "no." It's like "Can a man make a feminist film?" my answer to that would be "Why the hell would a man want to *think* he was making a feminist film?" And frankly that response seems to be contradictory, having just said there is no inherent female (or black) aesthetic. But there *is* something in between essentialism and a complete denial of people's different positions and experiences, and I think that the more concrete one's analysis of film culture, the more possibilities for it there are.

Looking at the three films at the focus of today's debate (*Handsworth Songs, Playing Away,* and *Passion of Remembrance*), you can see very clearly that there are common issues in black politics with which all three are engaging while aesthetically they're all very different. Just from seeing these three films it's obvious that there isn't one black aesthetic. In the light of all this I would say that any kind of oppositional or any questioning cinema is going to have to engage with both mainstream and avant-garde practices, and perhaps challenge that very dichotomy—which after all rests on all those high culture/low culture ideas. Colin MacCabe talked about the outmoded counterposition between realist and avant-garde aesthetics, but I'm going into it in more detail because I think you have to find ways to engage with *both* of them. The eliding of these two "good/bad" polarities, with the white film-reactionary-bad/black film-progressive-good dichotomy and the mainstream film-realist-bad/avant-garde film-difficult-good dichotomy just marrying each other, lets you fill the avant-gardeness with, say, a black cinema, so you have a black, avant-garde cinema and it can function as the other to white mainstream Hollywood stuff. I'm simply trying to draw attention to that other binary structure which I think has already begun to adhere to the first one, and to pull apart all those four corners, white, black, avant-garde, mainstream.

This is where I want to come back to audiences, because I think audiences do matter. I don't see how you can talk about oppositional or political film without talking about audiences. I really don't. I never have done. Audiences *do* matter. It's not enough to say, "Oh well, everything's fractured, everything's just diverse"—that's not adequate if you are to be political. If you're political you do want to reach people beyond your buddies; I think lots of issues arise here which aren't specific to black cinema but which are important to it. There are lots of obstacles as well. There's the kind of right-on-ness of the workshop movement, into which the black groups have come fairly late, and it is a problem that the movement as a whole has

never successfully grappled with, the question of audiences. Obviously it's a complicated issue and partly it's tied up with funding, money, dependency. The problem
that I'm talking about though is that the struggle to set up the workshops, which I
myself was involved in, was such a big one that once they were established and
funded there was a huge sigh of relief and then people forgot to talk about the products, the actual films.

Thinking about actual films and how they work—I'm glad also that Stuart
brought up *My Beautiful Laundrette* because outside the *Screen* circles that I to some
extent move in, a lot of people I know who are not at all theoretical just love *My
Beautiful Laundrette*. They love it! And many of them are *not,* for example, people
who have thought at all about heterosexism. I'm thinking maybe of neighbors, old
school friends, not people that I know professionally. It has in some way reached out
to people. As Stuart said, it's been a highly *enjoyed* film. In some ways it's an absolutely classic romance. You're just dying for those people to kiss—and they're both
men. And one is black and the other is white. And you're sitting there in the role of
the classic Hollywood spectator thinking "Are they going to get off with each other?
Is he going to say it? Will he be late?" The cinematic structures that it employs are
completely mainstream: it is not an avant-garde film in its form at all. There's nothing that interesting about it visually. I don't want to be rude to the makers but it is not
a formally exciting work. And yet it had this enthusiastic reception just about everywhere except in what you might call the *Screen* world, where it was, well, to put it
bluntly, kind of sneered at by all those people who are anti-mainstream. I'm afraid
I'm drawing on what I actually hear people say but they don't print, and I'm sorry to
do that, but otherwise these things don't get properly aired. I think these issues are
too important to let them slip by in odd remarks—because, as I keep saying, audiences really are important.

So my personal benchmark of one aspect of political filmmaking would be that
you would want your film—I would want my film—to reach some people, maybe
not the whole of the people, maybe not a mass audience, but to reach *some* people
who aren't already engaged in the kinds of debates we've been talking through, certainly to reach people outside the sometimes esoteric or privileged arena of film theory. This is a very rough-and-ready definition, but it brings the issue of audiences
back without saying either this must speak for the whole black community or this
must speak for all women, or this must speak for everybody. You simply want your
work to reach *somebody* outside your own circles, or at least that's what I want.

And in coming back to audiences I think we are coming back to the question of
class. I know that what I'm saying might be challenged by the kind of postmodernist
analysis that sees everything as already fragmented, but when we're talking about
mainstream cinema and why people enjoy a film like *Laundrette* we are talking

about class, if not in a completely rigid sense, at least in the sense that Bourdieu addresses when he talks about "cultural capital"—some level of education into film language and forms.

For about the first five years that I ever watched avant-garde work, I found it really difficult; it was incredibly hard to learn to expect different things from films, not to expect resolution, not to expect closure, not to expect to care about the characters and so on. *Now,* I can truthfully say that some avant-garde movies are among my absolutely favorite films. But the point is you don't just sit down one day and find "difficult" films really enjoyable. Without confronting that fact and its connection with class I think we're deceiving ourselves. The reason that I got to be able to like avant-garde films is because I had all that time in college, and if you don't want to call it class, call it education or call it cultural capital, to take up Bourdieu's useful term.

We're talking a lot nowadays about race and gender, and their relation to representation is being very highly theorized at the moment. But it's interesting that we haven't talked so much about class and representation, because it does raise major formal issues and that is where you come back to notions of difficulty which aren't just to be put aside. I mean the difficulty which is something to do with having a class or educational position different to the one where you learn to sit through *Wavelength* without getting fidgety. Now I can do it, but it took me a long time! And these are really things we have to think about.

Having started with my position as a critic, I'll end by thinking from the viewpoint of a filmmaker, because I think a key issue in all this is the problem of *learning*. It's very out of date at the moment to talk about learning the skills of your medium, but nevertheless that's something that filmmakers have to do, just as learning to watch rather more difficult films than usual is something that audiences have to do. The whole oppositional movement has a lot to learn about cinematic pleasure. That isn't to say, "Let's make films in a totally conventional way," but to say, "Let's reclaim certain kinds of pleasurable cinematic experience without throwing them out with the politically unacceptable bathwater." Any kind of progressive new cinema involves learning how to make films that can engage and be appealing without necessarily running back to precisely the same old realist modes. And part of that learning is actually listening to what people say about the films they see.

I'm not holding that up as the only factor in making a film, but I'm emphasizing it and I'm finishing on it because I think it's a thing which has been missing in many of these debates. A cavalier attitude to audiences is the very opposite of a politics that's concerned with people changing their perceptions. This may seem to have moved off the subject of black cinema, but perhaps it is a sign of the strength of black filmmaking practice in Britain now that we can stop asking "What *is* black cinema" and start addressing some of the more complex questions raised by actual films and their audiences, questions which all oppositional filmmakers could learn from.

Works Cited

Bourdieu, P. 1984. *Distinction: A Social Critique of the Judgement of Taste.* Cambridge: Harvard University Press.

Mercer, K. 1988. "Diaspora Culture and the Dialogic Imagination: The Aesthetics of Black Independent Film in Britain." In *Blackframes: Critical Perspectives on Black Independent Cinema,* ed. M. Cham and C. Andrade-Watkins. Cambridge: MIT Press.

Mulvey, L. 1975. "Visual Pleasure and Narrative Cinema." *Screen* (London) 16, no. 3.

Nine

The Cultural Context of Black British Cinema

Jim Pines

I

The 1980s have been a kind of watershed for black independent film and video in Britain. With the emergence of a new generation of practitioners whose work reflects a diverse range of thematic and formal concerns, there has been a significant shift not only in terms of accepted notions of "British" film culture, which hitherto ignored the work of black practitioners, but also in terms of institutional cultural (funding) policy. Through various mechanisms, including productions and associated screenings and representation on key institutional committees, black film and video independents have been able to revise the cultural agenda in relation to their own cultural and political concerns, as well as in relation to the way in which this intervention necessarily affects the wider society. The "recognition" of this black presence in the film and television culture has become a new and significant factor, particularly within the more liberal progressive areas of the British cultural scene, which has resulted in marked "adjustments" at the institutional level. However, these developments have not led to the complete radicalization of the cultural terrain, because black independent media practitioners to a very large extent are still hamstrung by, and thus are having to continue struggling against, recurrent institutional and cultural marginalization. In other words, the "dominant" cultural and funding bodies have thus far succeeded only in accommodating certain elements of change, without really altering the fundamental structures in their thinking and in their institutional practices.

Although resistance to exclusion and marginalization remains high on the agenda, other issues are now emerging into the forefront which are equally vital to the development of the sector, i.e., issues which one might define as black-specific in orientation—like the development of a genuinely independent black film culture, and concomitantly the shaping of an expressive film "language" which draws on and addresses in very specific ways particular features of black cultural experiences. This has led to a number of new tendencies emerging within the sector, such as an interest in formal experimentation, particularly among more theoretically aware practitioners, and a growing concern with practical matters like distribution and exhibition, which earlier black practitioners were simply unable to undertake. Indeed, the widening circulation of black and Third World films in Britain in the past couple of years has opened the possibility for new and more effective means of consolidating important areas of film-related cultural work, mainly, but not exclusively, through the promotion of black-owned distribution and exhibition networks. Of course more work still needs to be done on audience-building, especially given the fact that many people, black and white, still tend to approach black films with a sense of uncertainty at best. But recent experience indicates that this area of cinema is becoming increasingly "less difficult" or more viable both in a cultural and a (quasi-) commercial sense.

In an important sense, these developments within the black independent film and video sector in Britain have to be seen against the backdrop of eighties cultural politics, which in terms of black politics signaled the break with old-style "race relations" and multiculturalism. For many practitioners, the old preoccupation with conventional race-relations motifs had become more or less redundant. The privileging of black-white relations in the classic "race problem" sense was therefore seriously called into question, as it became patently obvious that this orientation was (is) really inappropriate in the context of "post-multicultural" Britain in the 1980s. The emphasis thus shifted toward a broader, more critical orientation which stresses a completely different set of political and cultural concerns, such as the need to retrieve and re-present black people's own histories through "archival excavation" (black historiography), and the importance of deploying motifs which convey a more complex sense of contemporary black (British) experiences from a black perspective. Within this framework, "race relations" is strategically repositioned within a broader set of sociopolitical and cultural concerns, thus making it possible—for the first time in the British context—to address black themes without having to directly involve otherwise omnipresent white figures in the narrative.

A good example of this radical departure into new territory is Sankofa's compelling drama *The Passion of Remembrance* (1986), which links together questions of race, class, sexuality, and gender, and explores the way in which these issues relate specifically to black communities, i.e., relations among black people, rather than between blacks and whites per se. In a similar vein, Black Audio Film Collective's documentary *Handsworth Songs* (1986) takes us along another path of resistance, through the creative blending of archival footage, political reportage, and historical symbolism, and signals a formidable challenge to the British race-relations documentary tradition (which for decades has been immensely effective in promulgating problem-oriented sociological representations of "race" in Britain). These films offer new insights into the nature of the black experience in postimperial Britain, and they also suggest new possibilities in representing black social, political, cultural, and historical realities which (again) could not have been contemplated in previous decades. These developments challenge critics, theorists, historians, and practitioners interested in the evolution of black (British) cinema to reassess old paradigms and to take into fuller account the political and cultural significance of black-produced (oppositional) imagery in representations of contemporary Britain.

II

Black independent film production in Britain dates back to around the mid-1960s, but it was at least a decade before cultural institutions started to recognize or make provisions for this activity within "official" cultural funding policy. Thus, the handful of black independents at the time operated in a characteristically entrepreneurial fashion, financing small to modest productions out of their own pockets or by other, more "unconventional" means. For example, Horace Ové's engaging documentary *Reggae* (1970) was financed by a black independent record producer. In sharp contrast to the situation today, earlier black independents did not engage in institutional cultural politics to any great extent, preferring instead to remain outside the white-dominated structures which in any case showed no interest in nonwhite film cultural activity. Even during the mid-1970s, the height of film theory and cultural expansion in Britain (which centered largely around *Screen* magazine and the British Film Institute's regional policy), there was precious little to be heard relating to black cultural production.

Ironically, this exclusion from the main cultural debates and policy initiatives of that era tended to reinforce a feeling of cultural and creative independence among many black practitioners. However, it also helped to perpetuate the dangerous notion that black people were either not seriously engaged in film- and video-related activity, or, if they were, that their work was not relevant to a wider constituency. It was therefore relatively easy for the cultural mandarins and their so-called enlightened clients to turn a blind eye to black-related cultural matters, despite the fact that much of it actually had a great deal to say about Britain in the sixties and seventies.

Of course these institutional responses were part of a much broader cultural debate which, needless to add, the handful of black independents at the time did not participate in. Without putting too fine a point on it, this period witnessed a sort of crisis within British film culture, in which the whole field of production, distribution, exhibition, and film cultural theory was being contested. The notion of subsidized independence became one of the central themes in the debates, particularly for those (progressive white) independents wanting to develop their craft outside (or in opposition to) the mainstream industry, and this led eventually to the grant-aided independent sector as we know it today. But because black independents had no input in these developments, they failed to get an early footing in the organization of the independent film and video sector. Consequently, they continued to be marginalized, even by the liberal progressive wing of the culture industry.

But whether black filmmaking would have developed more rapidly or more prolifically if it had been incorporated into the main independent sector at the time, we shall never know. What does seem clear, however, is that the lack of an organizational base from which to promote their activities prevented black independents from making a bigger impact on the cultural scene, and this inevitably affected the way in which black film and video developed through the 1970s. However, it would be a mistake to push this line of argument too far, because in a very real sense the cultural milieu in which black film and video practitioners lived and worked during the sixties and seventies was largely incompatible with the culture of the white independent sector and its institutional support structure. Although they shared similar problems, such as funding, the white and black independents did not share the same preoccupation regarding film cultural theory. This was to come in the 1980s, with the emergence of a new generation of black film/video practitioners well-versed in issues of theory.

Black filmmaking as an oppositional (cultural) practice refers to the complex relationship between black-produced imagery and dominant representation. It is more than simply a matter of black filmmakers projecting "positive" images of black people, although this is an important consideration; it denotes the way in which historically black-related themes and imagery have been tied inextricably to the exegesis of "official" race-relations discourse. Documentary realism is particularly relevant in this context, not only because of its colonial legacy and the fact that it has been the principal form of dominant representations of "race" in Britain, but also because it has had a profound impact on the form and content of black British films and videos, both documentaries and narrative fiction. This is also one of the ways in which black films are marked off from other kinds of independent work, because institutionalized "race relations" has a marginalizing effect structurally and tends to reinforce rather than ameliorate the "otherness" of the subject—which documentary realism historically and representationally embodies. Within this set of relations, therefore, it has been difficult for black practitioners to evolve a cinematic approach which is largely unaffected by the determinants of race-relations discourse or which works outside documentary realism. This is not as negative as it sounds, however, because a closer look at the history of black films in Britain will reveal numerous instances of filmmakers manipulating, if not entirely subverting, the codes of race relations and multiculturalism, and constructing narratives which go some way toward critiquing the "official" discourse, mainly at the level of content, not form.

Nevertheless, it should be stressed that the propensity for creative cinematic expression, in terms of style and content, was strongly evident during a brief period in the early years of black independent filmmaking, i.e., prior to the institutionalization of British "race relations" which would eventually permeate all aspects of racial discourse and representation from the late 1960s onward. A good example is Lionel Ngakane's allegorical short film *Jemima and Johnnie* (1964), where the race-relations story is developed cinematically without the narrative being hamstrung by the racial theme. This charming film is one of the earliest attempts to seriously explore the dynamics of British "race relations" in narrative fiction from a black point of view, and its "rediscovery" several years ago reaffirmed the existence of an interesting history of black filmmaking in Britain. The story follows the exploits of two children—one black, the other white—who happily run off to play together in the streets, their "disappearance" causing the distressed parents to join in the search for them. The film used this simple but effective device to comment on the stupidity of racial intolerance, at a time when racial antagonisms were running high in Britain. The final image of unconditional friendship between the children, in contrast to the adults' uneasy interracial cooperation, struck an optimistic note, invoking the possibility of racial harmony in the face of growing prejudice and suspicion. Despite the "obviousness" of the story situation, the film achieves its effect not so much through the use of a stereotypical (racial) narrative, but as a result of Ngakane's marvelous sense of cinematic expression, which is clearly rooted in a quality of social realism prevalent in the British left-liberal independent film movement during the 1950s and 1960s.

In a similar vein, though with quite different intentions, Frankie Dymon Jr.'s "pop fantasy," *Death May Be Your Santa Claus* (1969), constructs a Dantesque narrative centering on a black hero's imaginary journey through a nightmarish world of political violence, alienation, and eventual self-rediscovery. The film draws heavily on the themes and imagery of sixties cultural politics like black power, Che Guevara, the underground movement, pop culture, "flower power," Vietnam, and so on, which are all worked into the nonrealist narrative in a typically iconoclastic manner. Interestingly, the film was inspired by the director's involvement (as an actor) in Jean-Luc Godard's British film *One Plus One*. While Dymon's iconoclasm is largely instinctive and "untheorized," it nevertheless exemplifies the degree to which early black practitioners were quite responsive to a wide range of cinematic techniques and practices. Of course this fascination with pure cinematic expression— which in this example touches on the avant-garde—completely disappeared by the early seventies, though, happily, aspects of it have reappeared in some recent works by the present generation of black film/video practitioners.

So, from these two quite different examples, we can see how early black film-making was not only inventive in its approach to political (racial) themes, but also sensitive to the creative film process itself. It's also worth mentioning in this context that while a number of the filmmakers were trained at the London Film School (now the London International Film School), renowned for its highly motivated students, the majority in fact received no such formal training, but worked in other disciplines like writing and acting. What they all shared in common was an immense enthusiasm for the medium, and a burning desire to extend their creative energies into this otherwise highly expensive art form. Significantly, there was little interest in straightforward documentary forms of filmmaking, and more in feature-length production with a somewhat commercial or entertainment orientation in mind. This did not mean the abandonment of serious social issues, however, but rather a desire to incorporate these kinds of themes into narrative fiction and on a fairly grand ("serious") scale. Interestingly, the Hollywood entertainment films (especially those with Sidney Poitier) and the European "art movies" both provided useful, albeit contradictory, models.

III

Although black filmmakers started to receive a degree of recognition by the early 1970s, institutional support for black films remained notably lacking, with only perhaps the occasional race-relations-supported project receiving significant funding from any major institution. However, a turning point came when the British Film Institute's Production Board funded Horace Ove's first feature, *Pressure* (1974), which was also the first British-made feature film by a black director. It is a classic "race-relations" drama which draws on a number of familiar themes, such as the "immigrant problem" and the problem of assimilation, and reworks them into the film's documentary-like fictional narrative. In the context of the 1970s, the story of a British-born black school-leaver's disillusionment and growing politicization as he encounters rampant racism and discrimination had a timely message which highlighted from a black perspective—perhaps for the first time in any British film—the contradictions and impossibilities inherent in the idea of "black British." In this respect, certain aspects of the film can be "read" as a critique of the race-relations "industry," which of course has been instrumental in "professionalizing" race relations, and of (British) society's failure to progress even in the light of a new generation of British-born black people who are patently not "immigrants" in the stereotypical race-relations sense.

Identity is a central theme in *Pressure* and is most sharply articulated in the context of the boy's family. Thus, the black family represents the site of intense intergenerational conflict, an archetypal theme in sociological race relations, with the conflict revolving around the British-born youth's precarious sense of "Britishness." The boy's unstable identity gradually disintegrates as the story progresses; he is pulled in two ideologically opposing directions. On the one hand, his "first-generation immigrant" parents, especially the mother, try to impose a set of values and expectations which are based on an ideal notion of the complete assimilation of their British-born progeny, while an opposing set of values is represented by the boy's Caribbean-born militant brother, who constantly chides him about his lifestyle and exposes the contradictions and futility in "trying to be like the English." The boy's angst is further compounded by his encounters in the outside world, which have a traumatic impact on his whole being and lead him inevitably to a "non-English," stridently black, identity position. Hence his politicization through his identification with the brother's values and the concomitant rejection of his parents' view of the world. Despite the apparent radicalness of this narrative, the film's closing image of black political protest is less progressive or "positive" than it might appear, being more pessimistic in effect. But a more serious criticism is the film's representation of women, which leaves much to be desired, particularly the image of the "misguided" mother figure who is identified as the cause of the family's "failure to make it in Britain," and that of the militant leader who "seduces" the boy into the movement. These stereotypical motifs betray the film's chauvinism and, in my view, effectively undermine any possibility of a more enlightened sense of gender relationships from being developed in the narrative.

Menelik Shabazz's *Burning an Illusion* (1981), the second black feature film funded by the British Film Institute, marked an important advance in terms of addressing questions of "race" and black cultural politics in black narrative fiction. It is not concerned with "race relations" as such, but focuses instead on interpersonal relationships within a black community setting, particularly between men and women, and how these relationships change with black consciousness and cultural politicization. Like *Pressure,* the narrative has a linear structure and centers on the political awakening of the central character, in this case a black woman, whose initial social conformity and political naivete gradually evolve into an active political consciousness. This political transformation is framed by the young woman's relationship with her proud-hearted boyfriend whose arrest, imprisonment, and ill treatment by the authorities propel her to "decolonize" her mind, as a black woman. Thus, she gradually strips herself of "bourgeois" values and identifications (e.g., the desire for conformist respectability) and begins to adopt a more strident black presence (e.g., her "straightened" hair becoming "locks"). In a sense, she changes her identity.

Whereas the identity crisis in *Pressure* centers largely on the dissolution of "black Britishness," in *Burning an Illusion* it is built around the notion of black identity being defined positively within its own terms of reference, that is, in relation to "the black community." The question of "Britishness," therefore, does not arise as a central issue. It has no real relevance in the context of the film's representation of black experiences. Consequently, racial victimization—i.e., the image of blacks as "victims," a familiar motif in race-relations discourse—is not a major concern here, despite its appearance at key moments in the story. Rather, it functions as a plot device which drives the narrative along, nothing more. Indeed, the police raid on the black club is presented as a given occurrence which needs no further development in terms of "race relations." Instead, the film uses this "moment" as a way of signaling how these kinds of racial antagonism have an impact upon relationships between black people within "the community," especially politically. In stressing these kinds of intraethnic or intrablack community concerns, *Burning an Illusion* helped to bring a more militant tone to representing black experiences in narrative fiction. It also captured much of the mood of a new generation of British blacks who would challenge the whole basis of British race relations by the early 1980s.

Pressure and *Burning an Illusion* are both landmark films, and they aptly reflect the major concerns of the periods in which they were made. Needless to say, the years separating them also indicate the extent to which black independent filmmaking has been marginalized in Britain, especially in terms of feature-film production. Ahmed Jamal's *Majdhar* (1984) and Horace Ove's *Playing Away* (1986) are the only other notable features that have come out of the black independent sector in recent years, although the latter might well qualify as a "mainstream" film by virtue of its million-pounds-plus budget! *Majdhar* is especially interesting because, like the two earlier black features, it focuses on the theme of (cultural) identity, although in an Asian context. The story concerns a young Pakistani woman who is forced to adopt a new lifestyle when she is abandoned by her unfaithful husband and left to fend for herself in Britain. Her new "independence" leads to a series of "discoveries" about the outside world, and after some anxious moments she gradually begins to adopt more "Western" (British) attitudes and lifestyles. While not having quite the same political thrust as *Burning an Illusion,* and being somewhat ambivalent about the morality of the central character's transformation, *Majdhar* is nonetheless an interesting film and, significantly, is similar in its essentially male-oriented representation of black women's identity and politicization.

IV

Of course none of these films really comes to grips with (black) women's political consciousness. At best, they deploy women characters as emblematic figures whose identities are constructed ultimately through men and through (black) male notions of politicized black femininity. Hence the significance of Sankofa's *The Passion of Remembrance* (1986), which not only signals the most recent break with conventional race relations and multicultural representation in British-made black films, but also takes on broad questions of gender and sexuality from a black "feminist" perspective. The "story" is constructed around a series of dramatic moments, in which characters' personal histories intertwine with the history of political protest in ways that defy simple explanations based on race politics alone. The film makes extensive use of archival footage, which is reprocessed and re-presented in the form of montages celebrating political struggle and solidarity. These documentary "moments" are framed by vignettes of black family life, social interactions, and relationships which cut across generational differences and highlight the diversity of black experiences. There is no homogeneous "black community" in this construction, only "black communities" in the explicitly plural sense.

The drama is set against the backdrop of crisis-ridden Britain in the 1980s, although it is not specifically concerned with the "British crisis." Rather, it uses this motif to develop the theme of black people living through and (re-)defining their identities for themselves, and not in relation to the dominant. This is built around the idea of historical memory and how our sense of the past—historic moments in black people's political struggle, for example—is brought to bear on the present. As the film's title suggests, these reverential moments of remembering are fraught with ambiguities and contradictions, in the sense that each successive generation seems to immortalize its own contributions to history and to imbue its own struggles with highly charged symbolism, which subsequent generations are compelled to live through. While acknowledging the importance of this often mythologized historical past, the film nevertheless invites us to reappraise precisely what it entails in terms of how black people define and experience their reality, psychically as well as politically, and to consider its implications for the future. Thus, the hitherto neglected subject of black women's role in political struggle—for example, the relationship between black women (the mythical tea-makers) and black men (the mythologized action figures)—becomes a crucial one which the film explores with lucid forcefulness. The result is an engaging critique of black political culture which, more than just redressing the gender balance in black narrative, goes a long way toward recasting black themes and imagery in a form otherwise absent in British film and television (racial) representation.

In the broader context of British independent cinema, it has to be stressed that this kind of formal experimentation with (black) narrative and representation could only be a main preoccupation within the grant-aided workshop sector, where political, cultural, aesthetic, and pedagogic debates are an integral part of film and video cultural practice. But it would be a mistake to therefore ignore the importance of non-workshop independents, or to evaluate their contributions pejoratively in comparison, just because of their relatively mainstream orientation. The fact is, this quasi-commercial sector is not "protected" or cushioned by a structure of grants and subsidies and, therefore, it is obliged to compete in the highly competitive commercial marketplace. By definition, the nature of their practice does not allow them the "space" for formal experimentation. Nevertheless, they have made important interventions in terms of penetrating mainstream media institutions—for example, in the area of employment in the film and television industries—and in that respect they have worked toward demarginalizing black film and television production. Moreover, despite growing institutional support for black film and video, cultural and professional marginalization remains a critical problem which affects black practitioners as a whole, irrespective of their individual creative or artistic proclivities. In other words, the whole of the black independent film/video sector is obliged to engage in some form of institutional struggle, in order to secure greater access to otherwise limited (and rapidly diminishing) resources.

This is partly the reason why recent initiatives around black film/video distribution and exhibition are so important, because in a very real sense these areas of film culture provide some chance of longevity for the black independent sector as a whole. Of course there is no sense in which we can conceive black audiences as a homogeneous entity, because in reality they are not. Therefore, black film and video practitioners are obliged to think seriously about ways of addressing these different (black) audiences, and about how to promote different kinds of black and Third World films generally. It is no longer simply a matter of showing the films, but rather building into film distribution and programming strategy some form of pedagogic practice, to enable audiences to participate directly in the cultural debates around black and Third World film cultures. Some work in this area has already begun, for example, in the screenings and distribution-related projects organized by a number

of workshops and other media-related black organizations. A number of white independent venues like regional film theaters are also beginning to make an effort to
include more black and Third World films in their programs. But perhaps the most
significant development in recent years has been the growing number of black community-based venues across the country—such as social clubs, community centers,
and cultural associations—which are becoming increasingly involved in film and
television exhibition and in other media education–related activities. In some respects, this has been one of the most fertile areas of growth within the black
film/video sector, encompassing a fairly broad constituency including both young
and older-generation black people. The emergence of these community-based
venues is also interesting because it represents a potentially stable network of exhibition outlets, where the whole range of film cultural issues can be taken up, debated,
and consolidated for the future.

These new developments clearly point to the emergence of a definable black film
and video sector in Britain, which encompasses not just production, but distribution,
exhibition, educational work, and critical practice as well. It is this sense of growing
cohesion, which has been evolving steadily since the early 1980s, that prompts one
to think in terms of an emerging black film culture, although we are still at an embry-
onic stage in this regard. Obviously the sector comprises disparate groups and practices, whose creative expressions are informed by different histories and cultural
experiences. But this should not detract from the real advances which have already
been made within the black independent film and video sector, and the impact that
they have had on the wider British cultural scene. And though the pervasive power of
dominant representation, along with that of institutional marginalization, has
tended to impose serious constraints on black film practice historically, e.g., by pi-
geonholing it in "race relations," the signs today are that these constraints are gradually being whittled away by black cultural practitioners themselves. Moreover, black
film/video practice clearly has a cultural dynamic of its own which cannot (and
should not) be reduced simply to the exegesis of oppositional practice. We therefore
need to begin developing critical methods which are capable of addressing this dynamic in fairly specific terms, and with the aim of securing the important relationship between the practitioner, the critic, and the audience in a much more
meaningful way.

Ten

De Margin
and De Center

*Isaac Julien
and Kobena Mercer*

Film culture in the eighties has been marked by volatile reconfigurations in the relations of "race" and representation. Questions of cultural difference, identity, and otherness—in a word, ethnicity—have been thrown into the foreground of contestation and debate by numerous shifts and developments. Within the British context, these trends have underpinned controversies around independent films like *Handsworth Songs, My Beautiful Laundrette,* and *The Passion of Remembrance*—films which have elicited critical acclaim and angry polemic in roughly equal measure. The fragmented state of the nation depicted from a black British point of view in the films themselves contradicts (literally, speaks against) the remythification of the colonial past in mainstream movies such as *Gandhi* or *A Passage to India*; yet, the wave of popular films set in imperial India or Africa also acknowledge, in their own way, Britain's postcolonial condition insofar as they speak to contemporary concerns. The competing versions of narrative, memory, and history in this conjuncture might be read symptomatically as a state of affairs that speaks of—articulates—conflicting identities within the "imagined community" of the nation.

In the international context, certain moments and trends suggest further shifts, adjustments, in the articulation of ethnicity *as* ideology. The ratings success-story of *The Cosby Show*—"number one" in South Africa as well as the United States—has fulfilled the innocent demand for "positive images" with a (neoconservative) vengeance. And the very *idea* of a Hollywood director like Steven Spielberg adapting the Alice Walker novel *The Color Purple* (in the context of the unprecedented publication of black women writers) still seems extraordinary, however commercially astute. In addition, the widening circulation of Third World films among Western audiences, or the televisual "presence" of Third World spaces like Ethiopia via events such as Live Aid in 1985, implies something of a shift within the boundaries that differentiated the First and Third Worlds.

One issue at stake, we suggest, is the potential break-up or deconstruction of structures that determine what is regarded as culturally central and what is regarded as culturally marginal. Ethnicity has emerged as a key issue as various "marginal" practices (black British film, for instance) are becoming demarginalized at a time when "centered" discourses of cultural authority and legitimation (such as notions of a transhistorical artistic "canon") are becoming increasingly decentered and destabilized, called into question from within. This scenario, described by Craig Owens as a crisis, "specifically of the authority vested in Western European culture and its institutions" (1985, 57), has of course already been widely discussed in terms of the characteristic aesthetic and political problems of postmodernism. However, it is ironic that while some of the loudest voices offering commentary have announced nothing less than the "end of representation" or the "end of history," the political possibility of the *end of ethnocentrism* has not been seized upon as a suitably exciting topic for description or inquiry.[1] We would argue, on the contrary, that critical theories are just *beginning* to recognize and reckon with the kinds of complexity inherent in the culturally constructed nature of ethnic identities, and the implications this has for the analysis of representational practices.

We chose to call this the "last special issue" [on race in *Screen*] as a rejoinder to critical discourses in which the subject of race and ethnicity is still placed on the margins conceptually, despite the acknowledgment of such issues indicated by the proliferation of "special issues" on race in film, media, and literary journals.[2] The prob-

1. The assertion of the "end" of everything is exemplified in Baudrillard 1984 and Burgin 1986. More considered reflections on postmodernism, which focus on the problems of its ethnocentrism, are offered by Hall 1986 and Huyssens 1987.

2. For instance, "Black Experiences," *Ten. 8* (Birmingham), no. 22 (1986); "'Race,' Writing, and Difference," *Critical Inquiry* (Chicago) 12, no. 3 (1985) and 13, no. 1 (1986); "The

lem, paradoxically, is that as an editorial strategy and as a mode of address, the logic of the "special issue" tends to reinforce, rather than ameliorate, the perceived otherness and marginality of the subject itself. There is nothing intrinsically different or "special" about ethnicity in film culture, merely that it makes fresh demands on existing theories, methods, and problematics. Rather than attempt to compensate the "structured absences" of previous paradigms, it would be useful to identify the relations of power/knowledge that determine which cultural issues are intellectually prioritized in the first place. The initial stage in any deconstructive project must be to examine and undermine the force of the binary relation that produces the marginal as a consequence of the authority invested in the center.

At a concrete level the politics of marginalization is an underlying issue in the overview of black filmmaking in Europe sketched by Maureen Blackwood and June Givanni. The negotiation of access to resources in training, production, and distribution emerges as a common factor facing practitioners in a migrant or "minority" situation. While highlighting the different conditions stemming from the colonial past, the comparative dimension also draws attention to the specificity of British conditions in the present, where black filmmaking has flourished in the state-subsidized "independent" sector. Data compiled by June Givanni elsewhere[3] indicates some of the characteristics that constitute black British film as a "minor" cinema: the prevalence of material of short duration, shot on video, and in the documentary genre, indicates a pattern of underfunding, or rather, taking the variety of work into consideration, a considerable cultural achievement that has been won against the odds of meager resourcing. Moreover, shifts in the institutional framework of public funding in the U.K. were brought about in the eighties as a result of a wider social and political struggle to secure black rights to representation. It was said at the time of the 1981 "riots" that this was the only way in which those excluded from positions of power and influence could make themselves heard: in any case, the events were read and widely understood as expressing protest at the structural marginalization of the black presence in British public institutions.

The consequent demand for *black representation* thus informed shifts in multicultural and "equal opportunity" policy among institutions such as Channel Four, the British Film Institute, and local authorities such as the Greater London Council. More generally, this took place in the context of a rearticulation of the category "black" as a political term of identification among diverse minority communities of

---

Inappropriate Other," *Discourse* (Berkeley), no. 8 (1986); "Colonialism," *Oxford Literary Review* 9 (1987); and "The Nature and Context of Minority Discourse," parts 1 and 2, *Cultural Critique* (Minneapolis) (spring and fall 1987).

3. Compiled by Givanni and edited by North (1988); a transatlantic comparison is offered by Snead 1988.

Asian, African, and Caribbean origin, rather than as a biological or "racial" category. Together, these aspects of the cultural politics of "black representation" informed the intense debates on aesthetic and cinematic strategies within the black British independent sector. Far from homogenizing these differences, the concept has been the site of contestation, highlighted in numerous events and conferences, such as "Third Film Cinema" at the Edinburgh International Film Festival in 1986 and, more recently, the conference "Black Film/British Cinema" at the Institute of Contemporary Arts in London.[4] It has become apparent that what is at stake in the debates on "black representation" is not primarily a dispute over realist or modernist principles, but a broader problematic in cultural politics shaped, as Paul Gilroy suggests, by the tension between representation as a practice of depiction and representation as a practice of delegation.[5] Representational democracy, like the classic realist text, is premised on an implicitly mimetic theory of representation as correspondence with the "real": notionally, the political character of the state is assumed to "correspond" to the aspiration of the masses in society. However, not unlike the civil disruptions, aspects of the new wave in black British filmmaking have interrupted these relations of representation: in cinematic terms the challenge to documentary realism that features so prominently in more recent work, such as *Territories,* is predicated on a relational conception of representation as a practice of selection, combination, and articulation. At a textual level, such shifts have contested the hegemony of documentary realism underlying the formal codification of what Jim Pines calls the master discourse of the "race-relations narrative."[6] This also entails awareness of extratextual factors, such as funding, as important determinants on black filmmaking and its modes of enunciation, such as "the moral imperative which usually characterises black films, which empowers them to speak with a sense of urgency," as John Akomfrah of Black Audio Film Collective has put it.[7]

What is at issue in this problematic is the question of power, as Judith Williamson argues in her review of *The Passion of Remembrance:* "The more power any group has to create and wield representations, the less it is required to *be* representative."[8] Where access and opportunities are rationed, so that black films tend to get made only one-at-a-time, each film text is burdened with an inordinate pressure to be

4. Symposia organized by the Greater London Council in 1985 are documented in *Third Eye* 1986; the Edinburgh conference is documented in Pines and Willemen 1989; and the ICA conference is documented in Mercer 1988.
5. See Gilroy 1988 and Bourdieu 1984–85, 56–70.
6. See Pines, this volume, chap. 9, and Mercer 1988.
7. In Gilroy and Pines 1988, 11.
8. *New Statesman,* 5 December 1986.

"representative" and to act, as a delegate does, as a statement that "speaks" for the black communities as a whole. Martina Attille, producer of the film, suggests that the "sense of urgency to say it all" stems less from the artistic choices made by black filmmakers and more from the material constraints in which "sometimes we only get the *one* chance to make ourselves heard" (1986, 101). Contemporary shifts have brought these problems into view, for as Williamson adds, in relation to the invisible demand to be "representative" implicit in the rationing and rationalization of public funding, "what is courageous in Sankofa's project is that they have chosen to speak *from*, but not *for*, black experience(s) in Britain."

Marginality circumscribes the enunciative modalities of black film as cinematic discourse and imposes a double bind on black subjects who speak in the public sphere: if only *one* voice is given the "right to speak," that voice will be heard, by the majority culture, as "speaking for" the *many* who are excluded or marginalized from access to the means of representation. This of course underlines the problem of tokenism: the very idea that a single film could "speak for" an entire community of interests reinforces the perceived secondariness of that community. The double bind of expedient inclusion as a term for the legitimation of more general forms of exclusionary practice is also the source of a range of representational problems encountered not just by black subjects, but by other groups marginalized into minority status. In the gay documentary *Word Is Out* (Mariposa Film Group, 1978) the nature of this problematic is pointed out in a performative mode by a black woman who carefully describes the predicament she is placed in as a result of the editing strategy of the text:

> What I was trying to say when I asked you if I would be the only black lesbian in the film is: do you know we come in all shapes and colours and directions to our lives? Are you capturing that on the film? As a black lesbian-feminist involved in the movement, so often people try to put me in the position of speaking for all black lesbians. I happen to be *a* black lesbian among many, and I wouldn't want to be seen as *this is how all black lesbians are.* (Adair and Adair 1978, 203)

Within such a regime of representation, the restricted economy of ethnic enunciation is a political problem for at least two important reasons. First, individual subjectivity is denied because the black subject is positioned as a mouthpiece, a ventriloquist for an entire social category which is seen to be "typified" by its representative. Acknowledgment of the *diversity* of black experiences and subject positions is thereby foreclosed. Thus, second, where minority subjects are framed and contained by the monologic terms of "majority discourse," the fixity of boundary relations between center and margin, universal and particular, returns the speaking subject to the ideologically appointed place of the stereotype—that "all black people are the same."

Stuart Hall's account of the shifts taking place in contemporary black British cultural production offers a means of making sense of the "politics of representation" at issue here. His argument that current shifts demand the recognition of the "end of the innocent notion of the essential black subject" enables us to analyze and unpack the burden of racial representation. The recognition that "black" is a politically and culturally constructed category, and that our metaphorical fictions of "white" and "black" are not fixed by Nature but by historical formations of hegemony, brings into play "the recognition of the immense diversity and differentiation of the historical and cultural experiences of black subjects." This has major consequences for the critical evaluation of different aesthetic and discursive strategies that articulate race at the level of language and representation.

> Films are not necessarily good because black people make them. They are not necessarily "right-on" by virtue of the fact that they deal with the black experience. Once you enter the politics of the end of the essential black subject you are plunged headlong into the maelstrom of a continuously contingent, unguaranteed, political argument and debate: a critical politics, a politics of criticism. You can no longer conduct black politics through the strategy of a simple set of reversals, putting in the place of the bad old essential white subject, the new essentially good black subject. (Hall, this volume, chap. 7; see also chap. 5)

The deconstruction of binary relations thus entails the relativization and rearticulation of "ethnicity." This is an important *enabling* argument as it brings a range of critical issues into an explanatory structure, however tentative.

At one level, it contextualizes Salman Rushdie's point, expressed in his polemic against *Handsworth Songs,* that "celebration makes us lazy."[9] Because black films have been so few and far between, up till now, there has been a tendency to "celebrate" the fact that they ever got made at all; but this has inhibited the formulation of criticism and self-criticism and perpetuated the moral masochism of "correctness" so pervasive in oppositional "left" cultural politics (especially in Britain). Judith Williamson takes up this point and argues that the moralism of being ideologically "right-on" has been conflated with aesthetic judgment and thus the formal properties of the recent "experimental" films have been subsumed into their "blackness" (that is, the racial identity of the authors), giving the films an "aura of untouchability" that further preempts critical analysis. The problem which arises is that such responses threaten to frame the films as merely replacing the avant-garde

9. "*Songs* Doesn't Know the Score," *Guardian,* 12 January 1987.

(as the "latest thing") rather than as displacing the orthodoxies that have led the Euro-American vanguard (especially its formalist variant) into its current stasis. At another level, Perminder Dhillon-Kashyap argues that the debates on black British film have in turn made Asian experiences and interventions "secondary," thus risking the replication of essentialist versions of race precisely when the rearticulation of subaltern ethnicities as "black" seeks to undermine the "ethnic absolutism" (anchoring the culturalist terms of the "new racism" that fixes hybridized experiences in terms of alien cultures).[10] Coco Fusco's assessment of two major conferences in the U.S. examines the way in which two kinds of essentialist tendency, manifest in the contradictory reception of black British film, mutually forestall the politics of criticism. The impetus to "celebrate" black cinema, on the one hand, invokes a unitary notion of blackness that precludes elucidation of "internal" differences and diversity. The desire to "correct" the omissions of the past within the Western avantgarde, on the other hand, has led to a one-sided fixation with ethnicity as something that "belongs" to the other alone: thus white ethnicity is not under question and retains its "centered" position; more to the point, the white subject remains the central reference point in the power ploys of multicultural policy. The burden of representation thus falls on the other, because as Fusco argues, "to ignore white ethnicity is to redouble its hegemony by naturalizing it."

While such discursive events acknowledge contemporary shifts, their logic evades the implications of Hall's insight that the point of contestation is no longer between multiculturalism and antiracism, but *inside* the concept of ethnicity itself. Within dominant discourses, "ethnicity" is structured into a negative equivalence with essentialist versions of "race" and "nation" which particularize its referent, as the pejorative connotation of "ethnic minority" implies (*who*, after all, constitutes the "ethnic majority"?). On the other hand, just as it was necessary to reappropriate the category "black," Hall argues that "ethnicity" is a strategically *necessary* concept because it

> acknowledges the place of history, language, and culture in the construction of subjectivity and identity, as well as the fact that all discourse is placed, positioned, situated, and all knowledge is contextual. Representation is possible only because enunciation is always produced within codes that have a history, a position within the discursive formations of a particular space and time. (This volume, chap. 7)

In this sense, "we are all *ethnically* located," but the cultural specificity of white ethnicity has been rendered "invisible" by the epistemic violence that has, historically,

10. Discursive formations of British racism are discussed in Gilroy (1991), where he proposes the concept of syncretism to examine cultural resistance in the "hybridized" context of black Britain (see esp. chap. 5, "Diaspora, Utopia, and the Critique of Capitalism").

disavowed difference in Western discourses. The rearticulation of ethnicity as an epistemological category thus involves

> The displacement of the *centered* discourses of the West [and] entails putting into question its universalist character and its transcendental claims to speak for everyone, while being itself everywhere and nowhere.

Richard Dyer's article "White" inaugurates a paradigmatic shift by precisely registering the reorientation of "ethnicity" that Hall's argument calls for. Dyer shows how elusive white ethnicity is as a representational construct (and the difficulties this presents for constituting it as a theoretical object of analysis) and notes, "Black is, in the realm of categories, always marked as a colour . . . is always particularising; whereas white is not anything really, not an identity, not a particularising quality, because it is everything." In other words, whiteness has secured universal consent to its hegemony as the "norm" by masking its coercive force with the invisibility that marks off the other (the pathologized, the disempowered, the dehumanized) as all too visible—*colored*.[11] Significantly, in relation to the films that Dyer discusses, whiteness only tends to become visible when its hegemony is under contestation.

The complex range of problems now coming into view in film studies around the site of ethnicity, partly as a result of developments elsewhere in literary and social theory,[12] enables a more adequate understanding of contemporary forms of contestation. The "differences" between various black independent film practices have, to some extent, been overplayed, as the key underlying objective across each of the strategies is to displace the binary relation of the burden of representation, most clearly pinpointed by Horace Ove (1987):

> Here in England there is a danger, if you are black, that all you are allowed to make is films about black people and their problems. White film-makers on the other hand, have a right to make films about whatever they like.

Theoretically, the displacement of binarisms has been most important in the analysis of stereotyping—the marginalization of ethnicity has been held in place by the logical impasse of the "positive/negative" image polarity. *Screen* has contributed

11. The term "people of color" operates in the U.S. as a political term analogous to "black" in the British context. In both instances, such terms have engendered intense semantic ambiguity and ideological anxiety as the racial mythology of "color" is put *under erasure,* canceled out but still legible, in a deconstructive logic that depends on the same system of metaphorical equivalences and differences. Semantic determinacy as a condition of political contestation is discussed in Laclau and Mouffe 1985.

12. See Hall, this volume, chap. 1; Said 1978 and 1984; Spivak 1987; West 1986; "Race and Social Theory," in Davis et al. 1987; "Marxist Theory and the Specificity of Afro-American Oppression," in Nelson and Grossberg 1988.

to the productive displacement of this stasis in a number of ways: from Steve Neale's analysis of the impossibility of the "perfect image" sought by idealist and realist arguments, to Homi Bhabha's influential reading of colonial discourse, which emphasizes the psychic ambivalence, the fear and fascination, that informs the "Manichaean delirium" of classical regimes of racial representation (Neale 1979–80, 32–33; Bhabha 1983, 18–36). However, the range of textual readings here suggests that we need to go much further toward a reflexive examination of the mutual inscription of self and other in the analysis of ethnic boundaryness. This involves questioning the way that, during its "centered" role in the discursive formation of film theory during the 1970s, *Screen* participated in a phase of British left culture that inadvertently marginalized race and ethnicity as a consequence of the centrifugal tendency of its "high theory."

During this period, one was more likely to encounter the analysis of racial stereotyping in sociology than cultural theory, where class and gender took precedence in debates on ideology and subjectivity.[13] Furthermore, without imputing maleficent intentions (because such relations are beyond the control of individual intentionality), it can be said that even within *Screen*'s important acknowledgment of ethnic difference in previous "special issues,"[14] the explanatory concept of "otherness" distances and particularizes ethnicity as something that happens far away, either in the U.S. or in the Third World.[15] Space prohibits an adequate exploration of the intellectual milieu that *Screen* helped to form, but recent comments on the institutionalization of film studies have argued that "*Screen* theory," so-called, came to function as a kind of corporate "name of the father," a "theoretical superego" or even a "phallic mother"—a centered point of reference that, like a doctrine or orthodoxy, featured a number of "disciplinary" characteristics.[16] Jane Gaines recalls that, in the translation of "*Screen* theory" into the North American academic environment in the seventies, leftist enthusiasm for theoretical "correctness" was heard to speak in an unmistakably English accent.

13. In both Weberian and Marxist variants, see Husband 1975 and Hall et al. 1978. Cultural struggles over media racism are documented in Cohen and Gardener 1982. CARM's BBC *Open Door* program is discussed in Hall et al. 1981.

14. "Racism, Colonialism, and the Cinema," *Screen* (London) 24, no. 2 (March/April 1983), and "Other Criticisms," *Screen* (London) 26, nos. 3–4 (May–August 1985).

15. Black British perspectives have rarely been featured in *Screen*, but see Carby 1980, 62–70; Gilroy 1983, 130–36; and Crusz, this volume, chap. 4.

16. The description of a "theoretical superego" in film studies is made by Paul Willemen (1982 and 1987). The characterization of orthodoxies in terms of the demand of a "phallic mother" is made by Lesley Stern (1988) in her tribute to Claire Johnston. An interesting case of another translation, this time in the postcolonial periphery, is produced by Felicity Collins (1982).

This background is important because what emerges in the current situation is not a "new" problematic, but a critical *return* to issues unwittingly "repressed" in some of the "old" problematics and debates. It would be useful, therefore, to tentatively draw out some of the directions in which the field is being remapped and in which the lacunae of previous paradigms are excavated.

First, the analysis of ethnic binarisms at the level of narrative codes returns to the question of how dominant ideologies naturalize their domination, underlying previous debates on the classic realist text. Clyde Taylor's intertextual examination of racialized repetition across two "epic" Hollywood films suggests that the ethnic iconography that drives the reproduction of racist ideology is not simply indicative of capitalist commodification or a bourgeois world view. *Star Wars*, argues Taylor, repeats the "blood and purity" mythology of *The Birth of a Nation,* not as a defiant assertion of Wasp "superiority" but as an embattled recoding of the master text in response to the encroaching presence of the Third World. The racial discourse subtextualized by binary oppositions acknowledges the crises of (U.S.) hegemony. The "liberal" inflections in the films discussed by Richard Dyer also acknowledge the destabilization of prevailing race relations, albeit within a different set of generic and narrative conventions. Common to both readings is a concern to "typify" textual structures that position racial and ethnic signifiers in the fixed relation of a binary opposition, whether it be one of antagonism, accommodation, or subordination.

There is, in addition, a historical emphasis that relativizes the kinds of claims once extrapolated from the formal structures of the CRT, as it was known. Aspects of Bhabha's theorization of the stereotype in colonial discourse replicate this transhistorical or dehistoricized emphasis.[17] The move toward a more context-oriented view, on the other hand, indicates that although dominant discourses are characterized by closure, they are not themselves closed but constantly negotiated and restructured by the conjuncture of discourses in which they are produced. The way in which ethnic "types" are made afresh in contemporary movies like *An Officer and a Gentleman* and *Angel Heart*—or more generally in current advertising—demands such a conjunctural approach. The theory of the stereotype cannot be abandoned as it also needs to be able to explain how and why certain ethnic stereotypes are at times recirculated, in the British context, in the work of black film and television authors.[18]

Second, there is a note of caution about reproducing binarisms at the level of theory. Cameron Bailey's reading of the accretion of "ethnic" signifiers around the

17. Methods employed by Homi Bhabha and Gayatri Spivak are the subject of a critique by Benita Parry (1987).

18. An issue raised in Jim Pines's 1981 reading of sociological stereotypes in Horace Ove's *Pressure* (1975). Some of the paradoxical consequences of documentary realism in black independent film are also discussed in Mercer 1988.

construction of (white) femininity as a source of pleasure and danger in *Something Wild* demonstrates that, rather than the familiar "race, class, gender" mantra, analysis needs to take account of the intersections of differences, in particular of the representation of sexuality as a recurring site upon which categories of race and gender intersect. Feminist theories of the fetishistic logic inherent in the sexualization of gender-difference have provided an invaluable inventory for the reading of the eroticized othering of the black (male and female) subject. Yet, as Jane Gaines argues, the gender binarism implicit in the heterosexist presumption so often unwittingly reproduced in feminist film theory, or FFT (the acronym already indicates an orthodoxy), remains "color blind" to the racial hierarchies that structure mastery over the "look." The scenario voyeurism, sadism, and the objectification played out across Diana Ross's star image in *Mahogany* enacts a patriarchal discourse of masculine "desire," but also demands a historical understanding of the pretextual and the contextual discourses of race that placed the black woman in the "paradox of nonbeing"—a reference to the period in Afro-American history when the black female did not signify "woman" on account of the racial ideology that made the black subject less than human.

The historical violation of black bodies in social formations structured by slavery gives rise to a discourse (encoded in both the rationalization of and resistance to such premodern forms of power as lynching) which has indeed the countervailing force to rival the problematic of castration rhetorically placed at the center of psychoanalytic theory by the Oedipal grand narrative. Just as lesbian critiques of FFT have questioned the explanatory capacity of Freudian and Lacanian theory to account for the inscription of female pleasure and desire[19]—demonstrating the contradictory subject positions occupied by different spectators—the reorientation of the spectatorship problematic in the articles by Gaines and Manthia Diawara identifies the ethnocentrism of psychoanalytic discourse as a barrier to further inquiry. Both question the universalist claims anchored in the Oedipus story and imply that uncritical adherence to psychoanalytic theory (however enabling as a method) risks the disavowal of its Eurocentric "authority"; Freud closes his essay on fetishism by commenting that the acknowledgment and disavowal of difference "might be seen in the Chinese custom of mutilating the female foot and then revering it like a fetish after it has been mutilated" (1977, 357)—surely this culturebound aesthetic judgment is the starting point for a more circumspect appropriation of psychoanalytic theory.

Diawara identifies the mythic "castration" and "visual punishment" of the black male as a term of the "narrative pleasures" offered by Hollywood spectacle

19. See Stacey 1987, 48–61; reprinted in a slightly different version in Gamman and Marshment 1988.

(and also as a narratological term of closure, analogous to the "punishment" of feminine transgression in film noir). By raising the issue of spectatorial resistance, Diawara opens up an interesting question about the place of the black spectator in the ideological machinery of interpellation. How is the black subject sutured into a place that includes it only as a term of negation? *What* does the black spectator identify with when his/her mirror image is structurally absent or present only as other? In the past, it was assumed that all social subjects acceded to the narcissistic pleasure of the "mirror phase" in their misrecognition of themselves as the subject of enunciation, returned thus as normalized and passified "subjects" of ideological subjection (this was the basis of Barthes's distinction [1975] between "pleasure" and "bliss"). But what if certain social categories of spectator do not have access, as it were, to the initial moment of *recognition?* The question of how black subjects psychically manage to make identifications with white images is thus signposted as an important area for further inquiry.[20] Perhaps one reason why, for example, *The Cosby Show* is so popular among black audiences is that it affords the pleasure of a basic or primary narcissism even though it interpellates the minority subject, in particular, into ideological normalization.[21] A contemporary black star, like Eddie Murphy—popular with both white and black audiences—offers another source of "bad pleasure," partly on account of the pastiche of the stereotype that he performs in his star-image as the street-credible, but ideologically unthreatening, macho loudmouth.

This is also where class comes back into the calculation of difference. An appreciation of differentiated regimes of racial representation necessitates acknowledgment of different audiences or, taken together, recognition of the different forms of ideological articulation characteristic of First and Second Cinemas, as described by the concept of Third Cinema.[22] The inscription of ethnic indeterminacy does not take place "inside" the text, as if it were hermetically sealed, but in-between the relations of author, text, and reader specific to the construction of different discursive formations. Blackness is not always a sign of racial codification (as the term "film

20. This again is by no means a "new" topic. The starting point for James Baldwin's autobiographical reflections on cinema is his adolescent identification with Bette Davis's star image; see Baldwin 1976, pp. 4–7.

21. *The Cosby Show* is the subject of two conflicting readings—as a "breakthrough" and as a "sell-out": cf. Mel Cummings's "Black Family Interactions on Television," presented at the International Television Studies Conference, London, 1986, and Pat Skinner's "Moving Way Up: Television's 'New Look' at Blacks," presented at the International Television Studies Conference, London, 1988. Both ITSC conferences were sponsored by the British Film Institute and the Institute of Education, University of London.

22. The concept of "Third Cinema" was originally sponsored by Fernando Solanas and Octavio Gettino (1976). It has been subsequently expanded, with particular reference to African cinema, by Teshome Gabriel (1982).

noir" admits): its representational aura in auteurist and avant-garde traditions conventionally serves to mark off the status of the author (as white subject of enunciation) in relation to the discourse authorized in the text (as black subject of the statement). Ethnic alterity is a consistent trope of modernist differentiation in various Euro-American canons: the play of black signs that inscribe the authorial voice self-referentially in Jonathan Demme's *Something Wild* can be seen as drawing on elements of the romanticist image-reservoir, where blackness is valorized as emblematic of outsiderness and oppositionality, that might be read off Jean Genet's *Chant d'amour* (1953), Jean-Luc Godard's *One Plus One/Sympathy for the Devil* (1969), or Laura Mulvey and Peter Wollen's *Riddles of the Sphinx* (1976). This arbitrary list (indexing disparate debates on independent filmmaking)[23] is made merely to point out another set of questions; namely, how to differentiate diverse appropriations of the same stock of signs and meanings built up around different discursive formations of "race" and ethnicity? This question bears upon the broader underlying issue of the multiaccentual nature of the signs characteristic of the flashpoints of ideological contestation and cultural struggle.[24] It also alludes to the paradox identified in Richard Dyer's reading of Paul Robeson as a cinematic icon that meant different things to racially differentiated readers:

> Black and white discourses on blackness seem to be valuing the same things—spontaneity, emotion, naturalness—yet giving them a different implication. Black discourses see them as contributions to the development of society, white as enviable qualities that only blacks have. (1987, 79)

The issue of "envy" confirms that white identifications are as problematic (conceptually) as the ability of black readers—or readers of subaltern status—to appropriate alternative "subtextual" readings from the racial discourse of dominant cultural texts. *King Kong*—to cite one of the most centered mythologies of modern popular cinema—has been read as the tragic story of a heroic beast and/or the fate of a black man punished for the transgressive coupling with the white woman that he/the monster desires. These questions appear to be "new," hence very difficult, yet we have returned, by a rather circuitous route, to the hotly contested terrain of the

23. Jean Genet's film is the subject of intense debate in the Cultural Identities seminar "Sexual Identities: Questions of Difference," in *Undercut* (London), no. 17 (1988). Maxine, the black woman in *Riddles of the Sphinx*, is identified as a signifier of "dark continent" mythology in Judith Williamson's critique of the film (1986, 134). Frankie Dymon Jr. was involved in Godard's *One Plus One* and subsequently directed his own film, *Death May Be Your Santa Claus* (1969), described as a "pop fantasy" by Jim Pines (this volume, chap. 9).

24. Identified as indicative of class struggle in Volosinov 1973. From another point of view, similar concepts are explored by Homi Bhabha (1988, 20–22) in a reinterpretation of Frantz Fanon's *Wretched of the Earth* (1970).

debates on class and culture, hegemony and subjectivity that were territorialized with such passion in the mid seventies.[25] We must conclude that this cannot possibly be the last word on "race" as these complicated issues are only now coming into view as a result of the critical dialogue that has engaged with the blind spots and insights of earlier conversations. And further, that such dialogism is a necessary discursive condition for understanding contestation in film culture and other formations of cultural practice and cultural politics.

25. See Coward 1977, 75–105, and for a response, Chambers 1977–78, 109–19. On authorship, enunciation, and textual analysis, see Willemen 1978, 41–69. And on critiques of "*Screen* theory" from the Centre for Contemporary Cultural Studies, see Morley 1980 and Hall et al. 1980.

Works Cited

Adair, N., and C. Adair, eds. 1978. *Word Is Out: Stories of Some of Our Lives.* New York: New Glide/Delta.

Attille, M. 1986. "The Passion of Remembrance: Background and Interview with Sankofa." *Framework* (London), no. 32/33.

Baldwin, J. 1976. *The Devil Finds Work.* London: Michael Joseph.

Barthes, R. 1975. *The Pleasure of the Text.* New York: Hill and Wang.

Baudrillard, J. 1984. *Simulations.* New York: Semiotext(e).

Bhabha, H. 1983. "The Other Question: The Stereotype and Colonial Discourse." *Screen* (London) 24, no. 6 (November–December).

———. 1988. "The Commitment to Theory." *New Formations* (London), no. 5.

Bourdieu, P. 1984–85. "Delegation and Political Fetishism." *Thesis Eleven* (Sydney), no. 10/11.

Burgin, V. 1986. *The End of Art Theory.* London: Macmillan.

Carby, H. 1980. "Multiculture." *Screen Education* (London), no. 34 (spring).

Chambers, I. 1977–78. "Marxism and Culture." *Screen* (London) 18, no. 4 (winter).

Cohen, P., and C. Gardner, eds. 1982. *It Ain't Half Racist, Mum.* London: Comedia/Campaign against Racism in the Media.

Collins, F. 1982. "The Australian Journal of Screen Theory." *Framework* (London), no. 24.

Coward, R. 1977. "Class, 'Culture,' and the Social Formation." *Screen* (London) 18, no. 1 (spring).

Davis, M., et al., eds. 1987. *The Year Left 2.* London: Verso.

Diawara, Manthia. 1988. "Black Spectatorship: Problems of Identification and Resistance." *Screen* (London) 29 (Autumn).

Dyer, R. 1987. "Paul Robeson: Crossing Over." In *Heavenly Bodies: Film Stars and Society.* London: British Film Institute/Macmillan.

———. 1988. "White: The Representation of Whiteness as an Ethnic Category in Mainstream Film." *Screen* (London) 29 (Autumn).

Freud, S. 1977. "Fetishism." In *On Sexuality*. Pelican Freud Library, vol. 7. Harmondsworth: Penguin.

Gabriel, T. 1982. *Third Cinema in the Third World: The Aesthetics of Liberation*. Ann Arbor: UMI Research Press.

Gaines, Jane. 1988. "White Privilege and Looking Relations: Race and Gender in Feminist Film Theory." *Screen* (London) 29 (Autumn).

Gamman, L., and M. Marshment, eds. 1988. *The Female Gaze*. London: Women's Press.

Gilroy, P. 1983. "C4—Bridgehead or Bantustan?" *Screen* (London) 24, nos. 4–5 (July–October).

———. 1988. "Nothing but Sweat inside My Hand: Diaspora Aesthetics and Black Arts in Britain." In *Black Film/British Cinema*, ed. K. Mercer. ICA Document 7. London: Institute of Contemporary Arts/British Film Institute Production Special.

———. 1991. *There Ain't No Black in the Union Jack*. London: Hutchinson, 1987. Reprint, Chicago: University of Chicago Press.

Gilroy, P., and J. Pines. 1988. "Handsworth Songs: Audiences/Aesthetics/Independence." An interview with Black Audio Film Collective. *Framework* (London), no. 35.

Givanni, J., and N. North. 1988. *Black and Asian Film List*. London: British Film Institute Education.

Hall, S. 1986. "On Postmodernism and Articulation." An interview edited by Lawrence Grossberg. *Communications Inquiry* (Iowa City) 10, no. 2.

Hall, S., et al. 1978. *Policing the Crisis*. London: Macmillan.

———. 1980. "Recent Developments in Theories of Language and Ideology: A Critical Note." In *Culture, Media, Language*, ed. S. Hall et al. London: Hutchinson.

———. 1981. "The Whites of Their Eyes: Racist Ideologies and the Media." In *Silver Linings: Some Strategies for the Eighties*, ed. G. Bridges and R. Brunt. London: Lawrence and Wishart.

Husband, C. 1975. *White Media and Black Britain*. London: Arrow.

Huyssens, A. 1987. "Mapping the Post-Modern." In *After the Great Divide*. London: Macmillan.

Laclau, E., and C. Mouffe. 1985. *Hegemony and Socialist Strategy*. London: Verso.

Mercer, K. 1988. "Diaspora Culture and the Dialogic Imagination: The Aesthetics of Black Independent Film in Britain." In *Blackframes: Critical Perspectives on Black Independent Cinema*, ed. M. Cham and C. Andrade-Watkins. Cambridge: MIT Press.

———, ed. 1988. *Black Film/British Cinema*. ICA Document 7. London: Institute of Contemporary Arts/British Film Institute Production Special.

Morley, D. 1980. "Texts, Readers, Subjects." In *Culture, Media, Language*, ed. S. Hall et al. London: Hutchinson.

Neale, S. 1979–80. "The Same Old Story: Analysis, Stereotypes, and Difference." *Screen Education* (London), nos. 32–33 (autumn/winter).

Nelson, C., and L. Grossberg, eds. 1988. *Marxism and the Interpretation of Culture*. London: Macmillan.

Ove, H. 1987. Interview with Sylvia Paskin. *Monthly Film Bulletin* (London) 54, no. 647.

Owens, C. 1985. "The Discourse of Others: Feminists and Post-Modernism." *Postmodern Culture,* ed. H. Foster. London: Pluto Press.

Parry, B. 1987. "Problems in Current Theories of Colonial Discourse." *Oxford Literary Review* 9.

Pines, J. 1981. "Blacks in Films: The British Angle." *Multiracial Education* (London) 9, no. 2.

Pines, J., and P. Willemen, eds. 1989. *Third Cinema: Theories and Practices.* London: British Film Institute.

Said, E. 1978. *Orientalism.* London: Routledge.

———. 1984. *The World, the Text, and the Critic.* London: Faber and Faber.

Snead, J. 1988. "Black Independent Film: Britain and America." In *Black Film/British Cinema,* ed. K. Mercer. ICA Document 7. London: Institute of Contemporary Arts/British Film Institute Production Special.

Solanas, F., and O. Gettino. 1976. "Towards a Third Cinema." In *Movies and Methods,* ed. B. Nichols. Berkeley: University of California Press.

Spivak, G. 1987. *In Other Worlds.* London: Methuen.

Stacey, J. 1987. "Desperately Seeking Difference." *Screen* (London) 28, no. 1 (winter).

Stern, L. 1988. "Remembering Claire Johnston." *Film News* (Sydney), no. 35.

Taylor, Clyde. 1988. The Master Text and the Jeddi Doctrine; Comparisons between the *Star Wars* trilogy and *Birth of a Nation.*" *Screen* (London) 29 (Autumn).

Third Eye: Struggles for Black and Third World Cinema. 1986. London: Greater London Council, Race Equality Unit.

Volosinov, V. 1973. *Marxism and the Philosophy of Language.* New York: Seminar Press.

West, C. 1986. "The Dilemma of a Black Intellectual." *Cultural Critique* (New York) 1, no. 1.

Willemen, P. 1978. "Notes on Subjectivity—On Reading Edward Branigan's 'Subjectivity under Seige.'" *Screen* (London) 19, no. 1 (spring).

———. 1982. "An Avant-Garde for the Eighties." *Framework* (London), no. 24.

———. 1987. "The Third Cinema Question: Notes and Reflections." *Framework* (London), no. 34.

Williamson, J. 1986. "Two or Three Things We Know about Ourselves." In *Consuming Passions.* London: Calder and Boyars.

Eleven

Cultural Identity and Cinematic Representation

Stuart Hall

Both the new "Caribbean cinema," which has now joined the company of the other "Third Cinemas," and the emerging cinemas of Afro-Caribbean blacks in the "diasporas" of the West, put the issue of cultural identity in question. Who is this emergent, new subject of the cinema? From where does it speak? The practices of representation always implicate the positions from which we speak or write—the positions of *enunciation*. What recent theories of enunciation suggest is that, though we speak, so to say "in our own name," of ourselves and from our own experience, nevertheless who speaks, and the subject who is spoken of, are never exactly in the same place. Identity is not as transparent or unproblematic as we think. Perhaps, instead of thinking of identity as an already accomplished historical fact, which the new cinematic discourses then represent, we should think, instead, of identity as a "production," which is never complete, always in process, and always constituted within, not outside, representation. But this view problematizes the very authority and authenticity to which the term "cultural identity" lays claim.

In this paper, then, I seek to open a dialogue, an investigation, on the subject of cultural identity and cinematic representation. The "I" who writes here must also be thought of as itself "enunciated." We all write and speak from a particular place and time, from a history and a culture which is specific. What we say is always "in context," *positioned*. I was born into and spent my childhood and adolescence in a lower-middle-class family in Jamaica. I have lived all my adult life in England, in the shadow of the black diaspora—"in the belly of the beast." I write against the background of a lifetime's work in cultural studies. If the paper seems preoccupied with the diaspora experience and its narratives of displacement, it is worth remembering that all discourse is "placed," and the heart has its reasons.

There are at least two different ways of thinking about "cultural identity." The first position defines "cultural identity" in terms of the idea of one, shared culture, a sort of collective "one true self," hiding inside the many other, more superficial or artificially imposed "selves," which people with a shared history and ancestry hold in common. Within the terms of this definition, our cultural identities reflect the common historical experiences and shared cultural codes which provide us, as "one people," with stable, unchanging, and continuous frames of reference and meaning, beneath the shifting divisions and vicissitudes of our actual history. This "oneness," underlying all the other, more superficial differences, is the truth, the essence, of "Caribbeaness." It is this identity which a Caribbean cinema must discover, excavate, bring to light, and express through cinematic representation.

Such a conception of cultural or national identity played a critical role in all the postcolonial struggles which have so profoundly reshaped our world. It lay at the center of the vision of the poets of "Negritude," like Aimé Césaire and Léopold Senghor, and of the Pan-African political project, earlier in the century. It continues to be a very powerful and creative force in emergent forms of representation among hitherto marginalized peoples. In postcolonial societies, the rediscovery of this identity is often the object of what Frantz Fanon once called a "passionate research . . . directed by the secret hope of discovering beyond the misery of today, beyond self-contempt, resignation and abjuration, some very beautiful and splendid era whose existence rehabilitates us both in regard to ourselves and in regard to others." New forms of cultural practice in these societies address themselves to this project for the very good reason that, as Fanon puts it, in the recent past, "Colonisation is not satisfied merely with holding a people in its grip and emptying the native's brain of all form and content. By a kind of perverted logic, it turns to the past of the oppressed people, and distorts, disfigures and destroys it" (1968, 170).

The question which Fanon's observation poses is, what is the nature of this "profound research" which drives the new forms of visual and cinematic representation? Is it only a matter of unearthing that which the colonial experience buried and overlaid, brining to light the hidden continuities it suppressed? Or is a quite different practice entailed—not the rediscovery but the *production* of identity? Not an identity grounded in the archaeology but in the *retelling* of the past?

We cannot and should not, for a moment, underestimate or neglect the importance of the act of imaginative rediscovery. "Hidden histories" have played a critical role in the emergence of some of the most important social movements of our time. The photographic work of a visual artist like Armet Francis, a Jamaican-born photographer who has lived in Britain since the age of eight, is a testimony to the continuing creative power of this conception of identity within the practices of representation. His photographs of the peoples of the Black Triangle, taken in Africa, the Caribbean, the U.S., and the U.K., attempt to reconstruct in visual terms "the underlying unity of the black people whom, colonisation and slavery distributed across the African diaspora." His text is an act of imaginary reunification.

Crucially, his images find a way of imposing an imaginary coherence on the experience of dispersal and fragmentation, which is the history of all enforced diasporas. He does this by representing or "figuring" Africa as the mother of these different civilizations. His Triangle is, after all, "centered" in Africa. Africa is the name of the missing term, the great aporia, which lies at the center of our cultural identity and gives it a meaning which, until recently, it lacked. No one who looks at these textual images now, in the light of the history of transportation, slavery, and migration, can fail to understand how the rift of separation, the "loss of identity," which has been integral to the Caribbean experience only begins to be healed when these forgotten connections are once more set in place. Such texts restore an imaginary fullness or plenitude, to set against the broken rubric of our past. They are resources of resistance and identity, with which to confront the fragmented and pathological ways in which that experience has been reconstructed within the dominant regimes of cinematic and visual representation of the West.

There is, however, a related but different view of cultural identity, which qualifies, even if it does not replace, the first. This second position recognizes that, as well as the many points of similarity, there are also critical points of deep and significant *difference* which constitute "what we really are": or rather—since history has intervened—"what we have become." We cannot speak for very long, with any exactness, about "one experience, one identity," without acknowledging its other side—the differences and discontinuities which constitute, precisely, the Caribbean's "uniqueness." Cultural identity, in this second sense, is a matter of "becoming" as well as of "being." It belongs to the future as much as to the past. It is not something which already exists, transcending place, time, history, and culture. Cultural identities come from somewhere, have histories. But, like everything which is historical, they undergo constant transformation. Far from being eternally fixed in some essentialized past, they are subject to the continuous "play" of history, culture, and power. Far from being grounded in a mere "recovery" of the past, which is waiting to be found, and which, when found, will secure our sense of ourselves into eternity, identities are the names we give to the different ways we are positioned by, and position ourselves within, the narratives of the past.

It is only from this second position that we can properly understand the truly traumatic character of "the colonial experience." The ways we have been positioned and subjected in the dominant regimes of representation were a critical exercise of cultural power and normalization, precisely because they were not superficial. They had the power to make us see and experience ourselves as "other." Every regime of representation is a regime of power formed, as Foucault reminds us, by the fatal couplet, "power/knowledge." And this kind of knowledge is internal, not external. It is one thing to place some person or set of peoples as the other of a dominant discourse. It is quite another thing to subject them to that "knowledge," not only as a matter of imposed will and domination, by the power of inner compulsion and subjective conformation to the norm. That is the lesson—the somber majesty—of Fanon's insight into the colonizing experience in *Black Skin, White Masks.*

This expropriation of cultural identity cripples and deforms. If its silences are not resisted, they produce, in Fanon's vivid phrase, "individuals without an anchor, without horizon, colourless, stateless, rootless—a race of angels" (1968, 176). Nevertheless, it also changes our conception of what "cultural identity" is. In this perspective, cultural identity is not a fixed essence at all, lying unchanged outside history and culture. It is not some universal and transcendental spirit inside us on which history has made no fundamental mark. It is not once-and-for-all. It is not a fixed origin to which we can make some final and absolute Return. Of course, it is not a mere phantasm, either. It is *something*—not a mere trick of the imagination. It has its histories—and histories have their real, material, and symbolic effects. The past continues to speak to us. But this is no longer a simple, factual "past," since our relation to it is, like the child's relation to the mother, always-already "after the break." It is always constructed through memory, fantasy, narrative, and myth. Cultural identities are the points of identification, the unstable points of identification or suture, which are made within the discourses of history and culture. Not an essence but a *positioning*. Hence, there is always a politics of position, which has no absolute guarantee in an unproblematic, transcendental "law of history."

This second view of cultural history is much less familiar, and unsettling. But it is worth spending a few moments tracing its formations. We might think of Caribbean identities as "framed" by two axes or vectors, simultaneously operative: the vector of similarity and continuity and the vector of difference and rupture. Caribbean identities always have to be thought of in terms of the dialogic relationship between these two axes. The one gives us some grounding in, some continuity with, the past. The second reminds us that what we share is precisely the experience of a profound discontinuity. The peoples dragged into slavery by the triangular Atlantic trade came predominantly from Africa—though when that supply ended, it was temporarily refreshed by indentured labor from the Asian subcontinent. This neglected fact explains why, when you visit Guyana or Trinidad, you suddenly see, symbolically inscribed in the faces of their peoples, the paradoxical "truth" of Christopher Columbus's mistake: you *can* find "Asia" by sailing west, if you know where to look! The great majority of slaves were from Africa—already figured, in the European imaginary, as "the Dark Continent." But they were also from different countries, tribal communities, villages, languages, and gods. African religion, which has been so profoundly formative in Caribbean spiritual life, is precisely *different* from Christian monotheism in having, not one, but a proliferation of gods. These gods live on, in an underground existence, in the pantheon of black saints which people the hybridized religious universe of Latin American Catholicism. The paradox is that it was the uprooting of slavery and transportation and the insertion into the plantation economy (as well as the symbolic economy) of the Western world that "unified" these peoples across their differences, in the same moment as it cut them off from direct access to that past.

Difference, therefore, persists—in and alongside continuity. And this is so, not only for the past but in the present. To return to the Caribbean after any long absence is to experience again the shock of the "doubleness" of similarity and difference. As a Jamaican returning for the First Caribbean Film Festival, I "recognized" Martinique instantly, though I was seeing it for the first time. I also saw at once how different Martinique is from, say, Jamaica: and this is no mere difference of topography or climate. It is also a profound difference of culture and history. And the difference *matters*. It positions Martiniquains and Jamaicans as *both* the same *and* different. Moreover, the boundaries of difference are continually repositioned in relation to different points of reference. Vis-à-vis the developed West, we are very much "the same." We belong to the marginal, the underdeveloped, the periphery, the "other." We are at the outer edge, the "rim," of the metropolitan world—always "South" to someone else's *El Norte*.

At the same time, we do not stand in the same relation of "otherness" to the metropolitan centers. Each has negotiated its economic, political, and cultural dependency differently. And this "difference," whether we like it or not, is already inscribed in our cultural identities. In turn, it is this negotiation of identity which makes us, vis-à-vis other Latin American people with a very similar history, different. Caribbeans—*les Antilliennes:* "islanders" to their mainland. And yet, vis-à-vis one another, Jamaican, Haitian, Cuban, Guadeloupean, Barbadian, etc. . . .

How, then, to describe this play of "difference" within identity? The common history—transportation, slavery, colonization—has been profoundly formative. It was also, metaphorically as well as literally, a translation. The inscription of difference is also specific and critical. I use the word "play" because the double meaning of the metaphor is important. It suggests, on the one hand, the instability, the permanent unsettlement, the lack of any final resolution. On the other hand, it reminds us that the place where this "doubleness" is most powerfully to be heard is "playing" within the varieties of Caribbean musics. This cultural "play" could not be represented, cinematically, as a simple, binary opposition—"past/present," "them/us." Its complexity exceeds this binary structure of representation. At different places, times, in relation to different questions, the boundaries are resited. They become, not only what they have, at times, certainly been—mutually excluding categories, but also, what they sometimes are—differential points along a sliding scale.

One trivial example is the way Martinique both *is* and *is not* "French." Superficially, Fort de France is a much richer, more "fashionable" place than Kingston—which is not only visibly poorer, but itself at a point of transition between being "in fashion" in an Anglo-African and Afro-American way—for those who can afford to be in any sort of fashion at all. Yet, what is distinctively "Martiniquais" can only be described in terms of that special and peculiar supplement which the black and mulatto skin adds to the "refinement" and sophistication of a Parisian-derived *haute couture:* that is, a sophistication which, because it is black, is always transgressive.

To capture this sense of difference which is not pure "otherness," we need to deploy the play on words of a theorist like Jacques Derrida. Derrida uses the anomalous *a* in his way of writing "difference"—*différance*—as a marker which sets up a disturbance in our settled understanding or translation of the concept. It sets the word in motion to new meanings without obscuring the trace of its other meanings. His sense of *différance*, as Christopher Norris puts it, thus "remains suspended between the two French verbs 'to differ' and 'to defer' (postpone), both of which contribute to its textual force but neither of which can fully capture its meaning. Language depends on difference, as Saussure showed . . . the structure of distinctive propositions which make up its basic economy. Where Derrida breaks new ground . . . is in the extent to which 'differ' shades into 'defer' . . . the idea that meaning is always deferred, perhaps to the point of an endless supplementarity, by the play of signification" (1982, 32). This second sense of difference challenges the fixed binaries which stabilize meaning and representation and shows how meaning is never finished or completed in this way, but keeps on moving to encompass other, additional or supplementary meanings, which, as Norris puts it elsewhere, "disturb the classical economy of language and representation" (1987, 15). Without relations of difference, no representation could occur. But what is then constituted within representation is always open to being deferred, staggered, serialized.

Where, then, does identity come into this infinite postponement of meaning?

Derrida does not help us as much as he might here—and this is precisely where, in my view, he has permitted his profound theoretical insights to be reappropriated into a celebration of formal "playfulness," which evacuates it of its political meaning. For if signification depends upon the endless repositioning of its differential terms, meaning, in any specific instance, depends on the contingent and arbitrary stop—the necessary and temporary "break" in the infinite semiosis of language. This does not detract from the original insight. It only threatens to do so if we mistake this "cut" of identity—this *positioning,* which makes meaning possible—as a natural and permanent, rather than an arbitrary and contingent "ending." Whereas I understand every such position as "strategic"—and arbitrary, in the sense that there is no permanent equivalence between the particular sentence we close, and its true meaning, as such. Meaning continues to unfold, so to speak, beyond the arbitrary closure which makes it, at any moment, possible. It is always either over- or undetermined—either an excess or a supplement. There is always something "left over."

It is possible, with this conception of "difference," to rethink the positionings and repositionings of Caribbean cultural identities in relation to at least three "presences," to borrow Aimé Césaire's and Léopold Senghor's metaphor: Présence Africaine, Présence Européenne, and the third, most ambiguous, presence of all—the sliding term, "Présence Américaine." I mean America, here, not in its "First World" sense—the big cousin to the North whose "rim" we occupy, but in the second, broader sense: America, the New Found Land, the "New World," *Terra Incognita.*

"Présence Africaine" is the site of the repressed. Apparently silenced beyond memory by the power of the new cultures of slavery, it was, in fact present everywhere: in the everyday life and customs of the slave quarters, in the languages and patois of the plantations, in names and words, often disconnected from their taxonomies, in the secret syntactical structures through which other languages were spoken, in the stories and tales told to children, in religious practices and beliefs, in the spiritual life, the arts, crafts, musics, and rhythms of slave and postemancipation society. Africa, the signified which could not be represented, remained the unspoken, unspeakable "presence" in Caribbean culture. It is "hiding" behind every verbal inflection, every narrative twist of Caribbean cultural life. It is the secret code with which every Western text was "reread." *This* was—is—the "Africa" that "is alive and well in the diaspora" (Hall and Jefferson 1976).

When I was growing up as a child in Kingston, I was surrounded by the signs, music, and rhythms of this Africa of the diaspora, which only existed as a result of a long and discontinuous series of transformations. But, although almost everyone around me was some shade of brown or black (Africa "speaks"!), I never once heard a single person refer to themselves or to others as, in some way, or as having been at some time in the past, "African." It was only in the 1970s that this Afro-Caribbean identity became historically available to the great majority of Jamaican people, at home and abroad. In this historic moment, the great majority of Jamaicans discovered themselves to be "black"—just as they discovered themselves to be the sons and daughters of "slavery."

This profound cultural discovery, however, was not, and could not be, made directly, without "mediation." It could only be made through the impact on popular life of the postcolonial revolution, the civil rights struggles, the culture of Rastafarianism and the music of reggae—the metaphors, the figures or signifiers, of a new construction of "Jamaican-ness." This is a "new" Africa, grounded in an "old." Africa, now, as part of a spiritual journey of discovery that led, in the Caribbean, to an indigenous cultural revolution. "Africa," as we might say, necessarily "deferred"—as a spiritual, cultural, and political metaphor.

It is the presence/absence of the "otherness" of Africa, in this form, which made it also the privileged signifier of new conceptions of Caribbean identity. Everyone in the Caribbean, of whatever ethnic background, must sooner or later come to terms with this African presence. Black, brown, mulatto, white—all must look "Présence Africaine" in the face, speak its name. But whether it is, in this sense, an *origin* of our identities, unchanged by four hundred years of displacement, dismemberment, transportation, to which we could in any final or literal sense, return, is more open to doubt. The original "Africa" is no longer there. It too has been transformed. History is, in that sense, irreversible. We must not collude with the West which, precisely, "normalizes" and appropriates Africa by freezing it into some timeless zone of the "primitive, unchanging past." Africa must at last be reckoned with, by Caribbean people. But it cannot in any simple sense be merely recovered. It belongs irrevocably, for us, to what Edward Said once called an "imaginative geography and history," which helps "the mind to intensify its own sense of itself by dramatizing the difference between what is close to it and what is far away" (1979). It "has acquired an imaginative or figurative value we can name and feel" (Said 1979, 55). Our belongingness to it constitutes what Benedict Anderson calls "an imagined community." To *this* "Africa," which is a necessary part of the Caribbean imaginary, we can't literally go home again.

The character of this displaced "homeward" journey—its length and complexity—comes across vividly, not yet in the Caribbean cinemas, but in other texts. Tony Sewell's text and documentary archival photographs, *Garvey's Children: The Legacy of Marcus Garvey*, tells the story of a "return" to an African identity for Caribbean people which went, necessarily, by the long route—through London and the United States. It "ends," not in Ethiopia but with Garvey's statue in front of the St. Ann Parish Library in Jamaica, with the music of Burning Spear and Bob Marley's "Redemption Song." This is our "long journey" home. Derek Bishton's remarkably courageous visual and written text, *Black Heart Man*—the story of the journey of a *white* photographer "on the trail of the promised land"—starts in England, and goes, through Sashamene, the place in Ethiopia to which many Jamaican people have found their way on their search for the Promised Land, and the story of slavery; but it ends in Pinnacle, Jamaica, where the first Rastafarian settlement was established, and "beyond"—among the dispossessed of twentieth-century Kingston and the streets of Handsworth, where Bishton's voyage of discovery first began. This symbolic journey is necessary for us all—and necessarily circular.

This is the Africa we must return to but "by another route": what Africa has *become* in the New World, what we have made of "Africa." "Africa"—as we retell it through politics, memory, and desire.

What of the second, troubling, term in the identity equation—the European presence? For many of us, this is a matter, not of too little but of too much. Where Africa was a case of the unspoken, Europe was a case of that which is endlessly speaking—and endlessly speaking *us.* The European presence thus interrupts the innocence of the whole discourse of "difference" in the Caribbean by introducing the question of power. "Europe" belongs irrevocably to the question of power, to the lines of force and consent, to the pole of the *dominant* in Caribbean culture. In terms of colonialism, underdevelopment, poverty, and the racism of color, the European presence is that which, in visual representation has positioned us within its dominant regimes of representation: the colonial discourse, the literatures of adventure and exploration, the romance of the exotic, the ethnographic and traveling eye, the tropical languages of tourism, travel brochure, and Hollywood, and the violent, pornographic languages of *ganja* and urban violence.

The error is not to conceptualize this "presence" in terms of power, but to locate that power as wholly external to us—an extrinsic force, whose influence can be thrown off like the serpent sheds its skin. What Frantz Fanon reminds us, in *Black Skin, White Masks,* is how its power is inside as well as outside: "the movements, the attitudes, the glances of the other fixed me there, in the sense in which a chemical solution is fixed by a dye. I was indignant; I demanded an explanation. Nothing happened. I burst apart. Now the fragments have been put together again by another self" (1967, 109). This "look," from—so to speak—the place of the other, fixes us, not only in its violence, hostility, and aggression, but in the ambivalence of its desire. This brings us face to face, not simply with the dominating European presence as the site or "scene" of integration where those other presences which it had actively disaggregated were recomposed—reframed, put together in a new way—but as the site of a profound splitting and doubling: what Homi Bhabha has called "the ambivalent identifications of the racist world," the "'otherness' of the self-inscribed in the perverse palimpsest of colonial identity" (introduction to Fanon 1967, xv).

The dialogue of power and resistance, of refusal and recognition, with and against "Présence Européenne" is almost as complex as the so-called dialogue with Africa. In terms of popular cultural life, it is nowhere to be found in its pure, pristine state. It is always already fused, syncretized, with other cultural elements. It is always-already creolized. Not lost beyond the Middle Passage, but ever-present, the harmonics in our musics to the ground-bass of Africa, traversing and intersecting our lives at every point. How can we stage this dialogue so that, finally, we can place it, without terror, rather than being forever placed by it? Can we ever recognize its irreversible influence, while resisting its imperializing eye? The enigma is impossible, so far, to resolve. It requires the most complex of cultural strategies. Think, for example, of the dialogue of every Caribbean filmmaker, one way or another, with the dominant cinemas of the "West"—of European and American filmmaking. Who could describe this tense and tortured dialogue as a "one-way trip"?

I think of the third, "New World" presence, not so much in terms of power, as of ground, place, territory. It is the juncture-point where the other cultural tributaries met, the "empty" land (the European colonizers emptied it) where strangers from every other part of the globe met. None of the people who now occupy the islands— black, brown, white, African, European, American, Spanish, French, East Indian, Chinese, Portuguese, Jew, Dutch—originally "belonged" there. It is the space where the creolizations and assimilations and syncretisms were negotiated. The New World is the third term—the primal scene where the fateful/fatal encounter was staged between Africa and the West. It has to be understood as the place of displacements: of the original pre-Columbian inhabitants, the Arawaks, permanently displaced from their homelands; of peoples displaced in different ways from Africa, Asia, and Europe; the displacements of slavery, colonization, and conquest. It stands for the endless ways in which Caribbean people have been destined to "migrate"; it is the signifier of migration itself—of traveling, voyaging, and return as fate, as destiny; of the Antillean as the prototype of the modern or postmodern New World nomad, continually moving between center and periphery. This preoccupation with movement and migration Caribbean cinema shares with many other "Third Cinemas," but it is one of our defining themes, and is destined to cross the narrative of every film script or cinematic image.

Présence Américaine also has its silences, its suppressions. Peter Hulme, in his essay "Islands of Enchantment" (1987) reminds us that the word "Jamaica" is the Hispanic form of the indigenous Arawak name of the island—"land of wood and water"—which Columbus's renaming ("Santiago") never replaced. The Arawak "presence" remains a ghostly one, visible in the islands mainly in their museums and archaeological sites, part of the barely knowable or usable "past." It is not represented in the emblem of the Jamaican National Heritage Trust, for example, which chose, instead, the figure of Diego Pimienta, "an African who fought for his Spanish masters against the English invasion of the island in 1655"—a deferred, metonymic, sly, and sliding representation of Jamaican identity if ever there was one! Peter Hulme recounts the story of how Prime Minister Edward Seaga tried to alter the Jamaican coat-of-arms, which consists of two Arawak figures holding a shield with five pineapples, surmounted by an alligator. "Can the crushed and extinct Arawaks represent the dauntless character of Jamaicans? Does the low-slung, near extinct crocodile, a cold-blooded reptile, symbolise the warm, soaring spirit of Jamaicans?" Prime Minister Seaga asked, rhetorically.[1] There can be few political statements which so eloquently testify to the complexities entailed in the process of trying to represent a diverse peoples with a diverse history through a single, hegemonic "identity." Fortunately, Mr. Seaga's invitation to the Jamaican people, who are overwhelmingly of African descent, to start their "remembering" by first "forgetting" something else, got the comeuppance it so richly deserved.

Thus I think of the New World presence—America, Terra Incognita—as itself the beginning of diaspora, of diversity, of difference: as what makes Afro-Caribbean people already the people of a diaspora. I use this term here metaphorically, not literally. I do not mean those scattered tribes whose identity can only be secured in relation to some sacred homeland to which they must at all costs return, even if it means pushing other people into the sea. This is the old, the imperializing, the hegemonizing, form of "ethnicity." We have seen the fate of the people of Palestine at the hands of this backward-looking conception of diaspora—and the complicity of the West with it. The diaspora experience as I intend it here is defined, not by essence or purity, but by the recognition of a necessary heterogeneity, diversity; by a conception of "identity" which lives with and through, not despite, difference; by *hybridity*. Diaspora identities are those which are constantly producing and reproducing themselves anew, through transformation and difference. One can only think here of what is uniquely—"essentially"—Caribbean: precisely the mixes of color, pigmentation, physiognomic type; the "blends" of tastes that is Caribbean cuisine; the aesthetics of the "crossovers," of "cut-and-mix," to borrow Dick Hebdige's telling phrase, which is the heart and soul of black music.

Young black cultural practitioners and critics in Britain are increasingly coming to acknowledge and explore in their work this "diaspora aesthetic": "Across a whole range of cultural forms there is a 'syncretic' dynamic which critically appropriates elements from the master-codes of the dominant culture and 'creolises' them, disarticulating given signs and re-articulating their symbolic meaning. The subversive force of this hybridising tendency is most apparent at the level of language itself where creoles, patois and black English decentre, destabilise and carnivalise the lin-

1. *Jamaica Hansard* 9 (1983–84):363, quoted in Hulme 1987.

guistic domination of 'English'—the nation-language of master-discourse—through strategic inflections, reaccentuations and other performative moves in semantic, syntactic and lexical codes" (Mercer 1988, 57).

It is because this "New World" is constituted for us as place, a narrative of displacement, that it gives rise so profoundly to a certain imaginary plenitude, recreating the endless desire to return to "lost origins," to be one again with the mother, to go back to the beginning. Who can ever forget, when once seen rising up out of that blue-green Caribbean, those islands of enchantment. And yet, this "return to the beginning" is like the Imaginary in Lacan—it can neither be fulfilled nor requitted, and hence is the beginning of the symbolic, of representation, the infinitely renewable source of desire, memory, myth, search, discovery—in short, the reservoir of our cinematic narratives.

I have been trying, in a series of metaphors, to put in play a different sense of our relationship to the past, and thus a different way of thinking about cultural identity, which might begin to constitute new points of recognition in the discourses of the emerging Caribbean cinema. I have been trying to speak of identity as constituted, not outside but within representation; and hence of cinema, not as a second-order mirror held up to reflect what already exists, but as that form of representation which is able to constitute us as new kinds of subjects, and thereby enable us to discover who we are. Communities, Benedict Anderson argues in *Imagined Communities* (1983, 15) arc to be distinguished, not by their falsity/genuineness, but by the style in which they are imagined. This is the vocation of a modern Caribbean cinema: by allowing us to see and recognize the different parts and histories of ourselves, to construct those points of identification, those positionalities we call "a cultural identity."

"We must not therefore be content," Fanon warns us, "with delving into the past of a people in order to find coherent elements which will counteract colonialism's attempts to falsify and harm. . . . A national culture is not a folk-lore, nor an abstract populism that believes it can discover a people's true nature. A national culture is the whole body of efforts made by a people in the sphere of thought to describe, justify and praise the action through which that people has created itself and keeps itself in existence" (1968, 188).

Works Cited

Anderson, B. 1983. *Imagined Communities: Reflections on the Origin and Spread of Nationalism*. London: Verso. Rev. ed., London: Verso, 1991.

Fanon, F. 1967. *Black Skin, White Masks*. New York: Grove Press.

———. 1968. *The Wretched of the Earth*. New York: Grove Press.

Hall, S., and T. Jefferson, eds. 1976. *Resistance through Rituals: Youth Subcultures in Postwar Britain*. London: Hutchinson.

Hulme, P. 1987. "Islands of Enchantment." *New Formations* (London), no. 3 (winter).

Mercer, K. 1988. "Diaspora Culture and the Dialogic Imagination: The Aesthetics of Black Independent Film in Britain." In *Blackframes: Critical Perspectives on Black Independent Cinema,* ed. M. Cham and C. Andrade-Watkins. Cambridge: MIT Press.

Norris, C. 1982. *Deconstruction: Theory and Practice.* London: Methuen.

———. 1987. *Derrida.* Cambridge: Harvard University Press.

Said, E. 1979. *Orientalism.* New York: Vintage Books.

Twelve

British Cultural Studies and the Pitfalls of Identity

Paul Gilroy

It is only in the last phase of British imperialism that the labouring classes of the satellites and the labouring classes of the metropolis have confronted one another directly "on native ground." But their fates have long been indelibly intertwined. The very definition of "what it is to be British"—the centrepiece of that culture now to be preserved from racial dilution—has been articulated around this absent/present centre. If their blood has not mingled extensively with yours, their labour power has long since entered your economic blood-stream. It is in the sugar you stir: it is in the sinews of the infamous British "sweet tooth": it is the tea leaves at the bottom of the "British cuppa."

Stuart Hall

Whenever I felt an inclination to national enthusiasm I strove to suppress it as being harmful and wrong, alarmed by the warning examples of the peoples among whom we Jews live. But plenty of other things remained over to make the attraction of Jewry and Jews irresistible—many obscure emotional forces, which were the more powerful the less they could be expressed in words, as well as clear con-sciousness of inner identity, the safe privacy of a common mental construction. And beyond this there was a perception that it was to my Jewish nature alone that I owed two characteristics that had become indispensable to me in the difficult course of my life. Because I was a Jew I found myself free from many prejudices which restricted others in the use of their intellect; and as a Jew I was prepared to join the Opposition and to do without agreement with the "compact majority."

Freud

This short piece cannot hope to provide a comprehensive exposition of the concept of identity, its surrogates, and kin terms in the diverse writings of cultural studies. Indeed if the discrepant practices that take place under the tattered banners of British cultural studies can be unified at all, and that must remain in doubt, exploring the concept of identity and its changing resonance in critical scholarship is not the best way to approach the prospect of their unity. Reflecting upon identity seems to unleash a power capable of dissolving those tentative projects back into the contradictory components from which they were first assembled. Highlighting the theme of identity readily flushes out disagreements over profound political and intellectual problems. It can send the aspirant practitioners of cultural studies scuttling back toward the quieter sanctuaries of their old disciplinary affiliations where the problems and the potential pleasures of thinking through identity are less formidable and engaging. Anthropologists utter sighs of relief; psychologists rub their hands with glee; philosophers relax, confident that their trials are over; sociologists mutter discontentedly about the illegitimate encroachments of postmodernism while literary critics look blank and perplexed. Historians remain silent. These characteristic reactions from the more secure positions of closed disciplines underline that few words in the conceptual vocabulary of contemporary cultural analysis have been more flagrantly contested and more thoroughly abused than "identity."

The history of the term, which has a lengthy presence in social thought, and a truly complex philosophical lineage that goes back to the pre-Socratics, is gradually becoming better known (Gleason, 1983, 69; Calhoun 1994; Hall 1992b). However, though it has received some attention in debates over modernity and its anxieties, little critical attention has been directed toward the specific puzzle involved in accounting for identity's contemporary popularity. Though the philosophical pedigree of the term is usually appreciated by today's users, identity is invoked more often in arguments that are primarily political rather than philosophical. The popular currency of the term may itself be a symptom of important political conflicts and a signal of the altered character of postmodern politics, especially in the overdeveloped countries. Another clue to this change is provided by the frequency with which the noun "identity" appears coupled with the adjective "cultural." This timely pairing is only the most obvious way in which the concept "identity" directs attention toward a more elaborate sense of the power of culture and the relationship of culture to power. It introduces a sense of *cultural* politics as something more substantial than a feeble echo of the *political* politics of days gone by. This cultural politics applies both to the increased salience of identity as a problem played out in everyday life and to identity as it is managed and administered in the cultural industries of mass communication that have transformed understanding of the world and the place of individual possessors of identity within it.

The stability and coherence of the self has been placed in jeopardy in these overlapping settings. This may help to explain why identity has become a popular, valuable, and useful concept. Though the currency of identity circulates far outside the walls of the academy, much of its appeal derives from a capacity to make supple connections between scholarly and political concerns. These days, especially when an unsavory climate created by the unanswerable accusation of "political correctness" makes too many critical scholars, political thinkers, and cultural activists hypersensitive about professional standards and the disciplinary integrity of their embattled work, identity has become an important idea precisely because of these bridging qualities. It is a junction or hinge concept that can help to maintain the connective tissue that articulates political and cultural concerns. It has also provided an important means to both rediscover and preserve an explicitly political dynamic in serious interdisciplinary scholarship.

It would be wrong, however, to imagine that the concept of identity belongs exclusively to *critical* thought, let alone to the emancipatory intellectual and political projects involved in enhancing democracy and extending tolerance. Identity's passage into vogue has also been mirrored in conservative, authoritarian, and right-wing thought, which have regularly attempted to use both inquiries into identity and spurious certainty about its proper boundaries to enhance their own interests, their capacity to explain the world, and to legitimate the austere social patterns that they favor. The crisis involved in acquiring and maintaining an appropriate form of *national* identity has appeared repeatedly as the principal focus of this activity. It, too, makes a special investment in the idea of culture, for nations are presented as entirely homogeneous cultural units staffed by people whose hypersimilarity renders them interchangeable.

Apart from these obviously political claims on identity, the concept has also provided an important site for the erasure and abandonment of *any* political aspirations. Clarion calls to comprehend identity and set it to work often suggest that mere politics has been exhausted and should now be left behind in favor of more authentic and powerful forms of self-knowledge and consciousness that are coming into focus. Thus, if the idea of identity has been comprehensively politicized, it has also become an important intellectual resource for those who have sought an emergency exit from what they see as the barren world of politics. Identity becomes a means to open up those realms of being and acting in the world which are prior to and somehow more fundamental than political concerns. Any lingering enthusiasm for the supposedly trivial world of politics is misguided, untimely, and therefore doomed to be frustrating. It too corrodes identity and can profitably be replaced by the open-ended processes of self-exploration and reconstruction that take shape where politics gives way to more glamorous and avowedly therapeutic alternatives.

This type of reorientation has occurred most readily where reflection on individual identity has been debased by simply being equated with the stark question "Who am I?" This deceptively simple question has been used to promote an inward turn away from the profane chaos of an imperfect world. It is a problematic gesture that all too often culminates in the substitution of an implosive, and therefore antisocial, form of *self*-scrutiny for the discomfort and the promise of public political work which does not assume either solidarity or community but works instead to bring them into being and then to make them democratic. That memorable question ends with a fateful and emphatically disembodied "I." It refers to an entity that is represented as both the subject of knowing and a privileged location of being. When it sets out in pursuit of truth, this "I" can be made to speak authoritatively from everywhere while being nowhere, if only the right methods are brought to bear upon its deployment. This fateful fiction has a long and important history in the modern world, its thinking, and its thinking about thinking (Taylor 1989; Haraway 1991). This "I" can readily become a signature and cipher for numerous other problems to which the sign "identity" can help to supply the answers. For example, if we are committed to changing and, hopefully, improving the world rather than simply analyzing it, will political agency be possible if the certainty and integrity of that "I" have been compromised by its unconscious components, by tricks played upon it by the effects of the language through which it comes to know itself, or by the persistent claims of the body that will not easily accept being devalued in relation to the mind and the resulting banishment to the domain of unreason? Is the "I" and the decidedly modern subjects and subjectivities to which it points a product or symptom of some underlying history, an effect of individual insertion into and constitution by society and culture? At what point or under what conditions might that "I" bring forth a collective counterpart, a "We"? These are some of the troubling questions that spring to mind in a period when the previously rather contradictory idea of "identity politics" has suddenly begun to make sense.

This is a time in which *what* (no longer even who) you are can count for a great deal more than anything that you might do, for yourself and for others. The slippage from "who" to "what" is absolutely crucial. It expresses a reification (thingification) and fetishization of self that might once have been captured by the term "alienation," which was itself a significant attempt to account for the relationship between the subject and the world outside it upon which it relied. Today, social processes have assumed more extreme and complex forms. They construct a radical estrangement that draws its energy from the reification of culture and the fetishization of absolute cultural difference. In other words, identity is inescapably political, especially where its social workings—patterns of identification—precipitate the retreat and contraction of politics.

. . .

No inventory currently exists—either inside or outside the flimsy fortifications of existing cultural studies—of the ways in which identity operates politically and can change political culture, stretching political thinking so that modern secular distinctions between private and public become blurred and the boundaries formed by and through the exercise of power on both sides of that line are shown to be permeable. Before the preparation of that precious inventory can proceed, we must face how the concept of identity tangles together three overlapping but basically different concerns. This suggestion involves a degree of oversimplification but it is instructive to try to separate out these tangled strands before we set about making their symptomatic interlinkage a productive feature of our own thinking and writing. Each cluster of issues under the larger constellation of identity has an interesting place in the checkered history of the scholarly and political movement that has come to be known as cultural studies.

The concept of identity points initially toward the question of the self. This is an issue that has usually been approached in the emergent canon of cultural studies via histories of the subject and subjectivity.[1] We should note, however, that it has not been the exclusive property of cultural studies' more theoretically inclined affiliates. These ideas and the characteristic language of inwardness in which they have been expressed are extremely complex and immediately require us to enter the wild frontier between psychological and sociological domains. On this contested terrain we must concede immediately that human agents are made and make themselves rather than being born in some already finished form. The force of this observation has had a special significance in the development of modernity's oppositional movements. Their moral and political claims have arisen from a desire to estrange social life from natural processes and indeed from quarrels over the status of nature and its power to determine history.

Feminist thought and critical analyses of racism have made extensive use of the concept of identity in exploring how "subjects" bearing gender and racial characteristics are constituted in social processes that are amenable to historical explanation and political struggle. The production of the figures "woman" and "Negro" has been extensively examined from this point of view (Beauvoir 1960; Fanon 1986; Schiebinger 1993). The emergence of these durable but fictive creations has been understood in relation to the associated development of categories of humanity from which women and blacks have been routinely excluded. This kind of critical investigation has endowed strength in contemporary political thinking about the modern self and its contingencies. This is not solely a matter of concern to the "minorities" who have not so far enjoyed the dubious privileges of inclusion in this official humanism.

The obligation to operate historically and thereby to undermine the idea of an invariant human nature that determines social life was readily combined with psychological insights. This blend provided not only a means to trace something of the patterned processes of individual becoming but to grasp, through detailed accounts

---

1. This was a strong component of the early analyses of subculture produced by Paul Willis, Iain Chambers, Dick Hebdige, and Angela McRobbie. See also Probyn 1994.

of that variable process, the kind of protean entity that a human agent might be (Geertz 1985). The endlessly mutable nature of unnatural humanity can be revealed in conspicuous contrast between different historically and culturally specific versions of the boundedness of the human person. Labor, language, and lived interactive culture have been identified as the principal media for evaluating this social becoming.

Each of these options stages the dramas of identity in a contrasting manner. Each, for example, materializes the production and reproduction of gender differences and resolves the antagonistic relationship between men and women differently. All raise the question of hierarchy and the status of visible differences whether they are based on signs like age and generation or the modern, secular semiotics of "race" and ethnicity. The ideal of universal humanity certainly appears in a less attractive light once the unsavory exclusionary practices that have surrounded its coronation at the center of bourgeois political culture are placed on display. Nietzsche showed long ago how an archaeological investigation of the modern self could lead toward this goal.

Identity can be used to query the quality of relations established between superficial and underlying similarities in human beings, between their similar insides and dissimilar outsides. By criticizing the compromised authority invested in that suspect, transcendent humanity, identity—understood here as subjectivity—presents another issue: the agent's reflexive qualities and unreliable consciousness of its own operations and limits. Posed in this way, the theoretical coherence of identity unravels almost immediately. The concept is revealed to be little more than a name given to one important element in the interminable struggle to impose order on the flux of painful social life.

The impossible modern quest for stable and integral selfhood points toward the second theme that has been (con)fused in the compound inner logic of identity. This is the equally complicated question of sameness. It too has psychological and psychoanalytic aspects. In this second incarnation, identity becomes visible as the point where a concern with individual subjectivity opens out into an expansive engagement with the dynamics of identification: how one subject or agent may come to see itself in others, to be itself through its mediated relationships with others, and to see others in itself. Dealing with an agent's consciousness of sameness unavoidably raises the fact of otherness and the phenomenon of difference. Politics enters here as well. Difference should not be confined exclusively to the gaps we imagine between whole, stable subjects. One lesson yielded up by the initial approach to identity as subjectivity is that difference exists within identities—within selves—as well as between them. This means that the longed-for integrity and unity of subjects is always fragile.

In many of the political movements where the idea of a common identity has become a principle of organization and mobilization, there is an idea of interplay between "inner" and "outer" differences that must be systematically orchestrated if their goals are to be achieved. For example, differences within a group can be minimized so that differences between that group and others appear greater. Identity can emerge from the very operations it is assumed to precede and facilitate. The investment in ideas of essential difference that emerges from several different kinds of feminist thinking as well as from many movements of the racially oppressed and immiserated confirms that deeper connections have been supposed to reside unseen, hidden beneath or beyond the superficial, nonessential differences that they may or may not regulate.

Identity as sameness can be distinguished from identity as subjectivity because it moves on from dealing with the formation and location of subjects and their historical individuality into thinking about collective or communal identities: nations, genders, classes, generational, "racial," and ethnic groups. Identity can be traced back toward its sources in the institutional patterning of identification. Spoken and written languages, memory, ritual, and governance have all been shown to be important identity-producing mechanisms in the formation and reproduction of imagined community. The technological and technical processes that create and reproduce mentalities of belonging in which sameness features have also come under critical scrutiny. Exploring the link between these novel forms of identification and the unfolding of modernity has also provided a significant stimulus to politically engaged interdisciplinary research (Gillis 1994). So far, Benedict Anderson's groundbreaking discussion of the role of print cultures in establishing new ways of relating to the power of the nation-state and experiencing nationality has not acquired a postmodern equivalent. The mediation and reproduction of national and postnational identities in cyberspace and on virtual paper await a definitive interpretation. The changing resonance of nationality and the intermittent allure of subnational and supranational identities demand that we note how theorizing identity as sameness unfolds in turn into a concern with identifications and the technologies that mediate and circulate them. We must acknowledge the difficult work involved in thinking about how understanding identification might transform and enrich political thought and action.

Analysis of communal and collective identity thus leads into the third issue encompassed by identity: the question of solidarity. This aspect of identity concerns how both connectedness and difference become bases on which social action can be produced. This third element moves decisively away from the subject-centered approach that goes with the first approach and the intersubjective dynamic that takes shape when the focus is on the second. Instead, where the relationship between identity and solidarity moves to the center stage, another issue, that of the social constraints upon the agency of individuals and groups must also be addressed. To what extent can we be thought of as making ourselves? How do we balance a desire to affirm the responsibility that goes with accepting self-creation as a process and the altogether different obligation to recognize the historical limits within which individual and collective subjects materialize and act? This reconciliation usually proceeds through an appeal to supraindividual identity-making structures. These may be material, discursive, or some heuristic and unstable combination of them both. Attention to identity as a principle of solidarity asks us to comprehend identity as an effect mediated by historical and economic structures, instantiated in the signifying practices through which they operate and arising in contingent institutional settings that both regulate and express the coming together of individuals in patterned social processes.

Apart from its extensive contributions to the analysis of nationality, "race," and ethnicity, the term "identity" has been used to discern and evaluate the institution of gender difference and of differences constituted around sexualities. These unsynchronized critical projects have sometimes coexisted under the ramshackle protection that cultural studies has been able to construct. Conflicts between them exist in latent and manifest forms and have been identified by several authoritative commentators as a key source of the intellectual energy and perversely as a sign of the seriousness in some cultural studies writing (Hall 1992a). These tensions have also been presented as part of a corrective counternarrative that has been pitched against some inappropriately heroic accounts of political scholarship and pedagogy in the institutional wellspring of cultural studies: the Centre for Contemporary Cultural Studies at Birmingham University. Undermining those overly pastoral accounts of the Birmingham experience that might obstruct the development of today's cultural studies by mystifying it and sanitizing its embattled origins may be useful. However, those conflicts—which are usually presented as phenomena that arose where the unity of class-oriented work supposedly crumbled under the impact of feminisms and antiracist scholarship—are only half the story.

In assessing the importance of the concept of identity to the development of cultural studies it is important to ponder whether that concept and the agenda of difficulties for which it supplies a valuable shorthand might have played a role in establishing the parameters within which those conflicts were contained and sometimes made useful. I am not suggesting that the term "identity" was used from the start in a consistent, rigorous, or self-conscious way to resolve disagreements or to synchronize common problems and problematics. But rather that, with the benefit of hindsight, it is possible to imagine a version of the broken evolution of cultural studies in which thinking about identity—as subjectivity and sameness—can be shown to have been a significant factor in the continuity and integrity of the project as a whole. It may be that an interest in identity and its political workings in a variety of different social and historical sites provided a point of intersection between the divergent intellectual interests from which a self-conscious cultural studies was gradually born. I will suggest below that a tacit intellectual convergence around problems of identity and identification was indeed an important catalyst for cultural studies and by implication, that identity's capacity to synthesize and connect various inquiries into political cultures and cultural politics is something that makes it a valuable asset even now—something worth struggling with and struggling over.

. . .

There is an elaborate literature surrounding all three aspects of identity sketched above. It includes work in and around the Marxist traditions that contributed so much to the vision, verve, and ethical commitments demonstrated in British cultural studies' early interventionist ambitions. Much feminist writing has also made use of the concept of identity and generated a rich discussion of the political consequences of its deployment (Fuss 1990; Haraway 1991; Riley 1990). But before that generation of feminist scholar-activists was allowed to find its voice, the themes of identity as sameness and solidarity emerged in the political testing ground provided by the urgent commentary on the changing nature of class relations: conflict, solidarity, and what we would now call identity. A new understanding of these questions was being produced as new social and cultural movements appeared to eclipse the labor movement and old political certainties evaporated under pressure from the manifest barbarity of classless societies, a technological revolution, and a transformed understanding of the relationship between the overdeveloped and underdeveloped parts of the planet that had been underlined by decolonization and mass migration. These half-forgotten debates over class are a good place to consider subjectivity, sameness, and solidarity because they took place beyond the grasp of body-coded difference in a happy interlude when biology was not supposed, mechanically, to be destiny and classes were not understood to be discrete biosocial units. No one dreamed back then of genes that could predispose people to homelessness or drug abuse.

If a deceptive oblique stroke was sometimes placed between the words culture and identity, this was done to emphasize that the latter was a product of the former—a consequence of anthropological variation. This literature on class encompassed research into both historical and contemporary social relations. It was governed by political impulses that were not born from complacent application of anachronistic Marxist formulae but rather from an acute comprehension of the political limits and historical specificity of Marxist theory. This stance suggested that class relations were an integral part of capitalist societies but that they were not, in themselves, sufficient to generate a complete explanation of any political situation. Insights drawn from other sources were needed to illuminate the process in which the English working class had been born and in order to comprehend the more recent circumstances in which it might be supposed to be undergoing a protracted death. The subtle and thoughtful concern with class and its dynamics yielded slowly and only partially to different agendas set by interpretation of countercultural movements and oppositional practices that had constituted new social actors and consequently new politicized identities. Women, youth, "races," and sexualities: under each of these headings interest in subjectivity, sameness, and solidarity developed and acquired quite different emphases that did not necessarily complement the order of priorities that had taken shape as a result of exploring class. Partly, this was because an important divergence existed between political movements and consciousness in which the body was an immediate and inescapable issue and those where the relationship to phenotypical variation, though certainly present, was more attenuated, arising, as it were, at one remove. Historical materialism as a political and philosophical doctrine was strongest where the politicization of the body and the consequent grasp of embodiment as the guarantor of shared identity were weakest. The reluctance to engage biology or the semiotics of the body produced a heavy theoretical investment in the idea of labor as a universal category that could transcend particularity and dissolve differences. Willingness to accept the exclusion of the body from the domains of rational cognition and scientific inquiry was thought to establish the hallmark of intellectual enterprise. The abstraction "labor power" was offered as a means to connect the actions and experiences of different people in ways that made the kind of body in which they found themselves a secondary and often superficial issue. Marx's cryptic observation that there is a "historical and moral element" that affects the differential price paid for the labor power of different social groups suggests otherwise and is an important clue to comprehending how these superficial differences could resist the embrace of a higher unity. This unity was situational. Consciousness of solidarity and sameness as well as collective class-based subjectivity grew from common submission to the regime of production and its distinctive conceptions of time, right, and property.

Edward Thompson's 1963 *Making of the English Working Class* broke with the complacent moods of mechanical materialism and productivism and reformulated class analysis in an English idiom that supplied later cultural studies with vital political energy and a distinctive ethical style. Recognizing the strongly masculinist flavor of this important intervention should take nothing away from contemporary attempts to comprehend how it could have grown as much from the context supplied by CND, the New Left, and "practical political activity of several kinds [that] undoubtedly prompted [Thompson] to see the problems of political consciousness and organisation in certain ways." Thompson's famous statement of the dynamics of class formation is relevant here:

> We cannot have love without lovers, nor deference without squires and la-bourers. And class happens when some men, as a result of common experiences (inherited or shared), feel and articulate the identity of their interests as between themselves, and against other men whose interests are different from (and usually opposed to) theirs. (1980, 14)

This is not the place to attempt some hasty resolution of the difficult issues implicit in this formulation such as the base and superstructure relationship, the tension between different forms of consciousness, and the epistemological valency of immediate experience. Nor is this an appropriate moment in which to try to chart the convoluted debates arising from the need to conceptualize the material effects of ideology and the materializing capacities of discourse (Butler 1993). Thompson's celebrated formulation links identity to selfhood, interests, and political agency. To say that his politicized notion of identity derived from an engagement with powers which operate outside of and sometimes in opposition to those rooted in production, for example, in the residential community, would be too simple. An interest in identity was not injected into the thinking of the labor movement and its scholarly advocates by an alternative feminist historiography. An explicit and implicit concern with the political mechanisms of identity emerged directly if not spontaneously from complex analyses of past class relations. This work by Thompson and others was produced in a continuous dialogue with the urgent obligation to understand the present by seeking its historical precedents. Almost without being aware of the fact, these analyses reached beyond themselves not toward an all-encompassing holy totality but, in the name of discomforting complexity, toward deeply textured accounts of bounded and conflictual consciousness that could illuminate contemporary antagonisms.

Though he makes use of the idea of identification rather than the concept of identity, something of the same political and imaginative enterprise can be detected in the closing pages of Raymond Williams's *The Long Revolution* (1961, 354). Grasping for the "new creative definitions" through which that oppositional process might be maintained if not completed, Williams wrote of "structures of feeling—the meanings and values which are lived in world and relationships" and "the essential language—the created and creative meanings—which our inherited reality teaches and through which new reality forms and is negotiated" (293). Williams's conclusion seeks to make the individualization effect of contemporary society into a problem. It is not therefore surprising that he avoids the ambiguities of identity—a term which has a strongly individualistic undertone. However, the theme of political identity as an outcome of conflictual social and cultural processes rather than some fixed invariant condition is clearly present:

> the reasonable man . . . who is he exactly? And then who is left for that broad empty margin, the "public opinion of the day"? I think we are all in this margin; it is what we have learned and where we live. But unevenly, tentatively, we get a sense of movement, and the meanings and values extend. (354–55)

. . .

It took me a long time to appreciate how the founding texts of my own encounter with English cultural studies could be seen to converge around the thematics of identity. The key to appreciating this architecture lay in the ideas of nationality and national identity and the related issues of ethnicity and local and regional identity. Structures of feeling and the forms of consciousness that they fostered were nationally bounded. Similarly, for Thompson, the magical happening of class was something that could only be apprehended on a national basis. Along with Thompson's *Making* and Williams's *Revolution,* Richard Hoggart's *The Uses of Literacy* (1957) can be positioned so that it triangulates the rather ethnocentric space in which cultural development and cultural politics got configured as exclusively English national phenomena. Though each of these critical thinkers had his own subnational, regional, and local sensitivities and obligations, culture and its political forms were comprehended by all of them on the basis that nationality supplied. To be sure, the nation was often recognized as riven with the antagonist relations that characterized the struggle to create and maintain the domination of one group by others. But the boundaries of the nation formed the essential parameters in which these conflicts took shape. Though by no means always celebratory in tone, none of these important texts conveyed a sense of Britain and British identity being formed by forces, processes that overflowed from the imperial crucible of the nation-state. Williams's fleeting mentions of jazz or Hoggart's scarcely disguised apprehension about the catastrophic consequences of uniform "faceless" internationalism (his code for the leveling effects of American culture) suggest other conclusions and revealed their authors' direct interest in what might be worth protecting and maintaining amid the turmoil of the postwar reconstruction of British social life.

Each of these founding texts in the cultural studies canon can be read as a study of becoming: as an examination of class-based identity-in-process—transformed by historical forces that exceed their inscription in individual lives or consciousness and, at the same time, resisting that inevitable transformation.

This often unspoken fascination with the workings of identity has several additional facets. It does not always initiate the tacit collusion with Englishness that has been the festive site of cultural studies' reconciliation to a bunting-bedecked structure of feeling that its democratic, libertarian, and reconstructive aspirations once threatened to contextualize if not exactly overturn.

The significantly different political alignments and hopes of these writers as well as their contrasting stances within the generative political context that the New Left supplied for their attempts to grapple with class, popular culture, and communications (Thompson 1981) should not be played down. That the direction of Hoggart's investigations was parallel to those of Thompson and Williams was signaled in the force of his opening question, "Who are the working classes?" His thoughtful and stimulating book elaborated the distinguishing features of working-class English cultural identity. They were apprehended with special clarity even as they were assailed by the insidious forces of Americanism and commercialism: as they yielded "place to new" in a process he understood exclusively in terms of diminution and loss—"the debilitating mass trends of the day." The diseased organs of a vanishing working-class culture were anatomized in a sympathetic conservationist spirit. This mournful operation captured the pathological character of their extraordinary post-1945 transformation.

Hoggart's interest in the class-based division of the social world into "them" and "us" and his enthusiasm for the "live and let live" vernacular tolerance that thrived there could not be sustained once the insertion of postcolonial settler-citizens was recognized as a fundamental element in the transformation of Britain that alarmed and excited him. Immigration would become something that tested out the integrity and character of national and class identities in ways that he was not able to imagine. Hoggart's interesting speculations about the lack of patriotism in the working class, their spontaneous antiauthoritarianism and "rudimentary internationalism" sounded hollow. This was not only because complications introduced into the analysis of class and nationalism by the existence of a "domestic" fascism were somewhat brushed over (Mosley 1946) but, more important, because he was entirely silent about the social and political problems that mass black settlement was thought to be introducing into the previously calm and peaceable urban districts of England and Wales. It is not illegitimate to point to the narrowness of Hoggart's concerns or in the light of the subsequent patterning of British racial politics, to remind ourselves that his enigmatic silences on that subject could be used to undermine the authority of his pronouncements overall.

This is not just a question of hindsight. Before Hoggart's great book was published, Kenneth Little's 1947 *Negroes in Britain* had included a section entitled "The Coloured Man through Modern English Eyes" (1947, 240–68). Michael Banton's *The Coloured Quarter* (which had preceded Hoggart into print by some two years) had drawn explicit attention to the problems precipitated by large scale "Negro immigration" into "the large industrial cities of the North and the Midlands, in particular Leeds, Sheffield and Birmingham" (1955, 69). By this time the morality and injustices of the British color bar had been extensively discussed in a wide range of publications including the *Picture Post* (Kee 1949, 23–28). The moral and physical health status of "colonial coloured people" had been given a good public airing by this time and associated panics over the proliferation of half-caste children, Negro criminality, and vice were all established media themes by the time Hoggart's book was published.[2] Learie Constantine attempted to sum up the situation in 1955 when, as Harold Macmillan has revealed, the Conservative government discussed the possibility of using Keep Britain White as its electoral slogan (Macmillan 1973, 73–74). Constantine's insightful view of the class and gender topology of English racism in the same period that produced *The Uses of Literacy* is worth quoting at length. It is a valuable reminder to anyone who would suggest that a sensitivity to the destructive effects of racism did not arise until after the 1958 "race riots" in London's Notting Hill and Nottingham (Pilkington 1988):

> After practically twenty-five years' residence in England, where I have made innumerable white friends, I still think it would be just to say that almost the entire population of Britain really expect the coloured man to live in an inferior area devoted to coloured people, and not to have free and open choice of a living place. Most British people would be quite unwilling for a black man to enter their home, nor would they wish to work with one as a colleague, nor to stand shoulder to shoulder with one at a factory bench. This intolerance is far more marked in lower grades of English society than in higher, and perhaps it disfigures the lower middle classes most of all, possibly because respectability is so dear to them. Hardly any Englishwomen and not more than a small proportion of Englishmen would sit at a restaurant table with a coloured man or woman, and inter-racial marriage is considered almost universally to be out of the question. (Constantine 1955, 67)

Repositioned against the backdrop of this minoritarian history, it seems impossible to deny that Hoggart's comprehensive exclusion of "race" from his discussion of postwar class and culture represented clear political choices. His work certainly exemplifies a wider tendency to render those uncomfortable political issues invisible. The same fate awaited the unwanted "coloured immigrants" to whose lives the problems of "race" in Britain became perversely attached. It may be too harsh to judge his inability to perceive the interrelation of "race," nationality, and class as a

---

2. For a preliminary survey of the English political discussion of race during this period, see Carter, Harris, and Joshi 1967. See also Smith 1967 and Rich 1986, 14–20.

form of myopia induced by an indifferent ethnocentrism and complacent cryptona-tionalism but that is exactly how it seemed to me as a student of cultural studies on the twentieth anniversary of the publication of *The Uses of Literacy*.

What is more important to me now, some twenty years later still, is the possi-bility that the distinctive sense of cultural politics created by those precious New Left initiatives supplied critical resources to the investigation of identity. And further, that mingled with insights drawn from other standpoints, these very resources en-couraged us to see and to transcend the limits of the quietly nationalistic vision ad-vanced by British cultural studies' imaginary founding fathers.

Thankfully these days, the writing of contemporary cultural history has become a less self-consciously ethnocentric affair than it was in the 1950s. Stuart Hall's un-compromising insistence that contrary to appearances, "race" was an integral and absolutely internal feature of British political culture and national consciousness made a solid bridge not so much from scholarly nationalism to internationalism but toward a more open, global understanding of where Britain might be located in a decolonized and postimperial world order defined by the Cold War. Hall's consis-tent political engagements with the identity-(re)producing actions of Britain's mass media allocated substantial space to the issue of racism and used it as a magnifying glass through which to consider the unfolding of authoritarian forms that masked their grim and joyless character with a variety of populist motifs.

Particularly when appreciated in concert with the interventions of Edward Said, whose study of the Orient as an object of European knowledge and power endowed cultural studies with new heart in the late 1970s, Hall's work has supplied an invigo-rating corrective to the morbidity and implosiveness of figures like Williams, Thompson, and Hoggart. Said and Hall are both thinkers whose critiques of power and grasp of modern history have been enriched by their own experiences of migra-tion and some ambivalent personal intimacies with the distinctive patterns of colo-nial social life in Palestine and Jamaica. Both draw explicitly upon the work of Antonio Gramsci and implicitly on the legacy of the itinerant Anglophile Trinida-dian Marxist C. L. R. James. With the supplementary input of these intellectual but nonacademic figures, cultural studies' evaluations of identity were comprehensively complicated by colonialism as well as the enduring power of a different, non-Eu-ropean, or marginal modernity that had been forged amid the cultures of terror that operate at the limits of a belligerent imperial system.

The nation-state could not remain the central legitimizing principle brought to bear upon the analysis of the cultural relations and forms that subsumed identity. It was not only that core units of modern government and production had been consti-tuted from their external activities and in opposition to forces and flows acting upon them from the outside. Henceforth, identities deriving from the nation could be shown to be competing with subnational (local or regional) and supranational (diaspora) structures of belonging and kinship.

. . .

The main purpose of this inevitably cursory and oversimplified genealogy of identity is not to rake over the fading embers of the "Birmingham school" or to endorse a specific canon for cultural studies' institutional expansion. It has been to prompt inquiries into what cultural studies' committed scholarship might have to offer to contemporary discussions, not of culture but of multiculture and multiculturalism. Today, the volatile concept of identity belongs above all to the important debate in which multiculturalism is being redefined outside the outmoded conventions that governed its earlier incarnations, especially in the educational system. The obvious reply to this demand for a new theory of multicultural society that can yield a timely strategy for enhancing tolerance and respect renounces innocent varieties of orthodox pluralism and starts afresh by rethinking cultural difference through notions of hierarchy and hegemony. This is surely valuable but can only be a beginning. Multiculturalism in both Britain and the United States has retreated from reexamining the concept of culture in any thoroughgoing manner and drifted toward a view of "separate but equal" cultures. These parcels of incompatible activity may need to be rearranged in some new compensatory hierarchy or, better still, positioned in wholesome relations of reciprocal recognition and mutual equivalence that have been denied hitherto by the unjust operations of power which is not itself comprehended in cultural terms. In this approach, power exists outside of cultures and is therefore able to distort the proper relationship between them. The best remedy for this unhappy state of affairs is supposedly to be found in strengthening political processes and modernity's neutral civic identities so that cultural particularity can be confined and regulated in appropriately private places from which the spores of destructive incommensurability cannot contaminate the smooth functioning of always imperfect democracy. A political understanding of identity and identification—emphatically *not* a reified identity politics—points to other more radical possibilities in which we can begin to imagine ways for reconciling the particular and the general. We can build upon the contributions of cultural studies to dispose of the idea that identity is an absolute and to find the courage necessary to argue that identity formation—even body-coded ethnic and gender identity—is a chaotic process that can have no end. In this way, we may be able to make cultural identity a premise of political action rather than a substitute for it.

Works Cited

Banton, M. 1955. *The Coloured Quarter*. London: Jonathan Cape.

Beauvoir, S. de. 1960. *The Second Sex*. London: Four Square Books.

Butler, J. 1993. *Bodies That Matter*. New York: Routledge.

Calhoun, C., ed. 1994. *Social Theory and the Politics of Identity*. Oxford: Basil Blackwell.

Carter, B., C. Harris, and S. Joshi. 1967. "The 1951–1955 Conservative Government and the Racialization of Black Immigration." *Immigrants and Minorities* (London) 6, no. 3.

Constantine, L. 1955. *Colour Bar*. London: Stanley Paul and Co.

Fanon, F. 1986. *Black Skin, White Masks*. London: Pluto Press.

Fuss, D. 1990. *Essentially Speaking*. New York: Routledge.

Geertz, C. 1985. "The Uses of Diversity." *Michigan Quarterly Review* (Ann Arbor) 23.

Gillis, J. R., ed. 1994. *Commemorations: The Politics of National Identity*. Princeton: Princeton University Press.

Gleason, P. 1983. "Identifying Identity: A Semantic History." *Journal of American History* 69.

Hall, S. 1992a. "Cultural Studies and Its Theoretical Legacies." In *Cultural Studies*, ed. L. Grossberg et al. New York: Routledge.

———. 1992b. "The Question of Cultural Identity." In *Modernity and Its Futures*, ed. S. Hall et al. Oxford: Polity Press.

Haraway, D. 1991. "Situated Knowledges: The Science Question in Feminism and the Privilege of Partial Perspective." In *Simians, Cyborgs, and Women: The Reinvention of Nature*. New York: Routledge.

Hoggart, R. 1957. *The Uses of Literacy*. London: Chatto and Windus.

Kee, R. 1949. "Is There a British Colour Bar?" *Picture Post* (London) 44, no. 1 (2 July).

Little, K. 1947. *Negroes in Britain*. London: Routledge and Kegan Paul.

Macmillan, H. 1973. *At the End of the Day, 1961–1963*. Basingstoke: Macmillan.

Mosley, O. 1946. *My Answer*. Horley: Mosley Publications/Invicta Press.

Pilkington, E. 1988. *Beyond the Mother Country*. London: I. B. Tauris and Co.

Probyn, E. 1994. *Sexing the Self*. New York: Routledge.

Rich, P. B. 1986. "Blacks in Britain: Response and Reaction, 1945–1962." *History Today* (London) 36 (January).

Riley, D. 1990. *Am I That Name?* Basingstoke: Macmillan.

Schiebinger, L. 1993. *Nature's Body*. Boston: Beacon Press.

Smith, G. 1967. *When Jim Crow Met John Bull: Black American Soldiers in World War II Britain*. London: I. B. Tauris and Co.

Taylor, C. 1989. *Sources of the Self: The Making of Modern Identity*. Cambridge: Harvard University Press.

Thompson, E. 1980. *The Making of the English Working Class*. Harmondsworth: Pelican.

———. 1981. "Culturalism." In *People's History and Socialist Theory*, ed. R. Samuel. London: Routledge.

Williams, R. 1961. *The Long Revolution*. London: Chatto and Windus.

Thirteen

Beyond the Boundary:
The Work of Three Black
Women Artists in Britain

Gilane Tawadros

The artistic practice of gathering and re-using is said to have been invented in Paris in the Twenties by Picasso, a Spaniard. "Jazz Age" Paris jumped for joy at the "discovery" of Africa and her artifacts and stole them . . . [but] gathering and re-using has always been a part of Black creativity. . . . Gathering and re-using is like poetry, a gathering of words, sounds, rhythms and a re-using of them in a unique order to highlight, pinpoint and precisely express. A real poem does not decorate a page it changes a world. . . . Gathering and re-using takes time, measurable in hours certainly but also a sense of time having passed before, a sense of history and most importantly a sense of survival. . . . Gathering and re-using is an essential part of Black creativity, it does not mimic and is inextricably linked to economic circumstance. Each piece within the piece has its own history, its own past and its own contribution to the new whole, the new function. As Black women artists in the Black triangle in the twentieth century we must continue this process of gathering and re-using.

Lubaina Himid, "Fragments"

Two black women, their bodies clothed in a patchwork of colored fabrics, are running across a plain of pink cloth. Ahead of them, beyond the frame of pink are four black dogs, their leads gripped in the hand of the woman who fixes us with her gaze. The heads of two white men, trapped in dense particles of sand, are left behind the running women and their dogs. Lubaina Himid's *Freedom and Change* (1984) is a reworking of Pablo Picasso's *Two Women Running on the Beach* (1922). The small neoclassical image of two white women racing across a depopulated coastline, made by the Spanish artist in the years following the cessation of the Great War, has been appropriated by Himid and transformed. Picasso's appropriations of African tribal masks and ceremonial figures and the assimilation of "primitive" art into the work of modernist artists is challenged and reversed. While artists like Picasso absorbed the styles and forms of non-European art and translated them into the language of Western avant-gardism, Himid has visibly adapted Picasso's work to draw attention to the wider implications of the European process of gathering and reusing, a process

240

Lubaina Himid, *Freedom and Change,* 1984

wherein "Euro-American masters have stolen the genre, assimilated the methodology, oppressed the originators and claimed the prize" (Himid 1988, 8).

The significance of Himid's act of appropriation lies not only in the differing ramifications of gathering and reusing as a mode of creative expression but also in the sense of time which frames the work as a whole—a sense of history and a sense of the future—which stands in stark contrast to the consciousness of time articulated by the modern, avant-garde artist. There is a timeless, almost ahistorical quality to Picasso's *Two Women Running on the Beach,* evoked by the neoclassical figures who move through a deserted landscape devoid of any sense of time or place, which thus obscures the specificity of the historical and aesthetic framework in which the painting was made. Reaching away from an unseen past and stretching forward to an intangible future, these women emerge from the distinct context of post–World War I European society. Abandoning the traumatic memories of war which shook Western civilization, they are running toward a future progressively modern and, at the same time, continuous with the classical Graeco-Roman roots of European culture. In short, Picasso's *Two Women* visualizes a period of transition in the social and aesthetic history of Europe and denotes "modernity" insofar as that has been defined as "the consciousness of an epoch that defines itself in relation to the past of antiquity in order to view itself as the result of a transition from old to new" (Habermas 1987, 3). Moreover, it pictures a changed consciousness of time which emerged in the course of the nineteenth century and which, according to Jurgen Habermas, characterizes the project of "aesthetic modernity."

Lubaina Himid's *Freedom and Change* expresses a period of transition from old to new and can be defined as "modern" to the extent that this transition is articulated in relation to the past. There the similarity between the two works ends. For Himid asserts a very different relationship to the past and the future in her work. The past expressed by Picasso's *Two Women* is an abstract one, not fixed by historical time or place, wherein the contours of classical art are stretched quite literally to accommodate an unspecific and universalizing conception of the past. By contrast, the past in Himid's work, defined by the configurations of white men's heads, is designated as a place shaped and presided over by a white male presence. The history of the West, and indeed the history of Western art, has privileged the mark of male individuals and rendered invisible or inferior the place of black peoples (particularly black women) within these histories. Himid's cardboard cut-outs of white male heads point to the privileged site accorded both to the originators of the grand narratives of Western culture and also to the declared origins of Western civilization, in other words, the past of Graeco-Roman antiquity. The figurative remnants of the old order of Western culture which gave currency to notions of originality, origins, and authenticity have been thus consigned to the depths of the past. While their place in the present has been usurped by two black women who mediate between this past and a future defined by the contours of four black dogs.

Moving across a field of pink, these women designate a reign of freedom and change. The pink can be seen as emblematic, not of nationhood or national sovereignty, but of black womanhood which defies its relegation to the margins and enters the center ground to assert its place *in* history. Himid's women displace what Stuart Hall has called the "centered discourses of the West," but this does not imply that the grand narratives of Western culture are simply to be replaced by an alternative, totalizing narrative. Rather, this process of displacement "entails putting in question [Western culture's] universalist character and its transcendental claims to speak for everyone, while being itself everywhere and nowhere" (this volume, chap. 7). Whereas Picasso's women race across a space which aspires to the status of the universal and the transcendental and which paradoxically remains confined within the perimeters of the frame, Himid's women significantly tread a borderline which marks the threshold between real and imagined space, between lived experiences and expressions of that experience. In opposition to the universalizing tendencies of modernism, *Freedom and Change* assigns central importance to the position of difference. Himid articulates a "positive conception of the ethnicity of the margins, or the periphery . . . a recognition that we all speak from a particular place, out of a particular history, out of a particular experience, a particular culture without being contained by that position" (Hall, this volume, chap. 7). The particular place from which Himid's women assert their historical experience is the coastline, an ambivalent site which marks the frontier of slavery, colonialism, and migration but which also denotes the positivity of the *diasporan* experience. Like the separate pieces of a patchwork, Himid has embroidered together a number of diverse histories and varying categories of creative expression (from drawing as a signifier of the academy traditions of Western art to patchwork as a signifier of domestic, "feminine" craft) which contest the unequivocal order and monolithic perspective circumscribed by Picasso's earlier work. Himid weaves a web of cultural and historical meanings into the fabric of her work which derive both from the transformation of the original source and also from the assemblage of fragments which together dispute the authority of the established order (both historical and art historical) of Western culture.

What then are the implications of postmodernism for Lubaina Himid's *Freedom and Change*? Is her collage of fragments merely a "random cannibalization of all the styles of the past," as Jameson argues, and thus symptomatic of the "waning of our historicity" and our inability to fashion representations of our current experience? Can Himid's intimations of the illegitimacy of the grand narratives of the West be explained in terms of the death of the individual subject and a crisis of confidence in notions of progress and human emancipation? Or are these prescriptions for a postmodern condition themselves indicative of continuing periodic transformations in European thought? In this context, I would argue, Lubaina Himid's *Freedom and Change* does not substitute a history of aesthetic styles for "real" history. Rather, in positioning two black women between a specific past delimited by white male individualism and a particular vision of the future defined by the vivid contours of a black presence, Himid situates black women and black women's artistic discourse firmly *within* history. Thus the avowed collapse of the grand narratives of Western culture makes possible the articulation of black experience at the very center of history and the history of art. The process of gathering and reusing, far from affirming the fragmentation of the black subject in the terms of postmodernity, attests to the centrality and dynamism of the diasporan experience, of diverse cultural influences and discontinuous histories in opposition to the false unities of Western thought which reach their apogee in the "supreme fictions" of modernism (Foster 1987, ix–xvi).

The question which then poses itself and which frames this paper as a whole is whether Lubaina Himid's *Freedom and Change* and the cultural production of two other contemporary black women artists—Sonia Boyce and Sutapa Biswas—can be defined in terms of postmodernism and postmodernity. Or alternatively, whether the aesthetic and sociohistorical category of postmodernity as a particular moment within Western consciousness merely corresponds with and legitimates the historical and cultural configurations of black experiences and black creativity within the diaspora. These are the central questions which I aim to address within the parameters of the artistic practice of Himid, Boyce, and Biswas, although the work of other artists is cited to illustrate specific points or themes.

Modernism and Modernity

The most significant feature of modernism as a historical category of Western thought and artistic consciousness was its self-characterization as a period of transition and radical change which found expression through metaphors of the vanguard and the avant-garde. The military terminology which framed the artistic production of modernist practitioners was apposite insofar as this indicated the assaults that would be mounted on the fortresses of past tradition and the forays into an "as yet unoccupied future" (Habermas 1987, 5). The domain of artistic practice, it was claimed, would be transformed through stylistic innovation and radical new subject-matter in the same way that the arena of modern life had been transfigured irrecoverably by science and technology. As men "professionally engaged in the present and the future as opposed to being 'representatives of a prolonged and once-glorious past,'" modern artists could see themselves alternatively as scientists, priests, or engineers in the construction of a new and better world (Lynton 1980, 12).

Yet one of the paradoxes of modernity, as both Lyotard and Habermas have pointed out, is that in order to see itself as something essentially new and different, modernity must define itself in relation to the past. Thus the language of avant-gardism and stylistic innovation in modernism is consistently qualified by references to and even continuities with the past. So when, for example, the poet Filippo Tommaso Marinetti launched his program for Futurism in the form of a manifesto repudiating all the traditional values of the past, he exalted the "new form of beauty" exemplified by the racing car in comparative terms with the established canon of Hellenic art.[1] In order to understand fully the implications of this and the other paradoxes of modernism, it is necessary to differentiate, as Habermas has done, between the development of modernist European art and the "project of modernity" to which it is intimately tied. First of all, the concept of modernity itself is not confined to the historical epoch of modernism. The idea of modernity (and the contingent notion

1. "A racing car," wrote Marinetti, "its bonnet adorned with pipes like serpents with explosive breath . . . a racing car which seems to run on gunpowder is more beautiful than the Victory of Samothrace" ("The Foundation and Manifesto of Futurism" [1909], quoted in Lynton 1982, 87).

of progress) has appeared and reappeared intermittently in Western thought over the centuries since the time of Roman Christendom. What distinguishes modernism as part of the discourse of nineteenth-century Western thought is that rather than expressing itself in opposition to a specific historical period, it defines itself in relation to a vague and indefinite past:

> In the course of the 19th century, there emerged . . . that radicalized consciousness of modernity which freed itself from all specific historical ties. This most recent modernism simply makes an abstract opposition between tradition and the present. (Habermas 1987, 3–4)

Aesthetic modernity is historically only a part of cultural modernity, inheriting the project of modernity which involved three main developments: the separation of thought into autonomous spheres of science, morality, and art; the institutionalization and professionalization of art and its consequent distancing from the wider public; and finally, the expectation that this specialized domain of culture could be utilized to enrich everyday social life (Habermas 1987, 8–9). Thus, while the "radicalized consciousness of modernity" abandons fixed historical references to the past, the history of Western knowledge, and specifically, the emergence of cultural modernity in the Enlightenment, provides a historical context for understanding the discourse of modernism, its continuities, and its inconsistencies, as well as the paradox whereby modernism characterizes itself as progressive and innovative on the basis of its avowed affinity with the "primitive" and the "barbaric."

In a letter to Charles Morice in the spring of 1903, Paul Gauguin, traditionally cast as the founding father of modernist primitivism, declared: "I am a savage. And the civilised foresee it, for there is nothing surprising or confusing in my work except this savage-in-spite-of-myself. For that reason it is inimitable."[2] Artistic originality, it is implied, goes hand in hand with a seemingly visionary identification by the "civilized" modern artist with the forces of primitivism and the domain of the savage. The boundaries of traditional art would be transgressed, or so it was perceived, by a voyage beyond the established parameters of Western society, whether in a temporal or a geographical sense, into the margins of distance and difference (Solomon-Godeau 1989, 118–28). On the basis of an alliance with the perceived "other" of Western society, the modern artist could claim both originality and universal validity for his cultural production, as Abigail Solomon-Godeau has written in relation to Gauguin:

> Common to both the embrace of the primitive—however defined—and the celebration of artistic originality is the belief that both enterprises are ani-

---

2. Paul Gaugin's letter to Charles Morice, Atuana, Marquesas Islands, April 1903, reprinted in Chipp 1968, 84–85.

mated by the artist's privileged access, be it spiritual, intellectual or psychological, to that which is primordially internal. . . . [T]he artist "recognizes" in the primitive or the primitive artifact that which was immanent, but inchoate; the object from "out there" enables the expression of what is thought to be "in there." The experience of the primitive or of the primitive artifact is therefore, and among other things, valued as an aid to creation, and to the act of genius located in the artist's exemplary act of recognition (120).

As a subtext to the history of modern art, primitivism has been considered traditionally as just such an "aid to creation" or alternatively as a catalyst in the evolution of avant-garde art in Europe which, according to one art historian, "helped the [modern] artists to formulate their own aims because they could attribute to it the qualities they themselves sought to attain" (Goldwater 1967, 253). Thus Picasso's more or less direct citations of African sculpture in his painting *Les Demoiselles d'Avignon* (1907) is interpreted as a "watershed" in the development of modern art, while Mondrian's assimilation of non-Western systems of thought is obscured by the overriding significance of his innovative pictorial language in terms of the canon of European modernism. What is important here, however, is not the role, catalytic or otherwise, played by African and Oceanic art forms in the cultural production of the avant-garde. Nor is it my intention to rehearse the gamut of traditional art historical analyses and commentaries on modernist art. Rather, I am concerned with what Solomon-Godeau has defined as the "mythic speech of primitivism," that is, the mystification of actual social and economic relations in the discourse of primitivism (whether in terms of artistic practice or art historical accounts). The process of demystification necessitates the articulation, however briefly, of the configurations of power and knowledge within which this mythic speech is articulated and which makes it possible. Far from disturbing the boundaries between Western and non-Western cultures, the discourse of so-called modern primitivism effectively reinforces the separation of spheres of the modern and the primitive which significantly can be traced back to the Enlightenment:

> The primitive has served as a coded other at least since the Enlightenment, usually as a subordinate term in its imaginary set of oppositions (light/dark, rational/irrational, civilised/savage). This domesticated primitive is thus constructive, not disruptive, of the binary *ratio* of the West; fixed as a structural opposite or a dialectical other to be incorporated, it assists in the establishment of a western identity, center, norm and name.[3]

3. Hal Foster 1985, 196, quoted in Willis and Fry 1988–89, 6.

This imaginary set of oppositions between civilized and savage, self and other, superior and inferior operates as a *productive* function of the political and economic relations between European and non-European peoples in a particular historical period. In other words, the history of "modern primitivism" is bound up inextricably with the history of European colonialism in such a way that knowledge of other cultures and hence their appropriation can be subsumed into the language of modernism precisely because the hegemony of the West is not allowed to be contested:

> The "primitive" can be put on a pedestal of history (Modernism) and admired for what is missing in Western culture, as long as the "primitive" does not attempt to become an active subject to define or change the course of history. . . . Primitivism has little to do with the *actual* conditions of the peoples or cultures it refers to, but it is an idea in Western culture by which Others are defined in various periods of its recent history. As a projection and representation of non-European peoples and their cultures in Western philosophy or discourse, it in turn justifies colonial expansion and domination. In other words, Primitivism is a function of colonial discourse. (Araeen 1987, 8; my emphasis)

This point is made clear in a cartoon by Lubaina Himid and Maud Sulter, entitled *An A–Z of Picasso* (1988), which appeared in *Feminist Arts News*. The alleged innovation of a Picasso painting is juxtaposed with a representation which articulates the conjuncture between colonialism and "culture colonialism." The barrel of a rifle, wedged between an African mask and a ceremonial figure points to the intersection on a map between the continents of Europe (significantly, of southern Spain) and Africa. The text which accompanies this image and the following representation of the artist's studio, emphasizes the dissonance between Picasso's appropriations of African art (which signal the progressive development of European modernism) and the Western characterizations of African cultures as savage, barbaric, and essentially backward. The final image in the strip responds to the question posed at the beginning, "How inventive, who would ever think of doing such a thing," with the retort, "First look at African Art." The discourse of primitivism, Himid implies, and the contingent precepts of originality and innovation need to be located in the historical context of European colonialism. Consequently, the different epistemological status of the perceived other is rendered visible within the cultural map of Western knowledge and, furthermore, as a corollary to the differing political and economic status of non-European peoples within the geographical map of colonial conquest and annexation (Philippi 1987, 35).

It is necessary at this point to distinguish between Lyotard's thesis of postmodernity and the diagnosis of modernism and postmodernism put forward by Jurgen

Habermas and which to a great extent informs my argument here. Whereas Lyotard perceived the "decay of confidence" in the suppositions of modernity as the basic condition of an epoch and, furthermore, as evidence of the collapse of the "Enlightenment project" as a whole, Habermas contests this apparent demise of modernity and argues that the configurations of postmodernity rather stem from the fact that the project of modernity has been onesidedly and inadequately realized, that is, essentially incomplete. Consequently, the modernist consciousness needs to be understood as the product of an intersection of historical and utopian perspectives and if this particular model of modernity has been exhausted, this does not imply a priori that there has been a collapse of belief in the possibility of progress (or change) as such. The way in which postmodernity is defined or expressed, implies Habermas, depends on the way in which modernity is understood *historically*. Whereas Lyotard and other contemporary theorists have concentrated on the *effects* of modern consciousness and derived from this a prescription for the postmodern condition, Habermas emphasizes the importance of articulating the historical processes which determine this consciousness of modernity and which make it fallible and subject to criticism. This assertion of history, he suggests, can provide the necessary structures for understanding the present dynamically in relation to the past and pave the way for a grand narrative which is "neither 'metaphysical,' nor authoritarian, nor insensitive to the complexities of contemporary societies."[4]

In her essay "Sculpture in the Expanded Field," Rosalind Krauss defines postmodernism as a break with the aesthetic field of modernism (1987, 31–42). She argues that the "bounded conditions of modernism have suffered a logically determined rupture" which is consummated in postmodern artistic practice. According to Krauss, the logic of modern sculpture has led not only to its deconstruction (which she traces back to the late 1950s and early 1960s) but also to the "deconstruction of the modern order of the arts based on the Enlightenment order of distinct and autonomous spheres" (Foster 1987, xiii). The modernist demand for the purity and separateness of the various mediums, she claims, has been disrupted by postmodern practitioners who have dissolved the boundaries between the different mediums of sculpture, architecture, photography, and so on. As a direct consequence, the notion of the specialized domain of individual practice has been displaced by "continual relocation," a sort of "cultural nomadism" which characterizes the contemporary artist's movement across the space of postmodernism. Among the artists she cites as operating within this expanded field of postmodernism is Richard Long, who occupies the "nomadic position" described by Achille Bonita Oliva wherein the contemporary artist

4. For a full account of the respective positions of Lyotard and Habermas in relation to modernity and postmodernity, see Dews 1989, 27–40.

not only traverses different cultural mediums but also different cultural traditions, Western and non-Western, at a time when, it is claimed, "the declines of ideology, the loss of a general theoretical position pushes man into drifting."[5] Works by Long such as *Walking a Line in Peru* (1972), however, while contesting the Enlightenment notion of autonomous and distinct spheres of artistic activity, nonetheless suggest continuities not only with modernism but with the project of cultural modernity as a whole. Where the narrative of Krauss's critical analysis is informed consistently with the precepts of cultural modernity, that is, notions of rupture, innovation, and progress, Long's artistic practice perpetuates the modernist model of the white male artist who invades unknown territories (in this case, exemplified by the Peruvian terrain which implicitly shrouds the remnants of ancient Inca culture) to create original and innovative work which defies the boundaries of traditional Western art.

The interrelationship of Long's work with the project of modernity is borne out by two installations by Rasheed Araeen—*Arctic Circle* and *White Line through Africa*—which dispute Krauss's argument that the expanded field of postmodernist sculpture has broken conclusively with the aesthetic paradigm of modernism. Taking Long's work as a starting point for a critique of the appropriation by Western artists of "other" cultures, Araeen himself appropriates Long's interventions in the land of the "other." *Arctic Circle* (1982–88) consists of empty, discarded beer cans and wine bottles arranged to form a complete and geometrically correct circle. Such an act of dual reference both to modernism and to the high instance of alcoholism among Eskimo peoples renders visible the interdependency of the singular initiative of the individual artist and the economic and political interventions of Western society as a whole in the terrain of the "other." *White Line through Africa* (1982–88) more directly challenges the ethos of "romantic innocence" which cloaks the operations of cultural colonialism in Western art—both modern and postmodern. Composed of a line of bleached bones, thirty-five feet in length, it implicates Long's artistic practice:

> While high technology makes people leave the land and move to the shanties of the cities in search of food and shelter, the romantics of the affluent metropolis move out with their cameras into the "wilderness" to claim the earth again, and for themselves, and they do so in such a way that the act of the former is covered up. The world is touched again, ordered, depoliticised and reclaimed.[6]

The project of modernity, moreover, remains intact since Long's work maintains the implications of Enlightenment thought whereby artistic practice not only retains its

5. Achille Oliva (1982), quoted in Philippi 1987, 37.
6. Rasheed Araeen, quoted in *Artscribe*, March/April 1989, 74.

Rasheed Araeen, *White Line through Africa*, 1982–88. Photograph by Edward Woodman

distance from the social realities of everyday life but also functions as the cultural rationalization and mystification of socioeconomic relations, in this case, between European and non-European peoples. Where Krauss, Lyotard, Jameson, and others argue that postmodern cultural production marks a break with modernism and modernity, the works of Araeen and other contemporary black artists question whether postmodernism in reality expresses a rupture from the *conceptual* fabric of Western modernity (and from the structures of Western knowledge as a whole) as well as from the *aesthetic* configurations of modernism. Along the lines of Habermas's counterperspective on postmodernity, the work of black artists discussed here suggests not only a critique of cultural modernity, but also the assertion of a conceptual framework formulated within the diasporan experience, which defies the transcendental, hierarchical, and oversimplistic precepts of modernist consciousness. Furthermore, the agenda circumscribed by contemporary black cultural practice, as Paul Gilroy has argued, demands a theoretical shift from the restrictive opposition between modernism and postmodernism:

> Approaching contemporary black cultural politics by this route involves a sharp move away from the rigid nexus of modernism and postmodernism. . . . It is a tenacious challenge to the nascent orthodoxies of postmodernism which can only see the distinctive formal features of black expressive culture in terms of pastiche, quotation, parody and paraphrase rather than a more substantive, political and aesthetic concern with polyphony and the value of different registers of address. . . . Postmodernism fever is an ailment identified through symptoms that have been around within modernism for a long while. . . . These ties may be an indication that the grand narrative of reason is not currently being brought to an end but rather *transformed.* Forms of rationality are being created endlessly. Perhaps only European hubris claims that this particular moment of crisis is the fundamental moment of rupture, the new dawn. (Gilroy 1988–89)

The importance which Habermas assigns to establishing the historical roots of cultural modernity in the Enlightenment and hence its continuing presence in the postmodern arena is echoed in Gilroy's implication of postmodernity as merely a historical phase in the ensuing development of Western thought. The important point here is that it is the assertion of history and historical processes which puts sharply into focus the continuities of modernism and postmodernism with the project of modernity as a whole. It is also history, as opposed to nostalgia for, or reproduction of, the past, which informs and distinguishes the recent emergence of black artistic practice from the configurations of postmodernism. Thus in the face of Jameson's insistence upon the incompatibility of postmodernist nostalgia with "genuine historicity," black cultural production is about *history itself* (Jameson 1984, 65–66).

History, Historicism, and the Historiography of Art

Now to talk to me about black studies as if it's something that concerned black people is an utter denial. This is the history of Western Civilisation. I can't see it otherwise. This is the history that black people and white people and all serious students of modern history and the history of the world have to know. . . . I do not know, as a Marxist, black studies as such. I only know the struggle of people against tyranny and oppression in a certain social and political setting, and particularly, during the last two hundred years, it's impossible for me to separate black studies from white studies in any theoretical point of view. (James 1984, 194)

The assertion of history and historical processes in black cultural production can only be defined in relation to the historical narratives of Western society and culture in the same way that the history of black peoples can only be articulated in terms of the history of modern Europe. Against this background, the work of contemporary black artists will be seen to be derived from a "double consciousness" which not only affirms the interdependency of the histories of black peoples and Western civilization, but also questions the precepts of modern Western historiography, that is, the ordering of history in terms of the privileged concepts of tradition, evolution, source, and origin.

According to Michel Foucault's archaeology of Western knowledge, the end of the eighteenth century and the beginning of the nineteenth century mark a point of discontinuity in Western thought and the threshold of a modernity that we have not left behind. At this juncture, the theory of representation which throughout the classical age plays a constructive role in the knowledge of Western culture is eclipsed by a "profound historicity [which] penetrates into the heart of things [and] imposes upon them the forms of order implied by the continuity of time." Thus, Foucault argues (1986b), the discourses of the modern age are shaped according to the precepts of history and historicity. Hence the emergence of such human sciences as anthropology, psychology, and archaeology which not only posit man at the center of knowledge, but also imply a conception of history which is premised on principles of continuity and cohesion. This particular conception of history which still informs modern knowledge Foucault defines as "total history" and he contrasts this with the contours and methodologies of an alternative "general history," predicated on discontinuities, boundaries, differences of level, shifts, and chronological specificities. Total history, he maintains, "draws all phenomena round a single centre—a principle, a meaning, a spirit, a world-view, an overall shape," whereas general history deploys "the space of dispersion" (1986a, 3–17).

The significance of the conceptual framework of Foucault's general history lies in the fact that, while it maintains continuities with the project of modernity insofar as it sees itself in terms of a rupture from traditional history, it nonetheless contests notions of evolution, teleology, and origins, and asserts in their place the principles of dispersion and difference in history. While Foucault's structuralist theory of history (and this applies equally to poststructuralist theory) implies a rejection of traditional history and historicism, black cultural politics insists upon the importance of analyzing critically and redefining notions such as progress and origin in order to express history and historicism along the lines of resistance and change. This suggests three main themes or aspects underlying the forms and contents of black cultural production. First of all, it is predicated on an awareness of the historical limits of the modern, Western *episteme* which privileges notions of continuity, development, origins, and so on over and above notions of discontinuity, dispersion, and difference. Second, like the diasporan experience of black peoples, the artistic practice level derives from and is created within Western history as well as Western theories of history. Third, the art work, in this context, both involves a questioning of the political implications and "dubious legacies" of the conceptual framework of European history and also implies an alternative conception of history, historicism, and the historiography of art.

In opposition to the work of postmodern artists which reproduces notions of origins, originality, and authenticity based in the forms of classical art, some black cultural artists "imitate" the work of the "old masters" in order to dismantle the "theoretical scaffold" in which they were created. Lubaina Himid's *Michelangelo's David* (1982?), for example, quite explicitly copies the work of the artist who, according to Vasari, epitomizes the summit of Renaissance artistic achievement. Her painted wood reproduction of Michelangelos's *David,* however, rather than adapting the specific style of sixteenth-century Italian art in order to celebrate its past glories, deconstructs the conceptual fabric of Renaissance culture. For the figure of David has been subverted by the imposition, in the place of his penis, of a massive Graeco-Roman pillar. The alleged cultural origins of European art and art history, Himid suggests, are the roots of a patriarchal, racist, and subjective "grand narrative" which, by asserting the principles of progress and originality, conceals the historical processes which shape its ascendance in Western knowledge. Craig Owens writes:

> In the modern period the authority of the work of art, its claim to represent some authentic vision of the world, did not reside in its uniqueness or its singularity, as is often said; rather that authority was based on the universality modern aesthetics contributed to the *forms* utilized for the representation of vision. . . . As recent analyses of the "enunciative apparatus" of visual representation—its poles of emission and reception—confirm, the

representational systems of the West admit only one vision—that of the constitutive male subject—or, rather they posit the subject of representation as
absolutely centred, unitary, masculine. (1987, 58)

According to Owens, postmodernism attempts to upset the reassuring authority and
universal claims of this essentially modern, male-centered discourse. He argues that
at the intersection of postmodernism and contemporary feminism lies the epistemological and political challenge to the "master narratives" of the past, designated
by the dual questioning of the patriarchal order as well as of the structure of representation. Since the issue of feminism and the work of black women is discussed
below, I am more concerned at this point to examine the claims made for postmodernism by Owens and poststructuralist theory in general, in particular, the idea
put forward by Owens and others that postmodernism signals the West's "loss of
mastery" in the domain of both culture and politics. As a symptom of this recent
demise of the master narratives, he points to the resurrection of the "heroism" of
previous ages in art history and contends that contemporary artists at best can only
simulate mastery and that this simulacra of mastery thus testifies to its loss through
the act of disavowal (67).

There are two major questions raised by this assertion: the first relates to the
nature of the framework in which this alleged "loss of mastery" has taken place;
the second addresses whether the West in reality has surrendered its hegemony.
First of all, where postmodern practice and theory do contest notions of origins,
originality, and authenticity, the frame of reference appears to remain manifestly
Western.

It is in fact a narcissistic and introspective loss which has been proclaimed by
poststructuralist theory. The declaration of loss in itself, and the central position
which this occupies in contemporary thought, negates the possibility that the Western tradition may have been challenged before and elsewhere, in the margins of European thought. Furthermore, the loss of the grand narratives of Western culture or
the death of the white, male subject does not necessarily imply that alternative narratives or other subjects will be fixed within the center frame of European consciousness. That is to say, such losses may make possible the recognition of other cultures
and theoretical perspectives, but only as one amid a plurality of cultures, another
fragment amid the debris and "bric-a-brac" of the global museum:

> When we discover that there are several cultures instead of just one and con-
> sequently at the time when we acknowledge the end of a sort of cultural mo-
> nopoly, be it illusory or real, we are threatened with the destruction of our
> own discovery. Suddenly, it becomes possible that there are just *others*, that
> we ourselves are an "other" among others. All meaning and every goal hav-

ing disappeared, it becomes possible to wander through civilisations as if through vestiges and ruins. The whole of mankind becomes an imaginary museum. . . . We can very easily imagine a time close at hand when any fairly well-to-do person will be able to leave his country indefinitely in order to taste his own national death in an interminable, aimless voyage.[7]

This narrative which maps out so clearly the space of postmodernism testifies to Habermas's assertion (1987, 3–15) that postmodernity, and poststructuralism also, evacuates from its conceptual field of vision the specific imperatives of history and historical time. The exclusion of history from the theory and practice of postmodernism has several implications. It circumscribes the limits of a discourse which ignores, to a greater extent, the historical roots of concepts such as origins, originality, and authenticity, and of modern European thought generally. By ignoring the historical exigencies which contributed to the formulation of these concepts, postmodernism, then, can assert itself as a break or rupture from past tradition and hence fail to recognize the persistence of these notions both *outside* and *within* postmodernism itself. Finally, and most important, this evacuation of history enables postmodernism to deny the continuing hegemony of the West, both in the cultural sphere where it still prescribes and legitimates the artistic practice of its choosing and when it chooses, and also in the political sphere where the dispersion and changing forms of Western hegemony are mistaken for economic and political egality.[8] What distinguishes the black artistic practice again from postmodern practice and theory is the assertion of history and historiography unambiguously within the frame of cultural reference. Thus, the citation by Himid and other black artists of preexisting art forms from the history of Western art can be seen to be a part of a coherent political and aesthetic strategy based on an interrogation of Western history *through* history.

. . .

Martin Bernal (1987) has described in detail the ways in which racist ideology and the idea of progress determined the ascendancy of the Aryan model of history in Western knowledge. These two factors, as other writers have shown also, were bound together inextricably in the *episteme* of nineteenth-century Europe.[9] The notion that

7. Hilton Kramer (1980, 35), quoted in Crimp 1983, 44.
8. For example, Craig Owens (1987) seems to have mistaken the displacement of nineteenth-century configurations of colonialism by contemporary neocolonial forms as the demise of Western hegemony entirely, particularly where he writes: "It is clear that what has been lost is not primarily a cultural mastery, but an economic, technical and political one."
9. See, for example, Nisbet 1980 and Mosse 1978.

historical progress as a linear continuity would pave the way for human emancipation was founded on the belief that the present would supersede the past, but also on a philosophy of European racial superiority. Consequently, there emerged the paradox of Western historiography whereby non-European peoples in the present were relegated to the depths of the past and designated as statistically "primitive," while the declared Graeco-Roman past of Europe was mobilized as the paradigm of human progress. Racist ideology and the idea of progress intersect in Western knowledge, therefore, at the point where other non-European cultures are fixed *outside* of history, while the West moves forward unceasingly on the wheels of historical progress. As Partha Mitter (1977) has argued in relation to Hegel and art history:

> For Hegel, every nation had a preordained place in his "ladder" of historical progress and reflected a unique national "spirit." . . . The conclusion was that if we were to judge each particular type or tradition of art we must first of all see what particular national spirit it represented and to what particular point in history that nation in turn belonged. . . . Paradoxically, his dynamic principle of history, the dialectics of change, only helped to establish a fundamentally static image of Indian art, its immemorial immutability, its unchanging irrationality, and its poetic fantasy, all predetermined by the characterisation of the Indian "spirit." It needs to be repeated here that Hegel's characterisation of the Indian spirit was not based on empirical evidence but determined essentially by India's temporal position in Hegelian metaphysics. . . . It was thus condemned to remain always outside history, static, immobile, and fixed for all eternity.

Sutapa Biswas's diptych *Pied Piper of Hamlyn/Put Your Money Where Your Mouth Is* (1987) articulates concisely these conceptual ramifications of the Western notion of progress. A plump European man, seated in a rickshaw drawn by an Indian man in one panel of the painting, is followed by a procession of young children in the second panel. In the background to both panels stand the ancient remains of Indian architectural sculptures, chiseled from the contours of the hills. Such an explicit reference to the European fairy tale in which a piper cleanses a rat-infested town by leading the rats to be drowned along the melodic train of his music implicates the idea of progress as a sinister and misleading one. Through the notion of progress, Biswas implies, Western knowledge has rationalized the relative superiority of European culture over non-European civilizations, in defiance of the physical evidence. The mythology of racial superiority and the contingent concept of progress, like the fable of the pied piper of Hamlyn, erases non-Western cultures from the map of history, rendering them fixed and immobile in an ahistorical vacuum and in the background to the central imperatives of European progress. The price which this mythology and its historical repercussions exacts is the relative poverty and economic dependency which now engulf these non-European civilizations.

This alternative conception of history which can be discerned in Biswas's work and in the domain of black cultural production as a whole implies not only that the histories of black people and Western civilization are locked together inseparably, but also that history or historicity is a dynamic part of everyday life and human existence as opposed to being a conceptual or aesthetic archive from which specific periods or particular ideas can be invoked haphazardly. This leads me to C. L. R. James's theorization of Heidegger's notions of "historicality" and "temporality" which he identifies in the writings of the West Indian writer Wilson Harris. According to James (1980, 157–72), Heidegger's concept of *dasein* or "being there," that is to say, the idea that each man or woman's existence is predicated on a specific and individual consciousness of time—on an awareness of the past and a conception of the future—is particularly pertinent to black cultural experiences in the diaspora. He argues that Heidegger's distinction between "inauthentic existence" wherein "truth" is perceived to be in the perimeters of the mind and is pursued throughout the classification of facts and things on the one hand, and "authentic existence" or *dasein* on the other hand, implies a challenge to the precepts of modern European thought which has always existed in the margins of black experience and knowledge.

It is in this context that the concept of the *diaspora* assumes its full significance in relation both to *dasein* and historicality. In opposition to essentialist notions of race and the linear construction of history as progress, the term *diaspora* embraces a plurality of different cultures and discontinuous histories. Not removed or separated from each other as postmodernism would imply, except in a geographical sense, these cultures and histories are interrelated and are interwoven together in the tapestry of a wider history. More important, however, the notion of the diaspora rejects the restrictive limitations of "origins" and "essences," as decisively as the European prescriptions for nationhood and progress. As Gilroy writes in relation to black artist in Britain:

> The value of the term diaspora increases as its essentially symbolic character is understood. It points emphatically to the fact that there can be no pure, uncontaminated or essential blackness anchored in an originary moment. It suggests that a myth of shared origins is not a talisman which can suspend political antagonisms or a deity invoked to cement a pastoral view of black life that can answer the multiple pathologies of contemporary racism. (1988–89, 35)

Identity, Nation, Race

Stuart Hall has argued (this volume, chap. 7) that the new politics of black representation has a "profound and complex relationship" to the past which does not rely on nostalgia or simple reconstruction but which implicates the past dynamically in relation to the present. In terms of identity and black cultural production in contemporary Britain, this suggests that the identities of the present will be mediated by the ways in which racial and national identities have been and are defined presently in British consciousness. It suggests also that the diaspora as a historical experience will have implications for the ways in which black identity is constructed and represented in artistic practice.

In order to delineate the ways in which race and nation are articulated it should be emphasized that both racism and nationalism are shifting categories subject to historical and geographical transformations. Indeed, while they are able to maintain certain continuities with the past, the discourses of race and nation nonetheless assume new forms and different meanings according to their specific context. Against this background, Paul Gilroy has pointed to the distinctive features of "the new racism" in Britain and identified its relative novelty in terms of its capacity "to link discourses of patriotism, nationalism, xenophobia, Englishness, militarism and gender difference into a complex system which gives 'race' its contemporary meaning" (1991, 43). The significant hallmark of the politics of "race" in Britain today, according to Gilroy, is its grounding in concepts of national belonging and homogeneity which not only "blur the distinction between 'race' and nation but rely on that very ambiguity for their effect" (45). Notions of race and nation are locked together in the fabrication of "imagined communities" whose perimeters are being defined and redefined constantly by racism.

While this contemporary theorization of race, nation, and cultural identity is not the exclusive domain of the New Right, it is here that the perceived conflict between national identity and racial identity is most explicitly stated in terms of cultural difference. According to neoconservative thought, "the nation is constituted by homogeneity of culture, and the problem of race lies in the fact of cultural difference. Alien cultures . . . necessarily undermine social cohesion" (Seidel 1986, 112). The important point, here, is that the definition of "race" and ethnicity in contemporary Britain has been articulated on both sides of the color line, by left and right equally, in terms of *cultural* absolutes, that is to say, "race" as a cultural identity and not an unequivocal "biological" category. At the same time national identity is perceived not only as the basis for *cultural* homogeneity, but also as the result of a natural and continuous relationship with a hazy national past. In this respect, the fabrication of national identity and the discourse of "nation" in contemporary Britain relies upon a nostalgia for a mythical, premodern past neither threatened by cultural difference nor disrupted by the socioeconomic forces of modernity.

Jurgen Habermas has linked together the discourses of neoconservatism and postmodernity, hence provoking an intense debate in the circles of poststructuralist and postmodern theory. According to Habermas's counterperspective, postmodernism, like neoconservatism, rejects cultural modernism on the basis of a disenchantment with the historical effects of social and economic modernization. Neoconservatism, he argues, "shifts onto cultural modernism the uncomfortable burdens of a more or less successful capitalist modernization of the economy and society" (Habermas 1987, 7). In this displacement of discontent and negation onto the shoulders of cultural modernity, he identifies an analogy between neoconservative doctrine and the conceptual field of postmodernity, specifically its antimodernism. The "young conservatives," he states, "claim for their own the revelations of a decentered subjectivity" and on this basis, "they step out of the modern world" (14). This perspective, I would argue, provides a persuasive explanation for the ways in which identity is expressed in postmodern cultural practice. Furthermore, the construction of identity within the framework of postmodernism—as a decentered subjectivity which is located outside of modernity—stands in stark contrast to the concept of identity designated by the diaspora experience which is forged in modernity itself.

The notion of a "decentered subjectivity" is expressed most clearly in the writings of Fredric Jameson, and it is worth recapitulating here. The "critical distance" of cultural politics, that is, culture as an autonomous sphere which can distance itself from society, has been abolished in the new space of postmodernism. This is a direct consequence, Jameson argues, of the fact that it has become impossible for the postmodern subject to map his or her place in the postmodern world. That is to say, we are no longer able to locate or define ourselves as individual subjects in the expanded global map of postmodern society (Jameson 1984). Jameson's diagnosis of postmodernism and that of other postmodern theorists has been criticized elsewhere as a nostalgic longing for a distinct, individual subject who stands out against the structures of modern, capitalist society (see, e.g., Collins 1987, 11–26). However, I am less concerned at this point with Jameson's own position than with the implications of this notion of the "fragmented subject" for postmodern practice as well as for black cultural practice.

The conception of identity as disconnected and incoherent appears to be reflected in postmodern practice by an aesthetic articulation of the fragmentary and pluralistic nature of national and cultural identities, as in the work of Imants Tillers. The aesthetic configurations of Tiller's *The Nine Shots* (1985), for example, involves collating different cultural identities in the form of appropriated pictorial fragments to make up a new, fragmented whole. The resulting image, it is claimed, represents a "postmodern allegory of nationhood no longer able to be unified through 'imagined communities'" (Nairne 1987, 224). Yet, this mosaic of fragments merely affirms the existence of several self-contained and, above all, separate cultural identities even if these differentiated identities are presented as a contestation of the symbolic order of a homogeneous national identity or nationhood. Moreover, all these cultural strategies which are seen to articulate a "crisis of identity" in European consciousness in some way or another seem to me to corroborate Habermas's contention that contemporary cultural politics do not necessarily signal a transition from modernity to postmodernity, but rather a disaffection with the "consequences of *societal* modernization" (1987, 8). In addition to this, the assertion of different cultural or national identities in various ways within the space of postmodernism seems to indicate not the emergence of a politics of difference as such, but rather what Nelly Richard has called a "new, sophisticated economy of 'sameness.'" As she argues in relation to Latin American art:

> Postmodernism's first claim is that it offers room within itself for our Latin American space. This is the "decentered" space of the marginalised or peripheral subject faced with the crisis of centrality. It is adorned with the ciphers of plurality, heterogeneity and dissidence. . . . The fact is, however, that no sooner are these differences—sexual, political, racial, cultural—posited and valued, than they become subsumed into the meta-category of the "undifferentiated" which means that all singularities immediately become indistinguishable in a new, sophisticated economy of "sameness." Postmodernism defends itself against the destabilising threat of the "other" by integrating it back into a framework which absorbs all differences and contradictions. The centre, though claiming to be in disintegration, still operates as a centre: filing away any divergences into a system of codes whose meanings, both semantically and territorially, it continues to administer by exclusive right. (1987–88, 11)

Thus, the articulation of fragmented and plural identities in both postmodern theory and practice obscures the historical framework in which postmodernism can be understood meaningfully. Such a historical perspective would, as I have stated before, reveal the ways in which postmodernism is a specific historical discourse in European thought which maintains essentially the same old relationship between European and non-European cultures, that is, between the center and the periphery. More important, in the context of my argument here, this historical framework would clarify the limitations of poststructuralist thought insofar as it only holds up a mirror to the cultural manifestations of the European experience of "loss of identity" and the "fragmentation of the subject" and, hence, does not engage critically with the historical reasons for these contemporary cultural forms. Finally, if the fragmented identity of the postmodern subject or its corollary, the nostalgic fabrication of a cohesive national and cultural identity, were viewed from the perspective of history, as Habermas suggests, this would show that the "crisis of identity" in contemporary society is in reality a disenchantment and reaction to social and economic modernization. Against this background the expression of identity in black artistic practice represents the assertion of a cultural politics of difference which, far from rejecting cultural modernism or socioeconomic modernization, engages critically and historically with the construction of identity from the viewpoint of the present. Furthermore, it challenges the notion that there ever existed a coherent or unmediated cultural identity which can be resurrected or indeed superseded. And above all, the conception of identity articulated by black artists implies a *political* formulation of identity which resists the packaging of identity in racial or national absolutes. This is precisely what is meant by Frantz Fanon when he writes:

> I will not make myself the man of any past. I do not want to exalt the past at the expense of my present and my future. . . . If the question of practical solidarity with a given past ever arose for me, it did so only to the extent to which I was committed to myself and my neighbour to fight for all my life and with all my strength so that never again would a people on the earth be subjugated. It was not the black world that laid down my course of conduct. My black skin is not the wrapping of specific values. (1986, 229–30)

Frantz Fanon's words articulate concisely the arena in which black identity and "black arts" have been defined and contested in contemporary Britain. On the one hand, state policy and provision (including arts policy and funding) propose a separate and distinct category of "ethnic minorities" wherein racial identity is formulated along the lines of cultural and ethnic difference to the extent that "ethnicity" itself comes to comprise separate categories—"Afro-Caribbean" as opposed to "Asian." On the other hand, black artists and writers have insisted upon the formulation of "blackness" as a political strategy wherein cultural and racial absolutes are contested by a dynamic "unity of difference." Such a conception of identity diverges from postmodern theory and practice at the point where pluralism and heterogeneity cease to be a set of aesthetic or political codes based on negation—the negation of coherent identities or the negation of fragmented identities—but rather the assertion of the positive and political implications of difference. There is of course the danger that this "unity through difference" will become the constitutive feature of an alternative totalizing notion of identity and this has been addressed by black writers and artists alike. Yet, its potential to designate a new space of identity resides in the fact that unlike postmodernism, it articulates difference and specificity in terms of and through *history:*

> One is aware of the degree to which nationalism was/is constituted as one of those major poles or terrains of articulation of the self. I think it is very important the way in which some people . . . begin to reach for a new conception of ethnicity as a kind of counter to the old discourses of nationalism or national identity. Now one knows that these are dangerously overlapping terrains. All the same they are not identical. Ethnicity *can* be a constitutive

element in the most viciously regressive nationalism or national identity. But in our times, as an imaginary community, it is also beginning to carry other meanings, and to define a new space for identity. It insists on difference—on the fact that every identity is placed, positioned, in a culture, a language, a history. (Hall, this volume, chap. 5)

The category of "black arts" also has been defined historically as an artistic practice arising from a specific framework, as the cultural expression of a particular reality, that is, the historical and cultural reality circumscribed by the diasporan experience which one artist has described succinctly as "cultural domination by Western Euro-centricism, and marginality to it; the experience of exploitation, appropriation, slavery, inequality and racism" (Jantjes 1988, 44). Significantly, the diasporan experience constitutes a critical distance which Jameson claims has been abolished in the space of postmodern society. This critical distance, however, does not imply that black artists occupy an autonomous sphere, but rather, a radical position actually *within* modernity and one, furthermore, which does not coincide neatly with the contours of the British nation-state.

The fusion of diverse, non-European elements into the dominant order of British culture contests the notion that cultural expression, or indeed identity, is a univocal, homogenous entity. The cultural language, or more precisely, the cultural languages of the diaspora reflect the intersection of various specialized discourses and dialects. In short, black cultural production reflects a conception of identity—polyphonic, historical, and existential—which has always existed in the margins of Western consciousness but which, at this particular historical conjuncture, corresponds with European thought. If postmodern theory and practice has not yet realized the full possibilities and positivities of this alternative formulation of identity, then perhaps the cultural expression of the diaspora can provide the framework of resistance and change as opposed to that of negation and reaction.

. . .

Such a framework of resistance and change is predicated, as I have suggested above, on a political and historical conception of identity, such as the one which informs Gavin Jantjes's image *The First Real Amerikan Target* (1974). Appropriating Jasper Johns's *Target with Plaster Casts* (1955), Jantjes replaces the row of boxes and plaster casts of fragments of the human figure in the original collage with various photographic images of Native Americans. The significance of Jantjes's act of appropriation only becomes fully clear in the light of the image which Johns made directly before this one, namely, *Flag* (1955). This image which replicates the American flag in the form of a painterly surface projects a wholly ambivalent notion of identity which was an intentional strategy on the part of the artist. The image posed the question, "Is it a flag or is it a painting?" which, according to Fred Orton, distracted attention from the more important question of whether the image should be read as an "endorsement or a criticism of a certain kind of patriotic sensibility" (Orton 1987–88, 13). Whether or not the image is a critique of national identity or nationalism, it remains an equivocal cultural expression which results in foregrounding artistic means at the expense of content. It is this which Jantjes implicates in his work. National identity or the icons of national identity, he implies, are not a self-sufficient critical statement unless this critical statement is informed by a historical perspective. The construction and the mythologization of American national identity, he asserts, obscure the historical and economic initiatives which characterized the formation of the American nation-state. Furthermore, the intersection of the different histories from which "Americanness" derives become overshadowed in Johns's cultural production by a unitary history of nationhood as well as of art. Finally, Johns's artistic practice in many ways prefigures the dual formulation of identity by postmodernism—on the one hand, an identity of reconstructed cohesion and, on the other, an identity of fragments.

Sonia Boyce's *Lay Back, Keep Quiet, and Think of What Made Britain So Great* (1986) again represents a very different articulation of identity. Divided into four separate panels which are linked by the dominant iconography, this image affirms the status of identity as the sum total of the intersection of diverse but related histories and cultures. A wallpaper design, originally conceived as a tribute to the fiftieth year of Queen Victoria's reign has been appropriated and transformed. The red rose, symbol of British nationhood, has been eclipsed by the abiding presence of a *black* rose which appears repeatedly in every panel. The notion of ambivalence which characterizes Johns's work assumes a very different meaning in the context of Boyce's image. The equivocal nature of the rose, the fragility and beauty of the flower combined with the sharpness and intractability of its thorns, becomes a metaphor for the ambivalence not only of "Britishness" but also of "blackness." The colonial and imperial character of Britain's past is weaved into the contours of the decorative paper, but so also is the resistance of non-European peoples—the native South Africans and Australians whose figures can be discerned only slightly in its midst. The black woman who stares out at us from the final panel—a self-portrait of the artist herself—suggests that this English rose, as woman or as identity, inherits a history of resistance as well as a history of oppression, that is, separate histories but ones which at the same time are locked together inextricably.

The notion of ambivalence is asserted not in spite of but *because* black artistic practice recognizes that identity is a politically and historically constructed category. As A. Sivanandan writes:

Gavin Jantjes, *The First Real Amerikan Target*, 1974. Screenprint

Sonia Boyce, *Lay Back, Keep Quiet, and Think of What Made Britain So Great,* 1986

Creating ourselves in terms of our culture and reshaping our society in terms of that creation are part and parcel of the same process. To abstract our culture from its social milieu in order to give it coherence is to lose out on its vitality. And once a culture loses its social dynamic, identity becomes an indulgence. . . . [I]dentity may emanate from the consciousness of our culture, but its operational function can only be meaningful in political terms. . . . A culture that takes time off to refurbish itself produces a personality without purpose. There is no point in finding out who I am if I do not know what to do with that knowledge.[10]

Race, Gender, Artistic Production

The process of requestioning and rethinking the legitimacy of the "grand narratives" of the West, according to Alice Jardine, potentially signifies a redefinition of the world in terms of the "*en-soi*, Others, without history—the feminine." In the configurations of postmodernity (which she prefers to call "modernity"), she identifies a development which she has described as "gynesis" or "the putting into discourse of woman" (Jardine 1985, 72). Craig Owens, too, in a slightly different way, sees an intersection between the "feminist critique of patriarchy and the postmodernist critique of representation" (1987, 57–82). Both argue that feminism and postmodernism announce a crisis in the legitimizing function of the grand narratives which has shaken the foundation stones of European thought. While it is claimed

10. A. Sivanandan (1970), quoted in Steyn 1988, 4.

that both these discourses challenge the structures of signification, I would argue that the deconstruction or dispersion of the dominant order does not in itself serve to question established meanings and identities. However, black women's creativity, it seems to me, proposes an alternative discourse of resistance and change through the articulation of the positive and political function for the periphery.

I have suggested the ways in which postmodernism, in spite of its diverse and even divergent aesthetic and political configurations, remains confined to a manifestly Western framework which is contested by black critical practice. The focus of postmodern theory and practice, for the most part, remains circumscribed by the demise of *European* grand narratives and *European* subjectivity so that the relationship between the center and the periphery persists to greater extent. The same can be said for feminism insofar as that has been articulated in the first instance as a resistance and contestation of patriarchy as a whole. As a direct consequence, feminist discourse often fails to take into account the broader ramifications of a conjuncture between patriarchal structures and imperial, colonial, or neocolonial initiatives. That is to say, a totalizing theory of patriarchy and female oppression obscures the complex relations which pertain to the economic and political hegemony of the West vis-à-vis non-European peoples. In this context, many black women have challenged repeatedly what they have defined as "imperial feminism":

> A definition of patriarchal relations which looks only at the power of men over women without placing that in a wider economic framework has serious consequences for the way in which relationships within the Black community are viewed. . . . [A]rguments of radical feminists who see patriarchy as the primary determining feature of women's oppression ignore totally the inapplicability of such a concept in analysing the complex of relations obtaining in Black communities both historically and in the present. . . . Our very positions as Black women in a racist society has meant that we have been forced to organize around issues relating to our very survival. The struggle for independence and self-determination and against imperialism has meant that for Black and Third World women in Britain and internationally, sexuality as an issue has often taken a secondary role and at times not been considered at all. (Amos and Parmar 1984, 9–12)

The implication of this is that the identity of black women is expressed not in terms of sexuality alone nor in terms of male-female relations as the primary determining factor. Rather, the identity of black women is represented consistently within an economic and historical context which binds together sexual and racial politics. An excellent example of this would be Sonia Boyce's *Missionary Position II* (1985). Part of a series of images, this picture depicts a black woman, lying down on the floor in a posture of resistance rather than submission, holding out one hand to the kneeling figure of a black man who is praying, his eyes closed. The title and the image itself state explicitly the analogies between sexual and colonial relations and between religion and colonialism. The holy sanctity of a sexual position which imposes submission and capitulation on women, Boyce asserts, finds its equivalence in the application of Christianity as a system of beliefs which justifies the oppression of non-European peoples and the annexation of their lands. The text inscribed on the image reads: "They say keep politics out of religion and religion out of politics. Laard but look my trials nuh—but when were they ever separate? Laard give me strength." Once more, Boyce affirms the notion of ambivalence. In this case, the ambivalence not only of avowed female oppression (the woman depicted here is clearly a source of resistance not submission) but also of religion. In the same way that the languages of the dominant order are appropriated by black people and transformed, religion too is transmuted into a liberating force and becomes the "site of oppositional meaning and collective strength" (Gilroy 1991, 213–14).

The translation of the personal into the political and the assertion of political resistance in Boyce's *Missionary Position II* lead me to the question of the limitations imposed by the postmodernist (and also the feminist) embrace of psychoanalytic theory. Specifically, the ways in which the assimilation of Lacanian theory raises problems for feminism and conflicts with the precepts of black women's work. Sheila Tebbatt has pointed to the ways in which the psychoanalytic framework of Jacques Lacan places women "firmly and squarely in a negative relationship to language and the whole symbolic order" (1988, 22–27). This has resulted, according to Tebbatt, in a situation where women perceive problems in expressing themselves in a "man-made language" and thus, finding they have no voice, are relegated to a position of silence. Some examples would be the theoretical writings of women like Luce Irigaray, Xaviere Gauthier, and Hélène Cixous or the creative writing of Marguerite Duras, especially the script for the film *Natalie Granger* (1972) in which the two main women characters express female resistance quite literally through silence (Kaplan 1983, 91–103). As a consequence of their negative status, Tebbatt argues, women become "unable to enter [the social world] on any other terms than patriarchal," and furthermore, "without the power to alter it" (1988, 26). In opposition to this, she asserts the importance of Valentin Volosinov's conception of language which identifies language as a social construct rather than a fixed process, hence admitting for language and meaning to be redefined through political struggle, that is, to be restructured and reconstituted.[11]

It should already be clear that this is precisely the conception of language and

11. Tebbatt refers specifically to Volosinov's *Marxism and the Philosophy of Language* (1973).

meaning which informs the cultural practice of black artists under discussion here. What Bakhtin defines as the "carnivalization" or dispersal of the dominant order pertains to the cultural languages and meanings formulated in the space of the diaspora (Bakhtin 1981, 259–422). In other words, the works of Himid, Boyce, and Biswas are not fixed in a negative position in relation to the dominant order, but in a positive position of resistance to and disruption of the prevailing cultural and political system. Their artistic production does not lie beyond the perimeters of British culture but within it. In short, the cultural politics of the margins represents not a passive spectator but an active intruder, so to speak, into the hegemonic system.

This leads me to my final point, which relates to Tania Modleski's analysis (1986, 37–52) of Baudrillard's theorization of mass culture. By way of summary, Modleski argues that Baudrillard extends psychoanalytic definitions of woman to a political analysis of the masses whereby the "silent majority," according to Baudrillard's definition, are passive and hence "feminine" as opposed to being active and implicitly therefore "masculine."

The important point to make here is that black women's creativity does not occupy a passive position in relation to the political and aesthetic structures of Western society and knowledge. Lubaina Himid's *Freedom and Change* and Sonia Boyce's *Missionary Position II* locate black women, and hence the politics of the periphery, at the center of European modernity. They identify black women as a force of resistance and change as opposed to being a source of "mute acquiescence." Moreover, the conception of femininity which emerges from the work of these women points to a notion of femininity which is far from passive or inert. Sutapa Biswas's *Housewives with Steak-knives* (1985) asserts femininity as equivocal, that is, both fragile and strong at the same time. Such a conception of femininity effectively dismantles the binary opposition between "masculine" and "feminine." Furthermore, it contests the delineation of separate spheres between private and public or between personal and political. That is to say, femininity in the space of the diaspora is conceived in terms of an intersection of those distinct and essential absolutes of European thought. In this context, the idea of differentiated and binary realms has been contested by black artists and writers alike, not on the basis of what Baudrillard calls the "circularity of signaling" at this particular historical moment, but rather on the basis that no such clear division is realized *historically* by the diasporan experience.

Finally, black femininity implies a rejection of such totalizing discourses as postmodernism or feminism, which remain confined within the perimeters of European consciousness and which, moreover, draw their often transcendental and globalizing conclusions in a conceptual field which in many cases has been evacuated of wider historical and economic perspectives. This last point suggests that neither postmodernity nor feminism are the most appropriate or coherent theoretical structures in which to study black women's creativity. The possibility that there may be alternative and transient "grand narratives" in the history of Western thought means that the artistic production of Himid, Boyce, and Biswas could be understood more meaningfully within an alternative framework. The conceptual framework which I propose is one of "small narratives," or *petits récits*, to corrupt Lyotard's original phrase. Such "small narratives," I would argue, clarify the broader political and aesthetic project which informs black women's creativity and from which it derives.

The iconography of Biswas's image *Housewives with Steak-knives* is the clearest enunciation of the notion of black femininity as a form of creative resistance. The picture depicts a strong multiarmed woman wearing a necklace of men's heads while brandishing a vast steak knife in one hand, the head of a white man in another, and a rose and flag in yet another of her four hands. Here, Hindu mythology is invoked to serve a political content which is quintessentially modern. The image of the goddess Kali, traditionally represented with a garland of men's heads around her neck and the head of a man in one of her many hands, has been appropriated by Biswas as a means of dissolving the absolute distinctions and binary oppositions which characterize European thought. In opposition to these false and essentialist categories, the precepts of Hindu culture reflect the ascendancy of ambivalence. Thus, the Western notion of "femininity" as essentially fragile and passive is contested by the ambivalent status of the goddess Kali who is at once the goddess of both war and peace. In adapting the Hindu iconography of Kali, then, Biswas asserts the ambivalence of femininity, both pacifist (as opposed to passive) and aggressive, both "feminine" in a traditional sense and strong. She also affirms the existence, in terms of the Hindu system of knowledge, of a "zone of indiscernibility," to borrow Gilles Deleuze's phrase, between myth and reality. Thus, Biswas implies, there is an element of the real in the mythologization of "femininity," and equally, an element of the myth in the reality of black womanhood. Furthermore, by introducing ancient icons and myths into her work, Biswas suggests a fusion between the past and the present, an intimation not only of the relevance of history to contemporary experience, but also, perhaps, of the abiding presence of black female resistance and creativity. Finally, Biswas's *Housewives* defies the distinction drawn between the private and avowedly "feminine" domestic sphere, in this case exemplified by the kitchen, and the public, allegedly "masculine" domain of political action. Resistance to white, male hegemony, it is implied, can be and has been the imperative of black women. Moreover, the domestic environment which black women inhabit circumscribes a defiant domesticity which reappears in another image by Biswas entitled *The Only Good Indian . . .* (1985). Here, a Indian woman is sitting watching the television, quietly peeling a potato which has metamorphosed into an uncanny resemblance to the for-

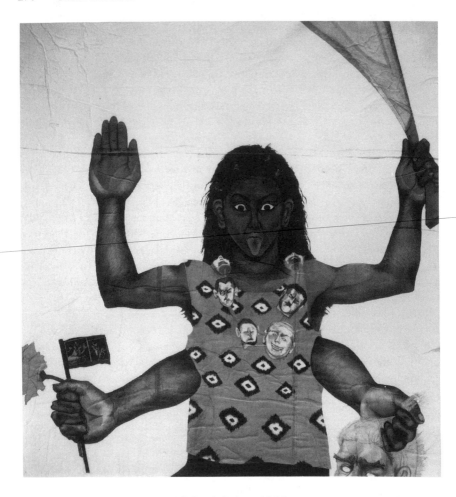

Sutapa Biswas, *Housewives with Steak-knives*, 1985

mer Home Secretary, Leon Brittan. Kitchen utensils have become the tools of defiance where the domestic space is conceived as the arena in which the hegemonic order is contested. In this case, the satirical visual iconography of *The Only Good Indian . . .* is a decidedly domestic response to the institution of increasingly exclusive nationality laws (for example, the Nationality Act of 1981).

The white hand (or head) of the Law, whether in the shape of a parliamentary act or of a religious canon, is represented consistently by these artists in the form of incomplete fragments—the cardboard cut-outs of men's heads in Himid's *Freedom and Change,* the garland of heads and the decapitated, sightless head in Biswas's *Housewives,* or the white palm of a hand severed from its body in Boyce's *Missionary Position I* (1985)—which stand in stark contrast to the pictorial and metaphoric centrality assigned to black women. In the specific context of Biswas's *Housewives,* the garland which the goddess Kali wears around her neck, symbolizing the evil which Kali was to destroy, here designates a more contemporary and allegorical meaning. The dominant order of white, male individuality, it is implied, will be overturned by black creative resistance. Furthermore, the former invisibility and marginalization of black women in European consciousness will be challenged by an assertion of their presence and their voices not on patriarchal terms but on the explicit terms of black women's cultural practice and historical experience.

The artistic means of this cultural practice is the distinct process of gathering and reusing by means of which the diasporan experience is reflected through a literal patchwork of experiences, cultures, and histories. As Himid writes, this is not an aesthetic strategy isolated from the domain of lived experiences. That is to say, black women's creativity does not represent an autonomous, cultural sphere but rather is constituted in and derived from historical necessity which finds its precedent in the activity of quilt-making:

> A quilt made from gathered pieces of cloth takes time to plan, design and make. Often several women have worked on one quilt. It can be made as a testimony to time spent as well as lives lived. It is made to go into the future as a used object for a "family" membership, as a talisman for the years ahead and a reminder of women past. (Himid 1988, 8)

Thus, in Himid's *We Will Be* (1983), the fabric of the woman's dress is a collage of visual references—decorative patterns, photographic reproductions, images of fish and fruit, and a sequence of words—which represent a patchwork of memories, dreams, and cultural signifiers. The written script, contained within the contours of the dress, echoes the voices of black women, "talking back," resisting the unity and homogeneity of Western consciousness and the singular progression of a total history, while at the same time affirming the fusion of different times (past and present) and different places (Europe, Africa, Asia, the Caribbean, the Americas) which characterize the space of the diaspora. In this way, Himid's iconography and those of the other artists here attest to a different mode of enunciation and an alternative conceptual framework which signals an interruption and a reconstruction of the dominant cultural terrain. Above all, they designate a female resistance through and in cultural language, but not in silence. In the words of bell hooks (1986–87):

> Moving from silence into speech is for the oppressed, the colonized, the exploited, and those who stand side by side, a gesture of defiance that heals, that makes new life, and new growth possible. It is that act of speech, of

"talking back" that is no mere gesture of empty words, that is the expression of moving from object to subject that is liberated voice.

The aesthetic configurations of this "gesture of defiance" are articulated, as I have illustrated above, through an alternative conception of femininity as creative resistance. This takes the material form of patchwork and collage, a reusing of fragments from diverse sources which assume different meanings and create a new frame of reference. It also takes the form of works which use pastels and crayons as the primary artistic means. Both these creative modes have been characterized as the domain of "women's art." They are, according to the discourse of nineteenth-century Europe, an extension of women's domestic role in society, that is, "quintessentially feminine, delicate and decorative."[12] Yet, once again, black women's creativity assigns a very different meaning to the notion of "feminine arts" as it does to "femininity." The hierarchy of art forms which pertains to the classification and stratification of different categories of art in Western art history is subverted by the application of "feminine arts" to a specific cultural and political project. Pastels and chalks in the works of Biswas and Boyce particularly are mobilized in the service not of quiet, delicate images but of huge and assertive political statements. Like patchwork and collage, the use of pastels by these artists forges links with the history of women's creativity. Furthermore, it sustains the idea of an ambivalent femininity which defies simplistic categorization as inherently passive and apolitical. And finally, it corroborates the historical and cultural conjuncture of the personal and political and the private and public in the diasporan experience.

It is in this context that the home and the domestic environment can be seen to define the space of black women's creativity. It is a space, first of all, in which the past and the present become fused together, where the discontinuous histories of black peoples and the history of Western civilization are locked together inextricably. As in the wallpaper which shapes the configurations of Boyce's *Lay Back, Keep Quiet . . .*, history circumscribes the present; it is contained in the very walls of lived experience and domestic relationships. Moreover, the designs which decorate these personal spaces are the means by which links are forged with the historical past. But, in contrast with the work of Gilbert and George where decorative motifs signify the continuity of an unmediated and unequivocal national past, via modern technology, into the present; in Boyce's work, decorative pattern and design signal the ambivalence and dissonance of different histories meshed together.[13] Against this background, the genre of the "conversation piece" is transformed by intimations of

12. See Parker and Pollock 1981, particularly chapter 2, "Crafty Women and the Hierarchy of the Arts."

13. I am thinking especially of photoworks such as *England* (1980) or *Black God* (1983).

history in black women's creativity. Thus, in Boyce's *Conversational Piece* (1986), the hands of two black women trace in the decorative contours of a kitchen table-cloth the proximity and distance of their dreams and memories, a metaphor for the relative proximity and distance of the histories and experiences of black people in the diaspora, or, perhaps, of British history and diasporan history.

Above all, the domestic realm is a manifestly political space where there is no comfort from the configurations of history or lived experience. And at the point where the domestic is seen to be political, the "feminine" becomes politically resistant. Thus, the woman in Boyce's *In the Comfort of Your Own Home* (1986) meta-morphoses into a Medusa-like figure with a serpent's tongue, or more appropriately, a Medea-like figure—the woman of Greek mythology who is marginalized from the hegemonic order of Corinthian society on the basis of her avowed cultural difference, the woman whose resistance, furthermore, takes the form of a transfiguration of perceived notions of "femininity" and "domesticity."[14] Alternatively, as in Biswas's diptych *As I Stood, Listened, and Watched, My Feelings Were, This Woman Is Not for Burning* (1986), political defiance is the mirror image of domestic comfort.

The domestic environment also demarcates the arena of family relationships and the expression of personal identity, both of which are framed by ambivalence and uncertainty. In Sonia Boyce's *She Ain't Holding Them Up, She's Holding On (Some English Rose)* (1986), the artist was inspired, significantly, by the René Magritte painting *This Is Not a Pipe*.[15] The ambivalence between appearance and reality which informs the conceptual framework of Magritte's work here serves to articulate the tensions not only between private and public but between past and present generations, imaginary identity, and "real" identity. The picture bears witness to the conjuncture of the notion of family as a structural support and source of cultural identity and the idea that family is also the origin of discontinuity and dissonance. The point at which the woman's hands touch the base of the family unit here marks the point of connection, but also the point of separation. And once again, the black rose which appears and reappears consistently in Boyce's work, here embroidered into the fabric of the woman's dress, signifies the ambivalence of identity, the fusion and disjuncture simultaneously of "blackness" and "Britishness."

Thus, the space of black women's creativity does not designate the impossibility of mapping the black female subject within history and lived experience as Jameson

14. According to Euripides' version of Medea, Medea contests Jason's ambitions to assume Corinthian sovereignty by murdering her children.

15. In an interview with the artist by the author, Boyce stated that she was drawn to the surrealist notion of ambivalence between appearance and reality and, particularly, to the surrealist production of Frida Kahlo, who is cited by Biswas also as a precedent for black women's creativity within the framework of modernity.

insists is the case with the fragmented subject in the postmodern world. Rather, the work of these artists attests to the importance of charting individual and personal subjectivity within the material structures of history and politics. In this context, the architectural framework or the physical environment which circumscribes the contours of the black subject is imbued with resonances of past experience and contemporary reality. It is not fragmentation which characterizes the cultural politics of Himid, Biswas, and Boyce, but rather a specific conception of ambivalence. The space of black creativity is, in the final instance, a "zone of indiscernibility" which contests the political and aesthetic absolutes which delineate the conceptual scaffolding of European consciousness.

Conclusion

Black cultural practice cannot be defined in terms of postmodernism or postmodernity precisely because it does not attempt to divorce itself from the historical and political configurations of modernity. I have argued, following Habermas's counterperspective, that postmodernity does not constitute a break or rupture from the conceptual fabric of modernity. Rather, it articulates through artistic practice and theoretical structures a contemporary disaffection with the *effects* of societal modernization which takes the form of nostalgia for a cohesive and continuous historical past; or alternatively, the assertion of heterogeneity and fragmentation of contemporary experience. In some respects, even, postmodernism can be seen to represent continuities with the modern project insofar as it remains manifestly within the framework of Western knowledge. The constellation of voices and the plurality of meanings which are postulated by postmodernity serve to obscure its continuities with cultural modernism and suggest, perhaps, that this may not be a fissure or "new dawn" in European consciousness but merely a transformation of the grand narratives of the West. In this context, the "populist modernism" of black cultural practice, I would argue, signals a critical reappropriation of modernity which stems from an assertion of history and historical processes.

Black women's creativity in particular expresses the ambivalence of identity and the redundancy of exclusive and unambiguous absolutes. It dissolves the fixed boundaries between past and present, public and private, personal and political. The important point is that the "zone of indiscernibility" which characterizes the space of the diaspora and the cultural practice of Himid, Boyce, and Biswas does not attest to the primacy of difference and dispersion over and above historical and political exigencies. Rather, the cultural expression of the margins and of the periphery represents an aesthetic and political project which is predicated on resistance and change. That is to say, the banishment of utopian ideals is not a unilateral and self-sufficient contestation of the grand narratives of Western knowledge. In opposition to the theoretical structures of postmodernism, black cultural politics insists upon the ascendancy of a broader aesthetic and political project which redefines the agenda of modernity through a critical interrogation of the past and according to the political imperatives of the present. The last words belong to those black women artists who have drawn the "thin black line" which demarcates the boundaries of European consciousness and the possibilities which lie beyond those boundaries:

> The thin black line
> is long
> is slender (but not delicate)
> is cord, not thread
> is a long, slender cord
> taut when stretched[16]

16. Marlene Smith, *The Thin Black Line,* from the exhibition of the same name, Institute of Contemporary Arts, London, 1985.

Works Cited

Amos, V., and P. Parmar. 1984. "Challenging Imperial Feminism." *Feminist Review* (London) 17 (autumn).

Araeen, R. 1987. "From Primitivism to Ethnic Arts." *Third Text* (London) 1 (autumn).

Bakhtin, M. 1981. "Discourse in the Novel." In *The Dialogic Imagination.* Austin: University of Texas Press.

Bernal, M. 1987. *Black Athena.* New Brunswick: Rutgers University Press.

Chipp, H., ed. 1968. *Theories of Modern Art.* Berkeley and Los Angeles: University of California Press.

Crimp, D. 1983. "On the Museum's Ruins." In *The Anti-Aesthetic,* ed. H. Foster. Port Townsend, Wash.: Bay Press.

Collins, J. 1987. "Postmodernism and Cultural Practice: Redefining the Parameters." *Screen* (London) 28, no. 2 (spring).

Dews, P. 1989. "From Poststructuralism to Postmodernity." In *Postmodernism,* ed. L. Appignanesi. London: Free Association Books.

Fanon, F. 1986. *Black Skin, White Masks.* London: Pluto Press.

Foster, H. 1985. *Recodings.* Port Townsend, Wash.: Bay Press.

———. 1987. "Postmodernism." Preface to *Postmodern Culture,* ed. H. Foster. London: Pluto Press.

Foucault, M. 1986a. Introduction to *The Archaeology of Knowledge,* trans. A. M. Sheridan Smith. New York: Tavistock Publications.

———. 1986b. *The Order of Things.* New York: Tavistock Publications.

Gilroy, P. 1988–89. "Cruciality and the Frog's Perspective." *Third Text* (London) 8–9.

———. 1991. *There Ain't No Black in the Union Jack.* London: Hutchinson, 1987. Reprint, Chicago: University of Chicago Press.

Goldwater, R. 1967. *Primitivism in Modern Art*. London: Vintage Books.

Habermas, J. 1987. "Modernity—An Incomplete Project." In *Postmodern Culture*, ed. H. Foster. London: Pluto Press.

Himid, L. 1988. "Fragments." *F.A.N. (Feminist Arts News)* (London) 2, no. 8 (autumn).

hooks, b. 1986–87. "Talking Back." *Discourse: Journal for Theoretical Studies in Media and Culture* (Berkeley), no. 8 (winter).

James, C. L. R. 1963. *Beyond a Boundary*. London: Hutchinson.

———. 1980. "On Wilson Harris" (1965). In *Sphere of Existence: Selected Writings*. London: Allison and Busby.

———. 1984. "Black Studies and the Contemporary Student" (1969). In *At the Rendezvous of Victory: Selected Writings*. London: Allison and Busby.

Jameson, F. 1984. "Postmodernism, or The Cultural Logic of Capitalism." *New Left Review* (London), no. 146 (July–August).

Jantjes, G. 1988. "Art and Cultural Reciprocity." In *The Essential Black Art*. London: Chisenhale Gallery.

Jardine, A. 1985. *Gynesis: Configurations of Woman and Modernity*. Ithaca: Cornell University Press.

Kaplan, A. 1983. "Silence as Female Resistance in Marguerite Duras' *Natalie Granger*." In *Women and Film*. New York: Methuen.

Kramer, H. 1980. "Does Gérôme Belong with Goya and Monet?" *New York Times*, 13 April, sec. 2.

Krauss, R. 1987. "Sculpture in the Expanded Field." In *Postmodern Culture*, ed. H. Foster. London: Pluto Press.

Lynton, N. 1980. "The New Age: Primal Work and Mystic Nights." In *Abstraction: Towards a New Art, 1910–1920*. London: Tate Gallery.

———. 1982. *The Story of Art*. Oxford: Phaidon Press.

Mitter, P. 1977. *Much Maligned Monsters*. Oxford: Clarendon Press.

Modleski, T. 1986. "Femininity as Masquerade: A Feminist Approach to Mass Culture." In *High Theory, Low Culture*, ed. C. MacCabe. New York: St. Martin's.

Mosse, G. 1978. *Toward the Final Solution: A History of European Racism*. New York: Fertig.

Nairne, S. 1987. *State of the Art: Ideas and Images in the 1980s*. London: Chatto and Windus.

Nisbet, R. 1980. *History of the Idea of Progress*. New York: Basic Books.

Oliva, A. B. 1982. *Im Labyrinth der Kunst*. Trans. Isolde Eckle. Berlin: Merve Verlag.

Orton, F. 1987–88. "Present the Scene . . . Selves, the Occasion of Ruses." *Block* (East Barnet, U.K.) 13 (winter).

Owens, C. 1987. "The Discourse of Others: Feminists and Postmodernism." In *Postmodern Culture*, ed. H. Foster. London: Pluto Press.

Parker, R., and G. Pollock. 1981. *Old Mistresses: Women, Art, and Ideology*. London: Routledge and Kegan Paul.

Philippi, D. 1987. "The Conjuncture of Race and Gender in Anthropology and Art History." *Third Text* (London) 1 (autumn).

Richard, N. 1987–88. "Postmodernism and the Periphery." *Third Text* (London) 2 (winter).

Seidel, G. 1986. "Nation and 'Race' in the British and French Right." In *The Ideology of the New Right,* ed. R. Levitas. Cambridge: Polity Press.

Sivanandan, A. 1970. "Culture and Identity." *Liberator* (New York) 10, no. 6 (June).

Solomon-Godeau, A. 1989. "Going Native." *Art in America* (New York), July.

Steyn, J. 1988. Introduction to *Along the Lines of Resistance.* Barnsley: Cooper Gallery.

Tebbatt, S. 1988. "Women in Theory." *Ten.8* (Birmingham), no. 31 (winter).

Volosinov, V. 1973. *Marxism and the Philosophy of Language.* New York: Seminar Press.

Willis, A.-M., and T. Fry. 1988–89. "Art as Ethnocide: The Case of Australia." *Third Text* (London) 5 (winter).

Fourteen

Just Looking for Trouble: Robert Mapplethorpe and Fantasies of Race

Kobena Mercer

How does "race" feature in the politics of antipornography? Well, it does and it doesn't. "Race" is present as an emotive figure of speech in the rhetoric of certain feminist antipornography arguments; yet "race" is also markedly absent since there appears to be no distinctly black perspective on the contentious issues of sexuality, censorship, and representation that underpin the volatile nature of the antiporn debate. Although Audre Lorde and Alice Walker made important contributions early on in the debate in the United States over a decade ago, the question of pornography has hardly been a top priority on the agenda of black feminist politics in Britain in the 1980s and early 1990s (Lorde 1980; Walker 1980). If it is indeed the case that white and black women have not been equally involved in the antiporn movement, or have not made it a shared political priority, then we have to ask: What role does "race" play in the discourse of antipornography which has come mainly from white women?

"Race" as an Issue in Antipornography Feminism

When "race" is invoked to mobilize moral support for antipornography positions, it tends to function as a rhetorical trope enabling a race and gender analogy between violence against women and incitement to racial hatred. In their recent campaigns, Labour MPs Clare Short and Dawn Primarolo have frequently used this analogy to argue that just as black people are degraded by racist speech and hurt by racial violence, so women are harmed and victimized by sexist and misogynist representations which portray, and thus promote, the hatred and fear of women that erupt in all acts of male violence. It follows, so the argument goes, that just as the law is supposedly empowered to prohibit and punish incitement to racial hatred, new regulative legislation is needed to "protect" women from the harm and danger of male violence that pornography represents. Yet the 1965 Race Relations Act, which sought to prohibit racist speech, has never been particularly beneficial to black people—more often than not it has been used against black people to curtail our civil rights to representation, and was proved to be notoriously useless and ineffective by the rise of new racist and fascist movements in the 1970s. Just as most black people know not to entrust our survival and protection to the state, one ought to question any argument, feminist or otherwise, that seeks to extend the intervention of the state in the form of prohibitionary legislation.

Indeed from a black perspective, the problem lies with the very analogy between racial hatred and male violence because it is based on a prior equation between those sexually explicit words and images labeled "pornographic" and those acts of violence, brutality, and homicide that do indeed take place against women in "real life." This equation—that "pornography is the theory, rape is the practice"—is central to the radical feminist antipornography argument that gained considerable influence in the U.S.A. during the 1980s and is gaining ground in Britain now. One of the most worrying aspects of these developments is the strange alliance that has evolved between radical feminists demanding censorship in the name of women's freedom, and the antiobscenity lobby of the New Right, whose demands for the prohibition of sexual representations have always been part of the moral agenda of mainstream conservatism. For entirely different reasons, these two groups seek further state regulation of pornography, yet their convergence on this objective has created a wider constituency of support for a policy of cultural censorship. Where do black people stand in relation to this unhappy alliance?

While antiporn feminists are more likely than their neoconservative counterparts to observe that pornography itself is violently racist, one has to question the highly emotive way in which "race" is used only to simplify complex issues and polarize opinion, as if everything were a matter of black and white, as if everything depended on whether you are simply for or against pornography and, by implication, male violence. In a theoretical defense of the radical feminist view that pornography does not merely reflect male violence but is itself a form of violence even as representation, Susanne Kappeler uses "race" precisely in this way—not only to justify the unproven equation between images of sexual violence and actual violence experienced by women, but to elicit a moral response of horror and outrage that lends further credence to the antiporn argument. At the beginning of her book *The Pornography of Representation,* by means of a graphic description of photographs depicting a black African man—one Thomas Kasire of Namibia—shown mutilated, tortured, and obliterated for the gratification of his white male European captors, Kappeler hopes to persuade us that, essentially, all pornography entails that women experience the same kind of actual violence as the brutal, sadistic, and murderous violence of the colonial racism that resulted in the death of this black man.[1] Not only does this analogy reduce "race" to rhetoric—whereby the black/white polarity serves to symbolize an absolute morality based on an either/or choice between good and evil—but it offers no analysis of racial representation in pornography, nor of black people's experiences of it, as Kappeler nowhere acknowledges the relative absence of black women in defining the feminist antiporn agenda, or the fact that black feminism, in all its varieties, has certainly not prioritized the issue as a touchstone of revolutionary morality.

Each of these issues concerning race, representation, and sexual politics has arisen in the very different context of Robert Mapplethorpe's avowedly homoerotic photography, which was at the center of a major controversy in the United States during 1989 and 1990. Paradoxically, as a result of the campaign led by Senator Jesse Helms to prevent the National Endowment for the Arts from funding exhibitions of so-called indecent and obscene materials, Mapplethorpe's photographs have come to the attention of a far wider audience than at any point in his career before his death, from AIDS, in 1989. Although Helms's proposed amendment to NEA funding criteria was eventually defeated, the virulent homophobia that characterized his campaign against Mapplethorpe's "immoral trash" has helped to create a climate of popular opinion favorable to cultural repression. Just as self-censorship has become routine among art-world decision makers, so the policing and prosecution of cultural practitioners—from feminist performance artist Karen Finley to the black rap group 2 Live Crew—has also become commonplace. What is truly disturbing about these trends is both the way in which the New Right has successfully hijacked and appropriated elements of the feminist antipornography argument, and the way in which some feminists have themselves joined ranks with the law-and-

1. Kappeler 1986, 5–10. One important alternative to the race and gender analogy is to open the debate to include racism both in pornography and in the women's movement. This is an important point, raised in the context of a historical overview of the mutual articulation of gender and sexuality in racial oppression, discussed in Gardner 1980.

order state. An instance of this occurred in Cincinnati in 1990 when feminist campaigners aligned themselves with the city police department to close down the touring Mapplethorpe retrospective and prosecute the museum director responsible for the exhibition, Dennis Barrie, for the violation of "community standards."

Mapplethorpe's Black Male Nudes

In this context, I would like to offer a contribution to the debate on pornography that is based on my reading of Mapplethorpe's troublesome images of nude black men. Although the attack on Mapplethorpe focused mainly on his depictions of gay male sadomasochism and portraits of naked children, his black male nudes are equally, if not more, problematic—not only because they explicitly resemble aspects of pornography, but because his highly erotic treatment of the black male body seems to be supported by a whole range of racist myths about black sexuality.

To shock was always the key verb in the modernist vocabulary. Like other audiences and spectators confronted by the potent eroticism of Mapplethorpe's most shocking images, black audiences are not somehow exempt from the shock effect that Mapplethorpe's images so clearly intend to provoke. Indeed, it was this sense of outrage—not at the homoeroticism, but at the potential racism—that motivated my initial critique of the work, from a black gay male perspective. I was shocked by what I saw: the profile of a black man whose head was cropped—or "decapitated," so to speak—holding his semitumescent penis through the Y-front of his underpants, which is the first image that confronts you in Mapplethorpe's 1982 publication *Black Males*. Given the relative silence of black voices at the time of Mapplethorpe's 1983 retrospective at the Institute of Contemporary Arts in London, when the art world celebrated his "transgressive" reputation, it was important to draw critical attention to the almost pornographic flamboyance with which Mapplethorpe, whose trademark is cool irony, seemed to perpetuate the racist stereotype that, essentially, the black man is nothing more than his penis.

Yet, as the context for the reception and interpretation of Mapplethorpe's work has changed, I have almost changed my mind about these photographs, primarily because I am much more aware of the danger of simply hurling the accusation of "racism" about. It leads only to the closure of debate. Precisely because of the hitherto unthinkable alliance between the New Right and radical feminism on the issue of pornography, there is now every possibility that a critique which stops only with this kind of moralistic closure inevitably plays into an antidemocratic politics of censorship and cultural closure sought by the ascendant forces of the New Right. In what follows, I explain how and why I changed my mind.[2]

2. See Mercer 1986 and, for the revision of the initial analysis, Mercer 1991. Related work on the cultural politics of black masculinity may be found in Julien and Mercer 1988. The black

Picture this: two reasonably intelligent black gay men pore over Mapplethorpe's 1986 publication *The Black Book*. When a friend lent me his copy, this was exactly how it circulated between us: as an illicit and highly troublesome object of desire. We were fascinated by the beautiful bodies and seduced by the pleasure in looking as we perused the repertoire of images. We wanted to look, but we didn't always find what we wanted to see. This was because we were immediately disturbed by the racial dimension of the imagery and, above all, angered by the aesthetic objectification that reduced these individual black men to purely abstract visual "things," silenced in their own right as subjects and serving mainly as aesthetic trophies to enhance Mapplethorpe's privileged position as a white gay male artist in the New York avant-garde. In short, we were stuck in a deeply ambivalent structure of feeling. In an attempt to make sense of this experience, I drew on elements of feminist cultural theory.

The first thing to notice about Mapplethorpe's black males—so obvious that it goes without saying—is that all the men are nude. Framed within the generic conventions of the fine-art nude, their bodies are aestheticized and eroticized as "objects" to be looked at. As such, they offer an erotic source of pleasure in the act of looking. But whose pleasure is being served? Regarding the depiction of women in dominant forms of visual representation, from painting to advertising or pornography, feminist cultural theory has shown that the female image functions predominantly as a mirror-image of what men want to see. As a figment of heterosexual wish-fulfillment, the female nude serves primarily to guarantee the stability of a phallocentric fantasy in which the omnipotent male gaze sees but is never itself seen. The binary opposition of seeing/being seen which informs visual representations of the female nude reveals that looking is never an innocent or neutral activity, but is always powerfully loaded by the gendered character of the subject/object dichotomy in which, to put it crudely, men look and women are there to be looked at.

In Mapplethorpe's case, however, the fact that both artist and model are male sets up a tension of sameness which thereby transfers the *frisson* of "difference" from gender to racial polarity. In terms of the conventional dichotomy between masculinity as the active control of the gaze, and femininity as its passive visual object, what we see in Mapplethorpe's case is the way in which the black/white duality of "race" overdetermines the power relations implicit in the gendered dichotomy between subject and object of representation.

In this sense, what is represented in Mapplethorpe's photographs is a "look," or a certain "way of looking," in which the pictures reveal more about the absent and

---

male nude photographs referred to may be found in Mapplethorpe 1982 and 1986 and Marshall 1990.

invisible white male photographer who actively controls the gaze than they do about the black men whose beautiful bodies we see depicted in his photographs. Insofar as the pictorial space excludes any reference to a social, historical, cultural, or political context that might tell us something about the lives of the black models who posed for the camera, Mapplethorpe facilitates the projection of certain racial and sexual fantasies about the "difference" that black masculinity is assumed to embody. In this way, the photographs are very much about sexual investment in looking, because they disclose the tracing of desire on the part of the I/eye placed at the center of representation by the male gaze.

Through a combination of formal codes and conventions—the posing and posture of the body in the studio enclosure; the use of strong chiaroscuro lighting; the cropping, framing, and fragmentation of the whole body into parts—the "look" constructed not only structures the viewer's affective disposition toward the image but reveals something of the *mise en scène* of power, as well as desire, in the racial and sexual fantasies that inform Mapplethorpe's representation of black masculinity. Whereas the white gay male sadomasochist pictures portray a subcultural sexuality that consists of "doing" something, the black men are defined and confined to "being" purely sexual and nothing but sexual—hence hypersexual. We look through a sequence of individually named African-American men, but we see only sexuality as the sum-total meaning of their black male identity. In pictures like "Man in a Polyester Suit" (1980), apart from the model's hands, it is the penis, and the penis alone, that identifies him as a black man.

Mapplethorpe's obsessive focus on this one little thing, the black man's genitals, and the way in which the glossy allure of the quality monochrome print becomes almost consubstantial with the shiny, sexy texture of black skin, led me to argue that a certain racial fetishism is an important element in the pleasures (and displeasures) which the photographs bring into play. Such racial fetishism not only eroticizes the most visible aspect of racial difference—skin color—but also lubricates the ideological reproduction of "colonial fantasy," in which the white male subject is positioned at the center of representation by a desire for mastery, power, and control over the racialized and inferiorized black other. Hence, alongside the codes of the fine-art nude, Mapplethorpe seems to make use of the regulative function of the commonplace racist stereotype—the black man as athlete, mugger, or savage—in order to stabilize the invisible and all-seeing white subject at the center of the gaze, and thereby "fix" the black subject in its place not simply as the other, but as the object in the field of vision that holds a mirror to the fears and fantasies of the supposedly omnipotent white male subject.

According to literary critic Homi Bhabha, "an important feature of colonial discourse is its dependence on the concept of 'fixity' in the ideological construction of otherness" (this volume, chap. 3). Just as Mapplethorpe's photographs of female body-builder Lady Lisa Lyon seem obsessively to pin her down by processing the image of her body through a thousand cultural stereotypes of femininity, so the obsessive undercurrent in his black male nudes would appear to confirm this emphasis on fixity as a sign that betrays anxiety as well as pleasure in the desire for mastery. Mapplethorpe's scopic fixation on the luxurious beauty of black skin thus implies a kind of "Negrophilia," an aesthetic idealization of racial difference that merely inverts and reverses the binary axis of colonial discourse, in which all things black are equated with darkness, dirt, and danger, as manifest in the psychic representations of "Negrophobia." Both positions, whether they overvalue or devalue the visible signs of racial difference, inhabit the shared space of colonial fantasy. These elements for a psychoanalytic reading of fetishism, as it is enacted in the theater of Mapplethorpe's sex-race fantasy, are forcefully brought together in a photograph such as "Man in a Polyester Suit."

The use of framing and scale emphasizes the sheer size of the big black penis revealed through the unzipped trouser fly. As Fanon said, when diagnosing the terrifying figure of "the Negro" in the fantasies of his white psychiatric patients, "One is no longer aware of the Negro, but only of a penis: the Negro is eclipsed. He is turned into a penis. He *is* a penis" (Fanon 1986, 120). By virtue of the purely formal device of scale, Mapplethorpe summons up one of the deepest mythological fears in the supremacist imagination: namely, the belief that all black men have monstrously large willies. In the phantasmic space of the white male imaginary, the big black phallus is perceived as a threat not only to hegemonic white masculinity but to Western civilization itself, since the "bad object" represents a danger to white womanhood and therefore the threat of miscegenation, eugenic pollution, and racial degeneration. Historically, in nineteenth-century societies structured by race, white males eliminated the anxiety that their own fantastic images of black male sexuality excited through rituals of aggression in which the lynching of black men routinely involved the literal castration of the other's strange fruit.

The historical myth of penis size amounts to a "primal fantasy" in Western culture in that it is shared and collective in nature—and, moreover, a myth that is so pervasive and firmly held as a folk belief that modern sexology repeatedly embarked on the empirical task of actually measuring pricks to demonstrate its untruth. Now that the consensual management of liberal race relations no longer provides available legitimation for this popular belief, it is as if Mapplethorpe's picture performs a disavowal of the wish-fulfillment inscribed in the myth: *I know* (it's not true that all black guys have big willies), *but* (nevertheless, in my photographs they do).

Within the picture, the binary character of everyday racial discourse is underlined by the jokey irony of the contrast between the black man's exposed private parts and the public display of social respectability signified by the three-piece business suit. The oppositions hidden and exposed, denuded and clothed, play upon the Manichaean dualism of nature and culture, savage and civilized, body and mind, inferior and superior, that informs the logic of dominant racial discourse. In this way, the construction of racial difference in the image suggests that sexuality, and nothing but sexuality, is the essential "nature" of the black man, because the cheap and tacky quality of the polyester suit confirms his failure to gain access to "culture." The camouflage of bourgeois respectability fails to conceal the fact that the black man, as the white man's racial other, originates, like his dick, from somewhere anterior to civilization.

Conflicting Readings of Mapplethorpe

Notwithstanding the problematic nature of Freud's pathologizing clinical vocabulary, his concept of fetishism can usefully be adapted, via feminist cultural theory, to help conceptualize issues of subjectivity and spectatorship in representations of race and ethnicity. Its account of the splitting of levels of belief may illuminate the prevalence of certain sexual fantasies and their role in the reproduction of racism in contemporary culture. The sexual fetish represents a substitute for something that was never there in the first place: the mother's penis, which the little boy expected to see. Despite conscious acknowledgment of sexual difference, the boy's castration anxiety forces the repression of his initial belief, such that it coexists on an unconscious level and finds manifestation, in adult sexuality, in the form of the erotic fetish (Freud 1977). One might say that, despite anatomical evidence, the belief symbolized in the fantasy of the big black willy—that black male sexuality is not only "different" but somehow "more"—is one many men and women, black and white, straight or gay, cling onto, because it retains currency and force as an element in the psychic reality of the social fantasies in which our racial and gendered identities have been historically constructed.

Yet because Freud's concept of fetishism is embedded in the patriarchal system of sexual difference that it describes, treating sexual perversion or deviation as a symptom which reveals the unconscious logic of the heterosexual norm, it is less useful as a tool for examining the perverse aestheticism of the modern homoerotic imagination which Mapplethorpe self-consciously employs. Moreover, there are limits to the race and gender analogy drawn from feminist cultural theory in the preceding analysis of visual fetishism: it ignores the obvious homoerotic specificity of the work. As a gay male artist whose sexual identity locates him in a subordinate relation to heterosexual masculinity, Mapplethorpe is hardly representative of the hegemonic model of straight, white, bourgeois male identity traditionally privileged in art history as the centered subject and agent of representation. Above all, as the recent exhibition history of his work attests, far from demonstrating the stability of this supposedly centered white male subject, the vitriol and anxiety expressed in hostile attacks on Mapplethorpe's *oeuvre* (such as those of radical neoconservative art critic Hilton Kramer) would suggest that there is something profoundly troubling and disturbing about the emotional ambivalence experienced by different audiences through the salient shock effect of Mapplethorpe's work.

In the light of the changed context of reception, the foremost question is how different audiences and readers produce different and conflicting readings of the same cultural text. The variety of conflicting interpretations of the value of Mapplethorpe's work would imply that the text does not bear one, singular and unequivocal meaning, but is open to a number of competing readings. Thus Mapplethorpe's photographic text has become the site for a range of antagonistic interpretations. Once we adopt this view, we need to reconsider the relationship between artist and audience, or author and reader, because although we habitually attempt to resolve the question of the ultimate "meaning" of a text by appealing to authorial intentions, poststructuralist theory has shown, by way of the "death of the author" argument, that individual intentions never have the last word in determining the meaning or value of a text. This is because readers themselves play an active role in interpreting a multivalent and open-ended modernist cultural text.

One might say, therefore, that the difficult and troublesome question raised by Mapplethorpe's black male nudes—do they reinforce or undermine racist myths about black sexuality?—is strictly unanswerable, since his aesthetic strategy makes an unequivocal yes/no response impossible. The question is left open by the author and is thus thrown back to the spectator. Our recognition of the unconscious sex-race fantasies which Mapplethorpe's images arouse with such perverse precision does not confirm a stable or centered subject position, but is experienced precisely as an emotional disturbance which troubles the viewer's sense of secure identity.

The recent actual death of the author entails a reconsideration of the issue of authorship and intentionality, and the reciprocal role of the reader, because the articulation of race and homosexuality in Mapplethorpe's art can also be seen as a subversive move that begins to unravel the violent ambiguity at the interface of the social and the emotional. To clarify my suggestion that his black male nudes are open to an alternative evaluation from that of my initial reading, I should come clean with regard to the specific character of my own subject position as a black gay male reader.

My angry emphasis on racial fetishism as a potentially exploitative process of objectification was based on the way in which I felt identified with the black men depicted in the photographs, simply by virtue of sharing the same "categorical" identity as a black man. As the source of this anger, the emotional identification can be best described again in Fanon's words as a feeling that "I am laid bare. I am over-determined from without. I am the slave not of the 'idea' that others have of me but of my own appearance. I am being dissected under white eyes. I am fixed . . . Look, it's a Negro" (Fanon 1986, 82). It was my anger at the aestheticizing effect of Mapplethorpe's coolly "ironic" appropriation of racist stereotypes that informed the description of visual fetishism as a process of reduction, or dehumanization. This argument has many similarities with the early feminist critique of images of women in pornography.[3] But the problem with this view is that it moralizes images in terms of a reductive dichotomy between good and bad, "positive" and "negative," and thus fails to recognize the ambivalence of the text. If, on the other hand, we recognize that there is an important difference between saying that an image is racist and saying that it is "about" racism, then we need a more reflexive approach to the ambiguities set into motion in the destabilizing moment of Mapplethorpe's shock effect.

On this view, the strategic use of visual fetishism is not necessarily a bad thing, as it encourages the viewer to examine his or her own implication in the fantasies which the images arouse. Once I acknowledge my own location in the image reservoir as a gay subject—a desiring subject not only in terms of sharing a desire to look, but in terms of an identical object-choice already there in my own fantasies and wishes—then the articulation of meanings about eroticism, race, and homosexuality becomes a lot more complicated. Indeed, I am forced to confront the rather unwelcome fact that as a spectator I actually occupy the very position in the fantasy of mastery previously ascribed to the centered position of the white male subject! In other words, there was another axis of identification—between white gay male author and black gay male reader—that cut across the identification with the black men in the pictures. Could it not be the case that my anger was also mingled with feelings of jealousy, rivalry, or envy? If I shared the same desire to look, which would place me in the position of mastery attributed to the author, the anger in the initial critique might also have arisen from a shared, homosexual identification, and thus a rivalry over the same unobtainable object of desire. Insofar as the anger and envy were effects of my identification with both object and subject of the look, I would say that my specific identity as a black gay reader placed me in two contradictory positions at one and the same time. I am sure that emotions such as these are at issue in the rivalry of interpretations around Mapplethorpe's most contentious work. Black gay male readers certainly do not have a monopoly on the conflicted and ambivalent structures of feeling they create. My point here is not confessional, but to use my own experience as a source of data about the complex operations of identification and desire that posi-

3. The humanist critique of objectification is taken up by Essex Hemphill (1991).

tion us in antagonistic and contradictory relations of race, gender, and power, which are themselves partly constituted in representations. In revising my views, I have sought to reopen the question of ambivalence, because rather than simply project it onto the author (by asking whether he either perpetuates or challenges racism) one needs to take into account how different readers derive different meanings not only about race, but about sexuality and desire, in Mapplethorpe's work.

The Perverse Aesthetic

The whole point about the use of textual ambivalence in the modernist tradition is to foreground the uncertainty of any one, singular meaning—which, in the case of Mapplethorpe's double transgressions across race and homosexuality, is a risky business indeed. This is because the open-ended character of the images can provoke a racist reading as much as an antiracist one, elicit a homophobic reading as much as arouse a homoerotic one. A great deal depends on the reader and the social identity she or he brings to the text. The same statement—the black man is beautiful, say— retains the same denotative meaning, but acquires different connotational values when enunciated by different groups of subjects: the same sentence, uttered by a white man, a black woman, a black man, or a white woman, would inevitably take on a qualitatively different "sound." Similarly, once we situate the network of relations between author, text, and reader, in the contingent, context-bound circumstances in which Mapplethorpe's work currently stands, then we can examine the way in which the open-ended structure of the text gives rise to antagonistic readings that are informed by the social identity of the audience.

Without returning to a naive belief in the author as a godlike figure of authority, it is necessary to argue that it really does matter who is speaking whenever artists, because of their sexual, gender, or racial identity, are assigned "minority" status in the arts and in culture at large. Once we take the biographical dimension of Mapplethorpe's work as a gay artist into account it is possible to reinterpret the black male nudes as the beginning of an inquiry into the archive of "race" in Western culture and history, which has rendered black men into "invisible men," in Ralph Ellison's phrase. As Mapplethorpe put it in an interview shortly before his death, "At some point I started photographing black men. It was an area that hadn't been explored intensively. If you went through the history of nude male photography, there were very few black subjects. I found that I could take pictures of black men that were so subtle, and the form was so photographical." An awareness of the exclusion of the black subject from one of the most valued canonical genres of Western art— the nude—suggests that it is both possible and necessary to reread Mapplethorpe's work as part of an artistic inquiry into the hegemonic force of a Eurocentric aesthetics which historically rendered invisible not only black people but women, lesbians and gays, and others before the radical social transformations of the modern and postmodern period.

By virtue of a perverse aesthetic of promiscuous intertextuality, whereby the overvalued aura of the fine-art nude is contaminated by the filthy and degraded form of the commonplace stereotype, Mapplethorpe transgresses on several fronts to make visible that which is repressed and made invisible in the dominant, and dominating, tradition of the West against the rest. In the contemporary United States, for example, black males constitute one of the "lowest" social identities in the late-capitalist underclass: disenfranchised, disadvantaged, disempowered. Yet in Mapplethorpe's studio, some of the men who in all probability came from this class are elevated onto the pedestal of the transcendental aesthetic ideal of the male nude in Western culture, which had always excluded the black subject from such aesthetic idealization on account of its otherness. Mapplethorpe's achievement as a postmodern "society photographer" lies in the way he renders invisible men visible in a cultural system—art photography—that always historically denied or marginalized their existence. One can see in Mapplethorpe's use of homoeroticism a subversive strategy of perversion in which the liberal humanist values inscribed in the idealized fine-art nude are led away from the higher aims of "civilization" and brought face to face with that part of itself repressed and devalued as "other" in the form of the banal, commonplace stereotype in everyday culture. What is experienced in the salient shock effect is the disruption of our normative expectations about distinctions that imply a rigid separation between fine art and popular culture, or between art and pornography. Mapplethorpe's transgressive crossing of such boundaries has the effect of calling into question our psychic and social investment in these cultural separations.

Changing Political Climates

If I am now more prepared to offer a defense rather than a critique of Mapplethorpe's representations of race, because of the changed ideological context, it is because the stakes have also changed. I am convinced that it was not the death of the author so much as the cause of his death that was a major factor in the timing of the Helms campaign against the NEA. Almost all the discourse surrounding the furor noted that Mapplethorpe died of AIDS. The newfound legitimacy of political homophobia and the creation of new folk devils through the mismanagement of the AIDS crisis have proved fertile ground for the spread of popular authoritarian tendencies across the left/right spectrum. Yet the Mapplethorpe/NEA crisis in the U.S.A. was often perceived, like the Rushdie crisis in Britain, simply in terms of a straightforward opposition between censorship and freedom of artistic expression. This model of a crude binary frontier is unfeasible because what was at stake in the conflicting readings of Mapplethorpe was not a neat dichotomy between bigoted Philistines and enlightened cultured liberals but a new configuration of social actors, some of whom have engaged in unexpected alliances which have transformed the terrain of contestation.

In many ways the right's success in organizing a popular bloc of public opinion on issues like pornography derives from these new alliances. Just like the alliance formed between radical feminist antiporn activists and the local state legislature in the form of the Dworkin-MacKinnon-drafted Minneapolis Ordinance in 1984, or the appropriation of the feminist argument that pornography itself is violence in the official discourse of the Meese Commission in 1986, the Helms campaign has highlighted some significant developments in popular right-wing politics. In his original proposal to regulate public funding of art deemed "obscene and indecent," Jesse Helms went beyond the traditional remit of moral fundamentalism to add new grounds for legal intervention on the basis of discrimination against minorities. Helms wanted the state to intervene in instances where artistic and cultural materials "denigrate, debase or revile a person, group or class of citizens on the basis of race, creed, sex, handicap or national origin." By means of this rhetorical move, he sought to appropriate the language of liberal antidiscrimination legislation to promote a climate of opinion favorable to new forms of coercive intervention. In making such a move, the strategy is not simply to win support from black people and ethnic minorities, nor simply to modernize the traditional "moral" discourse against obscenity, but to broaden and extend the threshold of illegitimacy to a wider range of cultural texts. As the moral panic unfolds, more and more cultural forms transgress or come up against the symbolic boundary that such prohibitionary legislation seeks to impose. Consider the way in which parental warning labels on rap and rock albums have become commonplace: the Parents' Music Resource Center that helped to initiate this trend in the 1980s has also inspired prosecutions of rock musicians on the grounds that their cultural texts do not simply "deprave and corrupt," as it were, but have actually caused violence, in the form of suicides.

Under these conditions—when, despite its initial emancipatory intentions, elements of the radical feminist antiporn movement of the 1980s have entered into alliance with neoconservative forces—it is not inconceivable that a reading of Robert Mapplethorpe's work as racist, however well intended, could serve the ends of the authoritarian trend supported by this new alliance of social actors. The AIDS crisis has also visibly brought to light the way in which homophobia can be used to draw upon conservative forces within minority cultures. In black British communities, the antilesbian and antigay hostility expressed in the belief that homosexuality is a "white man's thing," and hence, because of the scapegoating of gay men, that AIDS is a "white man's disease," has not only helped to cement alliances between black people and the New Right (for example, in the local campaign on "Positive Images" in Haringey, London, in 1987) but has had tragically self-defeating consequences in the black community itself. Men and women have been dying, but the psychic mechanism of denial and disavowal in such fear of homosexuality has been particularly apparent in many black responses to AIDS.

Yet these contradictory conditions have also shaped the emergence of a new generation of black lesbian and gay cultural activists in Britain and the United States. Their presence is seriously important not only because they contest the repressive precepts of authoritarian politics in both white society and in black communities, but because their creativity points to new ways of making sense of the contemporary situation. Black lesbian and gay artists such as Isaac Julien, Pratibha Parmar, Michelle Parkerson, and Marlon Riggs in film and video, or Essex Hemphill, Cheryl Clarke, Barbara Smith, and Joseph Beam in writing and critique, or Sunil Gupta, Rotimi Fani-Kayode, or Lyle Harris in the medium of photography, have widened and pluralized the political and theoretical debates about eroticism, prohibition, transgression, and representation. In films such as Isaac Julien's *Looking for Langston* (1989) some of the difficult and troublesome questions about race and homosexuality that Mapplethorpe raised are taken on in a multifaceted dialogue on the lived experience of black gay desire. In his photographs, Rotimi Fani-Kayode also enters into this dialogue, not through a confrontational strategy but through an invitational mode of address which operates in and against the visual codes and conventions his work shares with Mapplethorpe's. But in this hybrid, Afrocentric, homoerotic image world, significant differences unfold as such artists critically "signify upon" the textual sources they draw from. In the hands of this new generation of black diaspora intellectuals rethinking sex, such "signifying" activity simultaneously critiques the exclusions and absences which previously rendered black lesbian and gay identities invisible, and reconstructs new pluralistic forms of collective belonging and imagined community that broaden the public sphere of multicultural society.

Such radical changes in black queer visibility were unthinkable ten or fifteen years ago, and one would hope that their emergence now suggests new possibilities for an alternative set of popular alliances that seek to open up and democratize the politics of desire. In the event that the legislation sought by those opposed to whatever can be called "pornographic" is ever successful in Britain, it is far more likely that it will first be brought to bear on independent artists such as these rather than on the corporations and businessmen who own the porn industry, edit the tabloids, or sell advertising. To propose to outlaw something the definition of which no one seems to agree upon is hardly in the interests of anyone seeking not just the protection of our existing civil rights and liberties (few as they are in Britain) but the necessary changes that would further democratize and deepen new practices of freedom.

Works Cited

Fanon, F. 1986. *Black Skin, White Masks*. London: Pluto Press.

Freud, S. 1977. "Fetishism." In *On Sexuality*. Pelican Freud Library, vol. 7. Harmondsworth: Penguin.

Hemphill, E. 1991. Introduction to *Brother to Brother: New Writings by Black Gay Men*, ed. E. Hemphill. Boston: Alyson Press.

Gardner, T. 1980. "Racism in Pornography and the Women's Movement." In *Take Back the Night: Women on Pornography*, ed. L. Lederer. New York: William Morrow.

Julien, I., and K. Mercer. 1988. "Race, Sexual Politics, and Black Masculinity: A Dossier." In *Male Order: Unwrapping Masculinity*, ed. R. Chapman and J. Rutherford. London: Lawrence and Wishart.

Kappeler, S. 1986. *The Pornography of Representation*. Cambridge: Polity Press.

Lorde, A. 1980. "Uses of the Erotic: The Erotic as Power." In *Take Back the Night: Women on Pornography*, ed. L. Lederer. New York: William Morrow.

Mapplethorpe, R. 1982. *Black Males*. Amsterdam: Gallerie Jurka.

———. 1986. *The Black Book*. Munich: Shirme-Mosel.

Marshall, R., ed. 1990. *Robert Mapplethorpe*. New York: Bullfinch Press.

Mercer, K. 1986. "Imagining the Black Man's Sex." In *Photography/Politics: Two*, ed. P. Holland, J. Spence, and S. Watney. London: Comedia.

———. 1991. "Skin Head Sex Thing: Racial Difference and the Homoerotic Imaginary." In *How Do I Look? Lesbian and Gay Film and Video*, ed. Bad Object Choices. Seattle: Bay Press.

Walker, A. 1980. "Coming Apart." In *Take Back the Night: Women on Pornography*, ed. L. Lederer. New York: William Morrow.

Fifteen

Black British Cinema: Spectatorship and Identity Formation in *Territories*

Manthia Diawara

You are an Englishman. Are you not loyal to them?

Yes, to England and to other things.
Lawrence of Arabia

According to the French film theorist Jean-Pierre Oudart, the assumptions behind the construction of the classical narrative of Hollywood film have masked the relation between the spectator and the image, while privileging the relation between images, and assigning the same position to the spectator and the character. For Oudart, the spectator, or the "filmic subject," is not to be confused with the character, or the "subject on film." While the character is only a signifier among the objects positioned on the screen, the spectator plays a role as important as the role of a "grammatical subject" in a sentence. In other words, just as the subject holds a sentence together through his/her/its relation to the different parts of the sentence, the spectator too occupies a position without which the film is a meaningless discursive fragment. Narration is always in a fragmentary state, and never closed, until it enters into a relation with the filmic subject. Every narration places the spectator in a position of agency; and race, class, and sexual relations influence the way in which this subjecthood is filled by the spectator.[1]

1. Drawing on J. A. Miller's formulations about the subject's relation to the object in the

Theories of identification assume a uniform regression in the movie theater. Until recently, race, gender, and sexuality did not constitute important categories within reception theory. It was assumed that we all regressed from the same point. While in recent years, feminist theory has made important gains in analyzing the gendered nature of the spectator, race has been neglected as a category for the identity formation of the spectator. I believe, however, that since race is an important structuring element in *every* Hollywood film, our analyses must also take it into account. The point, therefore, is not whether race is an acceptable category of film analysis, but how and when race enters into the discussion of identification. In a class discussing black spectatorship, a student asked me whether one goes to movies conscious of oneself as a black man, a white woman, or a gay person. I explained that I would not dispute the assumptions behind either the notion of regression during the process of identification or behind the theory of continuity editing.[2] I was interested in the moments of rupture in these two theories of spectatorship: i.e., the moments when the spectator retrieves his/her identities away from the film. The moments of rupture may be brief, but they enable the spectator to resist complete identification with the film's discourse, to break the aesthetic contract with the *Absent One*—"the Mother" in the mirror phase where the subject's desire is first constructed in her discourse[3]—and to use gender, class, race, and sexuality as elements for articulating resistance to the film's discourse. Thus the moment of rupture enables us as spectators to reclaim our identities as blacks, gays, Marxists, and so forth.

Oudart's distinction between *sujet filmique* (the spectator) and *sujet filmé* (the character or other objects on the screen) yields a better understanding of the centrality of rupture in the suturing process—the process of bringing the spectator into a relation with the images on the screen through the camera's disruptive technique.

---

mirror (Lacan's mirror phase), Oudart uses the term "suture" to stitch the spectator into the film narrative. Controversies surrounding the definition of suture and its distinction from shot/reverse shot have discouraged further discussions of the deconstructive potentials in the theory of suture. *Screen* (1975–78) has variously attempted to trace the theory back to Miller and Lacan, in the translation of Oudart's short and simple essays, and thereby helped to obscure the issue for American readers. See Oudart 1969; Dayan 1974; Rothman 1975; and Heath 1981.

2. Continuity, editing refers to the respect for the 180 degree rule in positioning the camera, which is positioned so that the cutting of images does not disrupt the continual flow of images.

3. See Heath 1981, 83. For David Bordwell, it is narration which is always already absent from the frame: "I have treated the 'Absent One' entailed by the image as the narration, not another character in the fiction" (1985). I use the Absent One interchangeably as Englishness, or blackness. In other words, as discourse. For more on the Absent One, see my essay "Englishness and Blackness: Cricket as a Discourse on Colonialism" (1990).

Oudart praises Robert Bresson for defining the character on the screen as a signifier, and for distinguishing it from the spectator, who is the filmic subject. He states that the spectator "may abstain from playing the role of the film's imaginary subject. In fact, he/she is able to play the role of filmic subject only from an angle different from the position of the Absent One, because he/she is not the Absent One."[4]

Sankofa Film and Video Collective—with such films as *Territories* (1985), *Passion of Remembrance* (1986), and *Looking for Langston* (1989)—uses experimental and documentary forms to dramatize the position of the spectator in order to reveal the terrain of identity formation, and the difference between the spectator and the Absent One, whose position is filled by the objects on the screen. In all Sankofa films, the first spectator is a black British who is trying to articulate his/her identity as a member of the African diaspora, as a citizen of Britain, and in terms of his/her location in class and sexual relations. The cinematic pleasure, or the illusion of immediacy, which is constituted in classical narratives by the confusion of the positions of the character and the spectator, is eclipsed in Sankofa films by the presence in each of the films of spectators who mark their positions as different from that of the Absent One. Sankofa films thus restore to spectators their difference; their right to abstain from occupying the same position as the subject on film or to put it in Oudart's words, "de la position du sujet filme." In Sankofa films, the emphasis is less on the event that is unfolding, and more on the questioning of a particular cinematic discourse in a single shot, or in a group of shots, and on the spectator's role as filmic subject which creates the conditions for the emergence of new and differentiated identities. The attempt to frame the spectator at the moment he/she is viewing an object (or a frame) that represents the discourse of an Absent One is Sankofa's way of giving back to the spectator his/her identities.

Until now, conventional theories of spectatorship have rendered invisible the effect of the spectator's identities on the image through their recourse to continuity editing or a homogeneous theory of regression. Sankofa films reveal the moments when the spectators' reading of the film contradicts the discourse of the Absent One. Sankofa films focus our attention on spectatorship by emphasizing frames within frames, spectators watching films while they are being filmed, and cameras being tracked while they are framing their subjects. The spectator and the objects on the screen are locked together in a struggle that modifies both their identities. Thus, Sankofa films depict the intersections, the contradictory and the intermediary spaces between blackness and Englishness, Britishness and Caribbeanness, and among race, class, and sexuality.

4. I have translated and adapted this passage from Oudart 1969 (part 1, 38), to my own text.

Suture as Rupture in *Territories*

To illustrate my point, I will now turn to the film *Territories* and analyze the relation between the spectator and the objects on the screen. I will emphasize the moment of rupture in the suturing process because I am interested in the intermediary spaces, during the process of identification, where the spectator recuperates his/her identities and interrupts the symbolic system of a master narrative. A film like *Territories,* for example, is concerned with the way in which narrative forms, such as conventional BBC documentaries, violently insert the Caribbean into European history. Focusing on the televisual representation of carnival by the BBC, the film comments on its strategies of containment, and omission of black cultural and subversive practices. *Territories*—a film in two parts, the first part dealing with the BBC rendition of the London carnival, and the second part deconstructing the BBC's version—depicts two young black British filmmakers at an editing table, watching and analyzing the representation of carnival by the BBC. From time to time, the two spectators can be heard on the soundtrack commenting on a particular scene of the documentary. They often bring some scenes from the documentary to the foreground of the film in order to interrupt the narrative flow, and to reveal the way in which the scenes participate in the reproduction of stereotypes about black people in London.

In order to account for the way spectatorship is delineated in *Territories,* it is important first to describe the formal disposition of the two spectators and the television monitor on the editing table on which they are watching the BBC documentary. The camera, which is positioned behind, shows the two spectators in the foreground and the monitor in the background. The camera pans left and right to show selected parts of carnival from the perspective of the spectators/filmmakers at the editing table. Then it zooms in on the monitor until its frames blend with those of the camera. On the soundtrack, the two spectators carry their deconstruction of the BBC documentary to its logical conclusion by stating that "conventional documentaries always return us to the Caribbean, to Trinidad in particular, to account for the meaning of carnival today for black people in Britain." The notion of differentiated spectator positions is also supported by the title of the film and by the attempt to depict what the film calls the "contradictory spaces which are the geographical expressions of a city" and the "territories of class, labor, race, and sex relations."

A look at the way *Territories* insists on the distinction between the positions of the narrator in the BBC documentary and the two black British spectators will inform our understanding of the process of inserting the spectator in the text. The goal of the film, in positioning the two spectators at different angles, which are themselves different from the position of the camera, is to reveal the power of the spectator as "filmic subject" to refuse at any time to play his/her role as subject of the documentary's discourse. Thus, images on the monitor screen are blurred whenever the camera attempts to occupy the position of one of the spectators to show selected scenes of carnival. The blurred images indicate that instead of "standing in the place of the Absent One" and reconstructing the narrative of carnival, the two spectators disrupt the continuity of the documentary through a selection of individual scenes which are analyzed in order to reveal the way the BBC projects a Eurocentric definition on carnival: i.e., the depiction of blacks as noble savages. The two spectators are interested in showing the distance between the specific context of carnival in London and the documentary, which ignores this historical specificity and retraces the event back to the West Indies as an exotic spectacle.

In one of the scenes that the two spectators select for analysis, the camera zooms in toward the television set until its frames blend with those of the movie screen. Then we see the BBC's images of carnival in close-up and in slow motion with the lines often blurred or dissolved into one big spot. On the soundtrack the spectators repeat after one another "that in conventional documentaries of carnival, we are routinely taken into a past, shown a plantocracy. We are told the ambiguities of mock revolutions. We are told the mimicry and parody of plantocrats and their manners. What do these conventional stories add up to? The same old story. A string of stereotypes about black culture. Carnival is neutralized and framed, contained as a site of spectacle."

The spectators' appropriation of this scene—the way they cut it out of the BBC story and brought it to the foreground to fill the screen—informs us about the differentiated locations of the Absent One and the spectator. When they occupy demarcated positions with the television set in the background, the images on the screen are clearer. However, whenever the camera assumes the same position as one of the spectators and blends the frames of the television with those of the big screen, it is significant to notice at that moment that the objects get blurred and move in slow motion on the big screen. Their chain of signification is ruptured.

These moments of rupture enable the two spectators to deconstruct the BBC discourse on carnival. According to them, the BBC associates the black subject in carnival with fun-loving people of the plantation, calypso, and cricket: "I would be whatever figure these foreign imaginations cared for me to be. It would be so simple to let others fill in for me . . . I know who I am, but you will never know who I am. I may in fact lose touch with who I am. I hid from my real sources, but my real sources were also hidden from me." The person behind the camera in the BBC documentary and the two spectators in *Territories* see different things when they look at carnival. Clearly, the film states that this difference is influenced by race, class, and sexual relations.

The reading of other sequences in the film demonstrates the power of the spectators to restructure the text, to alter its meaning by exposing its formal field to a new system of coherence. Thus, by selecting specific parts of the documentary and magnifying them, the two spectators show how the BBC defines carnival as a cathartic device that purges the frustrations of plantation slaves. For the BBC, carnival in the West Indies was concerned with mimicry and mock revolutions. From the documentary, one expects carnival in Britain, too, to be celebratory of the past and passive in its spectacle. For the BBC, carnival is a time to eat exotic Caribbean food, listen to music, and dance. For the two spectators, this commodification of London carnival depoliticizes it and turns it into a summer party where one can go and imitate the Trinidadians' mimicry of the plantocrats. The film states that, to preserve the party atmosphere and to suppress the subversive content of carnival (which led to the riots of 1959, 1966, and 1976), the London police require blacks to carry passes in order to attend the event. For the two spectators, this way of assigning an identity to every carnival participant is not only contrary to the production of many identities at the event, but also reminiscent of the apartheid system, which characterizes itself by constructing and constricting space for black people.

For the two spectators, the BBC's aestheticization of carnival fails, therefore, to take into account the use of the event by black people in Britain to defy racism, sexism, and unemployment. The BBC documentary obscures the use of carnival space to experiment with new battle strategies for the future, to exchange new musical sounds and dances, and to bring together the exploited groups from the Caribbean, Africa, Europe, and Asia.

The Burning of the Union Jack

The second part of *Territories* inaugurates a new cinematic discourse that defies the BBC's appropriation of carnival, and stages the event from the perspective of black British spectators. As I pointed out, the two black British in the film see in the BBC's strategy of reducing carnival to its original manifestations in the West Indies an attempt to erase or to conceal the ways in which carnival has been transformed to respond to the cultural and creative lives of black people in Britain. Their history of carnival must therefore deal with how the cultures of different territories are incorporated in carnival and used to express the political, social, and economic situation of blacks in Britain. *Territories* uses the leitmotif, "We're struggling to begin a story, a his-story, a her-story," at the beginning of every sequence in the film to show the new sets of complexities involved in the description of carnival in Britain. For the spectators, tracing the origins of carnival to Trinidad or to Africa, as the BBC documentary does, will not give an account of the new forms of performance that the event has taken in London. On the contrary, the return to a place of origin, such as Trinidad, is the BBC's way of colonizing the event and separating it from other events that are British. Similarly, the black British are always depicted as outsiders to British culture.

The new cinematic discourse that *Territories* employs to displace the conventional documentary style is characterized by the disposition of the images, the montage, and the soundtrack in a violent manner in order to establish the meaning of carnival in the British context. Unlike the BBC documentary, which sees carnival only as an event about the West Indies and its cultures, the film makes it clear at this point that the event is about Britain, about war between black youth and the police, and about the reclaiming of urban streets as expressive spaces for black culture. There are images of the Union Jack—the British flag—on fire. The flames burn through the middle of the flag, revealing black youth who confront policemen. The space is further confused by several shots of street scenes that are superimposed and dissolved onto each other. There are gay men embracing over a still photograph of policemen wearing helmets. The editing accentuates the transgression against the system by cross-cutting between images of youth and police. As the confrontation draws nearer, the two oppositional elements, i.e., desire and law, youth and police, are condensed into two shots: one a medium shot of a policeman and the other a close-up of a black man's defiant and transgressive-looking face. This linear style of narration—that is, the use of one policeman and one black man's face to represent the fight in the streets between youth and police—is soon subverted by a fusion of the synecdoches and the images they represent in the same shots. Later, I discuss how the film uses excess as a representational device. For the moment I would like to address the manner in which *Territories* posits violence both as form and as a way for black youth to reclaim the streets.

Clearly the confrontational editing enables us to understand the ways in which police and black youth construct each other: for the police, young blacks are the delinquents, the muggers, the threat to the system and, therefore, have to be kept off the streets (Hall et al. 1978). For youth, the police symbolize the militarization of Britain, e.g., the use of helmets, the oppressor of black people, the enemy that is restricting every expression of blackness in Britain. The opposition of police to youth is complemented by other oppositional elements in the film: the BBC's carnival and carnival in *Territories;* the decay of Britain and black British youth; the standardized English used by the BBC employees and the use of different voices and accents in the film; the BBC theme song and the use of new sound systems (of DJ toasting, African traditional music, American pop music, and nursery rhymes).

Thus, the second half of *Territories* uses force to push aside the police who symbolize the status quo, and to break down conventional storytelling forms such as those used by the BBC, in order to create its own space and its own story. *Territories* emphasizes local conflicts between youth and police, desire and law, which transform the content of carnival in Britain and distinguish it from carnival in Trinidad. In this respect, the film is not unlike C. L. R. James's *Beyond a Boundary,* which shows that West Indian cricket represents the taking-away and the appropriation of the game from Englishness. *Territories,* too, debunks the recourse to notions of origin to explain the significance of carnival in Britain. Accordingly, the film, by superimposing images, mixing private and public spaces, and using several voice-over commentators to repeat the same lines, sets in motion the transgression of the space delimiting the movement of blacks in Britain. The youth in the film, by burning the flag and by walking over the image of the police, take charge of opening up new spaces and of defining their Britishness on their own terms.

It seems to me crucial here to reflect further on the meaning of violence in *Territories* and the shape violence gives here to carnival as a specific black British cultural event. Certain aspects of Frantz Fanon's theory of violence may be useful here for understanding the way in which the concept is deployed in *Territories.* I am specifically referring to Fanon's description in *The Wretched of the Earth* (1968, 93) of violence as a process that sutures people into a common cause and as a category of historical and cultural production. When we consider violence as a suturing process, it is important to see that, for Fanon, the mobilization of the masses against the system that is oppressing them "binds them together as a whole, since each individual forms a violent link in the great chain, a part of the great organism of violence which has surged upward in reaction to the settler's violence in the beginning. The groups recognize each other and the future nation is already indivisible." There we have it: violence is a system or a machine, or, yet, a narrative, of which the individual desires to be a part in order to participate in the (re)construction of the nation. Furthermore, in order to be actualized, violence positions the masses in its chain of signification, "introduces into each man's consciousness the ideas of common cause, of a national destiny, and of a collective history." Violence—"this cement which has been mixed with blood and anger"—in this sense becomes the founding basis of the nation, the process through which the individual articulates his/her relation with the nation. This moment, when the individual takes his/her place in the chain of signification which forms the "body" of violence, when the individual identifies with the nation, is a key stage in Fanon's theory of violence, and it is equal to the mirror phase or the moment of screening where identity is articulated in relation to an Absent One.

It is unfortunate that Fanon focuses only on physical violence directed at settlers in a colonial situation to validate this important sociopsychoanalytic insight of seizing the moment of violence as space for identity formation. In turning to the Eurocentric formulations of sociopsychoanalytic theory, Fanon neglected to take into account the capabilities of African cultural formations, such as secret rituals, myths, and popular dances, to become sites of resistance. In dismissing these cultural sites,

Fanon shares with the settlers the view of precolonial African cultures as primitive. He does not seem to consider that the policing of metropolitan spaces such as Paris and London can be destabilized by the staging of black cultural forms. Fanon is thereby able to dismiss street dances and rituals of possession by "Zombies" and by "Legba" as mere "symbolical killings" (1968, 57).

But when we turn to *Territories,* it is important not to dismiss the role of artistic, cultural, and discursive violence, as well as the physical force, used by the black British to take their place in Britain. The material violence in *Territories,* which is linked to the burning of the Union Jack and the confrontation between youth and police, is reinforced equally by the artistic violence, symbolized by the disruption and altering of conventional cinematic forms; by the soundtrack, which combines defiant and revolutionary songs from Africa, America, and the West Indies; by the letting loose of desire in the public space, as demonstrated by gays, dancing in the streets; by the blurring of police space and youth space; and by the inscription of eroticism in close-up shots of such body parts as the nose, the eyes, and the neck.

These material, cultural, and artistic categories—taken together as aspects of violence against the attempts to maintain a decaying nation just for the privileges of one group—become the means for the submerging ethnicities to anchor themselves in the nation and to change its destiny. As the Union Jack burns, the opening cracks reveal the faces of black youth, new cultures and desires that are legitimized by flames burning through the flag. The burning of the Union Jack must therefore be seen as a civil war, a revolutionary war against the old institution, or, as the film puts it, against "the holding of one class's privileges in a declining system." Black youth declare their British nationalism by burning the flag and altering its shape. For Fanon, people's violent action in the process of liberating their nation sutures them as patriotic citizens: their action links them together, "they show themselves to be jealous of the results of their destiny, or the fate of their country in the hands of a living god" (1968, 94).

In his pioneering book *There Ain't No Black in the Union Jack* (1991), Paul Gilroy too has shown the complex relationship among race, class, and nation in Britain, and insisted on the notion that attacks on the police, as evidenced by the riots, fix the identities of black youth in British nationalism: "Violence is seemingly formed by or in relation to specific cultural institutions and events and identity is reproduced or transmitted by attacks on the police" (94). But Gilroy also stresses the role of artistic and cultural assaults on English ethnocentrism and its artistic conventions in order to construct black identities in Britain and address their rights as citizens. For Gilroy, such black artists as Culture Smiley in music, Lenny Henry in comedy, and Sonia Boyce in painting, decompose and recompose the sign systems of established conventions in order to infuse them politically with black structures of feeling and to redefine the meaning of Britishness. The presence of blacks in Britain, therefore, indicates not only specific ways in which Britishness modifies their identities, but also indicates the ways in which they transform, invert, and proliferate the symbols that stand for Britain. Thus, for Gilroy, black art, influenced by the black struggle, redefines Britishness in a manner that challenges white ethnic absolutists' exclusive claims to the signs of the empire. In discussing Culture Smiley's "Cockney Translation,' a song that breaks linguistic continuity by juxtaposing Jamaican-derived patois and Cockney, Gilroy shows how the artist sutures blacks in Britain and Britishness: "'Cockney Translation' conveys a view of these languages [patois and Cockney] as genuinely interchangeable alternatives disrupting the racial hierarchy in which they are usually arranged. It presents them as equivalent 'nation languages' facing each other across the desperate terrain of the inner city" (195).

Gilroy, in an essay entitled "This Island Race" (1990, 30-32), resumes the idea of a plural Britain in which the rising generation of blacks are transforming the configuration of British signs, finding ways of articulating their Britishness and ways of creating a sense of belonging to Britain. Gilroy sees in Sonia Boyce's repainting of such traditional symbols as the English rose an act of appropriation in which the monolithic sign of nationhood is eclipsed, and Britishness is redefined as the sum total of signs that are related to different but intersecting identities. For Gilroy, black artists "are already working to recompose understanding of English culture and their creativity needs to be complemented by a rereading of that culture's history" (31).

Similarly, in *Territories* artistic appropriation and transformation of established conventions along with the use of physical violence sutures blacks in Britishness. Through the use of the soundtrack and editing, the film inverts the meaning of the police's representation of youth as muggers and as a threat to Britishness and transforms it into youth as oppressed. As the image-track shows the police beating up young black men and taking them away, the soundtrack plays "The Ballad of Sacco and Vanzetti," which thematizes the police as oppressors and youth as innocent martyrs. Youths' rebellion against the police—their march over the images of helmeted policemen—is accompanied by an African popular song, "Mankene," as well as reggae beats, which are about hope and rebellion against the oppressor.

Also, the police's representation of the streets as dangerous for elderly white women is turned against itself. In one scene, an old woman clinging to her purse and looking frightened crosses a street full of young black males. The camera stays on her until she reaches the other end of the street, then the scene is reversed, sending her back to the beginning. Interpreted from the perspective of black youths' contestation of their construction by the police, this scene embodies several meanings. To begin with, it appropriates the discourse of the police and addresses the fears of the white woman for whom the image of the young black male connotes rape and mugging. In this sense, the presence of black youth turns the streets into hell, and crossing from one end to the other becomes a painful and long journey for the white woman. But, by running the same image in reverse, the film literally deconstructs the stereotypic police construction of black youth. The image in reverse, because it is comical—or a bad joke at the expense of the old woman—unseats the authenticity of the image of black youth the police have created in the woman's mind. The image in reverse, a backward double, imprints a new meaning on the traces of the first image, opening the possibility for black British to represent themselves in Britain. In other words, one of the tasks of black British film, too, is to "recompose" the signs of blackness and Britishness in Britain, to lift blackness from the pathological space created by police files, and to take the terms of documenting black lives away from the BBC and the police.

Carnivalesque Excess

To turn now to the use of carnivalesque excess in *Territories*,[5] I want to begin by submitting that, in a Foucauldian sense, the film is about discourses (territories) excluding, complementing, or traversing each other. Thus, the struggle over the meaning of signs discussed above concerns the police's attempt to keep youth off the streets, and vice versa. Some of the complementary spaces include the thematic songs on the soundtrack, and the defiant images of youth. The remainder of this discussion will be on the intersectionality of territories in the film. The use of carnival here both as subject of the film's deployment and as cinematic language is interesting. According to Kwesi Owusu and Jacob Ross, the masquerade of carnival is based on the privileging of ambivalence: "On the road with masquerade you don't see what you normally see. Voices hurry the boats to sea, shadows dance in the mind, blue-eyed dragons and sasabonsam inhale fire and belch out smoke. On the road with the masquerade you don't feel what you normally feel. Little chimes, arrow and shak-shak take a walk with Ananse and brigades of dancing feet along the valleys of the Kilimanjaro" (1987, 6).

The manner in which *Territories* translates this carnivalesque excess is not limited to simply putting the camera in front of the event called the London Carnival. The film also designs shots that contain intersecting bodies and objects. Crucially, the film posits excess by visualizing what it calls "the contradictory spaces which are the geographical expressions of a city: territories of race, labor, class, and sexual relations." The camera in *Territories*, like a Foucauldian archivist, maps discursive spaces and their articulations with the objects that traverse them. First we see contra-

5. For an application of Bakhtinian dialogism to black British cinema, see Mercer 1988a.

dictory bodies and objects that desire the same space: youth and police, desire and law, as well as sound systems, the burning flag, and dancing and embracing gay men. These bodies, which are sometimes aware of each other in an antagonistic manner, but which are most of the time oblivious of each other's presence, come together to define the geographical expression of space: i.e., the identities of the street. The film uses superimposed shots, and the soundtrack states that "behind each conflict, there is a his-story, a her-story," in order to convey the excess characterized by bodies possessed by the desire to cross spaces already occupied by other bodies.

The notion of bodies desiring different parts of the discursive space and defining the identities of that space through their movement is useful for an appreciation of the carnivalesque style adopted by *Territories*. Perhaps the clearest indication of desire's taking charge of different parts of the body and moving them horizontally, vertically, and on top of each other is seen through the film's weaving of superimposed close-ups of necks, noses, and eyes across the frames. The way desire causes bodies to traverse geographical spaces, under the watchful eyes of the police, shows the limits of restricting black youth to one space, or defining them as a monolithic community.

Carnivalesque style also enables *Territories* to move beyond the linear discourse of oppositionality that pits youth against police. For example, in one of the scenes described above, the film appropriates the logic of sequential narrative, and condenses the struggle between youth and police into two shots: a medium shot of a policeman and a close-up of a black man's defiant face. The oppositional elements are soon diffused, cut into pieces, pasted on top of each other, and made to share the same space. In other words, the film, in its attempt to posit the excess of a carnivalesque space, combines the documentary and the avant-garde, the linear and the circular, the symbol and the whole in the same space.[6]

Clearly, the second part of *Territories,* which uses excess as metaphor for carnival, takes us to a level of what may be called a cinematic masquerading. I use the masquerade here to convey the idea of mask, which in its African diasporic sense is a mediator and floating signifier among the ancestor figure, the bearer of the mask, and the community; and to convey the idea of movement, which is close to the sense that Teshome Gabriel uses for nomadic cinema (1988, 62–79). Masquerading as movement enables us to see the modification of the objects' identities as they move across spaces, and the transformation of spaces as new objects occupy them. It is in this sense that one understands Gilroy's thesis that blackness and Englishness permeate each other, and that ethnic absolutism is no longer tenable.

6. For a discussion of the use of realism and avant-garde techniques in black cinema, see Williamson, this volume, chap. 8, and Mercer 1988b.

Territories is a brilliant film, suturing and masquerading blackness in what used to be the exclusive spaces of whiteness and Englishness.

Works Cited

Bordwell, D., et al. 1985. *The Classical Hollywood Cinema*. New York: Columbia University Press.

Dayan, D. 1974. "The Tutor-Code of Classical Cinema." *Film Quarterly* (Berkeley), fall.

Diawara, M. 1990. "Englishness and Blackness: Cricket as a Discourse on Colonialism." *Callaloo* (Baton Rouge) 13, no. 2.

Fanon, F. 1968. *The Wretched of the Earth*. New York: Grove Press.

Gabriel, T. 1988. "Nomadic Cinema." In *Blackframes: Critical Perspectives on Black Independent Cinema*, ed. M. Cham and C. Andrade-Watkins. Cambridge: MIT Press.

Gilroy, P. 1990. "This Island Race." *New Statesman and Society* (London), 2 February.

———. 1991. *There Ain't No Black in the Union Jack*. London: Hutchinson, 1987. Reprint, Chicago: University of Chicago Press.

Hall, S., et al. 1978. *Policing the Crisis: Mugging, the State, and Law and Order*. London: Macmillan.

Heath, S. 1981. *Questions of Cinema*. Bloomington: Indiana University Press.

Mercer, K. 1988a. "Diaspora Culture and the Dialogic Imagination: The Aesthetics of Black Independent Film in Britain." In *Blackframes: Critical Perspectives on Black Independent Cinema*, ed. M. Cham and C. Andrade-Watkins. Cambridge: MIT Press.

———. 1988b. "Recoding Narratives of Race and Nation." In *Black Film/British Cinema*, ed. K. Mercer. ICA Document 7. London: Institute of Contemporary Arts/British Film Institute Production Special

Oudart, J.-P. 1969. "Suture." Parts 1 and 2. *Cahiers du Cinema* (Paris), no. 211 (April); no. 212 (May).

Owusu, K., and J. Ross. 1987. *Behind the Masquerade: The Story of Notting Hill Carnival*. London: Arts Media Group.

Rothman, W. 1975. "Against the System of Suture." *Film Quarterly* (Berkeley), fall.

Sixteen

The Art of Identity:
A Conversation

Sonia Boyce and
Manthia Diawara

S onia Boyce is at the center of a great deal of critical and artistic ferment in black Britain. Taking her place with such artists as Isaac Julien, Maureen Blackwood, and John Akomfrah in film, David A. Bailey and Rotimi Fani-Kayode in photography, and Keith Piper, Eddie Chambers, Lubaina Himid, Gavin Jantjes, Rasheed Araeen, and others in the visual arts, Sonia Boyce has been recognized as a chief exemplar of what's been called "diaspora aesthetics." (Her work has been widely shown in London, including recent exhibitions at the Institute for Contemporary Arts, the Whitechapel Gallery, and the Air Gallery.)

Drawing is her preferred medium, and its challenging linearity has proved well adapted for an art that is in many ways about lines—lines of descent and consent, lines that are broken and unbroken, lines of color, gender, class, and culture. Much of the work identified with the contemporary black arts movement in Britain is known for its insistent redefinitions of Britishness, its espousal of cultural hybridity, and its rejection of any ideology of purity or authenticity. And Boyce, too, has always refused to locate her work in any one cultural milieu. First she was concerned to express the multiplicity of her own identities, as someone who is British, black, Caribbean, European, and a woman. Now she seems to be looking for a space that is beyond identity, a creative space where contradictory desires intersect, juxtaposing past and present, the here-and-now with the there-and-then.

. . .

MANTHIA DIAWARA: Toni Morrison was once asked if she considered herself a writer or a black writer. She replied that she was a writer—and a black writer. She rejected the disjunction altogether.

SONIA BOYCE: Well, I am a black woman artist. That's not necessarily *who* I am, but *what* I am. And so I always feel nervous when people expect that what one *is* represents what one does . . . and represents anyone else who could come under that rubric. When I do a portrait of a black woman, it doesn't mean that I'm representing all black women—but it's taken as that.

MD: The question of representation has received a lot of discussion in the black British arts movement, if we can call it that. How do you feel about the idea of speaking for the black British community?

SB: I don't. I'm not representative at all. Nobody voted me to be a representative and I don't take up that position.

MD: In your case, there are other complications: there being so few black artists in Britain, it seems that the decision isn't in your hand any more. You become representative by default.

SB: I don't accept that. There have been quite a few black artists producing work. Now, because of the pressures within the fine arts world, and the additional challenge of being a black male or female artist working in the system, it's very, very difficult to survive and to develop as an artist. And when attention has been paid to black British art, there hasn't really been a discussion of the work, there's been discussion of things *around* the work. But I am not the only person; I am just one of the people who are quite well known.

MD: It's like the situation with black cinema. In the eighties, in the States, Spike Lee was *the* black filmmaker. And people would discuss his work in a singleminded way, focusing just on the race issue, debating whether he got it right or wrong, instead of looking at the coherence of his overall work.

SB: When he's taken up as the embodiment of black filmmakers, what happens is that one is enough. And so too in the art world. One is enough. Somehow that doesn't happen with other groups of people.

MD: That's true. But it's also the case that your work addresses some pretty encompassing themes. I'm thinking of works like *Missionary Position* and *British Rose,* and the way they evoke issues of colonialism and culture. It seems inevitable that it's going to cross the path of other people's experiences.

SB: I am not saying that I'm not trying to address common experiences. But having done that does not put me in the position of being a representative. That's always been a real problem: "one black represents all blacks." And there's been a quite firm refusal of that within the black arts sector, in particular. It questions the notion that one black equals all. Everyone has the right to speak of a common experience—but that doesn't mean it should get taken up in this way.

MD: Do you find yourself addressing an art community, or a black community, or some other amalgam? Who do you speak to?

SB: First and foremost I speak to myself. Which isn't as solipsistic as it sounds: I speak to myself because of what's going on around me, in order to try to clarify these things. And that can reflect a kind of black arts sector, or British culture in a larger way. So while I play around with the convention of the contemporary fine art practice, the work isn't necessarily about the medium I'm using. Usually, what's much more important are the various ideas going on at a particular time, including the whole, overstretched discussion that there has been around identity, which has taken place within the black arts sector, but which also happens, in a much broader way, within British society.

MD: You refer to the conversation around identity as "overstretched."

SB: Yes. In terms of black people, it's been overemphasized. Whatever we black people do, it's said to be about identity, first and foremost. It becomes a blanket term for everything we do, regardless of what we're doing. So within the last few years, I've been pushing up against this idea, trying to find other avenues that aren't to do with identity, even though people still try to place you under that blanket. And I'm reaching the point where I see this whole question of identity becoming a problem. This comes out of one's discussions within the black arts community, but the rhetoric of identity plays itself out in a much broader way as well.

MD: Many people have tried to resolve the problem by talking about *fragmented* identities, about the ways in which identities are not fixed, essential attributes. But they nonetheless hold onto notions of identity. Are you suggesting that the notion has been exhausted, that we drop it and turn to other areas of inquiry?

SB: I don't say that it should be abandoned. I say that *I* need to move away from that: you can get stuck in a groove. Am I only able to talk about who I am? Of course, who I am changes as I get older; it can be a lifelong inquiry. But why should I only be allowed to talk about race, gender, sexuality, class? Are we only able to say who we are, and not able to say anything else? If I speak, I speak "as a" black woman artist or "as a" black woman or "as a" black person. I always have to name who I am: I'm constantly being put in that position, required to talk in that place . . . never allowed to speak because I speak. I want to find out what other things I can talk about. I no longer want to describe who I am. So for myself, I have to move on, and say other things—and expect that at various points the issue of who I am may come up again. It's not the case that it's been abandoned, but the arena is much bigger than that.

. . .

MD: I'm intrigued by the fact that as an artist, your direct medium of expression is drawing, rather than painting. It reminds me of Madame de Staël's remarks on the differences between the northern and the southern Renaissance: one was supposed to be more alert to color, the other to form. And there's a sort of hierarchy established between the two.

SB: Back when I was twelve or fourteen I actually learned how to draw a figure, and how to use pastels and drawing materials. And it wasn't until I went to do my degree that it was made clear to me that drawing was considered to be preparation, preparation for something else. And so I had a lot of battles about that, about one medium being of less importance than another. And I attempted to paint; I did my first painting in my first year of my courses, and realized that I had more sympathy with drawing materials, and I couldn't think of any good reason why I couldn't use drawing materials for all I wanted to do. So on one level it was laziness; but it was also a kind of obstinacy, a refusal to enter into the hierarchy. I personally don't privilege any material above any other. It doesn't seem appropriate in contemporary practice to favor one medium over another. But it does have a different quality.

MD: I'm also struck by the element of self-portrait in your work. You see a young woman in most of your pictures, and, of course, one wonders about a moment of self-portraiture here.

SB: The reason I feature in a lot of the early work—I hardly do so now—was very practical. I went to school in a very small town in the West Midlands. There were fewer than ten African people and I knew very few of them. From the age of fourteen, I've been doing life-drawings, but there were almost no black models. So what I did was to start to draw myself; and that opened up the possibility of constructing the sort of images I wanted. As an artist, the biggest influence on me was Frida Kahlo. To me, she said all the things I wanted to say. And the format she uses is a self-portrait. It's almost like taking up a diary, like a natural autobiography, though I don't see it quite like that. When I look at Frida Kahlo's work, I see something broader and more political, not just self-portraiture.

MD: I'm thinking of your painting from 1984, *Big Women's Talk*. You see the big woman, and you see a younger woman, and the picture suggests a relation between the two, and yet you don't see the big woman's face.

SB: In a sense, it was about the relation of the child to the adult woman's body. It's a very close relationship, but in terms of the discussion invoked by the title, the child is not involved in the discussion: it's happening around the child, though the child is in some ways within it. You reach a cut-off point where the discussion is outside the frame.

MD: You were talking about the process of learning to draw figures. When I'm in Africa, I often see people standing by, drawing actors from posters. That's how people learn to draw in these places. Then they move to marketplaces, to saloons, hairdressing shops, anywhere they can go to draw people.

SB: I've heard about this sort of work, and the variety of ways in which art becomes part of everyday. I was in the Caribbean, in Barbados, not long ago, and the majority of what I saw fell into three particular camps. Of the painting, there was a lot of what once would have been called "naive": very colorful, local narrative. The best-known example of that kind of work is Haitian. There was another camp, which was that of the sculptors. Many of the sculptors—sculptors in wood—were Rastafarians. A lot of the influences there were of the various forms of African sculpture. The works were very much to do with figures or landscape, but using those stylistic forms. There was the notion of being rooted in an African heritage. And the third group, which seemed to be the "real" artist's group, in a way, were painters and sculptors largely influenced by Western contemporary art practices. To me their work seems very traditional: landscape, seascape, still life, portrait . . . abstracts. And even they work in quite traditional forms. That was the case across the board in Barbados.

MD: Did you find any of it related to your own art?

SB: The work I had the most sympathy for, and from which I derived the most pleasure, was the sculpture of the Rastafarians. Not as an influence on what I do, but I found it the most pleasing to engage with. But none of the formal work I saw in the Caribbean was as inspiring for me. The more established artists with connections to the galleries were completely bewildered with what I was doing. I think for them, the subject matter overshadowed the form, the medium, and I think they just couldn't understand why the work was so very political. They found it difficult to talk to me about the work and my ideas. I probably wouldn't be able to work in the Caribbean, because a lot of what I do requires a certain kind of tension, which exists here, and which is, in a way, the source material for the various ideas that I have.

MD: London gives you that? It strikes me that the multiplicity of identity is easier to conceptualize, and experience, in a big city.

SB: Yes, it's part of why I love it: to be able to be anonymous. And to mix with lots of different people. One can be lots of things in different places, you can change your role, you can play with changing the role in very short spaces of time, and I enjoy that. It can become a playful thing, rather than something that's just about survival.

MD: Did you encounter a stratum of "political art" in Barbados?

SB: I only met a couple of people you could consider to be political artists in Barbados, and much of what they were talking about was somewhere else; one had been doing work about South Africa. They engaged with something further away, rather than something that was immediately present. And then the Rastafarian artists were dealing with what I considered to be a very romanticized idea of Africa. Within that context, identity is almost a non-starter.

Of course, many Afro-Caribbean British people see the experience of the Caribbean as somewhat mystic, similar to how Afro-Americans envisage Africa. At the same time, there *are* these elements that directly relate to these places, and that have been passed on from generation to generation. My parents and their generation passed on quite a lot to their children's generation. And yet my generation was in a very peculiar situation. You know and you don't know what something means: you only partially understand the symbolic nature of something. And it's that partial knowledge that's so intriguing and draws you on to find out more. Hence the fascination among certain African Americans with folklore, religion, symbolism, and the way people have tried to retrieve and build a fuller picture of what the symbolism means—but from the position of having partial knowledge and feeling a certain inadequacy about that.

MD: One of your pictures that elaborates that theme is called *She Ain't Holding Them Up, She's Holding On*. You have a young woman standing in front, and behind her you have a family. It seems as if the idea of "holding on" can be a notion of holding on to the diaspora.

SB: One of the things I've always played with is this notion of a painting as a window through which you can look to see a reflection of the same world. I've always played with the idea of being able to enter that image. Everything is very close to the surface; it flits forward all the time, there's a vacillation between distance and presence. So, for example, in this piece, the family is much smaller than the main figure. It looks like they're quite a distance away; but at the same time, the way she holds on to them suggests that either she's moving back, which she obviously isn't, or that they're closer than that. Then there's the background made of different shades of brown. And that's what stops the idea of perspective, because it's one sheet that goes from top to bottom. That's so even with these birds, the sky, the tree, and the suggestion that there's something else, somewhere else behind that. But it's all very close to the surface at the same time.

MD: There seems to be a play of cultural memory in other works of yours as well. And of course, I think of your work in the production design of the film *Dreaming Rivers,* directed by Martina Attille, which is all about family, migration, and memory, but enacted within a very domestic tableau.

SB: To me, religion is centered in the home. There's a piece I did called *Sitting on the Mantelpiece,* which is part drawing, part photography. It has a person with eyes closed, either dreaming or dead. Then there are these two icons, both objects from my mother's house. One is a 1950s kitsch image of an African woman dancing. On the other side, there's an image of the Madonna. The person who's photographed is in the center of these two icons. And I've been engaged by the tradition of inquiry into folklore prior to making the film with Martina. What's really essential here is Zora Neale Hurston's "Sanctified Church." A lot of these issues grew out of the 1970s discussions of Rastafarianism, pan-Africanism, and so on, where you had to know your history, and understand the African elements. What strikes me about the American developments around "Afrocentrism" is how much they reprise the discussions we'd been having in this country in the seventies. Which I find quite odd, because there's always this assumption that what's happening in America is light-years ahead of what's happening anywhere else. There are, now, quite strong divisions between those who believe in a nationalist or pan-Africanist perspective, and those of us who have a much more pluralist perspective. I look forward to seeing how the discussion in America develops. I don't think that the pluralist perspective here excludes the possibility of a pan-Africanist or diasporic one.

MD: Actually, there's often a tension here between the pluralist approach and the pan-Africanist one, which in the States is sometimes called "Afrocentric," even though they're quite different; the Afrocentric approach is uniquely North American, whereas pan-Africanism could be British, African, Caribbean, and so on. But in some people's hands, pluralism and Afrocentrism tend to exclude each other. And the ideology of authenticity can take different forms. There's a suggestion you often encounter here that real "blackness" can only be found in the ghetto; the middle class is depicted as imitative, somehow less creative, less in touch.

SB: I think that's a non-starter. It's like the question "who is the most authentic . . ."—when there isn't *one* authentic black person. There is this idea that working-class people are more "real," more down-to-earth, and, in Western ideology, we know what is thought of the earth. So, as I say, I just think it's a non-starter, really.

MD: How could you describe the reception of African-American culture in Britain, and its influence upon you?

SB: People have been appreciative of the literature—and music, which may be America's greatest export. Because of the nature of publishing, there's very little in terms of theoretical texts, such as the work of black feminists, who seem more prolific in the States.

MD: Do you see common experiences? You talk about the black American obsession with slavery, for example.

SB: It seems as if the African American's psyche has been almost permanently damaged by slavery in America, and by having lived, for generations, with that experience alongside white America. And so much of their work always seems to me to start from that point. In Britain, not only is the experience of slavery and colonialism different, in terms of sheer numbers, Europe didn't live alongside the colonized: in general, the colonizer and the colonized didn't live together in the same place.

MD: Can we talk about a "black British school" of art at this point, or would that be jumping the gun?

SB: At the moment, it's hard to locate commonalities, save for a shared attempt to grapple with history, which we see particularly in the eighties. There was an ongoing conversation about migration, about identity after migration, and a concern with deconstructing cultural notions of race and gender. But I'd be resistant to any such claims beyond this shared intellectual context.

A Selected Bibliography

Ruth H. Lindeborg

I. Articles and Books

Akomfrah, John. "Black and White." Interview by Pervaiz Khan. *Sight and Sound* (London) 2 (May 1992): 30–31.

———. "Black Independent Film-making: A Statement by the Black Audio Film Collective." *Artrage* (London), no. 3/4 (1983): 29–30.

Amos, Valerie, and Pratibha Parmar. "Challenging Imperial Feminism." *Feminist Review* (London) 17 (1984): 9–12.

Appignanesi, Lisa, ed. *Identity*. ICA Document 6. London: Institute of Contemporary Arts, 1987.

Appignanesi, Lisa, and Sara Maitland, eds. *The Rushdie File*. London: Institute of Contemporary Arts, 1990.

Araeen, Rasheed. *The Essential Black Art*. Catalog of exhibit at Chisenhale Gallery. London: Black Umbrella/Kala Press, 1987.

———. *The Other Story*. Exhibition catalog. London: Hayward Gallery, 1989.

Art and Immigration. Special issue of *Third Text* (London) 15 (1991).

Attille, Martina, and Maureen Blackwood. "Black Women and Representation." In *Films for Women*, ed. Charlotte Brunsdon, 202–8. London: British Film Institute, 1986.

Auguiste, Reece. "Black Independents and Third Cinema: The British Context." In *Questions of Third Cinema*, ed. Jim Pines and Paul Willeman, 212–17. London: British Film Institute, 1989.

———. "Handsworth Songs: Some Background Notes." *Framework* (London) 35 (1988): 4–18.

Bailey, David, ed. *Black Experiences*. Special issue of *Ten. 8* (Birmingham) 22 (1986).

Banning, Kass. "Rhetorical Remarks Towards the Politics of Otherness." *CineAction!* (Toronto), spring 1989, 14–19.

Barker, Francis, et al., eds. *Europe and Its Others*. 2 vols. Colchester: University of Essex, 1985.

———. *Literature, Politics, and Theory*. London: Methuen, 1986.

Barker, Martin. *The New Racism: Conservatives and the Ideology of the Tribe*. 1981. Reprint, n.p.: University Publications of America, 1982.

Bhabha, Homi K. "The Commitment to Theory." In *Questions of Third Cinema,* ed. Jim Pines and Paul Willeman, 111–32. London: British Film Institute, 1989.

———. "DissemiNation: Time, Narrative, and the Margins of the Modern Nation." In *Nation and Narration,* ed. Homi K. Bhabha, 291–320. London: Routledge, 1990.

———. *The Location of Culture.* London: Routledge, 1994.

———. "Of Mimicry and Man: The Ambivalence of Colonial Discourse." *October* (Cambridge, Mass.) 28 (spring 1984): 125–31.

———. " 'Race,' Time, and the Revision of Modernity." In *Neocolonialism,* ed. Robert Young, 193–219. Special issue of the *Oxford Literary Review* 13 (1991).

———. "Signs Taken for Wonders: Questions of Ambivalence and Authority under a Tree outside Delhi, May 1817." In *Europe and Its Others,* ed. Francis Barker et al., 1:89–106. Colchester: University of Essex, 1985. Also in *"Race," Writing, and Difference,* ed. Henry Louis Gates, Jr., 163–84. Chicago: University of Chicago Press, 1986.

———. "The Third Space." In *Identity: Community, Culture, Difference,* ed. Jonathan Rutherford, 207–21. London: Lawrence and Wishart, 1990.

Bishton, Derek, and John Reardon. *Home Front.* London: Jonathan Cape, 1984.

Black Audio Film Collective. *"Expedition:* Extracts from a Tape-Slide Text in Two Parts." *Screen* (London) 26 (1985): 157–65.

Black Image/Staying On. Special issue of *Ten .8* (Birmingham) 16 (1984).

Black Women Writers in Britain. Special issue of *Wasafiri* (Canterbury), no. 17 (spring 1993).

Boyce, Sonia. Interview by John Roberts. *Literary Review* (Madison, N.J.) 34 (fall 1990): 109–19.

Brennan, Tim. "Writing from Black Britain." *Literary Review* (Madison, N.J.) 34 (fall 1990): 5–11.

Bridges, G., and R. Hunt, eds. *Silver Linings: Some Strategies for the 1980s.* London: Lawrence and Wishart, 1981.

"Brother to Brother: Black Gay Men and Film." Special section of *Black Film Review* (Washington, D.C.) 5 (1989): 12–22.

Bryan, Beverly, Stella Dadzie, and Suzanne Scafe. *The Heart of the Race: Black Womens' Lives in Britain.* London: Virago, 1985.

Butler, Alison. "Handsworth Songs." *International Documentary* (Los Angeles), winter/spring 1988, 19–23.

Carby, Hazel. "Multicultural Fictions." Occasional paper of the Centre for Contemporary Cultural Studies, Birmingham, 1980.

———. "Multiculture." *Screen Education* (London), no. 34 (1980): 62–70.

———. "Schooling in Babylon." In *The Empire Strikes Back: Race and Racism in Seventies Britain,* 183–211. Centre for Contemporary Cultural Studies. London: Hutchinson, 1982.

Centre for Contemporary Cultural Studies. *Culture, Media, Language.* London: Hutchinson, 1984.

———. *The Empire Strikes Back: Race and Racism in Seventies Britain.* London: Hutchinson, 1982.

Cham, Mbye, and Claire Andrade-Watkins, eds. *Blackframes: Critical Perspectives on Black Independent Cinema.* Cambridge: MIT Press, 1988.

Cohen, Philip. *It Ain't Half Racist, Mum.* London: Comedia/Campaign against Racism in the Media, 1982.

Cohen, Philip, and Harwant S. Bains, eds. *Multi-Racist Britain.* London: Macmillan Educational, 1988.

Daniels, Therese, and Jane Gerson, eds. *The Colour Black: Black Images in British Television.* London: British Film Institute, 1989.

Dhillon-Kashyap, Perminder. "Locating the Asian Experience." *Screen* (London) 29 (1988): 120–26.

Diawara, Manthia. "The Absent One. The Avant-Garde and the Black Imaginary in *Looking for Langston.*" *Wide Angle* (Athens, Ohio) 13, nos. 3 and 4 (July–October 1991): 96–109.

———. "Englishness and Blackness: Cricket as Discourse on Colonialism." *Callaloo* (Baton Rouge) 13 (1990): 830–44.

———. "The Nature of Mother in *Dreaming Rivers.*" *Third Text* (London) 13 (1991): 73–84.

Dorfman, Ariel. "Innocence and Neo-Colonialism." *Black Phoenix* (London), no. 2 (1978): 4–11.

Egbuna, Obi. *Destroy This Temple: The Voice of Black Power in Britain.* New York: William Morrow, 1971.

Ellis, Trey, Eric Lott, and Tera Hunter. "The New Black Aesthetic." *Callaloo* (Baton Rouge) 12 (1989): 233–51.

Fusco, Coco. *Young, British, and Black: A Monograph on the Work of Sankofa Film-Video Collective and Black Audio Film Collective.* Buffalo: Hallwalls Arts Centre, 1988.

Gilroy, Paul. "Art of Darkness: Black Art and the Problem of Belonging to England." *Third Text* (London) 10 (1990): 45–52.

———. *The Black Atlantic: Modernity and Double Consciousness.* Cambridge: Harvard University Press, 1993.

———. "Cruciality and the Frog's Perspective: An Agenda of Difficulties for the Black Arts Movement in Britain." *Third Text* (London) 5 (1988–89): 33–44.

———. Introduction to *d max: Photographs.* Birmingham: Clarkeprint, 1987.

———. "It Ain't Where You're At . . . : The Dialectics of Diasporic Identification." *Third Text* (London) 13 (1991): 3–16.

———. "Sounds Authentic: Black Music, Ethnicity, and the Challenge of a *Changing* Same." *Black Music Research Journal* (Nashville) 11 (1991): 111–36.

———. *There Ain't No Black in the Union Jack.* London: Hutchinson, 1987. Reprint, Chicago: University of Chicago Press, 1991.

———. "This Island Race." *New Statesman and Society* (London) 3 (2 February 1990): 30–32.

Grewal, Shabnam, et al. *Charting the Journey: Writings by Black and Third World Women.* London: Sheba, 1988.

Hall, Stuart. "Deviancy, Politics, and the Media." In *Deviancy and Social Control,* ed. M. McIntosh and P. Rock. London: Tavistock Publications, 1973.

———. "The Emergence of Cultural Studies and the Crisis of the Humanities." *October* (Cambridge, Mass.) 53 (1990): 11–24.

———. "Encoding and Decoding in Television Discourse." For the Council of Europe colloquy "Training in the Critical Reading of Televisual Language." Published in *Stencilled Occasional Papers in Media,* SP no. 7. Birmingham: University of Birmingham, Centre for Contemporary Cultural Studies, 1973.

———. "Gramsci's Relevance for the Study of Race and Ethnicity." *Journal of Communication Inquiry* (Iowa City) 10 (1986): 5–27.

———. *The Hard Road to Renewal: Thatcherism and the Crisis of the Left.* London: Verso, 1988.

———. "On Postmodernism and Articulation: An Interview." *Journal of Communication Inquiry* (Iowa City) 10 (1986): 45–60.

———. "The Problem of Ideology: Marxism without Guarantees." In *Marx 100 Years On,* ed. B. Matthews, 57–86. London: Lawrence and Wishart, 1983.

———. "The 'Structured Communication' of Events." For the Obstacles to Communication Symposium, UNESCO. Published in *Stencilled Occasional Papers in Media,* SP no. 5. Birmingham: University of Birmingham, Centre for Contemporary Cultural Studies, 1973.

———. "The Whites of Their Eyes: Racist Ideologies and the Media." In *Silver Linings: Some Strategies for the 1980s,* ed. G. Bridges and R. Hunt, 28–52. London: Lawrence and Wishart, 1981.

Hall, Stuart, et al. *Policing the Crisis: Mugging, the State, and Law and Order.* London: Macmillan Educational, 1978.

Hall, Stuart, and T. Jefferson. *Resistance through Rituals: Youth Subcultures in Post-war Britain.* London: Hutchinson, 1976.

Hall, Stuart, and Martin Jacques, eds. *New Times: The Changing Face of Politics in the 1990s.* London: Lawrence and Wishart, 1989.

———. *The Politics of Thatcherism.* London: Lawrence and Wishart, 1983.

Hazareesingh, Sandip. "Racism Cultural Identity: An Indian Perspective." *Dragon's Teeth* (London) 24 (1986): 4–10.

Hebdige, Dick. *Cut 'n' Mix: Culture, Identity, and Caribbean Music.* London: Methuen, 1987.

———. *Hiding in the Light.* 1979. London: Routledge, 1988.

James, Alby. "Black and British Temba Theatre Forges the Mainstream." Interview by Sandy Carpenter. *Drama Review* (Cambridge) 34 (spring 1990): 28–35.

Jones, Simon. *Black Culture, White Youth: The Reggae Tradition from Jamaica to the United Kingdom.* Basingstoke: Macmillan Educational, 1988.

Journal of Communication Inquiry (Iowa City) 10 (1986). Special issue on Stuart Hall.

Julien, Isaac. "States of Desire." Interview by bell hooks. *Transition* (Cambridge) 53 (1991): 168–84.

Julien, Isaac, and Colin MacCabe. *Diary of a Young Soul Rebel.* London: British Film Institute, 1991.

Kureishi, Hanif. "Bradford." *Granta* (Cambridge) 20 (1986): 147–70.

———. "The Rainbow Sign." In *My Beautiful Laundrette and the Rainbow Sign,* 7–38. London: Faber and Faber, 1986.

———. "Some Time with Stephen: A Diary." In *Sammy and Rosie Get Laid,* 59–127. New York: Penguin, 1988.

The Last "Special Issue" on Race? Special issue of *Screen* (London) 29, no. 4 (1988).

MacCabe, Colin, ed. *Futures for English.* Manchester: Manchester University Press, 1988.

Many Voices, One Chant. Special issue of *Feminist Review* (London) 17 (1984).

McFarlane, Cassie. "Towards a Critical Evaluation of Black British Film Culture." B.A. honors essay, London College of Printing, 1987.

Mercer, Kobena. "Black Art and the Burden of Representation." *Third Text* (London) 10 (1990): 61–78.

———. "Diaspora Culture and the Dialogic Imagination." In *Blackframes: Critical Perspectives on Black Independent Cinema,* ed. Mbye Cham and Claire Andrade-Watkins, 50–61. Cambridge: MIT Press, 1988.

———. "Monster Metaphors: Notes on Michael Jackson's *Thriller.*" *Screen* (London) 27 (1986): 26–43.

———. "Recoding Narratives of Race and Nation." *Independent* (New York) 12 (1989): 19–26.

———. "Welcome to the Jungle: Identity and Diversity in Postmodern Politics." In *Identity: Community, Culture, Difference,* ed. Jonathan Rutherford, 43–71. London: Lawrence and Wishart, 1990.

———, ed. *Black Film/British Cinema.* ICA Document 7. London: Institute of Contemporary Arts, 1988.

———. *Welcome to the Jungle: New Positions in Black Cultural Studies.* London: Routledge. 1994.

Miles. *The Two Tone Book for Rude Boys.* London: Omnibus, 1981.

Modood, Tariq. " 'Black' Racial Equality and Asian Identity." *New Community* (London) 14 (1988): 397–404.

Other Cinemas, Other Criticisms. Special issue of *Screen* (London) 26 (1985).

Over the Borderlines: Questioning National Identities. Special issue of *Screen* (London) 30 (1989).

Owusu, Kwesi, ed. *Storms of the Heart: An Anthology of Black Arts and Culture.* London: Camden Press, 1988.

———. *The Struggle for Black Arts in Britain.* London: Methuen, 1986.

Owusu, Kwesi, and Jacob Ross. *Behind the Masquerade: The Story of Notting Hill Carnival.* London: Arts Media Group, 1988.

Parry, Benita. "Problems in Current Theories of Colonial Discourse." *Oxford Literary Review* 9 (1987): 27–58.

Pines, Jim, and Paul Willemen, eds. *Questions of Third Cinema.* London: British Film Institute, 1989.

Racism, Colonialism, and the Cinema. Special issue of *Screen* (London) 24 (1983).

Rushdie, Salman. "Outside the Whale." *Granta* (Cambridge) 11 (1984): 123–38.

Rutherford, Jonathan, ed. *Identity: Community, Culture, Difference*. London: Lawrence and Wishart, 1990.

Sahgal, Nayantara. "The Schizophrenic Imagination." *Wasafiri* (Canterbury) 11 (1990): 17–20.

Sivanandan, A. "All That Melts into Air Is Solid: The Hokum of *New Times*." *Race and Class* (London) 31 (1989): 1–30.

———. *A Different Hunger: Writings on Black Resistance*. London: Pluto Press, 1982.

Solomos, John. *Black Youth, Racism, and the State: The Politics of Ideology and Policy*. Cambridge: Cambridge University Press, 1988.

———. *Race and Racism in Contemporary Britain*. Houndmills: Macmillan, 1989.

Spivak, Gayatri Chakravorty. "In Praise of *Sammy and Rosie Get Laid*." *Critical Quarterly* (Oxford) 31 (1989): 80–88.

Tawadros, Gilane. "Other Britains, Other Britons." *Aperture* (San Francisco) 113 (1988): 40–46.

Third Eye: Struggle for Black and Third World Cinema. London: Greater London Council, Race Equality Unit, 1986.

Third Scenario: Theory and the Politics of Location. Special issue of *Framework* (London) 36 (1989).

Toop, David. *The Rap Attack: African Jive to New York Hip Hop*. London: Pluto Press, 1984.

Twitchin, John, ed. *The Black and White Media Book*. Stoke-on-Trent: Trentham Books, 1988.

Widgery, David. *Beating Time: Riot 'n' Race 'n' Rock 'n' Roll*. London: Chatto and Windus, 1986.

Wilson, Amrit. *Finding a Voice: Asian Women in Britain*. London: Virago, 1978.

Young, Robert, ed. *Neocolonialism*. Special issue of the *Oxford Literary Review* 13 (1991).

II. Backgrounds: Historical, Theoretical, Comparative, and Cultural

Anderson, Benedict. *Imagined Communities: Reflections on the Origin and Spread of Nationalism*. Rev. ed., London: Verso, 1991.

Baker, Houston A., Jr. *Blues, Ideology, and Afro-American Literature: A Vernacular Theory*. Chicago: University of Chicago Press, 1984.

———. *Modernism and the Harlem Renaissance*. Chicago: University of Chicago Press, 1987.

Baraka, Amiri. *Black Music*. New York: Quill, 1967.

———. *Blues People*. New York: William Morrow, 1963.

Brathwaite, Edward. *Contradictory Omens: Cultural Diversity and Integration in the Caribbean*. Kingston: Savacou, 1974.

———. *The Development of Creole Society in Jamaica, 1770–1820*. Oxford: Clarendon, 1971.

Davis, Angela. *Women, Race, and Class*. New York: Random House, 1981.

dePestre, Rene. "Problems of Identity for the Black Man in the Caribbean." In *Carifesta Forum: An Anthology of Twenty Caribbean Voices*, ed. John Hearne, 61–67. Kingston, 1976.

Ellison, Ralph. *Shadow and Act*. New York: Random House, 1964.

Fanon, Frantz. *Black Skin, White Masks*. 1952. Trans. Charles Lam Markham. New York: Grove Press, 1967.

———. *The Wretched of the Earth*. 1963. Trans. Constance Farrington. New York: Grove Press, 1968.

Francis, Armet. *Children of the Black Triangle*. Trenton: Africa World Press, 1989.

Fryer, Peter. *Staying Power: The History of Black People in Britain*. London: Pluto Press, 1984.

Gates, Henry Louis, Jr., ed. *"Race," Writing, and Difference*. Chicago: University of Chicago Press, 1986.

Gellner, Ernest. *Nations and Nationalism*. Oxford: Basil Blackwell, 1983.

Gramsci, Antonio. *Selections from the Prison Notebooks*. Ed. Quintin Hoare and Geoffrey Nowell Smith. New York: International Publishers, 1971.

Grossberg, Lawrence. "Formations of Cultural Studies: An American in Birmingham." *Strategies* (Los Angeles) 2 (1989): 114–49.

Grossberg, Lawrence, Cary Nelson, and Paula A. Treichler, eds. *Cultural Studies*. New York: Routledge, 1992.

Heath, Stephen. *Questions of Cinema*. Bloomington: Indiana University Press, 1981.

Hiro, Dilip. *Black British, White British*. London: Eyre and Spottiswoode, 1971.

hooks, bell. *Ain't I a Woman: Black Women and Feminism*. Boston: South End Press, 1981.

———. *Talking Back: Thinking Feminist, Thinking Black*. Boston: South End Press, 1989.

James, C. L. R. *Beyond a Boundary*. 1963. Reprint, New York: Pantheon, 1984.

———. *Black Jacobins*. 1938. 2d ed., rev., New York: Vintage, 1963.

Jameson, Fredric. "Postmodernism, or the Cultural Logic of Late Capitalism." *New Left Review* (London), no. 146 (1984): 53–92.

———. "Third World Literature in the Era of Multinational Capitalism." *Social Text* (Madison) 15 (1986): 65–88. (See also Aijaz Ahmad's response: "Jameson's Rhetoric of Otherness and the 'National Allegory.'" *Social Text* [Madison] 17 [1987]: 3–25.)

Jordan, June. *Civil Wars*. Boston: Beacon Press, 1981.

Laclau, Ernesto. *Politics and Ideology in Marxist Theory*. London: New Left Books, 1977.

Laclau, Ernesto, and Chantal Mouffe. *Hegemony and Socialist Strategy: Towards a Radical Democratic Politics*. Trans. Winston Moore and Paul Commack. London: Verso, 1985.

Lamming, George. *The Pleasures of Exile*. 1960. Reprint, Ann Arbor: University of Michigan Press, 1992.

The Scarman Report: The Brixton Disorders, 10–12 April 1981. Harmondsworth: Penguin, 1986.

Marable, Manning. *From the Grassroots*. Boston: South End Press, 1980.

———. *Race, Politics, and Power: Comparative Political Movements in the Black Diaspora*. New York: Schocken, 1985.

———. *Race, Reform, and Rebellion*. 1984. 2d ed., Basingstoke: Macmillan Educational, 1991.

Mouffe, Chantal, ed. *Gramsci and Marxist Theory*. London: Routledge, 1979.

Nairn, Tom. *The Break-Up of Britain: Crisis and Neo-Nationalism.* London: Verso, 1977.

Nelson, Cary, and Lawrence Grossberg, eds. *Marxism and the Interpretation of Culture.* Urbana: University of Illinois Press, 1988.

Padmore, George. *Colonial and Coloured Unity.* Fifth Pan-African Congress, Manchester, England, 1945. 2d ed., London: Hammersmith Bookshop, 1963.

———. *Pan-Africanism or Communism?* 1956. Reprint, Garden City: Anchor, 1972.

Powell, Enoch. *Freedom and Reality.* Kingswood: Elliot Right Way Books, 1969.

———. *Still to Decide.* London: Batsford, 1972.

Ramdin, Ron. *The Making of the Black Working Class in Britain.* Brookfield, Vt.: Gower, 1987.

Robinson, Cedric. *Black Marxism.* London: Zed Press, 1982.

Said, Edward. *Culture and Imperialism.* New York: Alfred A. Knopf, 1993.

———. "Opponents, Audiences, Constituencies, and Community." *Critical Inquiry* 9 (1982): 1–26.

———. *Orientalism.* 1978. Reprint, New York: Vintage, 1979.

———. *The World, the Text, and the Critic.* Cambridge: Harvard University Press, 1983.

Spivak, Gayatri. *In Other Worlds: Essays in Cultural Politics.* 1987. London: Routledge, 1988.

———. *The Post-Colonial Critic: Interviews, Strategies, Dialogues.* Ed. Sarah Harasym. London: Routledge, 1990.

Visram, Rozina. *Ayahs, Lascars, and Princes: Indians in Britain, 1700–1947.* London: Pluto Press, 1986.

Walcott, Derek. "The Muse of History." In *Is Massa Day Dead? Black Moods in the Caribbean,* ed. Orde Coombs, 1–27. Garden City: Anchor, 1974.

West, Cornel. "The Dilemma of a Black Intellectual." *Cultural Critique* (Minneapolis) 1 (1986): 109–24.

———. "The New Cultural Politics of Difference." *October* (Cambridge, Mass.) 53 (1990): 93–109.

Williams, Raymond. *Culture and Society, 1790–1950.* 1958. Reprint, New York: Columbia University Press, 1959.

———. *Keywords: A Vocabulary of Culture and Society.* New York: Oxford University Press, 1976.

———. *Marxism and Literature.* New York: Oxford University Press, 1977.

III. Journals

Afterimage. Rochester, N.Y.: Visual Studies Workshop Photography/independent film/video/visual books.

Artrage. London: Minority Arts Advisory Service. International arts magazine.

Bazaar. London: South Asian Arts Forum.

Black Film Review. Washington, D.C.: University of the District of Columbia.

Black Phoenix (later incorporated in *Third Text*). London.

Dragon's Teeth. London. Examines racism in children's books and educational resources.

Framework. London. Film journal, particular interest in Third Cinema.

Independent. New York: Foundation for Independent Video and Film. Film and video monthly.

International Documentary. Los Angeles: International Documentary Association.

New Beacon Review. London: New Beacon Press.

New Community. London: Commission for Racial Equality.

New Formations. London: Routledge. Contemporary cultural studies and theory.

New Statesman and Society (incorporates the previously separate journals *New Statesman* and *New Society*). London.

Polareyes. London: Turnaround Distribution, Ltd. A journal by and about black women working in photography.

Race and Class. London: Institute for Race Relations.

Race Today. London.

Salisbury Review. London. "Britain's Most Reactionary Conservative Review."

Screen. London.

Spare Rib. London.

Strategies. Los Angeles: University of California. Theory, culture, and politics.

Ten .8. Birmingham: The Photographic Gallery.

Third Text. London. Third World perspectives on contemporary art and culture.

Undercut. London: London Filmmaker's Co-op.

Wasafiri. Canterbury: University of Kent. Caribbean, African, Asian, and associated literatures in English.

Contributors

HOUSTON A. BAKER, JR., is professor of English and Albert M. Greenfield Professor of Human Relations at the University of Pennsylvania, where he also directs the Center for the Study of Black Literature and Culture. Among his many publications is, most recently, *Black Studies, Rap, and the Academy* (1993).

STEPHEN BEST is assistant professor of English at the University of California, Berkeley.

HOMI K. BHABHA is professor of English at the University of Chicago. His publications include *Nation and Narration* (1990) and *The Location of Culture* (1994).

SONIA BOYCE is an artist in London whose work has been associated with the contemporary black arts movement and diaspora aesthetics.

HAZEL V. CARBY is professor of English at Yale University. She is the author of *Reconstructing Womanhood: The Emergence of the Afro-American Woman Novelist* (1989).

ROBERT CRUSZ is a member of the Sankofa Film and Video Collective and editor of *Framework.*

MANTHIA DIAWARA is professor of comparative literature and director of Africana Studies at New York University. He is the author of *African Cinema: Politics and Culture* (1992) and the editor of *Black American Cinema: Aesthetics and Spectatorship* (1992).

PAUL GILROY is lecturer in sociology at Goldsmith's College, University of London. His recent publications include *There Ain't No Black in the Union Jack* (1991) and *The Black Atlantic: Modernity and Double Consciousness* (1993).

STUART HALL is professor of sociology at the Open University, London. His recent publications include *Resistance through Rituals: Youth Subcultures in Post-War Britain,* edited with Tony Jefferson (1990), and *New Times: The Changing Face of Politics in the 1990s,* edited with Martin Jacques (1991).

323

DICK HEBDIGE teaches at the California Institute of the Arts. He is the author of *Cut 'n' Mix: Culture, Identity, and Caribbean Music* (1987) and *Hiding in the Light: On Images and Things* (1989).

ISAAC JULIEN is the director of the influential film *Looking for Langston* and is the author, with Colin MacCabe, of *Diary of a Young Soul Rebel* (1991).

RUTH H. LINDEBORG is assistant professor of English at the Ohio State University.

KOBENA MERCER is the author of *Welcome to the Jungle: New Positions in Black Cultural Studies* (1994).

JIM PINES is a freelance writer in London. He is the editor of *Questions of Third Cinema*, with Paul Willemen (1989) and *Black and White in Colour: Black People in British Television since 1936* (1992).

GILANE TAWADROS is art education officer at the South Bank Centre in London.

JUDITH WILLIAMSON is professor of cultural history at Middlesex University in England and is the author of *Decoding Advertisements: Ideology and Meaning in Advertising* (1978), *Consuming Passions: Politics and Images of Popular Culture* (1986), and *Deadline at Dawn: Film Criticism, 1980–1990* (1993). She has made a film entitled *A Sign Is a Fine Investment* (1983).

Index

Abraham, Karl, 104
Achille Oliva, Bonita, 248–49, 249n.5
advertising, 126, 142, 143, 145, 203, 282, 291
aesthetics: of black film, 175, 177–79, of diaspora, 220, 306; Eurocentric, 288
Africa, 7, 10, 141, 170; appropriations of artifacts as art objects, 240, 247; as the Dark Continent, 214; land rights, 81; music of, 219; photographs of, 212; precolonial, 301; retellings of, 218; sculpture, 246; slave trade in, 214
agency, 124, 227, 228, 230; political, 226, 233; of spectator, 293
AIDS, 280, 289, 290–91
Akomfrah, John, 197, 306
Althusser, Louis, 3, 12, 37–42, 45, 48, 49; *For Marx*, 37; *Reading Capital*, 37
America, 263, 312. *See also* United States
Anderson, Benedict, 229; *Imagined Communities*, 6, 217, 221. *See also* imagined communities
Angel Heart, 203
anthropology, 14, 83, 167, 224, 252; economic, 36–37; and colonialism, 124; project of, 125
antipornography: feminist debates on, 278–81, 287; legislation of, 290; politics of, 278–81. *See also* pornography
Appadurai, Arjun, 9, 9n.6
Arad, Ron, 148
Araeen, Rasheed, 249n.6, 251, 306; *Arctic Circle*, 249; *White Line through Africa*, 249, 250

Arawak culture, 219–20
art, 14; abstract, 242; and appropriation, 240, 241, 247, 249, 262; black British, 9–11, 302, 306–13; classical, 253; collage, 243, 262, 272; drawing, 306, 309, 310, 312; fine, 308; and freedom of expression, 289; historiography of, 252–57; history of, 243, 246, 253, 254, 256, 272, 285; and identity, 306–13; Indian, 256; institutionalization, 245; Latin American, 260; modern, 240–42, 244, 246, 248; performance, 280; practice of gathering and reusing, 240–41, 243, 271; painting, 301, 309, 310, 311; politics of, 10, 311; primitive, 240, 245; sculpture, 246, 248, 249, 310; self-portraiture, 309; and violence, 301. *See also* avant garde; modernism
articulation, 7, 12, 16–57, 195; concept of, 50; definitions of, 37–39, 40–43; and gender, 78; of labor, 44; language as domain of, 40; politics of, 118; and race, 166; thesis of, 36
artists: and audience, 286; black, 164–65, 251, 252, 257, 307; black gay and lesbian, 291; black women in Britain, 240–77, 307; ethnic, 169; gay, 282, 285, 288; independent, 291; postmodern, 253; white women, 249
Attille, Martina, 198, 312
audience, 10, 125, 179–82, 286; and artist, 286; avant-garde, 177; black, 110, 112, 113, 192, 193, 205, 281; as classic Hollywood spectator, 180; and dance, 137; and identity, 288;